D0216084

RENEWALS 458-457

WITHDRAWN
UTSA LIBRARIES

Computational Finance

A Scientific Perspective

Computational Finance

A Scientific Perspective

Cornelis A. Los

University of Adelaide, Australia

World Scientific

Singapore • New Jersey • London • Hong Kong

Published by

World Scientific Publishing Co. Pte. Ltd.

P O Box 128, Farrer Road, Singapore 912805

USA office: Suite 1B, 1060 Main Street, River Edge, NJ 07661

UK office: 57 Shelton Street, Covent Garden, London WC2H 9HE

British Library Cataloguing-in-Publication Data
A catalogue record for this book is available from the British Library.

COMPUTATIONAL FINANCE: A SCIENTIFIC PERSPECTIVE

Copyright © 2001 by World Scientific Publishing Co. Pte. Ltd.

All rights reserved. This book, or parts thereof, may not be reproduced in any form or by any means, electronic or mechanical, including photocopying, recording or any information storage and retrieval system now known or to be invented, without written permission from the Publisher.

For photocopying of material in this volume, please pay a copying fee through the Copyright Clearance Center, Inc., 222 Rosewood Drive, Danvers, MA 01923, USA. In this case permission to photocopy is not required from the publisher.

ISBN 981-02-4496-7

Printed in Singapore by World Scientific Printers

Library
University of Texas
at San Antonio

To:

Rosie

with
love, gratitude and a smile

Contents

Preface

0.1 Objective

Computational finance presents the mathematics of computer programs that realize financial models or systems. This book outlines the epistemic risks associated with the current valuations of different financial instruments and discusses corresponding risk management strategies. It covers most research and practical areas in computational finance. Starting from traditional fundamental analysis and using algebraic and geometric tools, it is guided by the logic of *science* to explore information from financial data without prejudice. In fact, this book has the unique feature that it is structured around the simple requirement of objective science:

> *the geometric structure of the data = the information contained in the data*

Models are abstractions, often of a mathematical nature, used to simplify our decision - making environment, since empirical reality is too complex and its complete analysis too time - consuming and expensive. Models must be realistic representations of a reality that we find to be written in the language of mathematics, in particular of algebraic geometry. Financial models are a subset of all generic models that deal with financial phenomena and data. Thus computational finance deals with the formulation, development and implementation of mathematical technology and software to realize financial models, so that an automatic mapping can take place between the available data and the model. Financial modeling is the subset of the general Theory of Modeling dealing with financial identification and realization. The objective is to produce a model, which can be used for experimentation, *c.q.*, for simulation and for extrapolation.

The reason for this book is that, in academic and commercial research in financial economics, as well as in the growing fields of mathematical finance and computational finance, all current expositions start with philosophical assumptions, on the basis of which mathematical model philosophies are erected. Next, the real world data are then forced into these assumed abstract frameworks. This top - down process leads to model mis-specification, data inconsistencies, and model instability. Thus, it provides an unreliable foundation for informed financial decision-making.

In contrast, this book follows the logic of the scientific method, which requires that we let the complete set of financial data speak for itself, without prejudice.

Therefore, it critically re-examines most of the currently existing inexact and exact valuation models of financial instruments.

Most current valuation models are simple finance models that, in top-down fashion, are derived from the axioms of economics utility theory and also from the notion of non-arbitrage. The latter leads to measure-theoretic notions of stochastic processes in general and of martingales in particular, under very restrictive and unrealistic assumptions of unconditional (wide and strict) stationarity and independence of the data points. That is, under the conventional i.i.d. (often Gaussian distribution) assumptions. In all these efforts, empirics does not lead the way, but has only been used to "statistically corroborate" the way, in a game-theoretic fashion. These measure-theoretic axioms and subjective probabilistic theorizing are at the core of most of the current exact valuation models and have little to do with inexact empirical science.

This book demonstrates that such "top-down reasoning models" often ignore the geometric structure and therefore the empirical information of the data. The geometric structure of many current exact valuation models does not fit the geometric structure of the empirical financial data. Otherwise stated: the information content of the current exact valuation models often differs from the information content of the financial data. There is often a conflict between the simply structured financial "model," like a single equation, that has been postulated and the complex, multi-equation model that the financial empiry of multi-dimensional data requires.

Indeed, recently much more sophisticated multi-dimensional-multi-variable, or mdmv modeling has been developed by mathematical system engineers. This often happened under the impact of direct $3D$ visualizations of the empirical data by sophisticated symbolic algebra and visualization software systems, like Matlab, Maple, Macsyma, and Mathematica.

To stimulate and promote this healthy interaction between engineering and finance, this book aims to carefully describe the exact mathematical structure of the current financial models and the epistemic uncertainty which surrounds them. It is intended for the (future) financial sector providers (in banks, funds, insurance companies and other financial intermediaries), who are interested not only in valuation models that are directly tied into empirical data, but who take also empirical financial risk management very seriously.

The book discusses efficient market theory, portfolio selection, risk analysis, and contingent-claim valuation theory and their relationships to each other and to empirical reality. Its empirical examples were gathered from the commercial practices of money management, financial (bank) intermediation, investment banking, corporate financing, capital budgeting and hedging procedures and global, multi-currency pension and insurance fund management. The Exercises contain many empirical examples gathered during my career as a Wall Street Economist. Instructor solutions for all Exercises are available from the author upon written request.

0.2 History

This book has a lengthy history. First, in the early 1980s I had many discussions about the shortcomings of theoretical econometrics with my Ph.D. thesis supervisor Dr. Phoebus J. Dhrymes, Professor of Econometrics at Columbia University. One evening, at his home, Dr. Dhrymes introduced me to his distinguished guest Dr. Tjalling C. Koopmans, * who, at that time somewhat surprisingly to me, agreed with several of my criticisms. My epistemological critique focused on the erroneous way Dr. Trygve Haavelmo and the Cowles Commission in the 1940s and 1950s had defined theoretical econometrics, in particular, its "probability approach " and its "estimation" of simultaneous equation models, respectively, but I could not (yet) formulate an alternative research method.†

Next, since 1985, the core argument of this book slowly emerged in long, intensive and sometimes painful discussions with Professor Rudolf E. Kalman, the 1985 winner of the Japanese Kyoto Prize for High Technology. After having earned my Ph.D. in 1984 from the Graduate School of Arts and Sciences of Columbia University, I was confronted with applied econometric practices in commercial financial environments. This first happened as an Economist, and then a Senior Economist, at the Federal Reserve Bank of New York (1981 - 87) and at Nomura Research Institute (America), Inc. (1987 - 90), and later as Chief Economist and Economic Advisor for ING Bank/ING Capital (1991-93) in New York City.

From those bruising empirical confrontations, I developed serious epistemological doubts about the established practices of econometrics, of financial analysis, and of conventional, probability theory based statistics in general. These doubts culminated initially in a series of Federal Reserve Research Papers in 1985, 1986 and 1987, which were eventually published in refereed journals in 1989, 1991 and 1992. Some of these papers led to vigorous, published academic debates. Dr. Kalman's and my ideas were severely criticized, e.g., by Bayesian probabilists like Professors E. T. Jaynes (Physics, Washington University in St. Louis, MO) and Arnold Zellner (Economics, University of Chicago), but were then decisively rebutted in the same scientific journals, sometimes to the public consternation of these critics.

In 1983, at the Fifth World Congress of The Econometric Society in Antipolis , Professor Kalman had delivered a scathing attack on econometrics and declared its death. Then I met him at the 7th IFAC/IFORS Symposium on "Identification and System parameter Estimation" in York, UK, 3 - 7 July 1985. He invited me to visit his research Center for Mathematical System Theory at the University of Florida in Gainesville, FL, over a period of seven years, two weeks every Spring and two weeks every Fall, until 1992. This became the Kalman - Los Project on System

---

*In 1975, jointly with Dr. Leonid V. Kantorovich, Dr. Tjalling Koopmans received the Nobel Memorial Prize in Economics for contributions to the theory of optimum allocation of resources.

†In 1989, despite our published misgivings and somewhat to his own personal consternation, Dr. Trygve Haavelmo received the Nobel Memorial Prize in Economics, for his clarification of the probability theory foundations of econometrics and his analyses of simultaneous economic structures.

Identification from Inexact Data, for which the Manifesto was formulated in 1986.[‡]

First, we discussed our mutual epistemological doubts about (financial) econometrics in great detail. Next, we attempted to develop a new approach to modeling under uncertainty, that does not rely on subjective statistical arguments. First, we followed in the footsteps of Ragnar Frisch, the 1969 (jointly with Jan Tinbergen) winner of the Nobel Memorial Prize in Economics.[§]

A crucial breakthrough came from my cracking of the Frisch $(4, 2)$ model problem, using Macsyma symbolic algebra. That solution was presented at the 8th IFAC/IFORS Symposium on Identification and System Parameter Estimation, in Beijing, People's Republic of China, 27 - 31 August 1988. This finding showed us clearly that Frisch's 1934 diagonal noise matrix assumption was also a prejudice, although a very subtle one. Our discovery led directly to my subsequent critique of Complete Capital Market Pricing (CCMP) theory and the (failed) Grand Unification Theory (GUT) of Finance proposal inherent in *RiskMetrics*[TM] (first developed by J. P. Morgan, Inc., but recently sold to Reuters, Inc.). Moreover, in addition to our rediscovery of the elementary (Grassmanian) projections in the information matrix (= inverse of the data covariance matrix), this breakthrough led directly to the Dr. Kalman's proof of the important *Complete* Least Squares (CLS) Projection Theorem in the winter of 1990/91, using Bekker's Lemma.[¶]

I made my first attempt at applying our new ideas of geometric model identification from inexact data in the field of Finance in a Lecture at the University of Zürich, Switzerland, on December 21 1990, by invitation of its Institute for Empirical Economic Research. In particular, I discussed the consequences for the CAPM and APT models and for portfolio mean-variance analysis. This Zürich Lecture I extended in the following year and on March 11, 1992, I summarized my collaborative research in a well attended Lecture on "A Scientific View of Economic and Financial Data Analysis" before The New York Academy of Sciences (NYAS). I gave my NYAS Lecture by invitation of Professors Lawrence Klein, the 1980 winner of the Nobel Memorial Prize in Economics,[||] and of Edmund Phelps (Professor of Economics at Columbia University) and Dominique Salvatore (Professor of International Economics, Fordham University).

My NYAS Lecture, together with the presented slides and a few supporting articles, was first disseminated to a limited circle of about four hundred cognoscenti and was finally published in 1995. My epistemological doubts regarding the (mis-)use of probability theory in uncertainty modeling were reinforced by Dr. Kalman's Lecture on "Stochastic Modeling Without Probability" on May 3, 1993 at the Sixth

---

[‡]The Manifesto is available in Appendix D. This formal collaborative research project lasted from 1986 through 1992. However, the project is still not finished and continues on an informal basis.

[§]For having developed and applied dynamic models for the analysis of economic processes.

[¶]CLS is not to be confused with the biased unidirectional projections of Generalized Least Squares (GLS).

[||]For the creation of econometric models and the application to the analysis of economic fluctuations and economic policies.

International Symposium on Applied Stochastic Models and Data Analysis at the University in Chania, Crete, Greece. There Dr. Kalman proved that there is very little, if any, scientific basis for Haavelmo's 1944 presumption of the empirical existence of Kolmogorov probability. The presumption of probability distributions does not contribute to the acquisition of scientific knowledge. It only detracts from the main task of model identification and can severely bias our conclusions.

Chapters 4, 5 and 6 of this book convincingly demonstrate that the presumption of probability is irrelevant for system identification, which requires an algebraic-geometric approach. I first presented my $2D$ and $3D$ maps of these Chapters in my NYAS Lecture; and next time, on March 16, 1992, in an Engineering and Statistics Seminar at M.I.T., with some help of Professor Paul A. Samuelson, the 1970 winner of the Nobel Memorial Prize in Economics.**

This was followed, on April 3, 1992 by an invited presentation on the identification of complex empirical systems at the Symposium on *The Interpretation of Quantum Theory: Where Do We Stand?* at the Italian Academy for Advanced Studies in America, at Columbia University. Next, there was a presentation in an intimate International Conference by invitation only, to Kenneth Arrow, the 1972 (jointly with Sir John R. Hicks), winner of the Nobel Memorial Prize in Economics,†† on "New Research on Identification in Econometrics", at the Department of Economics and Operations Research of Stanford University, Palo Alto, CA, November 4 - 6, 1992; and an International Symposium in Chania on Crete on May 4, 1993. A summary of the results was also presented that year at the 20th Annual Convention of the Eastern Economic Association in Boston by invitation of the (courageous) Editor of the *Eastern Economic Journal*, Professor Ingrid Rima.

Most of our arguments for *complete* identification from uncertain or noisy data, using a complete set of LS projections, have now been published. This book has benefitted from incorporating these published and properly acknowledged materials, which often emerged from my lectures. However, some lose ends remain, stimulating further research, *i.a.*, into the lack of stationarity and independence of financial data series.

0.3   Outline and Readers Guide

Following this Introduction, the book consists of five, nonconsecutive, parts:

1. Chapter 2 provides the basic formulas used in computational finance, while Chapter 3 provides the model valuations of the fundamental securities. It shows when and where exact, respectively, inexact modeling applies. For readers with a background in financial analysis, these two Chapters will be a (very) concise review, but within our new framework for discussion.

**For the scientific work through which he has developed static and dynamic economic theory and actively contributed to raising the level of analysis in economic science.

††For pioneering contributions to general equilibrium theory and welfare theory.

2. Chapters 4, 5 and 7 discuss inexact modeling and identification analysis, with applications to - systematic and unsystematic - financial risk analysis and management. It presents the critical material from the Kalman - Los 1986 - 1992 System Identification Research Project applied to financial computing. Appendices A, B, and C provide some further details for proofs and computations.

3. Chapters 8 - 13 discuss exact financial valuation models. Chapter 8 provides the basis of exact Complete Capital Market Pricing theory, on which the following five Chapters are based. Chapters 9 and 10 discuss exact option pricing theory. Chapters 11 and 12 discuss the exact systematic analysis of bonds and futures, with example of exact systematic financial risk management, while Chapter 13 uses the material of these two chapters to value exact swaps in three different, but equivalent fashions.

4. Chapters 6 and 14 discuss portfolio selection and optimization. Chapter 6 relates the systematic analysis of Chapters 4 and 5 to optimal portfolios, while Chapter 14 shows how the exact accounting analysis of Chapter 8 - 13 relates to the portfolio optimization of Chapter 6. Chapter 14 brings together the two strands of inexact and exact modeling in a common, international, investment growth accounting framework for portfolio selection and management and for return and risk attribution analysis.

Appendix E provides a list and a web site of journals publishing material on, or relatd to, computational finance.

0.4   Acknowledgements

I want to thank all those co-researchers and long-time friends, who have continued to have faith in me, despite many personal setbacks during my fifteen year research project. In particular, I thank my friend Rudolf Kalman (Professor Emeritus of the ETH in Zürich), who very patiently showed me the *via luminis* and who is not to be blamed for any remaining errors in my interpretation. I also thank Philip Cagan (Professor Emeritus of Columbia University) and Dominique Salvatore (Professor of International Economics of Fordham University). Both always replied kindly and generously to my long, critical letters.

I am also very grateful to all my former colleagues at the Federal Reserve Bank of New York, in particular Doctors Akhbar Akhtar, Paul Bennett, A. Steven Englander (now with Goldman Sachs, Inc.) Menahem Prywes (now with the World Bank). and Andy Hook (now with the International Monetary Fund (IMF)). They provided me with ample opportunities to present my ideas within the Federal Reserve System, challenged me on my views, and, in the mid - 1980s, often produced fresh evidence of severe model mis-specification, like the instability of the money demand equation, or the shaky credit-scoring of supervised commercial banks. Often they assisted me by sending recommendations on my behalf to the various institutions, which have consecutively provided me with gainful employment and made this research possible, despite resistance to the results. I also thank my Japanese and Dutch colleagues at Nomura Research Institute (America), Inc. and ING Bank/ING Capital in New York, respectively, for providing me with many additional empirical examples from the emerging markets, which were first used as illustrations in my published papers and then as case studies for my students and as Exercises in this book.

I'm deeply indebted to my colleagues and students in the Banking and Finance Division of the Nanyang Business School of the Nanyang Technological University in Singapore and of the School of Economics at Adelaide University in Adelaide, South Australia, respectively. Both universities provided me with the facilities to research, write and publish several academic articles and, finally, this book. It effectively grew out of my attempts in the years 1996 - 2000 to explain the scientific perspective on computational finance in semester lectures and tutorials. Several of my students in Singapore did collaborative research with me for their Honours projects and their questions and diligent work provided crucial research material and critical feedback. I would like to acknowledge, in Singapore, Au Yin Fung, Fong Yuen Chiang, Heng Miung Tse, Heng Puay Hiong, Hu Su Peng, Lee Lin Kew, Lim Cheer Hwi, Ng Tian Tat, Ng Yi Ee, Ong Sze Wei, Pee Chin Min, Ng Guan Mean, Shih Yueh, Tan Seow Min, Tan Su Lin, Tham Yein Mei, Wong Chi Wai, and my Master student Jeyanthi Karuppiah; and in Adelaide, Jason Boccaccio, Cheng Siu-Tin, Regan James Engelhardt, Michael Lamarca, Thi Thanh Huyen Nguyen, Michelle Tu Lu, and Phuong Truong.

Last but not least, my deepest gratitude is to my beautiful wife Rosie, who entered my life in 1990, by chance, on a flight between New York and Minneapolis, and who has ever since brightened my days with love and laughter.

Cornelis A. Los
Adelaide University

Chapter 1
A SCIENTIFIC PERSPECTIVE

1.1 Introduction

This book will provide you with a critical overview of the young field of *computational finance* . Its Chapters will provide you with an understanding of *exact* and *inexact modeling* based on real financial and economic data, while the exercises will give you practical experience with *spreadsheet programming* for financial modeling. The exercises form an integral part of this intensive book.

On the financial modeling side, the following Chapters will cover the mathematics of capital budgeting, the valuation of the fundamental assets of bonds and stocks and the valuation of the derivatives, like options, futures and swaps, using Complete Capital Markets Theory. Together with classical Markowitz' mean-variance analysis, new financial system identification techniques, based on information matrix analysis, will be introduced and applied to systematic risk analysis. Hedging strategies to deal with interest rate risk, credit risk measurement, and the important credit quality migration analysis, using Markov state transition theory, will also be discussed in detail. In the last Chapter, the book brings it all together with exact attribution analysis of multi-currency investment strategies, in combination with portfolio optimization, and it finishes with investment performance measurement.

On the programming side, the Exercises will cover how to scientifically analyze empirical financial data and how to identify and realize the various multivariate financial models discussed in the Chapters, using algebraic and geometric (graphical) modeling approaches in Windows 95 EXCEL spreadsheets. In addition, the Chapters and Exercises will also demonstrate some uses of financial visualization to stimulate interest in advanced (graduate level) research.

1.2 Financial Modeling and Computers

Let's first introduce some definitions, terminology and modeling principles to promote an intelligent discussion about financial modeling. *Computer-based financial models* are computer programs that realize financial models or systems. *Models* are abstractions , often of a mathematical nature, used to simplify our decision making environment , since the empirical reality is too complex and its complete analysis too time-consuming and expensive. Still models must be realistic representations of a reality that we find to be written in the language of mathematics, in particular of algebraic geometry . *Financial models* are a subset of all generic models that deal with financial (and economic) phenomena and data.

Computer-based financial modeling deals with the development and implementation of software to realize financial models, so that an automatic mapping takes place between the available data and the model. The objective is to produce a model which can be used for experimentation , *c.q.*, simulation and extrapolation. *Financial modeling* is the subset of the general *Theory of Modeling* which deals with finance. Therefore, in this book, we can borrow and implement some important principles from the general Theory of Modeling, which help us to clarify some problems that have baffled financial and economic analysts in past decades.

1.3   Epistemic Uncertainty : Exact and Inexact Models

Following fundamental research by Dr. Kalman (1985a & b, 1993), winner of the Japanese 1985 Kyoto Prize for High Technology and myself, we now can unequivocally state that the *logic of the scientific method* requires that we *let the complete set of (financial) data speak for itself, without prejudice* . This doesn't mean that we can not transform the original, or raw data before further analysis. We only have to be careful how we transform the raw data. Unique, one-to-one, exact conversions of the data don't change the internal (algebraic geometric) *structure* , or set of relationships, of the data, only the form of the data. This is of crucial importance, since

geometric structure of the data = information contained in the data

For example, exponentials, powers, or logarithmic transformation are exact and unique conversions of the *data frame of reference* . Unique conversions are *information invariant* . These unique conversions operate like lenses and bring salient details of the original data into focus.

However, the original data may be exact or inexact. In fact, empirical data are generically inexact . Correspondingly, the result of our modeling efforts may be exact or inexact, as follows.

realization = building a model S from available exact data D

A realization of the data D means that *all* the available (or more) data could have been produced by experimenting with the model.

This realization or exact system modeling led the mathematical system theorist Kalman to formulate the following important mathematical modeling principle (Kalman, 1985a & b).

Principle of Uniqueness : if the data are exact and complete (*i.e., as much as desired*), then the minimal model is unique. Implementation of this principle relies on checking certain rank conditions of the data and the system or model.

Remark 1 *In the system engineering literature the terms system and model are often used interchangeably. Both system and model are realizations when dealing with exact data. But most empirical data aren't exact and system engineers , including financial engineers have had to cope with the ill-understood problems created by inexact data.*

Building a model S from available *inexact* data D is called *identification* . An identification of the data means that *not all* of the available data could have been produced by experimenting with the model. The data contain some unidentifiable and unexplainable noise, or uncertainty.* The amount and the character of this noise depends on the modeling technique used, although there is a well-known physical limit to the amount of unidentifiable, unexplainable empirical uncertainty , due to the energy granularity of the universe.

Epistemic uncertainty is the uncertainty about the model induced by the inexactness of the data . In the context of financial modeling, epistemic uncertainty (= modeling risk) implies financial risk . This phenomenon of epistemic uncertainty, or noise, led Dr. Kalman to formulate a second important mathematical modeling principle (Kalman, 1985a & b; Los, 1992):

Principle of Epistemic Uncertainty : the inexactness of the data is expressed as uncertainty about the model.

In other words: "garbage in, garbage out." A model can only be as exact as the data used for its identification.

Remark 2 *If the empirical data are inexact, but the model resulting from some mathematical manipulation is exact, we know that some prejudices and biases have (often unconsciously, but always surreptitiously) been introduced by the research methodology and we must first find where and how these prejudices affect our research results.*

---

*According to Webster's *New Universal Unabridged Dictionary* (Deluxe Second Edition), Dorset & Baber, 1983, p. 1990):

> **un·cĕr 'tain·ty** = the quality or state of being uncertain; lack of certainty; doubt

and

> **un · cĕr 'tain** = 1. not certainly known; questionable; problematical.
> 2. vague; not definite or determined.
> 3. doubtful; not having certain knowledge; not sure.
> 4. ambiguous.
> 5. not steady or constant; varying.
> 6. liable to change or vary; not dependable or reliable

It should be emphasized that the amount of epistemic uncertainty or modeling noise is not immeasurable. In fact, signal processing (*e.g., sound*) engineers have always measured epistemic uncertainty by the *Noise/Signal ratio* (or, more often, by its inverse, the Signal/Noise ratio). The larger the Noise/Signal ratio, the more uncertain the identified model (= signal). The smaller the Noise/Signal ratio, the more certain the identified model (= signal). The importance of the measurement of the amount of noise or inexactness by the Noise/Signal ratio is derived from the following simple mathematical idea:

> exactness =
> inexactness (noise) and mathematical continuity
> and limit , with inexactness (noise) → 0

In other words, when the inexactness, or noise, in the data shows *mathematical continuity* , then in the limit, when the inexactness (noise) vanishes, we end up with the exact modeling situation. Thus in the limit and with continuity, model identification should result in model realization. Unfortunately, data are never continuous, since the universe isn't continuous. Even ostensibly analogue data are in essence discrete. There is a fundamental non-continuity and discreteness in data caused by the energy granularity of the universe. However, this fundamental data discreteness or inexactness is at a level much smaller than the computational accuracy of computers and should not be any hindrance to very precise modeling, despite the inexactness of the data. In particular this is of small (but not totally unimportant!) concern, when we are dealing with financial modeling, where the required accuracy is limited to only two digits after the decimal point, *i.e.*, to *cents*!

1.3.1 Exact Models , e.g., Financial Statements

Let us now first provide some examples of what is meant by exact data and their corresponding models. From our physics classes we are all familiar with some elementary physics . Kepler identified his elliptical planetary orbits from uncertain empirical observations of some planets in our solar system. But the next step was one of model realization:

Exact data: Kepler's exact elliptical planetary orbits .

Exact model: Newton's inverse square Universal Law of Gravitation

$$F = \frac{G \times m_1 \times m_2}{x^2} \tag{1.1}$$

where F is the gravitational (attraction) force, G is the universal gravitational constant , m_1 and m_2 the two masses, and x the radius or distance between the two masses. In logarithmic form this is a very simple additive model

$$\ln F - \ln G - \ln m_1 - \ln m_2 + 2 \ln x = 0 \tag{1.2}$$

Newton's realized model explains Kepler's theoretical elliptical orbits exactly.[†] In addition, this Newtonian model is probably one of the best empirically corroborated model in science , in the sense that it fits the modern laser generated observational orbital data almost exactly, with extremely little uncertainty left. This is a remarkable feat; the more so since this theory agreed with Newton's own observational data of planetary orbits only to within about 11%. From recent modern physics research at the atomic level with lasers , it is found that this theory applies equally well to the orbits of (slow-moving) electrons . By direct observation electrons are measured to follow elliptic (and not circular) orbits around the atomic nucleus . The attractive force between the electrons and the atomic nucleus is the Coulomb force.

However, what most people don't realize is that we have similar exact models in finance. Bookkeeping is the systematic recording of the monetary value of business transactions in a book of accounts . In 1494 by Luca Pacioli , a Franciscan monk, published an influential textbook on mathematics , *Summa de Arithmetica, Geometria Proportioni et Proportionalita*, which contains the first description of *double-entry bookkeeping* .[‡]

Figure 1   Luca Pacioli (1445-1517)

Bookkeeping is the preliminary record - keeping stage of *accounting* . The double entry system of bookkeeping enables a business to know at any given time the

---

[†]Johannes Kepler (1571 - 1630) identified his first law of elliptical planetary orbits in his *Astronomia nova* (New Astronomy), 1609. Isaac Newton (1643 - 1727) realized the theory of universal gravitation from Kepler's elliptical orbits in 1666 and published this first mathematical system realization result in his scientific master piece *Philosophiae Naturalis Principia Mathematica* (Mathematical Principles of Physics), 1687.

[‡]Historians generally credit 14th-century Italian merchants with developing the practice of double-entry bookkeeping, which is the basis for modern-day accounting. Luca Pacioli (1445-1517), a Franciscan monk, who tutored the sons and daughters of these wealthy Italian merchants, published his book, *Summa de arithmetica, geometria proportioni et proportionalita* (*Summary of Arithmetics, Geometry of Proportions and Abacus*) in 1494, just two years after Colum,bus "discovered" America. His treatise contained, along with discussions of arithmetic, algebra, geometry and trigonometry, a summary description of double-entry bookkeeping.

value of each item that is owned, or its Assets (A) , how much of this value is owed to creditors, its Liabilities (L) , and how much belongs to the business clear of debt, or its Equity (E) . Accordingly we have, as *double-entry bookkeeping model*:

Exact data: financial data, *i.e.*, accounting journal entries following Generally Accepted Accounting Principles (GAAP)

Exact model: two balance sheets , one at the beginning of the balance period and one at the end, plus the income statement during the balance period (plus the corresponding cash flow statement). The beginning and ending balance sheets are connected by the net profit at the bottom of the income statement for the period, while the cash flow statement can be uniquely derived from these three fundamental financial statements. Thus, financial statements - balance sheets, income and cash flow statements - are exact, because the data in them (*e.g.*, the journal entries) are recorded conforming to the original book value (but now more market value) Accounting Identity :

$$Assets = Liabilities + Equity \qquad (1.3)$$
$$\text{or } A = L + E \qquad (1.4)$$
$$\text{or, implicitly, } A - L + E = 0 \qquad (1.5)$$

This Accounting Identity is the basic model for most of exact financial modeling , since many financial instruments can be viewed as combinations of long and short positions of the fundamental securities , or $E = A - L$. Changes in the net equity position ΔE are produced by the

$$Net\ Income = Revenues - Expenses$$
$$= r_A A - r_L L$$
$$= \Delta A - \Delta L.$$
$$= r_E E$$
$$= \Delta E \qquad (1.6)$$

where r_A is the average Rate of Return on Assets (ROA) , r_L is the average rate of debt liability expense, and r_E is the average Rate of Return on Equity (ROE) .

The following is an example of a model of a fundamental security, which we will specify and elaborate on in Chapter 3:

Exact data: discount rate , maturity and maturity value

Exact model: value of a bond

When we introduce additional inexact or discrete data, like the grade or quality of the bond (which is a discrete measurement), we find that this model of a bond becomes inexact and the bond's value becomes uncertain.

1.3.2   Inexact Models , e.g., Behavioral Relationships

Next, we will provide a well-known economic example of inexact data and their corresponding model. Behavioral relationships , like the relationship between inventory and sales , are inexact, because the available empirical data do not conform to simple identities as in exact Newtonian physics . This does not mean that people have not philosophized about inventory theories , e.g., Baumol's (1972, Chapter 1, pp. 3 - 11) exact *optimal square-root inventory model*:

$$I = \sqrt{(2 \times b \times Q \times k)} \qquad (1.7)$$

in which I is the optimal (cost-minimizing) inventory, b is the fixed cost of reordering, k is the unit carrying of cost of inventory, and Q is the level of sales. Although in logarithmic form this is also a very simple additive model :

$$\ln I - 0.5.(\ln 2 + \ln b + \ln Q + \ln k) = 0 \qquad (1.8)$$

Baumol's inventory model is currently still an empirically uncorroborated, hypothesized model , based upon normative assumptions (about optimizing behavior). In fact, Baumol's normative model is not a scientific model realized from exact empirical data or even identified from inexact empirical data. Therefore, it should not be surprising to find that this model doesn't "fit" the empirical data well. There is inexactness in the data, which can be measured in four different projective directions, since there are four measured variables I, b, Q and k. Such multi-dimensional inexactness can lead to spurious measured covariances between the four data series. The problem then becomes how to decompose such measured covariance data into exact systematic and residual unsystematic covariances.

Remark 3 *Most of the current models are in the form of equations, and their visualizations, of increasing order, which have a long and illustrious history in science. Ca. 2000BC, the Babylonians solved quadratic equations in radicals. Next, it took three millennia before, in 1079AD Omar Khayyam (1050 - 1123) solved cubic equations geometrically by intersecting parabolas and circles. Ca. 1500AD, Renaissance mathematicians in Italy, like Luca Pacioli, solved cubic and quartic equations. In 1733 Edmund Halley (1656 - 1742) solved quadratic equations in trigonometric functions In 1858 Charles Hermite (1822 - 1901), Leopold Kronecker (1823 - 1891), and Francesco Brioschi (1824 - 1897) independently solved quintic equations explicitly in terms of elliptic modular functions.[§] In 1991 and 1992 David Dummit and, independently, Sigeru Kobayashi and Hiroshi Nakagawa gives methods for finding the roots of a general solvable quintic equation in radicals. The solutions of all these higher - order equations are now available in Mathematica. It is a remarkable fact that financial and economic models have not progressed much beyond the quadratic equations of a thousand years ago. Much scientific progress is therefore still to be expected in those fields.*

[§]The Taniyama-Shimura conjecture states that every elliptic curve is a modular form.

1.4   Identification, Simulation and Extrapolation

In addition to the concept of exact realization, there are three concepts that are often confused by modelers, in particular in financial and economic modeling: identification, simulation and extrapolation:

Identification is building a model from the available inexact data.

Simulation is experimenting with the model to produce new, additional data.

Extrapolation is producing new data with a model beyond the reference period of the available data.[¶]

Remark 4 *In this book, we will not use the statistical term "estimation," since that is based upon the assumption of stochastic , in particular, probabilistic phenomena . We will demonstrate that the assumption of probability is extraneous to modeling, although it can be used for playing sophisticated statistical games. Kalman and Los established that modeling can be executed by only algebraic and geometric, i.e., "non-statistical" methodologies . (Benzing and Dunleavy, 1992; Jaynes, 1989; Kalman, 1993; Los, 1989a & b, 1991, 1992a & b, 1994, 1995; Zellner, 1992)*

1.5   Pro Forma Financial Statement Projections

The identification of behavioral relationships, *i.e.*, the information in particular behavior, is important for simulation and extrapolation. *Pro forma* financial statements (balance sheet, income and cash flow statements) are financial statement projections in various time periods based on simulation and extrapolation, using the exact accounting identity $A = L + E$ in combination with identified behavioral relationships. They are thus complex combinations of exact and inexact models, using inertia properties of the data, *e.g.*, of the sales data, for extrapolation into the future. Benninga (1997) provides several detailed such *pro forma* balance sheet projections and uses them to optimize balance sheet structures in simulations.

1.6   Envisioning Information: Unique Mappings

Some inspiring examples of unique, exact, scientific mapping are provided by Hall (1993), mostly in the form of special visualizations :

- Navigational chart of Voyager 2

- Remote sensed Landsat maps of ocean floors

- Ultraviolet spectrometric map of the earth's ozone layer

[¶]Extrapolation has a more precise definition than the rather general and bland term "forecasting".

- Human genome maps.[||]

- Cartography of detected subatomic particles

- Hubble's law, which is a plot of the speed of recession of galaxies versus their distance

There is nothing that prevents us from similar unique scientific mapping in Finance, but, surprisingly, there are few multi-dimensional maps of financial instruments and financial systems in existence. The visualization of financial instruments has just started, thanks to the recent availability of user friendly 3-dimensional and 4-dimensional visualization[**] software packages (*Cf.* Wolff and Yaeger, 1993; Gallagher, 1994). Using such visualization software, empirical discoveries in finance are bound to happen in the near future.[††]

In this book, we will demonstrate several different kinds of financial maps and visualizations in two and three and more dimensions; like the 2−dimensional price - yield curve of a bond, the 3−dimensional ray structure of an Asset Pricing Theory model and the 6−dimensional surface structure of the Black - Scholes call option model . This is possible, since all these financial instruments are exact models, thanks to their particular expression of the exact Accounting Identity.

Option valuations are empirically inexact models. They look exact only because the assumption of continuity of the financial data is made, which allows the implementation of a limiting argument . However, visualization of the 6−dimensional Black - Scholes European call option model (Black and Scholes, 1973) shows substantial discrepancies between theory and empiry (Los, 1997). The Black-Scholes implied volatility differs from the directly measured price volatility, indicating a substantial source of inexactness and epistemic uncertainty. Furthermore, it appears that one of

---

[||]Positional DNA cloning to detect disease mutations actually involves four consecutive, ever more precise maps: (1) a genetic mapping between family studies and chromosome intervals, (2) a physical mapping between a chromosome interval and large - insert clones, (3) a transcript mapping between large-insert clones and candidate genes, and (4) a gene mapping (sequencing) between candidate genes and the disease mutation in the DNA sequence. In the last map the Noise/Signal Ratio is 1, so that repeated (ensemble) mapping is required. Huberman, Lukose and Hogg (1997) present a general method for combining such maps into new programs that are better than any of the component maps separately. Their method, based on notions of risk in economics, *i.e.*, Markowitz portfolio optimization (Cf. Chapters 6 and 14), offers a computational portfolio optimization procedure that can be used for problems involving the combinatorics of DNA sequencing.

[**]4-dimensional visualization is 3-dimensional visualization plus color coding or shading.

[††]In his Address to the Prussian Academy of Sciences in Berlin on January 27th 1921 :Geometry and Experience," Albert Einstein (1879 - 1955) emphasized the usefulness of higher-dimensional (non-Euclidean) visualization.. He stated: "To "visualise" a theory, or to bring home to one's mind, therefore means to give a representation to that abundance of experiences for which the theory supplies the schematic arrangement." and "...the human faculty of visualisation is by no means bound to capitulate to non-Euclidean geometry." Cf. Albert Einstein, *Sidelights on Relativity*, Dover Publications, Inc., New York, 1983, pp. 45 - 46 and p. 56, respectively.

its basic assumptions - the log-normality of the random walk innovations - cannot be corroborated by empirical data (Kalman, 1994, 1995). Currently option valuations must be deemed inherently speculative and, therefore, belong to the domain of mathematical games and not to the domain of scientific models , which explain real market behavior.

More importantly, empirical financial market relationships produce inexact models based upon inexact market behavior. Model identification is therefore (or, perhaps, we should say, should be) more prevalent than exact modeling, when the real world is encountered. However, we should keep the Platonian ideal , exact situation in our mind, to know in which direction our research should march forward with the most success for victory.

Of course, information about financial instruments and market relationships can always be envisioned in the form of (multi-dimensional) graphs, both for exact and for inexact data. But one should remain aware that often maps abstract from the inexactness and can be misleading. As researchers, we should always remain conscious of the fundamental prejudices and shortcomings of our maps and our models (cf... Hall, 1993), particularly in Finance, where prejudicial and misleading information about the systematic risk/return profiles of investment portfolios can have disastrous billion dollar consequences, e.g., the US' savings and loans crises in the 1980s, the Japanese stock market crash in 1990, the Barings Bank debacle in 1995, the Mexican currency crisis in 1994, and the ASEAN currency and bank debt crises in 1997.

1.7   Exercises

Exercise 5 *Basic EXCEL skills*

In EXCEL, learn the following skills (Fig. 2.): (a) Use of *toolbars* and *options*; (b) Setting *column width;* (c) Inserting and deleting *columns* and *rows;* (d) Formatting *cells* for currency, percentage, etc.; (e) Using *borders;* (f) *Naming cells & ranges;* (g) Display *formulas* instead of *values;* (h) *Relative* and *absolute referencing;* (i) Making *series* and filling *cells;* (j) Use of *auditing;* (k) Use of special *fonts. (cf...* Stultz, 1996) These skills will be applied in the following two questions and in all remaining Exercises.

Exercise 6 *Credit-Scoring Models*

The current Asian currency and banking crisis requires the quantitative determination of the likelihood of the default of bank loans. This is needed for proper discounting of existing distressed loan values for market-making purposes, *i.e.,* the securitization, pricing and trading of distressed bank loans. According to the credit risk literature, the following three practical approaches to estimating the probability of counterparty default exist:

The Excel Version 5 for Windows Screen

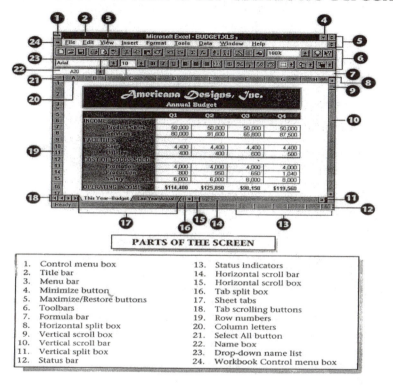

Figure 2   EXCEL spreadsheet: screen parts

1.	Control menu box	13.	Status indicators
2.	Title bar	14.	Horizontal scroll bar
3.	Menu bar	15.	Horizontal scroll box
4.	Minimize button	16.	Tab split box
5.	Maximize/Restore buttons	17.	Sheet tabs
6.	Toolbars	18.	Tab scrolling buttons
7.	Formula bar	19.	Row numbers
8.	Horizontal split box	20.	Column letters
9.	Vertical scroll box	21.	Select All button
10.	Vertical scroll bar	22.	Name box
11.	Vertical split box	23.	Drop-down name list
12.	Status bar	24.	Workbook Control menu box

Fundamental analytic accounting approach

The analytic accounting approach is uses a subjective valuation based on DuPont ratio analysis and is the method used by most rating agencies. Basically, it decomposes the Return on Equity (ROE) into its constituents of Profit Margin , Asset Turnover

($=$ Asset Utilization) and Asset/Equity Multiplier ($=$ Equity Leverage)[‡‡]. Thus

$$ROE = \text{Profit Margin} \times \text{Asset Turnover} \times \text{Asset/Equity Multiplier}$$
$$= \frac{\text{Profit}}{\text{Revenues}} \times \frac{\text{Revenues}}{\text{Assets}} \times \frac{\text{Assets}}{\text{Equity}}$$
$$= \frac{\text{Profit}}{\text{Equity}} \tag{1.9}$$

Statistical methods

The statistical methods encompass three basic approaches:

1. Qualitative dependent variable methods (logistic regression, probit/logit analysis);

2. Discriminant analysis (linear discriminant analysis; principal components analysis); and

3. Neural networks (self-organizing feature maps).

Option - theoretic methods

The option-theoretic methods are becoming fast the common academic paradigm for default valuation and is promoted by KMV Corporation as part of J.P. Morgan 's CreditMetrics^{TM} (cf. Introduction to CreditMetrics, 1997).

In this Exercise we will look at linear discriminant analysis, which applies a classification model to categorize (or score) which borrowing firms have defaulted versus which firms survived and compare it to the accounting analytic approach. The best example of linear discriminant analysis is Professor Edward Altman's Z-scores , first developed by Altman (1968) and commercially supplied by Zeta Services, Inc. (Altman et al., 1977). Commercial applications of neural networks are currently used in large volume, automatized, commercial credit allowance decisions, such as credit card, or quick bank loan authorizations.

Default Prediction Model of Altman

The Z-score of Altman is computed from the following Zeta model equation:

$$Z = 1.2X_1 + 1.4X_2 + 3.3X_3 + 0.6X_4 + 0.999X_5 \tag{1.10}$$

where the input variables are defined as follows in terms of the raw data:
$$X_1 = \frac{NetWorkingCapital}{TotalAssets}, \quad X_1 = \frac{RetainedEarnings}{TotalAssets}, \quad X_3 = \frac{EBIT}{TotalAssets},$$
$$X_4 = \frac{MarketValueofShares}{BookValueofDebt}, \quad X_5 = \frac{Sales}{TotalAssets}$$

[‡‡]Financial analysts use often much finer ratio decompositions.

Altman's 50/50 point is 2.675. His so-called "ignorance zone" is between 1.81 and 2.99. A higher value of Z is interpreted as less probability of bankruptcy, a lower value is interpreted as higher probability of bankruptcy.

Calculate the Z-score for a firm with $300 Net Working Capital , $2, 100 Total Assets , $700 Retained Earnings , $256 EBIT , $2, 900 Sales Revenues and the ratio of Market Value of Shares to Book Value of Debt equal to 138.6%.

Exercise 7 *Modeling Critique*

Suggest some fundamental technical deficiencies of this Z-score model. This model is used, in updated and patented form, *i.a.*, by international rating agencies (*e.g.*, Standard & Poors , Dun and Bradstreet) for credit grading and valuation, by credit analysis departments of banks, and by consultants, to determine the likelihood of corporate failures , and by central banks (*e.g.*, Federal Reserve System of U.S.) to determine the likelihood of commercial bank failures (Hooks, 1996; Los, 1989b). Professor Altman of the Stern School of Business of New York University and traders in fixed-income securities (*e.g.*, at ING Bank , Citibank , Bankers Trust) use this Z-model in a procedure to value distressed debt in emerging markets (Altman, 1996). But do not let these authorities deter you from critiquing the model and raising some epistemological doubts .

When you view this model, ask critical questions like: is this a representative model? Why or why not? Is this an exact or an inexact model? How do we know? How many relationships can exist among the six variables of the Z-model? Can you write them down in algebraic form? Why do you think that there is such a diversity of valuations and ratings in credit scoring ? How would you go about finding the coefficients of these behavioral models ? Based on your knowledge of financial analysis, can you suggest an exact accounting model to assess the likelihood of bankruptcy? What are the two main reasons for the appeal of Altman's Z-score? Would you recommend to commercial banks to use it, or not? Why?

1.8 Bibliography

Black, F. and Scholes, M. (1973) "The Pricing of Options and Corporate Liabilities," *Journal of Political Economy*, **81**, May - June, 637 - 659.

Bharadia, M. A. J., Christofides, N. and Salkin, G. R. (1995) "Computing the Black - Scholes Implied Volatility: Generalization of a Simple Formula," *Advances in Futures and Options Research*, **8**, 15-29.

Bharadia, M. A. J., Christofides, N. and Salkin, G. R. (1996), "A Quadratic Method for the Calculation of Implied Volatility Using the Garman - Kohlhagen Model, " *Financial Analysts Journal*, **52** (2), 61 - 64.

Bodie, Z. and Merton, R. C. (1995) "The Informational Role of Asset Prices: The Case of Implied Volatility," Chapter 6 in Crane, D. B. *et. al.* (Eds.), *The Global*

Financial System: A Functional Perspective, Harvard Business School Press, Boston, MA, pp. 197 - 224.

Clarke, R. G. (1992) "Short-Term Behavior of Option Prices: Hedging Relationships," Chapter 6 in *Options and Futures: A Exercise*, The Research Foundation of The Institute of Chartered Financial Analysts, Charlottesville, VA, pp. 57 - 68.

Derman, E., Kani, I. and Zou, J. Z. (1996) "The Local Volatility Surface: Unlocking the Information in Index Option Prices," *Financial Analysts Journal*, July - August, 25 - 36.

Gallagher, R. S. (Ed.) (1994) *Computer Visualization: Graphis Techniques for Scientific and Engineering Analysis*, CRC Press, Boca Raton, FL.

Gibson, R. (1991) *Option Valuation: Analyzing and Pricing Standardized Option Contracts*, McGraw-Hill, Inc., New York, NY.

Huberman, B. A., Lukose, R. M., and Hogg, T. (1997) "An Economics Approach to Hard Computational Problems," *Science*, **275**, 3 January, 51 - 54.

Hull, J. C. (1996) *Options, Futures and Other Derivatives,* (3rd ed.), Prentice Hall International, Inc., New York, NY.

Kalman, R. E. (1996) "Probability in the Real World as a System Attribute," *CWI Quarterly*, **9** (3), 181 - 204.

Kolmogorov, A. N. (1933) *Grundbegriffe der Wahrscheinlichkeitsrechnung*, Springer Verlag, Berlin. (Translated by Nathan Morrison: *Foundations of Probability*, Chelsea, New York, NY, 1950).

Los, C. A. (1997) "Visualization of Call Options and Implied Volatility," *MODSIM97 - International Congress on Modelling and Simulation Proceedings*, **3**, 8 - 11 December, Hobart, Tasmania, pp. 1311 - 1316.

Merton, R. C. (1975) "Theory of Finance from the Perspective of Continuous Time," *Journal of Financial and Quantitative Analysis*, **10** (4), November, 659 - 674.

Merton, R. C. (1995) "Influence of Mathematical Models in Finance on Practice: Past, Present and Future," Chapter 1 in Howison, S. D., Kelly, F. P. and Wilmott, P. (Eds.), *Mathematical Models in Finance*, Chapman & Hall, London, pp. 1 - 13.

Merton, R. C. (1998) "Applications of Option-Pricing Theory: Twenty-Five Years Later," *American Economic Review*, **88** (3), 323 - 349.

Nielson, G. M., Hagen, H. and Müller, H. (1997) *Scientific Visualization: Overviews, Methodologies and Techniques*, IEEE Computer Society, Los Alamitos, CA.

Pincus, S. and R. E. Kalman (1997) "Not All (Possibly) "Random" Sequences Are Created Equal," *Proceedings of the National Academy of Sciences (USA)*, **94**, April, 3513 - 3518.

Pincus, S. and B. H. Singer (1996) "Randomness and Degrees of Irregularity," *Proceedings of the National Academy of Sciences (USA)*, **93**, 2083 - 2088.

Risk/FINEX (1992) *From Black - Scholes to Black Holes*, Risk Magazine, Ltd, London.

Walmsley, J. (1992) "Options Applications," Chapter 17 in his book *The Foreign Exchange and Money Markets Guide*, John Wiley & Sons, Inc., New York, NY, pp. 363 - 403.

Wolff, R. S. and Yaeger, L. (1993) *Visualization of Natural Phenomena*, Telos/Springer Verlag, Boston, MA.

chapter:2,page:1

Chapter 2
CAPITAL BUDGETING AND ANALYTIC FORMULAS

2.1 Introduction

The purpose of financial analysis is to assess the return and risk prospects of investments and thus the value of business assets and liabilities. Under conditions of no risk (= no market price volatility and no credit risk), the *value of an asset* equals the *present value* (P) of all the future *cash flows* (CFs) which it generates, where these future cash flows are discounted at a risk - free discount rate . Under conditions of risk, the additional risk value of the asset is priced with options. First we will discuss the risk-free present value calculations and in later Chapters the additional risk valuation by options.

2.2 Present and Future Value Calculations

Present value calculations are "inverted" future value calculations. The process of computing future values is called *compounding* and the rate to use is the *compounding rate* x. The process of computing present values is called *discounting* and the interest rate to use is called the *discount rate* x. We have the following series of exact future and present value models :

Single period future value

$$
\begin{aligned}
F_1 &= X_0 + x_1 X_0 \\
&= X_0(1 + x_1)
\end{aligned}
\tag{2.1}
$$

Single period present value

$$
X_0 = \frac{F_1}{(1 + x_1)}
\tag{2.2}
$$

Multiperiod future value with different rates for each period

$$
F_n = X_0(1 + x_1)(1 + x_2)...(1 + x_n)
\tag{2.3}
$$

Multiperiod present value with different rates for each period

$$
X_0 = \frac{F_n}{(1 + x_1)(1 + x_2)...(1 + x_n)}
\tag{2.4}
$$

Multiperiod future value with one constant rate

$$F_n = X_0(1+x)^n \tag{2.5}$$

Multiperiod present value with one constant rate

$$X_0 = \frac{F_n}{(1+x)^n} \tag{2.6}$$

An important financial principle is the Value Additivity Principle, which enables the concatenation and accumulation of values from different cash flows.

Value Additivity Principle : the future, respectively present value of a series of cash flows equals the sum of the future, respectively present values of the individual cash flows.

An *annuity* is a series of equal periodic payments . Applying the Value Additivity Principle, the future value of an ordinary annuity, with payments at the end of the periods, or payments *in arrears* , is thus:

$$
\begin{aligned}
FA_n &= \sum_{t=0}^{n-1} CF(1+x)^t \\
&= CF \sum_{t=0}^{n-1} (1+x)^t \\
&= CF[(1+x)^0 + (1+x)^1 + (1+x)^2 + \dots + (1+x)^{n-1}]
\end{aligned} \tag{2.7}
$$

This future value of an annuity can be expressed more concisely. Pre-multiply this expression by $(1+x)$ and subtract the original expression from the result, so that

$$xFA_n = CF[(1+x)^n - 1] \tag{2.8}$$

Consequently, the future value of an annuity is

$$FA_n = \frac{CF[(1+x)^n - 1]}{x} \tag{2.9}$$

But then the present value of an annuity is

$$PA_0 = \frac{FA_n}{(1+x)^n} \tag{2.10}$$

which can easily be verified to be equivalent to

$$PA_0 = CF[\frac{1}{x} - \frac{1}{x(1+x)^n}] \tag{2.11}$$

2.3 Continuous and Discrete Compounding

Discrete compounding and discounting occurs when the compounding/discount rate, remains constant during each period and only changes between periods. The compounding/discount rate is a *step function* of time. *Continuous compounding* and *discounting* occurs when the compounding/discount rate changes continuously over time. The corresponding continuous time expressions for future , respectively present, values at any time t are:

$$F_t = X_0 e^{\rho t} \tag{2.12}$$
$$\text{and } X_0 = F_t e^{-\rho t} \tag{2.13}$$

The relationship between the discrete rate x and the continuous rate ρ is given by the unique conversion

$$(1 + x) = e^{\rho}, \tag{2.14}$$
$$\text{or } \rho = \ln(1 + x) \tag{2.15}$$
$$\text{or } x = e^{\rho} - 1 \tag{2.16}$$

Later, in Chapter 10 on Black - Scholes Option Pricing, we will use these transformations to find the Black - Scholes pricing formula as the limit of a binomial valuation process.

2.4 Expansions and Euler Formulas

In this Section we present some useful approximating functional *expansion series* and *exponential functions* , which are often used by financial analysts and, in particular, in the financial derivatives literature (*cf.* Chapter 10). Accents (′, ″, ‴, etc.) indicate derivatives of increasing degrees. Because these series are *approximations* , they all contain a *remainder term* , which we'll leave unspecified, although it is subject to specific conditions if the expansion series is to converge.

Taylor Series

Taylor's series* is an approximating expansion of a function at any point x_0:

$$f(x) = f(x_0) + f'(x_0)(x - x_0) + \frac{f''(x_0)}{2!}(x - x_0)^2 + \dots$$
$$+ \frac{f^{(n)}(x_0)}{n!}(x - x_0)^n + \frac{f^{(n+1)}(p)}{(n+1)!}(x - x_0)^{n+1} \tag{2.17}$$

---

*This series was first published in 1715 by the English mathematician Brook Taylor (1685 - 1731). But he did not grasp the fundamental importance that later Joseph Lagrange assigned to it. In his *Methodus Incrementorum Directa et Inversa* (1715), Taylor invented integration by parts and founded the calculus of finite differences. The series enables one to deduce more ready conclusions about complex functions and it provides estimates for irregularity ("errors").

where the last term is the remainder term, which is likely to be rather irregular .[†]

MacLaurin Series

MacLaurin's series[‡] is an approximating expansion at $x_0 = 0$, and thus a special case of a Taylor series:

$$\phi(x) = \phi(0) + \phi'(0)x + \frac{\phi''(0)}{2!}x^2 + ... + \frac{\phi^{(n)}(0)}{n!}x^n + \frac{\phi^{(n+1)}(p).x^{n+1}}{(n+1)!} \qquad (2.18)$$

Sinusoidal Series

Examples of MacLaurin's expansions are *sinusoidal* functions, when we express the angle θ as a dimensionless ratio in *radians* rather than degrees . First, the sinus function , $\phi(x) = \sin\theta$:

$$\sin\theta = \sin(0) + \sin'(0).\theta + \frac{\sin''(0)}{2!}.\theta^2 + ... + \frac{\sin^{(n)}(0)}{n!}.\theta^n + \frac{\sin^{(n+1)}(p)}{(n+1)!}\theta^{n+1} \qquad (2.19)$$

Since the derivatives of sines and cosines are cosines and sines with values within the closed finite range $[-1, +1]$, the remainder term will approach zero as $n \to \infty$ and thus the sinus function can be expressed as a converging infinite series :

$$\sin\theta = \sin(0) + \cos(0).\theta - \frac{\sin(0)}{2!}.\theta^2 - \frac{\cos(0)}{3!}.\theta^3 ... \qquad (2.20)$$

or

$$\sin\theta = 0 + \theta + 0 - \frac{\theta^3}{3!} + 0 + \frac{\theta^5}{5!}...$$
$$= \theta - \frac{\theta^3}{3!} + \frac{\theta^5}{5!} - \frac{\theta^7}{7!} + ... \qquad (2.21)$$

Notice all the "odd terms. "

Similarly, the cosine function :

$$\cos\theta = 1 + 0 - \frac{\theta^2}{2!} + 0 + \frac{\theta^4}{4!} + ...$$
$$= 1 - \frac{\theta^2}{2!} + \frac{\theta^4}{4!} - \frac{\theta^6}{6!} + ... \qquad (2.22)$$

Notice all the "even terms".

[†]The irregularity of this remainder term, expressed by its Lipschitz α coefficient, can now be measured via wavelet multiresolution analysis. (Cf. Mallat, 1989, and 1998, pp. 165 - 219).

[‡]The Scottish mathematician Colin MacLaurin, 1698 - 1746, provided in 1742 the first systematic and logical elaboration of Sir Isaac Newton's method of fluxions (derivatives). He did so in response to Bishop George Berkeley's attack on calculus for its lack of rigorous foundations. MacLaurin appealed to the geometrical methods of the ancient Greeks.

Exponential Series

Another MacLaurin expansion is the *exponential* function , $\phi(x) = e^x$:

$$e^x = e^0 + e^0 x + \frac{e^0}{2!}x^2 + \frac{e^0}{3!}x^3 + \frac{e^0}{4!}x^4 + ...$$

$$= 1 + x + \frac{x^2}{2!} + \frac{x^3}{3!} + \frac{x^4}{4!} + ... \tag{2.23}$$

As a special case, for $x = 1$

$$e = 1 + 1 + \frac{1}{2!} + \frac{1}{3!} + \frac{1}{4!} + ...$$

$$= 2.7182818539.... \tag{2.24}$$

Using the exponential function in combination with the sinusoidal series we can now derive the very useful *Euler relations*[§], using the concept of the *imaginary number* $i = \sqrt{-1}$, or, equivalently, $i^2 = -1$. Being the square root of a negative number , i is obviously not real valued; it is thus an imaginary number.

2.4.1 *Imaginary and Conjugate Complex Numbers and the Euler Relations*

By combining the sinusoidal series for $\sin\theta$ and $\cos\theta$ we find that the exponential series for $e^{i\theta}$ simplifies to the first Euler relation:

$$e^{i\theta} = 1 + i\theta + \frac{(i\theta)^2}{2!} + \frac{(i\theta)^3}{3!} + \frac{(i\theta)^4}{4!} + \frac{(i\theta)^5}{5!} + ...$$

$$= 1 + i\theta - \frac{\theta^2}{2!} - \frac{i\theta^3}{3!} + \frac{\theta^4}{4!} - \frac{i\theta^5}{5!} + ...$$

$$= \left[1 - \frac{\theta^2}{2!} + \frac{\theta^4}{4!} - \frac{\theta^6}{6!} + ...\right] + i\left[\theta - \frac{\theta^3}{3!} + \frac{\theta^5}{5!} - \frac{\theta^7}{7!} + ...\right]$$

$$= \cos\theta + i\sin\theta \tag{2.25}$$

where $i^2 = -1$. Similarly, we find the second Euler relation

$$e^{-i\theta} = \cos\theta - i\sin\theta \tag{2.26}$$

These two Euler relations represent *conjugate complex* numbers , *i.e.*, they are of the form $(h \pm i\omega)$ These numbers are *complex* since they consist of h, the *real* part and

---

[§]Leonhard Euler (1707-1783) was the most prolific mathematician in history. His 866 books and articles represent about one third of the entire body of research on mathematics, theoretical physics, and engineering mechanics published between 1726 and 1800. For example, he refined the notion of a function and made common many mathematical notations, including e, i, π and σ. He laid the foundation of analytical mechanics, especially in his *Theory of the Motions of Rigid Bodies* (1765). His teacher in Basel was Johann Bernouilli (1667-1748), the brother of Jacques Bernoulli (1654-1705), who published many articles on infinite series and did pioneering work in the theory of probability.

$i\omega$, the *imaginary* part, and they are *conjugate,* since they always exist as a pair, one with a positive and the other with a negative imaginary part. Notice that

$$\tan\theta = \frac{\sin\theta}{\cos\theta}$$
$$= \frac{\omega}{h}, (h \neq 0) \tag{2.27}$$

Cartesian and Polar Coordinates

When $h = R\cos\theta$ and $\omega = R\sin\theta$ we have

$$\sqrt{(h^2 + \omega^2)} = \sqrt{R^2(\cos^2\theta + \sin^2\theta)}$$
$$= R \tag{2.28}$$

Now we have three equivalent representations in three different *coordinate systems :*

$$h \pm i\omega$$
$$= R(\cos\theta \pm i\sin\theta) \tag{2.29}$$
$$= Re^{\pm i\theta} \tag{2.30}$$

The first representation, $h \pm i\omega$, is in *Cartesian form*[¶], the second, $R(\cos\theta \pm i\sin\theta)$, in *polar form* and the third, $Re^{\pm i\theta}$, in *exponential form*, with $(h,\omega) = Cartesian$ *coordinates*, and $(R,\theta) = polar$ *coordinates*. These relations are easy to visualize with an *Argand Diagram.*

Argand Diagram

In an Argand diagram, which is a circle with radius $R = 1$ (Fig.1.), h refers to the real *abscissa* and ω to the imaginary *ordinate* in a Cartesian coordinate system. Thus the expression $(h \pm i\omega)$ represents the Cartesian form of a pair of conjugate complex numbers.

[¶]The French philosopher Rene Descartes (1596 - 1650) is sometimes called the founder of modern philosophy. Writing at the beginning of the scientific revolution, he made major contributions to both philosophy and mathematics. His principal philosophical work, *Meditations on First Philosophy*, was first published in 1641, a year before Galileo died and Isaac Newton was born. One of his two main aims in philosophy was to provide a conceptual foundation for the new mechanical physics, which tried to explain everything in the created world external to human beings solely by geometry and motions of bodies. Because Descartes lived at a time when traditional ideas were being questioned, he also sought to devise a method for reaching the truth. This concern and his method of *systematic doubt and skepticism* had an enormous impact on the subsequent development of philosophy and science, in particular because of his epistemology of rationalism and empiricism. He unified algebra and geometry by use of his Cartesian coordinates.

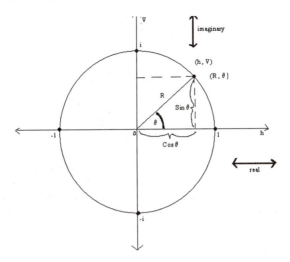

Figure 1   Argand Diagram

De Moivre's Theorem

It follows that,

$$(h \pm i\omega)^n = [R(\cos\theta \pm i\sin\theta)]^n$$
$$= R^n(\cos n\theta \pm i\sin n\theta)$$
$$= R^n e^{\pm in\theta} \tag{2.31}$$

Theorem 8 *(De Moivre's)* [||]

$$[R(\cos\theta \pm i\sin\theta)]^n = R^n(\cos n\theta \pm i\sin n\theta) \tag{2.32}$$

Some examples of the implementation of Euler's formulas are, for

$$\theta = n.\pi e^{i2\pi} = \cos 2\pi + i\sin 2\pi = 1 + i.0 = 1 = e^0 \tag{2.33}$$

[||] The French Hugenot and probabilist Abraham De Moivre (1667 - 1754) went after the withdrawal of the Edict of Nantes (1685) to England. He was a private teacher of mathematics who became a Member of the Royal Society (1714) and of the Academies of Paris and Berlin, but who never secured a university position, partly because of his non-British origin. Despite the long hours of tutoring necessary to support himself, De Moivre produced a considerable quantity of research on the laws of chance, which he published in the *Doctrine of Chances* (1718), containing more than fifty problems on probability, using rolling dice, drawing balls of various colors from a bag, and other games of chance, and questions relating to life annuities. He also developed the analytical side of of trignometrics in his *Miscellanea Analytica* (1730) in which he pubished his famous Theorem.

$$e^{i\pi/2} = \cos\frac{\pi}{2} + i\sin\frac{\pi}{2} = 0 + i.1 = i \tag{2.34}$$

$$e^{i\pi} = \cos\pi + i\sin\pi = -1 + i.0 = -1 \tag{2.35}$$

$$e^{-i\pi/2} = \cos\frac{\pi}{2} - i\sin\frac{\pi}{2} = 0 - i.1 = -i \tag{2.36}$$

Remark 9 *Notice that Euler's formulas and De Moivre's Theorem enable us to translate any imaginary exponential formula into an equivalent linear combination of trigonometric or sinusoidal functions. These are periodic functions , since they represent their values periodically, as the variable θ changes continuously.*

Exponential Function

The general form of an exponential function is

$$y_t = A_j e^{r_j t} \tag{2.37}$$

This is the expression of an initial investment A_i which grows at a constant rate of return of r_j, since the growth rate is defined by

$$\begin{aligned}
\frac{d\ln y_t}{dt} &= \frac{1}{y_t}\frac{dy_t}{dt} \\
&= \frac{r_j A_j e^{r_j t}}{A_j e^{r_j t}} \\
&= r_j \tag{2.38}
\end{aligned}$$

Such a growth rate may be conjugate complex, e.g., $r_j = h_j \pm i\omega_j$, so that the growth process may exhibit oscillatory behavior in addition to trend behavior.

Periodic Function

A periodic function y_t has the same value after a certain period T

$$y_t = y_{t+T} \tag{2.39}$$

Thus a function is periodic if its graph shows a repeating pattern. Therefore, trigonometric functions, like sinuses and cosines are periodic. More sophisticated examples of periodic function are the conjugate complex functions.

Conjugate Complex Function

This function consist of two imaginary exponential functions:

$$y_t = A_1 e^{(h+i\omega)t} + A_2 e^{(h-i\omega)t}$$
$$= e^{ht}(A_1 e^{\omega it} + A_2 e^{-\omega it}) \tag{2.40}$$

We can interpret this conjugate complex function as a circular function by using the Euler relations, so that

$$y_t = e^{ht}[A_1(\cos \omega t + i \sin \omega t) + A_2(\cos \omega t - i \sin \omega t)]$$
$$= e^{ht}[(A_1 + A_2)\cos \omega t + (A_1 - A_2)i \sin \omega t]$$
$$= e^{ht}(\alpha \cos \omega t + \beta \sin \omega t) \tag{2.41}$$

where $\alpha = (A_1 + A_2)$ and $\beta = (A_1 - A_2)i$.

Remark 10 *Since A_1 and A_2 are arbitrary constants, β is not necessarily imaginary, despite the fact that its expression contains the imaginary number i. For example, if A_1 and A_2 are a pair of conjugate complex numbers (say, $A_1, A_2 = m \pm in$) then α and β will both be real, since*

$$\alpha = (A_1 + A_2) = 2m \tag{2.42}$$

and

$$\beta = (A_1 - A_2)i = (2ni)i = -2n \tag{2.43}$$

a real number (integer).

2.5 Fourier and Wavelet Analysis

Fourier analysis is a branch of mathematics that is used to analyze periodic phenomena. Many natural and artificial phenomena occur in cycles that repeat constantly. These phenomena such as alternating currents, business cycles, high and low tides, the orbits of planets and artificial satellites, and the vibrations of electromagnetic waves – can be described by periodic functions. In the light of the preceding discussion about expansion series it should be no surprise that *any* function, periodic or otherwise, can be approximated as a Fourier series, but only when the functional processes are stationary (*cf.* Hsu, 1984).

2.5.1 Fourier Series

A one-dimensional Fourier** series expansion for a periodic function $y_t = y_{t+T}$ is the infinite series, represented by the equivalent *trigonometric form*, the *harmonic form*

**Jean Baptiste Joseph Fourier (1768-1830) was a French mathematician, who became famous for his *Theorie analytique de la chaleur (Analytical theory of heat)*, 1822, a mathematical treatment of the theory of heat. He established the partial differential equation governing heat diffusion and solved it by using an infinite series of trigonometric functions. His diffusion equation was used in 1973 to derive the Black-Scholes European option pricing model (Cf. Chapters 8 and 10).

and the *complex exponential form* , respectively:

$$y_t = \frac{\alpha_0}{2} + \sum_{n=1}^{\infty}(\alpha_n \cos n\omega_0 t + \beta_n \sin n\omega_0 t) \tag{2.44}$$

$$= C_0 + \sum_{n=1}^{\infty} C_n \cos(n\omega_0 t - \theta_n) \tag{2.45}$$

$$= \sum_{n=-\infty}^{\infty} c_n e^{in\omega_0 t} \tag{2.46}$$

Here, $\omega_0 = 2\pi f_0 = \frac{2\pi}{T}$ is the *angular frequency* , $f_0 = \frac{1}{T}$ the *fundamental frequency* , $\omega_n = n\omega_0$ the *nth harmonic*, C_0 the *harmonic amplitude* , and θ_n the *phase angle* . Simple conversion formulas exist between these three representations, which can easily be checked:
For $n \neq 0$ we have

$$c_n = \frac{1}{2}(\alpha_n - i\beta_n) \text{ and } c_{-n} = \frac{1}{2}(\alpha_n + i\beta_n) = c_n^*, \text{ its complex conjugate}$$

$$c_n = |c_n| e^{i\varphi_n}, \ |c_n| = \frac{1}{2}\sqrt{\alpha_n^2 + \beta_n^2}, \text{ and } \varphi_n = \tan^{-1}(-\frac{\beta_n}{\alpha_n})$$

$$\text{with } \alpha_n = 2\operatorname{Re}[c_n] \text{ and } \beta_n = -2\operatorname{Im}[c_n]$$

$$C_n = 2|c_n| = \sqrt{\alpha_n^2 + \beta_n^2} \text{ and } \theta_n = \tan^{-1}(\frac{\beta_n}{\alpha_n}) = -\phi_n$$

For $n = 0$ we have

$$\frac{\alpha_0}{2} = C_0 = c_0 \tag{2.47}$$

According to Parseval's Theorem , the *power content* of the periodic function $x(t)$, which is its mean-square value, can be represented by the infinite sum of the squared (exponential) Fourier coefficients.

Theorem 11 (Parseval for Fourier Series) *If a_0, a_n, and b_n are the coefficients in the Fourier expansion of a periodic function $x(t)$ with period T, then*

$$\frac{1}{T}\int_{-T/2}^{T/2} [x(t)]^2 \, dt = \frac{a_0^2}{4} + \frac{1}{2}\sum_{n=1}^{+\infty}(a_n^2 + b_n^2) \tag{2.48}$$

$$= c_0^2 + 2\sum_{n=1}^{+\infty}|c_n|^2 \tag{2.49}$$

$$= \sum_{n=-\infty}^{+\infty}|c_n|^2 \tag{2.50}$$

2.5.2   Fourier Transform

The continuous form of such a limiting approximation is called the continuous Fourier Transform. The *Continuous Fourier Transform (CFT)* of $x(t)$ (symbolized by $\mathcal{F}$) in the L^2 space is defined by:

$$F(\omega) = \mathcal{F}[x(t)]$$

$$= \int_{-\infty}^{+\infty} x(t)e^{-i\omega t}dt \tag{2.51}$$

The *inverse Fourier Transform* of $F(\omega)$ (symbolized by $\mathcal{F}^{-1}$) represents $x(t)$ as a sum of sinusoids

$$x(t) = \mathcal{F}^{-1}[F(\omega)]$$

$$= \frac{1}{2\pi} \int_{-\infty}^{+\infty} F(\omega)e^{i\omega t}d\omega \tag{2.52}$$

Remark 12 *These two equations are often called the Fourier Transform pair, symbolically denoted by:*

$$x(t) \leftrightarrow F(\omega) \tag{2.53}$$

The condition for the existence of $F(\omega)$ is given by

$$\int_{-\infty}^{+\infty} |x(t)| \, dt < \infty \tag{2.54}$$

In other words, the variable $x(t)$ must be absolutely integrable .

2.5.3   Wavelet Transform

A method analogous to the Fourier Transform makes use of a small mathematical fluctuation called a "wavelet" ψ and was developed in the late 1980s to tackle the issue of the non - stationarity of empirical time series (*cf.* Burke Hubbard, 1998). Wavelets are very finite Fourier kernels with limited support, in contrast to the sinusoidal bases $e^{-i\omega t}$ of the Fourier series, which have infinite support, *i.e.*, these are defined on a domain between $-\infty$ and $+\infty$. *Wavelet analysis* offers advantages in rapidly analyzing changing transient signals and in handling discontinuities in a body of data, for example, in *high frequency currency trading records with jumps*, that cannot be handled by the stationary Fourier analysis.

The *Continuous Wavelet Transform (CWT)* of $x(t)$ at the scale a and position τ is computed by correlating $x(t)$ with a wavelet atom $\psi_{\tau,a}^*(t)$

$$W(\tau, a) = \int_{-\infty}^{+\infty} x(t)\psi_{\tau,a}^*(t)dt$$

$$= \int_{-\infty}^{+\infty} x(t)\frac{1}{\sqrt{a}}\psi^*\left(\frac{t-\tau}{a}\right)dt \tag{2.55}$$

Thus the CWT is the correlation of the time series and the appropriate wavelets. The dilating and translating wavelet atoms act as a unique observation system, which allows various levels of resolution , like a microscope.

2.5.4 Multiresolution Analysis

For such a *multiresolution analysis (MRA)* of $x(t)$ one needs two closely related basic functions. In addition to the wavelet $\psi(t)$ which provides the details one needs a second basis function, called the *scaling function* , which provides the approximation . Mallat (1989) proved that, using a combination of these scaling functions and wavelets, a very large class of time series can be represented by the following decomposition equation of scaling functions and wavelets

$$
\begin{aligned}
x(t) &= A + D \\
&= \sum_{n=-\infty}^{+\infty} c_n \varphi_n(t) + \sum_{j=0}^{+\infty} \sum_{n=-\infty}^{+\infty} d_{j,n} \psi_{j,n}(t)
\end{aligned}
\tag{2.56}
$$

where the approximation (A) is provided by the one-dimensional linear combination of the scaling functions

$$
\begin{aligned}
A &= \sum_{n=-\infty}^{+\infty} c_n \varphi_n(t) \\
&= \sum_{n=-\infty}^{+\infty} c_n \varphi(t - n)
\end{aligned}
\tag{2.57}
$$

and the details (D) by the two-dimensional linear combination of the dyadic wavelet functions

$$
\begin{aligned}
D &= \sum_{j=0}^{+\infty} \sum_{n=-\infty}^{+\infty} d_{j,n} \psi_{j,n}(t) \\
&= \sum_{j=0}^{+\infty} \sum_{n=-\infty}^{+\infty} d_{j,n} \psi(2^{-j} t - n)
\end{aligned}
\tag{2.58}
$$

The coefficients of this MRA expansion are computed as inner products similar to Fourier Transform coefficients. The discrete *(approximation) scaling coefficients* are computed by the inner product

$$
\begin{aligned}
c_n &= \langle x(t) \phi_n(t) \rangle \\
&= \int_{-\infty}^{+\infty} x(t) \phi_n(t) dt, \text{ with } n \in \mathbb{Z}
\end{aligned}
\tag{2.59}
$$

The discrete (*detail*) *wavelet coefficients* are computed by the inner product

$$d_{j,n} = \langle x(t)\psi_{j,n}(t)\rangle$$
$$= \int_{-\infty}^{+\infty} x(t)\psi_{j,n}(t)dt, \text{ with with } j, n \in \mathbb{Z} \qquad (2.60)$$

The power content of any time series, periodic or non-periodic, continuous or discontinuous, can now be partitioned using this wavelet multiresolution analysis.

Theorem 13 *(Parseval for Wavelets)* *For the general wavelet expansion*

$$\int_{-\infty}^{+\infty} |x(t)|^2 \, dt = \sum_{n=-\infty}^{+\infty} |c_n|^2 + \sum_{j=0}^{+\infty} \sum_{n=-\infty}^{+\infty} |d_{j,n}|^2 \qquad (2.61)$$

with the energy in the expansion completely partitioned in time by n and in scale by j.[††]

2.6 Exercises

Exercise 14 *Become proficient with some of the special features of EXCEL (cf. Hallberg, 1995):*

1. Entering labels, numbers, ranges, and formula (Stulz, 1996, provides many simple exercises).

2. The difference between absolute and relative addressing

3. The special EXCEL functions for Statistics and Finance

Exercise 15 *From Markowitz (1987) refresh your memory about elementary matrix algebra and practice EXCEL's matrix algebra functions: TRANSPOSE(), MMULT(), MDETERM(), MINVERSE() by computing the 2 × 2 data covariance matrix of the weekly spot and futures prices of the German D-Mark given in the attached Table.*

Exercise 16 *Create a chart of these prices. What does it tell you? Do you find numerical confirmation of your impressions in the 2 × 2 data covariance matrix you've just computed? How?*

[††]The implications of Parseval's Theorem for Fourier and wavelet analysis of non-periodic time series are far reaching for financial analysis. Their advanced discussion is properly deferred to another another monograph.

Date	Spot DM	Futures DM
901228	1.4936	1.52625
910104	1.5045	1.49948
910111	1.5310	1.53374
910118	1.4995	1.51768
910125	1.4905	1.49098
910201	1.4673	1.48192
910208	1.4560	1.46306
910218	1.4821	1.48170
910222	1.5060	1.48854
910301	1.5400	1.53445
910308	1.5693	1.55497
910315	1.6075	1.58504
910322	1.6482	1.64042
910401	1.6683	1.69837
910405	1.6855	1.67673
910415	1.6695	1.68748
910419	1.7370	1.72801
910426	1.7520	1.75778
910503	1.7500	1.71910
910510	1.7230	1.73762
910517	1.7393	1.70765
910524	1.7040	1.71292
910531	1.7420	1.72622
910607	1.7720	1.75654
910614	1.7955	1.80310
910621	1.8035	1.81686
910628	1.8112	1.82249
910705	1.8260	1.84945
910712	1.7885	1.83251
910719	1.7475	1.76647
910726	1.7433	1.75408
910802	1.7410	1.76991
910812	1.7318	1.73100
910816	1.7643	1.75285
910823	1.7478	1.74064
910830	1.7473	1.74338
910906	1.7145	1.73913
910913	1.6869	1.69062
910920	1.6857	1.70882
910927	1.6695	1.69895
911004	1.6775	1.67420
911011	1.6895	1.70532
911018	1.6877	1.70619
911025	1.7010	1.70590
911101	1.6435	1.67954
911108	1.6453	1.65071
911115	1.6170	1.63666
911122	1.5843	1.60077
911129	1.6245	1.63532
911206	1.5665	1.58781
911216	1.5750	1.58378
911220	1.5345	1.57629
911227	1.5188	1.52532

Weekly spot and futures prices of the German D-Mark

2.7 Bibliography

Burke Hubbard, B. (1998) *The World According to Wavelets*, 2nd ed., A K Peters.

Hallberg, B. (1995) *Inside EXCEL for Windows 95*, New Riders Publishing, Indianapolis, IN.

Hsu, H. P. (1984) *Applied Fourier Analysis*, Harcourt Brace College Publishers, San Diego.

Mallat, S. G. (1989) "A Theory for Multiresolution Signal decomposition: The Wavelet Representation," IEEE Transactions on Pattern Analysis and Machine Intelligence, **11** (2), July, 674 - 693.

Mallat, S. G. (1998) *A Wavelet Tour of Signal Processing*, Academic Press, New York, NY.

Markowitz, H. M. (1987) "Appendix: Elements of Matrix Algebra and Vector Spaces," in *Mean-Variance Analysis in Portfolio Choice and Capital Markets*, Blackwell, Oxford, pp. 347 - 368.

Merton, R. C. (1989) "On the Application of the Continuous-Time Theory of Finance to Financial Intermediation and Insurance," The Geneva Papers on Risk and Insurance, **4** (52), 225 - 262.

Stulz, R. A. (1996) *Learn Microsoft Excel 7.0 for Windows^{TM} 95 in a Day*, Tech Publications Pte Ltd, Singapore.

chapter:3,page:1

Chapter 3
FUNDAMENTAL SECURITY VALUATION

3.1 Introduction

In this Chapter we'll discuss the valuation of Treasury bonds as exact financial models and graded corporate bonds as inexact financial models . We'll also show that the valuation of stocks is open-ended and inexact, but that by introducing the limit argument of a perpetually "ongoing concern," the valuation model of stocks becomes exact. O'Brien and Srivastava (1996) provide many fine two - dimensional visualizations of bond valuations.

3.2 Valuation of Bonds

A bond is a borrowing instrument and an obligation to pay an annuity with known, usually half year payments, called *coupon payments* CF, plus the *principal* B_T at *maturity* T. The value of a bond is a unique realization , since all the required data are exact and complete .

The (present) *value of a bond* is thus

$$PB_0 = PA_0 + X_0$$
$$= CF[\frac{1}{\frac{r}{2}} - \frac{1}{\frac{r}{2}(1+\frac{r}{2})^{2T}}] + \frac{B_T}{(1+\frac{r}{2})^{2T}} \tag{3.1}$$

Notice that, because of the semi-annual coupon payments, the number of payments of a bond is twice as high as the number of payments of an annuity with the same maturity T, but that conventional rate r is half its annual value.

The value of a US Treasury bond is an exact model with five variables; the value of the bond PB_0, the maturity T, the principal payment B_T, the coupon payment CF and the annual yield r:

$$PB_0 - PB_0(T, B_T, CF, r) = 0 \tag{3.2}$$

Since most bonds are in denominations of $B_T = 1000$, there are usually only four effective variables, PB_0, T, CF and r:

$$PB_0 - PB_0(T, CF, r) = 0 \tag{3.3}$$

The *yield-to-maturity* of a bond is the discount rate r that will make the PB_0 of a bond equal to its market price, which is determined by the required yield . Thus, there are three common market valuations:

When the coupon rate equals the required yield, a bond is valued *at par* with $\frac{PB_0}{B_T} = 100\%$. This is easy to check, since now

$$CF = \frac{c}{2}B_T$$
$$= \frac{r}{2}B_T \tag{3.4}$$

so that, by appropriate substitution into the formula for PB_0,

$$PB_0 = \frac{r}{2}B_T[\frac{1}{\frac{r}{2}} - \frac{1}{\frac{r}{2}(1+\frac{r}{2})^{2T}}] + \frac{B_T}{(1+\frac{r}{2})^{2T}}$$
$$= B_T \tag{3.5}$$

Similarly, when the coupon rate $<$ required yield, then the bond's price $<$ par and the bond is valued *at a discount* with $\frac{PB_0}{B_T} < 100\%$.

Finally, when the coupon rate $>$ required yield, the bond's price $>$ par, the bond is valued *at a premium* , with $\frac{PB_0}{B_T} > 100\%$.

3.3   Yield Curve and Term Structure Analysis

The *yield curve* of a particular grade (credit quality) bond is the relationship between its yield r and maturity T, for given principal B_T and coupon CF. For example, the yield curve of U.S. Treasury securities (which are default-risk free) forms the basis of many derivative bond valuations in the international financial markets.

A *zero coupon bond* (a "zero"), or *pure discount bond* , has zero coupons: $CF = 0$, so that its value is $PB_0 = \frac{B_T}{(1+r_T)^T}$. Zeros have been popular in many emerging markets , in particular in Latin America, because they are so easy to value and because there is a simple and unique relationship between the present value PB_0 and its rate r (*cf.* Dybvig and Marshall, 1996).

A T-year *spot interest rate* is the interest rate of a zero bond, which can be found by "inverting" the expression for the value of a zero coupon bond:

$$r_T = (\frac{PB_0}{B_T})^{-1/T} - 1 \tag{3.6}$$

The *term structure* of interest rates is the relationship between the spot interest rate r_T and the maturity T for a particular grade of obligations (*e.g.*, bills, notes and bonds). There are two major financial reasons for computing a term structure from various market yield curves: custom - fitting of bond maturities and computing forward rates (*cf.* Kawaller and Marshall (1996).

3.3.1 Custom-fitting of Bond Maturities

Every bond can be decomposed into a series of zero bonds of the same credit quality, since every coupon payment can be viewed as a separate zero bond principal to be discounted. Next, using the *Value Additivity Principle* , a bond of any maturity T, with any coupon payments CF and any principal B_T, can be re-composed out of zeros and *vice versa*. There are many coupon bonds with different maturities, but *there is only one term structure at any given time,* for a particular credit quality .

Furthermore, we will see later on that *any security* can be composed out of zero-coupon securities plus options , whereby the zeros price additively the risk - free value of that security and the options price its risk value.

3.3.2 Computing Forward Interest Rates

A *forward interest rate* $_1f_2 \equiv f_{t_1,t_2}$ is an interest rate on a zero to be issued at time t_1 and maturing at time t_2. Obviously, $t_2 - t_1 > 0$. Forward interest rates allow us to arrange and value financial transactions today that will take place during some time period in the future, *e.g.* swaps (*cf.* Chapter 12). Forward interest rates are computed from the concatenated term structure as follows:

$$(1 + r_2)^{t_2} = (1 + r_1)^{t_1}(1 +_1 f_2)^{t_2 - t_1} \tag{3.7}$$

so that, by "inversion,"

$$_1f_2 = \left[\frac{(1 + r_2)^{t_2}}{(1 + r_1)^{t_1}}\right]^{t_1 - t_2} - 1 \tag{3.8}$$

or, in continuous time,

$$e^{r_2 t_2} = e^{r_1 t_1} e^{_1 f_2(t_2 - t_1)} \tag{3.9}$$

so that, by "inversion,"

$$_1f_2 = \frac{(r_2 T_2 - r_1 T_1)}{T_2 - T_1} \tag{3.10}$$

3.4 Risk - Based Credit Ratings

When we introduce an additional discrete credit rating variable ξ to account for credit risk of corporate bonds or commercial bank loans , the value of a corporate bond or bank loan is no longer an exact model , since the relationship between the value of the bond and the discrete grade variable is inexact (Altman, 1968, 1996). The corporate bond model is inexact with six variables

$$PB_0 - PB_0(T, B_T, CF, r, \xi) \approx 0 \tag{3.11}$$

where PB_0 is the present value of the bond, T its maturity, B_T its principal, CF the coupon, r its yield and ξ its quality grade. Consequently, the value of a corporate bond, which is exposed to credit risk, is uncertain and can only be determined by projection and approximation . The model is inexact, since the credit rating is inexact.* Moreover, the relationship between the credit rating and the value of the bond PB_0 is also inexact and contains epistemic uncertainty . This relationship must be established by projections.

3.5   Valuation of Stocks by Dividend Discount Models

The *dividend discount model* (DDM) is a simulation model to compute the speculative intrinsic value of a stock. Its data are exact , but necessarily incomplete . Furthermore, its data are expected values and not historical or present values . The DDM values stock, *i.e.*, shares in equity, by discounting the expected future dividends, which is an open-ended series. The discount rate is the *cost of capital r*. For simplicity, assume that the cost of capital is constant. Then the *intrinsic value* of the stock is given by the infinite series

$$PS_0 = \sum_{t=1}^{\infty} \frac{D_t}{(1+r)^t}$$
$$= \frac{D_1}{(1+r)} + \frac{D_2}{(1+r)^2} + \frac{D_3}{(1+r)^3} + \dots \tag{3.12}$$

This discounted dividend series is infinite, based on the, admittedly, unrealistic legal abstraction of equity in an *ongoing concern* . Therefore, notice that the speculative intrinsic value of the stock is not the market value of the stock, but its speculative value. This speculative value can be higher than its market value, *i.e.*, the stock is *undervalued* by the market and warrants a "buy" recommendation . The speculative value can be lower than its market value, *i.e.*, the stock is *overvalued* by the market and warrants a "sell" recommendation . Or the two values can coincide and the stock is *properly valued* by the market and warrants a "hold" recommendation .

We distinguish two simulated valuations to produce closed form solutions :

(1) When the expected future dividends are assumed to remain constant, $D_t = D$, the value of the stock equals the value of an infinite annuity with payments in arrears . Thus we compute the finite limit of such a series, using the formula for the present value of an annuity, to calculate the intrinsic value of the stock:

$$PS_0 = \lim_{T \to \infty} \left[D\left[\frac{1}{r} - \frac{1}{r(1+r)^T}\right] \right] = \frac{D}{r} \tag{3.13}$$

---

*The credit rating procedures of Standard and Poors are trade secrets, but from what one can infer, the quantitative relationship between the credit rating and the underlying variables is determined by formal "scoring models," i.e., unidirectional projections with a subjective choice of regressors, "enhanced" by subjective value judgment. Moreover, the credit grade is a categorical variable and not a continuous variable.

The limit of this infinite summation series converges and is *finite* because the discount factor $0 < \frac{1}{1+r} < 1$, since $r > 0$.

(2) When the expected future dividends are assumed to grow at a constant growth rate $g < r$ (a necessary requirement for this model), then it is easy to show, using similar algebraic reasoning as before, that the intrinsic value of the stock is given by:

$$PS_0 = \frac{D}{r - g} \tag{3.14}$$

3.6 Cash Flow and Ratio Analysis

The value of an asset A_0, in addition to being the present value PS_0 of the future cash flows CFs which it generates, is also equal to a multiple of next year's forecasted economic earnings, with the multiple being the reciprocal of the discount rate r, *i.e.*, the required rate of return. The *economic earnings* (E) of an asset is any cash flow produced by the asset (like dividends for stocks and coupon payments for bonds), plus any change in its value in the subsequent period $A_1 - A_0$, *e.g.*, year. We will now show that this is the theoretical justification for the prevalent use of the *Price/Earnings (P/E) ratio* as the basis for stock valuation . Thus the value of any asset is

$$A_0 = \frac{CF_1}{(1+r)} + \frac{CF_2}{(1+r)^2} + \ldots + \frac{CF_n}{(1+r)^n} \tag{3.15}$$

Then pre-multiply by $(1 + r)$ and substitute by A_1, so that

$$(1 + r)A_0 = CF_1 + \frac{CF_2}{(1+r)} + \ldots \frac{CF_n}{(1+r)^{n-1}} = CF_1 + A_1 \tag{3.16}$$

But then

$$A_0 + rA_0 = CF_1 + A_1 \tag{3.17}$$

and thus

$$rA_0 = CF_1 + A_1 - A_0$$
$$= E_1 \tag{3.18}$$

the *expected economic earnings* in the next period, or

$$A_0 = \frac{1}{r}E_1 \tag{3.19}$$

The expected economic earnings in the next period are the sum of the cash payment in the next period CF_1 and the capital gain in the next period $(A_1 - A_2)$. This expression states that the value of an asset is determined only by the expected economic earnings in the next period and the discount rate . This is why financial analysts focus their attention on next year's economic earnings forecasts for business firms and why they don't have to forecast very far into the future, only one period. The fundamental Price/Earnings ratio is thus

$$\frac{P}{E} = \frac{A_0}{E_1}$$
$$= \frac{1}{r} \tag{3.20}$$

i.e., the inversion of the required rate of return. Since this rate r is usually small, changes in the required rate of return ("interest rates") have a major impact on stock prices for given predictions of earnings. Stocks are notoriously interest rate sensitive in an inverse way.

3.7 Exercises

Exercise 17 *Compute the intrinsic value of a $10-year$ Treasury bond with a $1,000 face value and a 5% coupon rate, when the interest rate varies between 2% and 10% (in steps of 100 basis points).*

Exercise 18 *Using EXCEL 's CHART WIZARD plot the price - yield curve of this bond. In the process learn to:*

1. Edit chart titles, writing $x-$axis and $y-$axis titles

2. Format axes and name the series

3. Add and delete legends

3.8 Bibliography

Altman, E. I. (1968) "Financial Ratios, Discriminant Analysis and the Prediction of Corporate Bankruptcy," *Journal of Finance*, **23** (3), 589 - 609.

    Altman, E. I. (1996) "Credit-Scoring Models and the Valuation of Fixed-Income Securities and Commercial Loans," CREFS Seminar presentation at SAB - NBS - NTU, 21 June, 1996, Singapore, 17 pages.

    Dybvig, P. H. and Marshall, W. J. (1996) "Pricing Long Bonds: Pitfalls and Opportunities," *Financial Analysts Journal*, January - February, 32 - 39.

    Fabozzi, F. J. (1993) *Bond Markets, Analysis and Strategies*, Prentice - Hall, Englewood Cliffs, NJ.

    Kawaller, I. G. and Marshall, J. F. (1996) "Deriving Zero-Coupon Rates: Alternatives to Orthodoxy," *Financial Analysts Journal*, May - June, 51 - 55.

    O'Brien, J. and Srivastava, S. (1996) *Investments, A Visual Approach: Bond Valuation and Bond Tutor*, South-Western College Publishing, New York, NY.

    chapter:4,page:1

Chapter 4
ANALYSIS OF INEXACT DATA I

4.1 Introduction

In Chapter 3 we discussed some exact valuation models of bonds and stocks, which realize data sets. These models are unique, *i.e.*, models based on sets of data which are exact and complete. They are based on finite sets of financial data adhering to the Accounting Identity, like balance, income and cash flow statements, or on completely defined and exact contractual data sets. We also noted that some financial models are not unique, because their exact data set is incomplete, like the Dividend Discount Model (DDM). However, when the data set for the DDM was completed, by closing it with a limit argument based upon the subjective assumption of an ongoing concern, a unique, but speculative, model could still be artificially created and a unique asset valuation model resulted.

In contrast, in this and the next Chapter, we will discuss linear models based upon *inexact* historical data .* In this Chapter, we'll discuss the bivariate , or two - dimensional data case. In the next Chapter, we'll discuss the multivariate or n - dimensional data case.

These *identification* models are identified from inexact data, *i.e.*, data series which are not exact linear combinations from each other, unlike the Accounting Identity models.[†] These inexact identification models are used to identify system behavior, for example, how the sales of a firm or an industry sector depend on the growth of the economy, or how the credit risk categorization of corporate bonds depends on various

---

*Although this Chapter has a 15 year history in the making, parts of it directly draw from two recent papers. First, Los (1999): this paper was presented at the 14th International Conference in Finance, Grenoble, France, June 23 - 25, 1997, and reprinted as article 34 on the AFFI97 Proceedings' CD-ROM. An earlier version had been presented at the International Symposium on Advanced Econometrics, Sophia Antipolis, France, June 3-5 1997. Second, "Valuation of Six Asian Stock markets: Financial System Identification in Noisy Environments", CREFS Working Paper 97-02, Nanyang Technological University, Singapore, 5 May, 1997, which was presented at the Econometric Society Australasian Meeting, Melbourne, Australia and reprinted in its Proceedings, Vol. 4, 2 - 4 July 1997, pp. 589 - 621. Both papers resulted from my 1990 Lecture in Zürich in December and my 1992 Lecture before the New York Academy of Sciences.

[†]The exact relationships implied by the Accounting Identity cause serious problems for optimization. However, these rank problems can be resolved by tensor algebra, as discussed in Chapter 14.

financial ratios of the issuing firm. Once these inexact linear models are identified from the observed covariances, and the stationarity of these covariances is checked by windowing, they can be used to extrapolate from the inexact existing data set to an inexact future data set, based upon the observed *inertia* and *homogeneity* of the data set. For example, a consensus forecast for the growth of the economy can be used in combination with the inexact identified model to produce an inexact forecast of the sales of the firm or the industry. Or, once the relative transition frequencies of the stationary risks of migrating corporate bonds have been established, one can make predictions about the credit quality of portfolios of these graded bonds a few periods from now.

To enable the model identification, we first create a complete, but still inexact, data set from the raw data set, by computing its *first and second moments* , *i.e.*, its means and covariances. This is useful, since *linear* models only use first and second moments for their identification. It is important to emphasize that by a *linear* model we mean a model linear in its coefficients only. The data may be nonlinear, *i.e.*, they may be *nonlinear transformations* of the raw, or original data, such as powers and logarithms.[‡]

4.2   First Two Moments

4.2.1   Expected Value and Variance

The first and second moments of a *raw*, or *original data* series , *i.e.*, the expected value (average , mean) and the variance , respectively, can *always* be computed. Let **y** be the *vector* (= single column array of *elements*) of order $T \times 1$. For example, let there be T observations on the quarterly rates of return on a stock, on the annual sales revenues of a firm, on the monthly yields of a $7-$year bond, or on the quarterly GDP growth rates of Singapore, presented in the $T \times 1$ vector:

$$\mathbf{y} - \begin{bmatrix} y_1 \\ y_2 \\ \dots \\ y_T \end{bmatrix} \tag{4.1}$$

with elements y_t for the integer t, $1 \leq t \leq T$.

Remark 19 *These elements y_t can also be nonlinear transformations of original data, e.g., raised powers , exponentials , first derivatives of logarithms , etc.*

[‡]This Chapter expands on material first introduced at an invited Lecture at the University of Zürich, Switzerland in December 1990 and presented in extended form in other invited Lectures before the New York Academy of Sciences and at the Quantum Theory Symposium at Columbia University in March and April 1992, respectively. The majority of this Chapter is new and can't be found in existing textbooks on multivariate (financial and economic) data analysis, but thanks its origination to the seminal influence of Professor Emeritus Rudolf E. Kalman, formerly (1972-1997) at the Eidgenossischen Technische Hochschule (ETH) in Zürich, Switzerland.

The *expected value* , or *mean* of the elements of vector **y** is the *scalar* (= single element of order 1×1)

$$\overline{y} = E(y_t)$$
$$= \frac{\sum_{t=1}^{T} y_t}{T} \tag{4.2}$$

The *deviations from the mean* $\overline{y}$ form the $T \times 1$ vector:

$$\mathbf{x}_1 = dev(y)$$
$$= \begin{bmatrix} y_1 - \overline{y} \\ y_2 - \overline{y} \\ \dots \\ y_T - \overline{y} \end{bmatrix}$$
$$= \mathbf{y} - \iota_T \overline{y} \tag{4.3}$$

where ι_T is the $T \times 1$ unit vector :

$$\iota_T = \begin{bmatrix} 1 \\ 1 \\ \dots \\ 1 \end{bmatrix} \tag{4.4}$$

Notice that the raw data vector is $\mathbf{y} = \mathbf{x}_1 + \iota_T \overline{y}$. Thus the data form the sum of their mean and their deviations from the mean. Therefore, we can always equivalently analyze the deviations $\mathbf{x}_1$ instead of the original data **y**. *Vice versa*, we can always reconstruct the original data from the deviations and the mean, by using the expression

$$\mathbf{y} = \mathbf{x}_1 + \iota_T \overline{y} \tag{4.5}$$

Also, the expected value of the deviations always equals a $T \times 1$ vector of zeros: $E(\mathbf{x}_1) = \mathbf{0}$.

The *variance* of the elements of the vector **y** is the scalar

$$\sigma_{yy} = Var(y_t)$$
$$= \frac{\sum_{t=1}^{T} (y_t - \overline{y})^2}{T}$$
$$= \frac{[dev(y)]' dev(y)}{T}$$
$$= \frac{\mathbf{x}_1' \mathbf{x}_1}{T} \tag{4.6}$$

where $\mathbf{x}_1'$ represents the $1 \times T$ *transpose* of the $T \times 1$ vector $\mathbf{x}_1 = dev(\mathbf{y})$, *i.e.*,

$$\mathbf{x}_1' = dev(\mathbf{y})' \tag{4.7}$$
$$= \begin{bmatrix} y_1 - \overline{y} & y_2 - \overline{y} & ... & y_T - \overline{y} \end{bmatrix}$$

Thus the variance of a series of data can be computed as a *scalar product* of deviations from the mean of that series.

The *standard deviation* of the elements of vector $\mathbf{y}$ is the scalar

$$\sigma_y = stdev(y)$$
$$= \sqrt{Var(y_t)} \tag{4.8}$$

In computational finance, the standard deviation of price or rate of return data is the measure of *price volatility* , *return volatility* , or *risk* .

4.2.2   Covariance Matrix and Correlations

Let $\mathbf{x}$ be the *matrix* (= rectangular array of elements) of deviations of order $T \times n$, *i.e.*, with n column vectors with each T deviations from the respective means. For example, let there be rates of return on n assets over T periods for which we have computed the respectively expected rates of return in the following $T \times n$ matrix

$$\mathbf{x} = [x_{ti}]$$
$$= \begin{bmatrix} y_{11} - \overline{y_1} & y_{12} - \overline{y_2} & ... & y_{1n} - \overline{y_n} \\ y_{21} - \overline{y_1} & y_{22} - \overline{y_2} & ... & y_{2n} - \overline{y_n} \\ ... & ... & ... & ... \\ y_{T1} - \overline{y_1} & y_{T2} - \overline{y_2} & ... & y_{T_n} - \overline{y_n} \end{bmatrix}$$
$$= \begin{bmatrix} \mathbf{x}_1 & \mathbf{x}_2 & ... & \mathbf{x}_n \end{bmatrix} \tag{4.9}$$

The *data covariance matrix* of these n data series is the $n \times n$ *symmetric* matrix of averaged products of deviations from the respective means

$$\Sigma = \frac{\mathbf{x}'\mathbf{x}}{'1'}$$
$$= \frac{\begin{bmatrix} \mathbf{x}_1 & \mathbf{x}_2 & ... & \mathbf{x}_n \end{bmatrix}' \begin{bmatrix} \mathbf{x}_1 & \mathbf{x}_2 & ... & \mathbf{x}_n \end{bmatrix}}{T} \tag{4.10}$$

or

$$\Sigma = \begin{bmatrix} \mathbf{x}_1'\mathbf{x}_1 & \mathbf{x}_1'\mathbf{x}_2 & ... & \mathbf{x}_1'\mathbf{x}_n \\ \mathbf{x}_2'\mathbf{x}_1 & \mathbf{x}_2'\mathbf{x}_2 & ... & \mathbf{x}_2'\mathbf{x}_n \\ ... & ... & ... & ... \\ \mathbf{x}_n'\mathbf{x}_1 & \mathbf{x}_n'\mathbf{x}_2 & ... & \mathbf{x}_n'\mathbf{x}_n \end{bmatrix} /T$$
$$= \begin{bmatrix} \sigma_{11} & \sigma_{12} & ... & \sigma_{1n} \\ \sigma_{21} & \sigma_{22} & ... & \sigma_{2n} \\ ... & ... & ... & ... \\ \sigma_{n1} & \sigma_{n2} & ... & \sigma_{nn} \end{bmatrix} \tag{4.11}$$

Notice that

$$\sigma_{ij} = \frac{\mathbf{x}_i' \mathbf{x}_j}{T} = \frac{\mathbf{x}_j' \mathbf{x}_i}{T} = \sigma_{ji} \tag{4.12}$$

for $i \neq j$ (symmetry). The diagonal elements of the covariance matrix, σ_{ii}, are *variances* , while its off-diagonal elements, σ_{ij} for $i \neq j$, are *covariances* . Each off-diagonal element of the data covariance matrix provides a simple "picture" of the bivariate *covariation* of two data series. There are $\frac{n(n+1)}{2}$ such independent, bivariate (2-dimensional) covariance pictures.

Remark 20 *Data analysis for the identification of an inexact (linear) model is quite different from the realization of an exact model. For inexact data the data covariance matrix is always positive definite and, consequently, invertible, so Σ^{-1} exists. Thus for inexact data*

$$\Sigma.\Sigma^{-1} = \Sigma^{-1}.\Sigma = I \tag{4.13}$$

where I is the identity matrix , i.e., a symmetric zero matrix with ones on the diagonal. A $n \times n$ positive definite matrix is a matrix which produces, when pre-and post-multiplied by a $n \times 1$ vector $\mathbf{w}$, a positive scalar , thus the quadratic form $\mathbf{w}'\Sigma\mathbf{w} = d > 0$. In contrast, for exact data, the data covariance matrix is singular and, consequently, invertible , so that Σ^{-1} does not even exist! A $n \times n$ singular matrix is a matrix which produces, when pre-and post-multiplied by any $n \times 1$ vector w, a zero, thus the quadratic form $\mathbf{w}'\Sigma\mathbf{w} = 0$.

A coefficient which plays an important role in bivariate data analysis is the *correlation coefficient* of two data series:

$$\rho_{ij} = \frac{\sigma_{ij}}{\sqrt{\sigma_{ii}.\sigma_{jj}}} \tag{4.14}$$

The correlation coefficient measures the bivariate correlation between the two series from zero correlation, $\rho_{ij} = 0$, to 100% correlation, $\rho_{ij} = 1$. Thus, in general, $0 \leq \rho_{ij} \leq 1$. For exact linear relationships $\rho_{ij} = 1$. For inexact relationships $0 < \rho_{ij} < 1$. Again, $\rho_{ij} = \rho_{ji}$ for $i \neq j$ (symmetry).

4.3 Iso-Information Ellipsoids

Data analysis is performed to identify models from inexact data. Based on the current state of knowledge of data analysis, which essentially uses linear algebra and geometry , the $n \times n$ covariance matrix of n data series, or *data covariance matrix* Σ, is its sole input. We will first illustrate data analysis for identification with the help of an algebraic *bivariate* example, which will then be generalized to the *n-variate* data series by matrix algebra. In the corresponding Exercise we extend the bivariate example numerically to a *trivariate* case.[§] The bivariate example of this Chapter will form the basis for the analysis of the CAPM in the next Chapter and will explain why the usual CAPM results are "downward" biased and why CAPM underestimates the relative market risk (Los, 1999).

4.3.1 Iso-Information Ellipsoids and Projections

Let there be T observations on 2 data series, $\mathbf{x} = \begin{bmatrix} \mathbf{x}_1 & \mathbf{x}_2 \end{bmatrix}$, so that their 2×2 data covariance matrix is

$$\Sigma = \frac{\mathbf{x}'\mathbf{x}}{T}$$
$$= \begin{bmatrix} \sigma_{11} & \sigma_{12} \\ \sigma_{12} & \sigma_{22} \end{bmatrix} \tag{4.15}$$

The inverse of the data covariance matrix

$$\Sigma^{-1} = \frac{Adj\Sigma}{|\Sigma|}$$
$$\text{or } \mathbf{I}.\,|\Sigma| = \Sigma.Adj\Sigma \tag{4.16}$$

is called the *information matrix* , where the *adjoint* , or *adjugate matrix* is

$$Adj\Sigma = \begin{bmatrix} \sigma_{22} & -\sigma_{12} \\ -\sigma_{12} & \sigma_{11} \end{bmatrix} \tag{4.17}$$

and the *determinant* is

$$|\Sigma| = \sigma_{11}.\sigma_{22} - \sigma_{12}^2$$
$$= \sigma_{11}.\sigma_{22}(1 - \rho_{12}^2) \tag{4.18}$$

The squared correlation coefficient ρ_{12}^2 is called the *coefficient of bivariate determination* . Both the determinant and the coefficient of bivariate determination inform about the *degree of inexactness* of the data.

The *iso-information ellipsoids* , or *data density contours* , are the affine invariant norm ellipsoids described by the quadratic equation

$$\widehat{\mathbf{x}}_t \Sigma^{-1} \widehat{\mathbf{x}}_t' = d \tag{4.19}$$

for any given value of the scalar $d > 0$ and all t.[¶] The hat ^ indicate certainty, or exactness. An affine transformation ellipsoid is an exact mathematical model which helps to visualize the geometric structure of the n - dimensional data scatter (Los, 1994; Nielson, Hagen and Müller, 1997).

[§] Without matrix algebra the symbolic algebra would quickly become rather dense.

[¶] In the $n = 2$ data space, these iso-information ellipses are identified from the data, by computing the information matrix, i.e., the inverse of the data covariance matrix. In 1865 Galton provided the original idea (Cf. Los, 1997).

Example 21 *For example, for the $n = 2$ variable case we have a (2×2) data covariance matrix Σ of two empirically observed financial - economic variables for Taiwan - the natural logarithms of its stock market index and its nominal GDP (one-quarter-ahead) for the period $1986Q1 - 1995Q3$ - is as follows:*

$$\Sigma = \begin{bmatrix} \sigma_{11} & \sigma_{12} \\ \sigma_{12} & \sigma_{22} \end{bmatrix}$$

$$= \begin{bmatrix} 0.4286 & 0.1184 \\ 0.1184 & 0.0861 \end{bmatrix} \quad (4.20)$$

with a determinant $|\Sigma| = 2.2884 \times 10^{-2}$. Two particular concentric information ellipses , based on this covariance matrix, are the following, scaled by the constants $d = 60$ and 150. The iso - information ellipsoid is computed by:

$$
\begin{aligned}
\widehat{\mathbf{x}}_t \Sigma^{-1} \widehat{\mathbf{x}}'_t &= \frac{\begin{bmatrix} \widehat{x}_{1t} & \widehat{x}_{2t} \end{bmatrix} \begin{bmatrix} \sigma_{22} & -\sigma_{12} \\ -\sigma_{12} & \sigma_{11} \end{bmatrix} \begin{bmatrix} \widehat{x}_{1t} \\ \widehat{x}_{2t} \end{bmatrix}}{\sigma_{11} \cdot \sigma_{22} - \sigma_{12}^2} \\
&= \begin{bmatrix} \widehat{x}_1 & \widehat{x}_2 \end{bmatrix} \begin{bmatrix} \frac{\sigma_{22}}{\sigma_{11}\sigma_{22}-\sigma_{12}^2} & -\frac{\sigma_{12}}{\sigma_{11}\sigma_{22}-\sigma_{12}^2} \\ -\frac{\sigma_{12}}{\sigma_{11}\sigma_{22}-\sigma_{12}^2} & \frac{\sigma_{11}}{\sigma_{11}\sigma_{22}-\sigma_{12}^2} \end{bmatrix} \begin{bmatrix} \widehat{x}_1 \\ \widehat{x}_2 \end{bmatrix} \\
&= \frac{\sigma_{22}\widehat{x}_{1t}^2 - 2\sigma_{12}\widehat{x}_{1t}\widehat{x}_{2t} + \sigma_{11}\widehat{x}_{2t}^2}{\sigma_{11} \cdot \sigma_{22} - \sigma_{12}^2} = d > 0 \quad (4.21)
\end{aligned}
$$

Implementing our numerical example, we have

$$
\begin{aligned}
\widehat{\mathbf{x}}_t \Sigma^{-1} \widehat{\mathbf{x}}'_t &= \begin{bmatrix} \widehat{x}_1 & \widehat{x}_2 \end{bmatrix} \begin{bmatrix} 3.7625 & -5.1739 \\ -5.1739 & 18.7292 \end{bmatrix} \begin{bmatrix} \widehat{x}_1 \\ \widehat{x}_2 \end{bmatrix} \\
&= 3.7625\widehat{x}_1^2 - 10.3478\widehat{x}_1\widehat{x}_2 + 18.7292\widehat{x}_2^2 = 60 \text{ and } 150 > 0 \quad (4.22)
\end{aligned}
$$

These two equations represent two concentric ellipses , or data density contours , in the 2D data scatter space, as can be seen in Fig. 1.[||] The size of these concentric ellipses is determined by the arbitrary constant d. Other 2D data scatter density contours can be plotted by varying the density level d.

4.3.2 Linear Loci of Certainty

The two variable, single equation, $(n, q) = (2, 1)$, orthogonal Least Squares projections , with coefficients from the rows of the information matrix , can be found by

---

[||]x_1 is plotted on the vertical axis and x_2 on the horizontal axis.

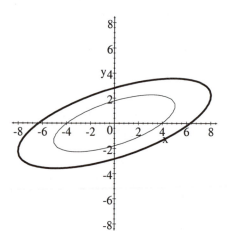

Figure 1 $\widehat{\mathbf{x}}\Sigma^{-1}\widehat{\mathbf{x}}=d$, exact concentric information ellipses

setting the first derivatives of the information ellipse equal to zero, as follows:

$$
\begin{aligned}
\frac{1}{2}\frac{\partial c}{\partial \widehat{\mathbf{x}}} &= \frac{1}{2}\frac{\partial \widehat{\mathbf{x}}\Sigma^{-1}\widehat{\mathbf{x}}}{\partial \widehat{\mathbf{x}}} \\
&= \Sigma^{-1}\widehat{\mathbf{x}} \\
&= \left[\begin{array}{cc} 3.7625 & -5.1739 \\ -5.1739 & 18.7292 \end{array}\right]\left[\begin{array}{c} \widehat{x}_1 \\ \widehat{x}_2 \end{array}\right] \\
&= \left[\begin{array}{c} \frac{\sigma_{22}\widehat{x}_{1t}-\sigma_{12}\widehat{x}_{2t}}{\sigma_{11}.\sigma_{22}-\sigma_{12}^2} \\ \frac{\sigma_{11}\widehat{x}_{2t}-\sigma_{12}\widehat{x}_{1t}}{\sigma_{11}.\sigma_{22}-\sigma_{12}^2} \end{array}\right] \\
&= \left[\begin{array}{c} 3.7625\widehat{x}_1 - 5.1739\widehat{x}_2 \\ -5.1739\widehat{x}_1 + 18.7292\widehat{x}_2 \end{array}\right] \\
&= \left[\begin{array}{c} 0 \\ 0 \end{array}\right]
\end{aligned}
\tag{4.23}
$$

from which we derive the two linear loci of partial optima

$$\widehat{x}_{1t} = \frac{\sigma_{12}}{\sigma_{22}}\widehat{x}_{2t}$$
$$= 1.3751\widehat{x}_{2t} \tag{4.24}$$
$$\text{and } \widehat{x}_{1t} = \frac{\sigma_{11}}{\sigma_{12}}\widehat{x}_{2t}$$
$$= 0.2762\widehat{x}_{2t} \tag{4.25}$$

Since this holds true for all t, we have for the two $T \times 1$ data vectors, two different optimal loci of certainty

$$\widehat{\mathbf{x}}_1 = \frac{\sigma_{12}}{\sigma_{22}}\widehat{\mathbf{x}}_2 \tag{4.26}$$
$$\text{and } \widehat{\mathbf{x}}_1 = \frac{\sigma_{11}}{\sigma_{12}}\widehat{\mathbf{x}}_2 \tag{4.27}$$

These linear loci represent all the points on the concentric iso-information ellipses , where a marginal change in one or the other data variable doesn't change the value of the iso-information ellipse. These are therefore the *loci of information certainty* .

Example 22 *These two linear loci are drawn in Fig 2. Each line is determined by the unique orthogonal projection of the data on one of the two data axes. These orthogonal LS projection lines form a convex cone in the 2D data scatter space "around" the principal axis of the information ellipse. The principal axis lies in the length of the ellipse, while the minor axis is orthogonal to the principal axis. The directions of these principal and minor axes are found from the coefficients of the eigenvectors of the information matrix Σ^{-1}. The relative lengths of these axes can be found by from the corresponding eigenvalues.** One of the orthogonal projection lines - of the "regression" of nominal GDP on the stock index - happens to lie very close to the principal axis and, therefore, appears to be statistically "most acceptable." In fact, the other orthogonal projection line - of the "reverse regression" of the stock index on nominal GDP - does not lie close to the principal axis. But such a situation isn't determinable a priori from the data alone. Therefore, an a priori distinction between "regressand" and "regressor" data variables is scientifically unjustified. It is necessary to take account of the complete set of data, i.e., the whole information matrix Σ^{-1}.*

But there is another, equivalent approach to this issue of how to extract certain information out of the uncertain data. As we will see, a Theorem tells us that the rows of the adjoint provide information about the *model structure* , which generated the inexact data, in particular about the *structural invariant* q. In fact, the adjoint

---

**The spectral decomposition of the data covariance matrix Σ into orthonormal matrices consisting of *eigenvectors* , and a matrix of *eigenvalues* , is discussed in Chapter 7

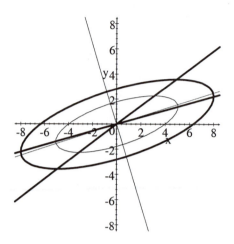

Figure 2   Exact information ellipses and orthogonal CLS projection lines

directly provides the values for the (*Grassmanian*) *coefficients* of the $q \times n$ matrix **A** of the *bivariate model*

$$\mathbf{A}\widehat{\mathbf{x}}' = 0 \tag{4.28}$$

where

$$\mathbf{x} = \widehat{\mathbf{x}} + \widetilde{\mathbf{x}} \tag{4.29}$$

such that the exact, or explained part of the data $\widehat{\mathbf{x}}$ is *orthogonal* to the inexact or unexplained part $\widetilde{\mathbf{x}}$, thus $\widehat{\mathbf{x}} \perp \widetilde{\mathbf{x}}$. This *orthogonality requirement* is imposed, so that what is logically explained by the model $\widehat{\mathbf{x}}$ will not be confused with what remains unexplained $\widetilde{\mathbf{x}}$, *i.e.*, the uncertainty or inexactness in the data. This orthogonality requirement implies the covariance decomposition

$$\begin{aligned} \Sigma &= \frac{\mathbf{x}'\mathbf{x}}{T} \\ &= \widehat{\mathbf{x}}'\widehat{\mathbf{x}} + \widetilde{\mathbf{x}}'\widetilde{\mathbf{x}} \\ &= \widehat{\Sigma} + \widetilde{\Sigma} \end{aligned} \tag{4.30}$$

where $\Sigma > 0$ is a *positive definite matrix* , and $\widehat{\Sigma} \geq 0$ and $\widetilde{\Sigma} \geq 0$ are both *positive semi-definite matrices* . Thus, the data covariance matrix can be decomposed into two parts: the matrix of the exact, explained, model covariance $\widehat{\Sigma}$ and the matrix of inexact, unexplained, noise or remainder covariance $\widetilde{\Sigma}$. Notice that

$$\mathbf{A}\widehat{\mathbf{x}}'\widehat{\mathbf{x}} = \mathbf{A}\widehat{\Sigma} = \mathbf{0} \tag{4.31}$$

and thus

$$\mathbf{A}\Sigma = \mathbf{A}\widetilde{\Sigma} \tag{4.32}$$

This last result means that linear combinations of the columns of the data covariance matrix are linear combinations of the uncertainty in the data, $\widetilde{\Sigma}$. Indeed, when the uncertainty, or inexactness , equals zero, $\mathbf{A}\Sigma = \mathbf{0}$, the columns of the empirical covariance matrix Σ are exact linear combinations. This is the situation of model realization, where the (Grassmanian) coefficients of $\mathbf{A}$ are an exact complement of the data covariance matrix and can therefore be directly read from the data covariance matrix self.

4.3.3 Bivariate Least Squares Projections

Because of the inexactness of the two data series of our simple example, we have at least *two* (extreme) orthogonal *Least Squares (LS) projections* , as follows. Concentrating on the first row of the adjoint [††]

$$\mathbf{A}\widehat{\mathbf{x}}' = \begin{bmatrix} \mathbf{A}_1 & \mathbf{A}_2 \end{bmatrix} \begin{bmatrix} \widehat{\mathbf{x}}_1 \\ \widehat{\mathbf{x}}_2 \end{bmatrix}$$

$$= \begin{bmatrix} \sigma_{22} & -\sigma_{12} \end{bmatrix} \begin{bmatrix} \widehat{\mathbf{x}}_1 \\ \widehat{\mathbf{x}}_2 \end{bmatrix}$$

$$= 0 \tag{4.33}$$

or

$$\sigma_{22}\widehat{\mathbf{x}}_1 - \sigma_{12}\widehat{\mathbf{x}}_2 = 0 \tag{4.34}$$

This is, of course, equivalent to the conventional Least Squares projection on variable $\mathbf{x}_2$:

$$\widehat{\mathbf{x}}_1 = \beta_2\widehat{\mathbf{x}}_2$$

$$= \frac{\sigma_{12}}{\sigma_{22}}\widehat{\mathbf{x}}_2 \tag{4.35}$$

Thus the $q \times n = 1 \times 2$ *projection coefficient matrix* for the orthogonal projection on $\mathbf{x}_2$ is

$$\mathbf{A}_2 = \begin{bmatrix} 1 & -\frac{\sigma_{12}}{\sigma_{22}} \end{bmatrix} \tag{4.36}$$

[††] The hats $\widehat{\mathbf{x}}_i$ indicate again the resulting exactness of the modeled variables.

However, we also have the not so conventional, but scientifically just as relevant, second projection (or "reverse regression") from

$$A\widehat{x}' = \begin{bmatrix} A_1 & A_2 \end{bmatrix} \begin{bmatrix} \widehat{x}_1 \\ \widehat{x}_2 \end{bmatrix}$$

$$= \begin{bmatrix} -\sigma_{12} & \sigma_{11} \end{bmatrix} \begin{bmatrix} \widehat{x}_1 \\ \widehat{x}_2 \end{bmatrix}$$

$$= 0 \qquad (4.37)$$

or

$$-\sigma_{12}\widehat{x}_1 + \sigma_{11}\widehat{x}_2 = 0 \qquad (4.38)$$

This is equivalent to the unconventional projection on variable x_1:

$$\widehat{x}_2 = \gamma_1\widehat{x}_1$$

$$= \frac{\sigma_{12}}{\sigma_{11}}\widehat{x}_1 \qquad (4.39)$$

or, mathematically equivalently,

$$\widehat{x}_1 = \beta_1\widehat{x}_2$$

$$= \frac{1}{\gamma_1}\widehat{x}_2$$

$$= \frac{\sigma_{11}}{\sigma_{12}}\widehat{x}_2 \qquad (4.40)$$

Thus the second 1×2 projection coefficient matrix for the orthogonal projection on x_1 is

$$A_1 = \begin{bmatrix} 1 & -\frac{\sigma_{11}}{\sigma_{12}} \end{bmatrix} \qquad (4.41)$$

Now we have the situation that the measured beta β lies between the parameter values of these two extreme orthogonal projections, $\beta_1 \geq \beta \geq \beta_2$, because any *linear combination* of these two extreme projections will also satisfy the data. In other words, uncertain, inexact data result in an infinite number of measured β's, with values lying between two extreme LS projections. In short: inexact data produce inexact measurements of linear relationships! The following relationship exists between the coefficient of bivariate determination and the parameter values resulting from the two extreme orthogonal LS projections :

$$\rho_{ij}^2 = \frac{\sigma_{12}^2}{\sigma_{11}\sigma_{22}}$$

$$= \beta_2 \cdot \gamma_1$$

$$= \frac{\beta_2}{\beta_1} \qquad (4.42)$$

Next, we will geometrically interpret this expression and then derive a useful Noise/Signal Ratio, as used by signal processing engineers . First, the *geometric interpretation* of the coefficient of bivariate determination is

$$\rho_{12}^2 = \beta_2 \cdot \gamma_1$$
$$= \tan(\theta_1) \cdot \tan(\theta_3)$$
$$= \frac{\tan(\theta_1)}{\tan(\theta_1 + \theta_2)} \tag{4.43}$$

where $\beta_2 = \tan(\theta_1)$, $\gamma_1 = \tan(\theta_3)$, $\beta_1 = \tan(\theta_1 + \theta_2)$ and, as in Fig. 3.:

$$\theta_1 + \theta_2 + \theta_3 = \frac{\pi}{2} \tag{4.44}$$

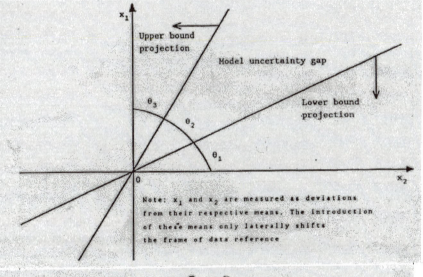

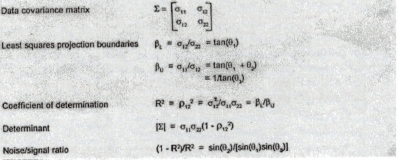

Data covariance matrix	$\Sigma = \begin{bmatrix} \sigma_{11} & \sigma_{12} \\ \sigma_{12} & \sigma_{22} \end{bmatrix}$
Least squares projection boundaries	$\beta_L = \sigma_{12}/\sigma_{22} = \tan(\theta_1)$
	$\beta_U = \sigma_{11}/\sigma_{12} = \tan(\theta_1 + \theta_2)$
	$= 1/\tan(\theta_3)$
Coefficient of determination	$R^2 = \rho_{12}^2 = \sigma_{12}^2/\sigma_{11}\sigma_{22} = \beta_L/\beta_U$
Determinant	$|\Sigma| = \sigma_{11}\sigma_{22}(1 - \rho_{12}^2)$
Noise/signal ratio	$(1 - R^2)/R^2 = \sin(\theta_2)/[\sin(\theta_1)\sin(\theta_3)]$

Figure 3: Orthogonal LS $(n, q) = (2, 1)$ projections: the model uncertainty gap

Thus the coefficient of bivariate determination is the product of the slope coefficients of the *two* orthogonal projections. It gives the percentage of explained bivariation . When in the limit $\theta_2 \to 0$, the two projection slopes coincide, the coefficient of bivariate determination equals unity. Such a limit is an abstraction, since with empirical data the slope coefficients will always differ because of fundamental data uncertainty.

Remark 23 *Conventional bivariate statistical analysis provides the value of β_2 and the value of ρ_{12}^2, but usually not the value of β_1. However,we can always recover β_1 from the expression*

$$\beta_1 = \frac{\beta_2}{\rho_{12}^2} \tag{4.45}$$

as we will see in Chapter 4 in an example of the CAPM using basic mutual funds data.

Since $\tan(\theta_i) = \frac{\sin(\theta_i)}{\cos(\theta_i)}$, by judicious substitution (*Cf.* Appendix A), we find that the *2D Noise/Signal Ratio for the bivariate model*

$$\begin{aligned} \frac{N}{S} &= \frac{(1 - \rho_{12}^2)}{\rho_{12}^2} \\ &= \frac{\sin(\theta_2)}{\sin(\theta_1)\sin(\theta_3)} \end{aligned} \tag{4.46}$$

This states that the Noise/Signal Ratio, or *relative uncertainty* in the bivariate model, can be expressed *algebraically* in terms of the coefficient of bivariate determination and *geometrically* in terms of the angles between the slopes of the projection lines and the reference frame of the data.

4.4 Envisioning Bivariate Modeling Uncertainty

We can now distinguish the following $(n, q) = (2, 1)$ uncertain model cases using *five* equivalent ways of presenting the same modeling uncertainty and, in the limit, modeling certainty, both algebraically and geometrically. Thus we can clearly *envision* bivariate modeling uncertainty and uncertainty of structural information by both algebraic and geometric means.

FIVE EQUIVALENT WAYS OF ENVISIONING
BIVARIATE MODEL UNCERTAINTY AND CERTAINTY

(1) Bivariate modeling uncertainty

(i) $|\Sigma| > 0$, the data covariance matrix is positive definite, *i.e.*, its determinant is positive;

(ii) $0 < \rho_{12}^2 < 1$, the coefficient of bivariate determination shows less than complete explanation, *i.e.*, inexact determination ;

(iii) $\beta_2 < \beta < \beta_1$, the upper and lower projection slopes do not coincide;

(iv) $0 < \theta_2 < \frac{\pi}{2}$, there exists an uncertainty gap in between the orthogonal frames of data reference ;

(v) $\frac{N}{S} > 0$, the noise/signal ratio is positive, since the inexact data contain some noise, together with the signal.

(2) Bivariate modeling certainty

(i) $|\Sigma| = 0$, the data covariance matrix is singular, *i.e.*, its determinant equals zero;

(ii) $\rho_{12}^2 = 1$, the coefficient of bivariate determination shows complete explanation or exact determination;

(iii) $\beta_2 = \beta = \beta_1$, the upper and lower projection slopes do coincide;

(iv) $\theta_2 = 0$, there exists no uncertainty gap in between the orthogonal frames of data reference;

(v) $\frac{N}{S} = 0$, the noise/signal ratio is zero, since the exact data consist only of the signal.

Remark 24 *Although one would think that the case of empirical modeling certainty is the limit of the case of modeling uncertainty, with uncertainty approaching zero, this may not be true (Kalman, 1994, 1995). The case of certainty is a theoretical abstraction that can be approached in empirical science by improved measurement, but that can empirically never be reached thanks to Heisenberg's Uncertainty Principle . The measurement uncertainty will show up in the finite inexactness of numerical computer computations, which are based on finite registers. In empirical science always $|\Sigma| > 0$. This fundamental uncertainty is the curse and the raison d'être of analytical empirical science.*

4.5   Exercises

Exercise 25 *Suppose we have the following data covariance matrix Σ of rates of return on three stocks and its inverse, the information matrix Σ^{-1}:*

$$\Sigma = \begin{bmatrix} 2.0596 & 0.3752 & 1.0775 \\ 0.3752 & 0.7903 & 0.3547 \\ 1.0775 & 0.3547 & 0.8673 \end{bmatrix}^{-1} \tag{4.47}$$

and

$$\Sigma^{-1} = \begin{bmatrix} 1.3999 & .14204 & -1.7973 \\ .14204 & 1.5642 & -.81618 \\ -1.7973 & -.81618 & 3.7197 \end{bmatrix} \tag{4.48}$$

1. Compute the three bivariate projection slopes .

2. Compute the three bivariate correlation coefficients .

3. Compute the three coefficients of bivariate determination and the corresponding bivariate Noise/Signal ratios .

4. Compute the three bivariate t-statistics and the Noise/Signal ratios? What do they measure?

5. How are the bivariate projection slopes, the correlation coefficients, the coefficients of determination, the t-statistics and the determinant of Σ related to each other?

6. How many linear relationships exist among these three variables and why?

4.6   Bibliography

Alexander, C. (1999) "Volatility and Correlation: Measurement, Models and Applications," Chapter 4 in Alexander, C. (Ed.) *Risk Management and Analysis, Volume 1: Measuring and Modelling Financial Risk*, John Wiley & Sons, New York, NY, 125 - 171.

Bring, J. (1996) "A Geometric Approach to Compare Variables in a Regression Model," *The American Statistician*, **50**, 57 - 62.

Campbell, J. Y., Lo, A. W. and MacKinlay, A. C. (1997) *The Econometrics of Financial Markets*, Princeton University Press, Princeton, NJ.

Galton, F. (1885) "Regression Towards Mediocrity in Hereditary Status," *Journal of the Anthropological Institute*, **15**, 246 - 263.

Hannah, J. (1996) "A Geometric Approach to Determinants," *The American Mathematical Monthly*, **103**, 401 - 409.

Herr, D.G. (1980) "On the History of the Use of Geometry in the General Linear Model," *The American Statistician*, **34**, 43 - 47.

Los, C. A. (1989a) "The Prejudices of Least Squares, Principal Components and Common Factor Schemes," *Computers & Mathematics With Applications*, **17** (8/9), 1269 - 1283.

Los, C. A. (1994) "The Accuracy of Social Science Observations: Kepler and Galton Compared," Research Report, EMEPS Associates, Inc., Jersey City, NJ, July, 19 pages.

Los, C. A. (1999) "Galton's Error and the Under-Representation of Systematic Risk," *Journal of Banking and Finance*, **23** (12), November, 1793 - 1828.

Margolis, M.S. (1979) "Perpendicular Projections and Elementary Statistics," *The American Statistician*, **33**, 131 - 135.

Nielson, G. M., Hagen, H. and Müller, H. (1997) *Scientific Visualization: Overviews, Methodologies, and Techniques*, IEEE Computer Society, Los Alamitos, CA, 1997, pp. 495 - 500.

Reilly, F. K. and Brown, K. C. (1997) *Investment Analysis and Portfolio Management*, The Dryden Press, Harcourt Brace College Publishers, New York, NY.

Rodgers, J.L., Nicewander, W. A. and Toothaker, L. (1984) "Linearly Independent, Orthogonal and Uncorrelated Variables," *The American Statistician*, **38**, 133 - 134.

Solnik, B., Boucrelle, C. and Le Fur, Y. (1996) "International Market Correlation and Volatility," *Financial Analysts Journal*, September - October, 17 - 34.

chapter:5,page:1

Chapter 5
ANALYSIS OF INEXACT DATA II

5.1 Introduction

In this Chapter, we'll continue with the identification of models from multivariate, or n - dimensional data. For that purpose. we'll introduce two very powerful identification Theorems. In the winter of 1990/91, after five years of intensive research, two Theorems were discovered by Kalman in collaborative discussions with Los , which permit us to do the CLS analysis. In this Chapter we'll state these Theorems in simplified form, without proof, and we probe their applications in the laboratory Exercises. *Cf.* Kalman (1991b) for the proofs of the Theorems and Los (1989a & b, 1992) for applications.

5.2 Complete Least Squares Projections

For *Complete Least Squares (CLS) Projections* we need to analyze the *complete* data covariance matrix . Conventional statistical multivariate analysis , which uses "Ordinary" and "Generalized" Least Squares projections , tends to *a priori* choose a particular projection direction and ignores most of the correlation information available in the data covariance matrix. Such analysis is therefore *scientifically incomplete* . The data needs to be completely examined, *i.e.*, from every possible *goniometric* projection angle to identify the linear model consistent with the data.*

5.2.1 Two Important System Identification Theorems

The first Theorem generalizes our procedure to detect if the model consists of a single equation , *i.e.*, a plane in n-data space, with model invariant $q = 1$, or not . If not, a more complex linear model structure than a plane must be identified from the information matrix, with the system invariant q such that $1 < q < n$.

Theorem 26 (Information Matrix) *The rows of the information matrix, i.e., the inverse of the data covariance matrix, provide us with all the available data information about the invariant linear structure generating the data. This includes information*

---

*The use of complete goniometric projections is accepted practice in 3 - dimensional crystallographic research of biometric protein models, for example. But it is not yet accepted scientific practice in financial econometrics and related empirical research subjects which deal with multivariate, multidimensional modeling.

about the degree of inexactness of the data, or, equivalently, the degree of modeling uncertainty .

Proof. *Follows from the matrix partition Lemma (Cf. Dhrymes, 1978, Proposition 30).* ∎

Remark 27 *It can be shown algebraically that each row of the information matrix is a single equation, "ordinary," or "elementary" "regression."* [†] *As remarked earlier, conventional statistical analysis a priori chooses one of those rows as its linear "model." This leads to incomplete analysis of all available covariance information, since the other rows contain additional structural model information, and, consequently, the single equation model may not be consistent with that additional information.*[‡]

Once we have determined the model rank q consistent with the data (Frisch, 1934; Kalman, 1991a & b; Los, 1987a, 1989a & b, 1999), the next Theorem allows us to compute the complete set of all possible model coefficient configurations, resulting from the complete set of projections for a particular model rank q.

Theorem 28 (Complete Least Squares, or CLS) *For all linear models $A\widehat{x}' = 0$ with* $rank(A) = q$, *which are identifiable from the data covariance matrix $\Sigma > 0$ and, which by definition, must satisfy the orthogonality requirement $\widehat{x} \perp \widetilde{x}$, it is true that the Least Squares noise covariance matrix*

$$\widetilde{\Sigma}^{CLS} = \Sigma A'(A\Sigma A')^{-1}A\Sigma$$

is the best , most efficient , or "smallest." This is true in the sense that any other noise matrix is "larger," so that for any noise matrix $\widetilde{\Sigma} = \widetilde{\Sigma}^{CLS} + Q$, where $Q \geq 0$, a positive semi-definite matrix .

Proof. *Kalman (1991b) used a Lemma of Bekker (1986) to proof this Theorem.* ∎

Remark 29 *Since the exact values of the model's (Grassmanian) projection coefficients A remain essentially undetermined, CLS noise remains essentially undetermined too.*[§] *Only the value of the structural model invariant q can be identified, while infinitely many different projection directions can be chosen. CLS noise is finite, since the data covariance matrix is finite.*

[†]The erroneous term "regression" is from Galton, 1885, but "it ain't ordinary." Cf. Los (1997).

[‡]Among the Exercises, we analyze a 3 × 3 data covariance, where the model consists of two simultaneous equations, $q = 2$, and not of one single equation, $q = 1$. Thus we have an $(n, q) = (3, 2)$ data example.

[§]The German linguist Hermann Grassman, a specialist in Sanskrit literature, who only taught at the secondary school level, developed in 1844 the concept of an n-dimensional vector space in his *Ausdehnungslehre (Expansion Theory)* and studied the geometric interpretation of negative quantities. His definition of n-dimensional (affine) space was made more precise in the 1862 revised edition of his book.

Remark 30 *For each projection and each corresponding coefficient matrix* **A**, *there exists a corresponding LS noise matrix* $\widetilde{\Sigma}^{CLS}$. *Since there are infinite projections possible based on linear combinations of the n orthogonal (data frame) projections, there are infinite model projection coefficients* **A**, *and corresponding noise matrices, compatible with the data. Thus the model projection coefficients of* **A** *cannot have a unique interpretation , as is often erroneously assumed in the very many disciplines of learning which use "regression."*

5.2.2 Noise and Signal Projections

The CLS Theorem has an important implementation. For a given $rank(\mathbf{A}) = q$, where q represents the number of simultaneous independent equations of the model, as determined from the information matrix, we can always compute the corresponding LS noise matrix, and thus the *LS projection uncertainty* , using the projection

$$\widetilde{\mathbf{x}}'^{CLS} = \widetilde{\Sigma}^{CLS}\Sigma^{-1}\mathbf{x}' \tag{5.1}$$

However, this means that the *exact LS signal* is given by

$$\begin{aligned}\widehat{\mathbf{x}}'^{CLS} &= \widehat{\Sigma}^{CLS}\Sigma^{-1}\mathbf{x}' \\ &= \left(\Sigma - \widetilde{\Sigma}^{CLS}\right)\Sigma^{-1}\mathbf{x}' \\ &= (\mathbf{I} - \widetilde{\Sigma}^{CLS}\Sigma^{-1})\mathbf{x}'\end{aligned} \tag{5.2}$$

since

$$\widehat{\Sigma}^{CLS} = \Sigma - \widetilde{\Sigma}^{CLS} \tag{5.3}$$

or, "signal = data - noise." Consequently, the systematic *LS projector* is:

$$\widehat{\mathbf{P}}^{CLS} = (\mathbf{I} - \widetilde{\Sigma}^{CLS}\Sigma^{-1}) \tag{5.4}$$

Remark 31 *It is an interesting algebraic exercise (try it!) to show that* $\widehat{\mathbf{P}}^{CLS}$ *is, indeed, a projector, since it has the projector property that* $(\widehat{\mathbf{P}}^{CLS})^2 = \widehat{\mathbf{P}}^{CLS}$.

After this necessarily succinct generalization, let's now first return to the bivariate model case to view an implementation of this theory and compute symbolically its *two* extreme noise and signal covariance matrices, assuming $\widetilde{\sigma}_{11} = 0$, respectively, $\widetilde{\sigma}_{22} = 0$.

The first orthogonal projection gave us the projection coefficient matrix

$$\mathbf{A}_1 = \begin{bmatrix} \sigma_{22} & -\sigma_{12} \end{bmatrix} \tag{5.5}$$

or, normalized

$$\mathbf{A}_1^N = \begin{bmatrix} 1 & -\frac{\sigma_{11}}{\sigma_{12}} \end{bmatrix} \tag{5.6}$$

The second projection gave us the projection coefficient matrix

$$\mathbf{A}_2 = \begin{bmatrix} -\sigma_{12} & \sigma_{11} \end{bmatrix} \tag{5.7}$$

or, normalized,

$$\mathbf{A}_2^N = \begin{bmatrix} 1 & -\frac{\sigma_{12}}{\sigma_{22}} \end{bmatrix} \tag{5.8}$$

Using *Theorem 2.* to compute the two corresponding extreme LS noise matrices $\widetilde{\Sigma}_1^{CLS}$ and $\widetilde{\Sigma}_2^{CLS}$, we find

$$\begin{aligned}
\widetilde{\Sigma}_1^{CLS} &= \Sigma \mathbf{A}_1'(\mathbf{A}_1 \Sigma \mathbf{A}_1')^{-1} \mathbf{A}_1 \Sigma \\
&= \begin{bmatrix} \frac{\sigma_{11}\sigma_{22}-\sigma_{12}^2}{\sigma_{22}} & 0 \\ 0 & 0 \end{bmatrix} \\
&= \begin{bmatrix} \frac{|\Sigma|}{\sigma_{22}} & 0 \\ 0 & 0 \end{bmatrix}
\end{aligned} \tag{5.9}$$

and

$$\begin{aligned}
\widetilde{\Sigma}_2^{CLS} &= \Sigma \mathbf{A}_2'(\mathbf{A}_2 \Sigma \mathbf{A}_2')^{-1} \mathbf{A}_2 \Sigma \\
&= \begin{bmatrix} 0 & 0 \\ 0 & \frac{\sigma_{11}\sigma_{22}-\sigma_{12}^2}{\sigma_{11}} \end{bmatrix} \\
&= \begin{bmatrix} 0 & 0 \\ 0 & \frac{|\Sigma|}{\sigma_{11}} \end{bmatrix}
\end{aligned} \tag{5.10}$$

Thus the LS noise resulting from the corresponding projections is

$$\begin{aligned}
\widetilde{\sigma}_{11} &= \frac{|\Sigma|}{\sigma_{22}} \\
&= \sigma_{11} - \frac{\sigma_{12}^2}{\sigma_{22}}, \text{ when } \widetilde{\sigma}_{22} = 0
\end{aligned} \tag{5.11}$$

and

$$\begin{aligned}
\widetilde{\sigma}_{22} &= \frac{|\Sigma|}{\sigma_{11}} \\
&= \sigma_{22} - \frac{\sigma_{12}^2}{\sigma_{11}}, \text{ when } \widetilde{\sigma}_{11} = 0
\end{aligned} \tag{5.12}$$

Appendix B contains a flow chart of the complete identification procedure, laid out as a recipe in 10 easy Steps for the computations.

5.2.3 Noise/Data Ratios in Two - Dimensional Data

Notice that the LS noise variance in variable x_1 equals the total amount of data noise in the two - dimensional data, as measured by the determinant $|\Sigma|$ of the data covariance matrix, relative to the variance of variable x_2. It is similar for the LS noise in variable x_2. This also implies that for the bivariate case the *percentage* of *epistemic uncertainty* (modeling uncertainty , or modeling risk) of the data is independent of the projection direction , since the Noise/Data Ratios in two-dimensional data are equal to each other:

$$
\begin{aligned}
\frac{N}{D} &= \frac{\widetilde{\sigma}_{11}}{\sigma_{11}} \\
&= \frac{\widetilde{\sigma}_{22}}{\sigma_{22}} \\
&= 1 - \frac{\sigma_{12}^2}{\sigma_{11}\sigma_{22}} \\
&= 1 - \frac{\beta_2}{\beta_1} \\
&= 1 - \rho_{12}^2
\end{aligned}
\tag{5.13}
$$

5.3 Hypotheses Non Fingo

When we have, for example, a trivariate data series

$$
\mathbf{x} = \begin{bmatrix} x_1 & x_2 & x_3 \end{bmatrix}
\tag{5.14}
$$

a considerably more complex modeling situation is encountered than in the bivariate case, since the model, or systematic relationship, of three variables can be a plane $(q = 1)$ or a ray $(q = 2)$ in the $n = 3$ data scatter space . Conventional statistics tends to *a priori* assume a plane, but in objective data analysis one should not contrive hypotheses, or as Newton wrote in 1713: *"Hypotheses Non Fingo"* (Translated by Kalman in 1991: *"I do not contrive hypotheses"*).

Again, the conventional statistical approach is scientifically incomplete with respect to the data. It is also unnecessarily incomplete, since from the adjoint of the data covariance matrix one can usually directly determine if a plane or a ray is the model consistent with the data (unless the inexactness is too large and a linear model would make no sense whatsoever). Ever more complex linear correlation structures $(q > 2)$ are encountered when the number of data series increases for $n > 2$, as we so often find in economics, finance and similar behavioral sciences. Of course, the integer q must be such that $1 \leq q \leq n - 1$.

Remark 32 *While q is the number of independent equations of the model, $n - q$ is the number of eigenvalues and factors , as used in both principal components analysis and factor analysis (Los, 1989a & b). "Principal components" and statistical "factors"* *are "bundles," or linear combinations , of the data. However, currently the choice of a particular linear combination (and projection) is still taught in conventional statistics as a subjective operation and a prejudiced choice of variables. Thus, it is not determined from the uncertain data alone. In contrast, our new complete identification methodology can objectively discover the true invariant q.*

5.3.1   Example of an Uncertain $(n, q) = (3, 2)$ Model

As we discussed in Chapter 4, affine transformations help to visualize information in $3D$ data scatter , in particular the affine invariant norm, which produces the information ellipsoid, or $3D$ density contour map, in $3D$ data scatter.[¶] The following example is based on a subset of data analyzed in Los (1997). This particular data set consists of three empirically observed financial economic variables for Taiwan - the natural logarithms of its stock market index, its nominal GDP (one-quarter-ahead) and its bank lending rate for the period $1986Q1 - 1995Q3$. These data are visualized in the $3D$ scatter plot in Fig. 1. by the black balls in the center, each ball representing a $3D$ data point. On the three sides of the data frame of reference are the $2D$ projections of these $3D$ data points represented by grey dots.One particular information ellipsoid based on the corresponding (3×3) data covariance matrix Σ is the following, scaled by the constant $d = 100$:

$$
\widehat{x}\Sigma^{-1}\widehat{x} = \begin{bmatrix} \widehat{x}_1 & \widehat{x}_2 & \widehat{x}_3 \end{bmatrix} \begin{bmatrix} 4.7529 & -4.3230 & -3.4514 \\ -4.3230 & 19.4717 & -2.9773 \\ -3.4514 & -2.9773 & 12.0409 \end{bmatrix} \begin{bmatrix} \widehat{x}_1 \\ \widehat{x}_2 \\ \widehat{x}_3 \end{bmatrix}
$$
$$
= 4.7529\widehat{x}_1^2 - 8.6460\widehat{x}_1\widehat{x}_2 - 6.9028\widehat{x}_1\widehat{x}_3 + 19.4717\widehat{x}_2^2 - 5.9546\widehat{x}_2\widehat{x}_3 + 12.0409\widehat{x}
$$
$$
= d
$$
$$
= 100 > 0 \tag{5.15}
$$

This quadratic equation represents an exact ellipsoid - a "cigar" - in the $3D$ data scatter space , as can be seen in Fig 2. Notice that the $3D$ plot has turned 90^0 to the left so that the ellipsoid's length can be better viewed and that the % scatter data have been multiplied by a factor of 100.[‖]

The volume of this information ellipsoid is determined by the arbitrary constant d. Otherwise stated, this information ellipsoid, or $3D$ data scatter density map

---

[¶]Analytic geometry was founded by the Frenchmen René Descartes (1596 - 1650) and Pierre Fermat (1601 - 1665) in the first half of the seventeenth century. *Elements of Curves*, a commentary on Descartes' *Geometry* by the Dutchman Jan de Witt (1625 - 1672), provided the first systematic treatment of conic sections, e.g., the parabola, ellipse and hyperbola. The earliest general classification of quadratic surfaces was given by Leonhard Euler, in his precalculus text *Introduction to Infinitesimal Analysis* (1748).

[‖]Since different software plotters had to be used at different times and at different universities, the following equivalence holds in these figures: the $x1$, $x2$ and $x3$ of Figures 1 and 4 correspond with the x, y and z, respectively of Figures 2 and 3. Figures 1 and 4 were produced by *Stanford Graphics* and Figures 2 and 3 by *Maple* embedded in *Scientific Workplace*, Version 3.0.

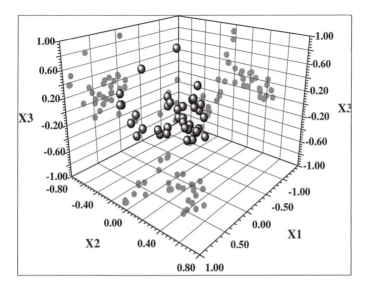

Figure 1   3D and 2D financial data scatter of Taiwan

, represents the data scatter density of $3D$ contour level d. Since d is arbitrary, other $3D$ contour levels, i.e., concentric ellipsoids of different volumes, can be plotted.[**]

Analogously to the $(n, q) = (2, 1)$ example in Chapter 4, the three 3-variable, single equation, $(n, q) = (3, 1)$, orthogonal Least Squares projections , with coefficients from the rows of the information matrix Σ^{-1}, can be found by setting the first

---

[**]Cf. Nielson, Hagen, and Müller, 1997, p. 500 (figure 20.70 and Color Plate 106) for an example of such visualization of the concentric information ellipsoids produced by this affine invariant norm. Their visualization uses transparent shading and shows the ellipsoids from different angles by rotation. Such rotational visualization of 3D contour ellipsoids is easily realized in recent PC software, such as Cyclone99.

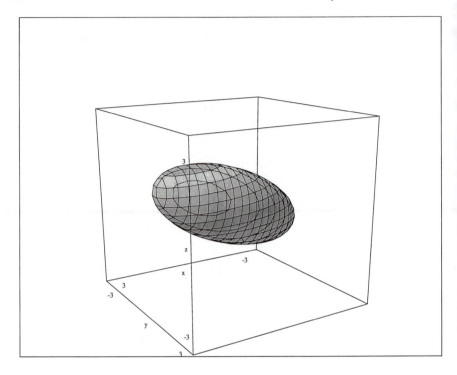

Figure 2   Exact information ellipsoid

derivatives of the information ellipsoid equal to zero, as follows:

$$\frac{1}{2}\frac{\partial \widehat{\mathbf{x}} \Sigma^{-1} \widehat{\mathbf{x}}}{\partial \widehat{\mathbf{x}}} = \Sigma^{-1}\widehat{\mathbf{x}}$$

$$= \begin{bmatrix} 4.7529 & -4.3230 & -3.4514 \\ -4.3230 & 19.4717 & -2.9773 \\ -3.4514 & -2.9773 & 12.0409 \end{bmatrix} \begin{bmatrix} \widehat{x}_1 \\ \widehat{x}_2 \\ \widehat{x}_3 \end{bmatrix}$$

$$= \begin{bmatrix} 4.7529\widehat{x}_1 - 4.3230\widehat{x}_2 - 3.4514\widehat{x}_3 \\ -4.3230\widehat{x}_1 + 19.4717\widehat{x}_2 - 2.9773\widehat{x}_3 \\ -3.4514\widehat{x}_1 - 2.9773\widehat{x}_2 + 12.0409\widehat{x}_3 \end{bmatrix}$$

$$= \begin{bmatrix} 0 \\ 0 \\ 0 \end{bmatrix} \tag{5.16}$$

Fig. 3 shows that these three LS projections form a convex cone of three planes in the $3D$ data scatter space. Each plane is determined by the orthogonal projection on two of the three axes of the data frame of reference .

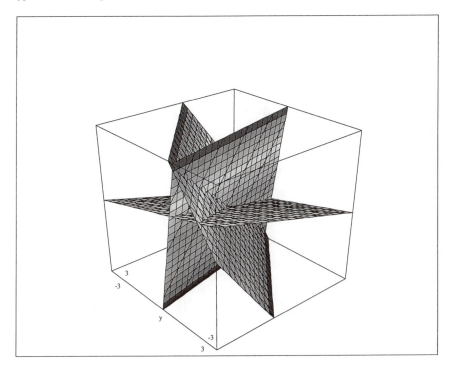

Figure 3   Three (n,q)=(3,1) CLS projection planes

These orthogonal LS projection planes form a convex cone "around" the principal axis of the information ellipsoid . This becomes obvious when the information ellipsoid and the three orthogonal LS projection planes are visualized together in the same data frame of reference , as in Fig. 4. The principal axis lies in the length of the ellipsoid, through its center. The directions of the principal and minor axes of the information ellipsoid can be found again from the eigenvectors of the information matrix Σ^{-1}. The length of these axes can be found from the absolute value of the corresponding eigenvalues .

In this case the orthogonal projection planes happen to almost "rotate" around the principal axis, providing strong evidence that a proper linear model for the data scatter would have a $(n, q) = (3, 2)$, instead of an $(n, q) = (3, 1)$ configuration. Each projection plane represents a single equation, $(n, q) = (3, 1)$ projection of one variable, the "regressand," on the other two. Fig. 3 again demonstrates that an *a priori* distinction between "regressand" and "regressor" data variables is scientifically unjustifiable , since each plane lies in a different direction, representing only part of the data. It is necessary to take account of the *complete set of data* , *i.e.*, the whole

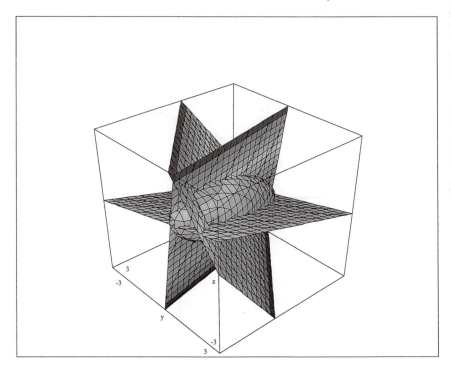

Figure 4   Exact information ellipsoid and $(n, q) = (3, 1)$ CLS projection planes

information matrix Σ^{-1}.

The three $(n, q) = (3, 1)$ planes cut each other to form three rays , as in Fig. 5.

Because these rays lie all in the same direction, as indicated by the sign - consistent row elements of the information matrix, we must conclude that the data should be represented by an $(n, q) = (3, 2)$ uncertain model. Such a model consists of two independent linear equations. Since there are $\binom{3}{2} = 3$ ways of choosing two independent linear equations from the three rows of the information matrix Σ^{-1}, there result three $(n, q) = (3, 2)$ uncertain ray models . The three resulting rays were obtained by plotting the three resulting $(n, q) = (3, 2)$ projection models:

$$\widehat{\mathbf{x}}'_i = \widehat{\mathbf{P}}^{CLS}_i \mathbf{x}'_i \text{ for } i = 1, 2, 3 \tag{5.17}$$

There is a positive systematic relationship between x_1 and x_2 as observed in the bottom (x_1, x_2) grid, a positive relationship between x_1 and x_3 as observed in the $(x1, x3)$ grid, and consequently, also a positive relationship between x_2 and x_3

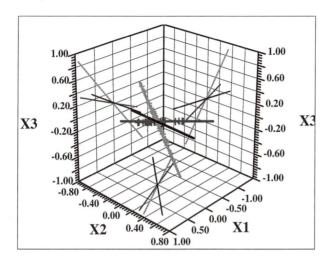

Figure 5   Three Complete Least Squares CLS(3, 2) projections in 3D data scatter

as observed in the $(x2, x3)$ grid. But the epistemic uncertainty does not allow us to choose which two equations out of the three to choose. In fact, two independent equations formed from linear combinations of the elementary equations here visualized , would also be allowed. That is what complete modeling means: to provide a complete honest presentation of the epistemic uncertainty of the empirical data.

Remark 33 *The number of* 3D *visualizations increases rather rapidly with the number of dimensions, since*

$$Number\ of\ 3D\ visualizations\ = n(n-1)(n-2)/6 \qquad (5.18)$$

For example, for $n = 3$ *data series there is one* 3D *visualization. For* $n = 4$, *there are four* 3D *visualizations. This can be cut down to one* 3D *visualization , when color is used. For* $n = 6$ *there are already* 20 *3D visualizations. Therefore, 3D visualization is useful for demonstration purposes, but it cannot be of much assistance for solving the higher-dimensional data problems occurring in finance. E.g., an option model has six variables. By using color, one can reduce the number of visualization dimensions to five, so that, using our formula, still* 10 *3D visualizations would be required to present the complete picture. When two more variables are fixed by timing, the unique empirical 3D visualization is possible for an option as in Fig. 4. of Chapter 10.*

5.3.2   Observed Relative Frequencies and Theoretical Distributions

Besides the identification of a model, there has been a related second issue. In the context of the discussion of *epistemic uncertainty* ,[tt] very often one encounters in statistics the assumption that the data are sampled from a universe ruled by a probability law, such as the *Gaussian distribution* , the *Poisson distribution* , the stable *Cauchy distribution* , the stable Lévi , or the *binomial distribution* .

Unfortunately, there is no scientific evidence that such an assumption is physically true, or can be physically true. In fact, there is much evidence that it is false, because of the finiteness of the observation systems (Kalman, 1994, 1995). To establish the usual probability laws for universes, one needs to possess infinite continuous random data , which is unrealistic and physically impossible. According to scientifically established laws of physics the Universe is finite and discontinuous , since exactness of measurement of the Universe is bounded, according to the Heisenberg Uncertainty Principle . Observable chaotic behavior , even at the quantum level, can be shown to result from finite, deterministic, nonlinear partial differential equations (For a very accessible mathematical explanation, *Cf.* Oliver, 1995). Consequently, the concept of probability may not even required as an "explanation" for a particular observable behavior. The measurement of relative frequencies can clearly not be extrapolated to probability laws without an extraordinary "leap of faith." An act of "faith" or the setting of a "level of confidence" is unallowed in *scientific* research, which is based on data and - true or false - logic .

In the context of modeling, a probability assumption does not assist or add to the linear identification of models from inexact data, since, as we have demonstrated, linear identification can proceed without it, using the first and second moments of data series as sole inputs.

Why are the theoretical concepts of probability law then used? The assumption of a probability law, to produce an abstract description of an actual relative frequency distribution , produces subjective game-theoretic constructions, like *hypothesis testing* (*e.g.*, based upon the assumption of a normal or Gaussian distribution). Speculative exact asset valuations , *i.e.*, financial instruments like Black - Scholes priced options, or binomially priced options, use the concept of probability law to introduce a closing limit argument to make a unique valuation possible, like in the case of the DDM (*Cf.* Chapters 3 and 10). In other words, scientifically unwarranted, but practically convenient, abstracting limiting arguments are introduced for closure of the expansion series to produce unique speculative valuations , which "fit" the abstract theory.

[tt]The ancient Greek word *episteme* = knowledge. Thus epistemic uncertainty = uncertainty about our knowledge.

5.4 Model Quality Measurement by Noise/Data Ratios

We will first demonstrate that, for the bivariate case, the conventional *t-statistic* does contain the same information we have already provided in our bivariate data analysis of the (2×2) data covariance matrix and that it doesn't add anything new by assuming an underlying probability law. The assumption of probability is extraneous to the data, but can add the element of the subjective game of hypotheses testing .

Next. we'll discuss how we can use our insights of the decomposition of financial risk into systematic and unsystematic risk in the n - dimensional data scatter . The following two subsections discuss the tool for measuring n - dimensional risk and epistemic uncertainty: the nD Noise/Data Ratio . Equivalent to the discussion of modeling in 2 - dimensional data scatter in Chapter 4, we'll present five equivalent ways to discuss certainty and uncertainty modeling in n - dimensional data.

5.4.1 The Directionless t-Statistic

The *t*-statistic is conventionally used in statistical research to "test" if the computed projection (slope) coefficient differs from zero. The *t*-statistic is defined by three equivalent expressions (*Cf.* Appendix A for the proofs). The first one, using the two extreme LS projection values of β, namely β_1 and β_2, is:

$$t = \frac{\beta_2}{\sqrt{\frac{\tilde{\sigma}_{11}}{\sigma_{22}}}}$$

$$= \frac{\beta_1}{\sqrt{\frac{\tilde{\sigma}_{22}}{\sigma_{11}}}} \tag{5.19}$$

This means that, in the bivariate case, the *t*-statistic is truly "directionless." It is independent of the chosen projection direction . This not so well-known fact becomes even more obvious when, after a few simple substitutions by the previously derived expressions for β_1, β_2 and $\tilde{\Sigma}_{11}$, respectively $\tilde{\Sigma}_{22}$, we find that the *t*-statistic is also equivalent to

$$t = \frac{\sigma_{12}}{\sqrt{\sigma_{11}\sigma_{22}(1 - \rho_{12}^2)}}$$

$$= \frac{\sigma_{12}}{\sqrt{|\Sigma|}} \tag{5.20}$$

Thus the *t*-statistic tests if the measured covariance between two data series, σ_{12}, is larger than the epistemic uncertainty in the data, as measured by the determinant of the data covariance matrix, $|\Sigma|$. The *t*-statistic provides a kind of *scientific reward/risk ratio* , the reward being the measured covariance and the risk being the data uncertainty.

Finally, from the preceding expression it immediately follows that the *t*-statistic is also equivalent to the following expression:

$$t = \sqrt{\frac{\rho_{12}^2}{1 - \rho_{12}^2}}$$

$$= \sqrt{\frac{S}{N}} \tag{5.21}$$

Thus the t-test is the square root of the inverse of the engineering Noise/Signal Ratio, where the (system) signal S is the data D minus the noise N, or $S = D - N$.

Summary 34 *In the bivariate case the t-statistic is essentially a test to see if the signal S is larger than the noise N in the data, be the data D stochastic , or (chaotically) deterministic , or not adhering to any probability law!*

5.4.2 Modeling n - Dimensional Financial Risk

In the modern financial literature, *financial risk* is measured by the variance, *c.q.*, the standard deviation of a series of values, be they asset values, market prices or rates of return. Financial risk can be decomposed in *systematic risk* and *unsystematic risk* . Thus, for one series i of return values, the variance is decomposed as $\sigma_{ii} = \widehat{\sigma}_{ii} + \widetilde{\sigma}_{ii}$. For n financial data series the covariance matrix is decomposed by data analysis as $\Sigma = \widehat{\Sigma} + \widetilde{\Sigma}$, where $\widehat{\Sigma}$ the systematic covariance matrix and $\widetilde{\Sigma}$ the unsystematic covariance matrix.

Only systematic risk is predictable , once the model $A\widehat{x}' = 0$ (or $A\widehat{\Sigma} = 0$) is identified, even though the model, *e.g.*, the value of the projection coefficients of A, remains uncertain. Systematic risk is identifiable and, assuming data inertia and data homogeneity , predictable. Unsystematic risk is, per definition, unidentifiable and thus unpredictable, although we can estimate its power, and, perhaps, determine its degree of dependence.

5.4.3 Noise/Data Ratios In n - Dimensional Data

In bivariate financial models , like the CAPM, the amount of systematic risk is often measured by the coefficient of determination ρ_{12}^2. The equivalent compact algebraic expression (yet) for the systematic risk of multivariate finance models embedded in n - dimensional data can be computed as the complete volume occupied by all possible Least Squares projections $\widehat{P}^{CLS}$ in the data space relative to the volume of the data space. The unsystematic risk is given by the determinant $|\Sigma|$. For example, for $n = 3$, we have for the percentage of unsystematic risk :

$$|\Sigma| = \sigma_{11}\sigma_{22}\sigma_{33}(1 - \rho_{12}^2 - \rho_{13}^2 - \rho_{23}^2 + 2\rho_{12}\rho_{13}\rho_{23}) \tag{5.22}$$

Thus the *Noise/Data Ratio* for 3 - dimensional data is:

$$\frac{N}{D} = \frac{|\Sigma|}{\sigma_{11}\sigma_{22}\sigma_{33}}$$

$$= (1 - \rho_{12}^2 - \rho_{13}^2 - \rho_{23}^2 + 2\rho_{12}\rho_{13}\rho_{23}) \tag{5.23}$$

The derivation of this Noise/Data Ratio, and its companion $3D$ Noise/Signal Ratio, can be found in Appendix C.

In general, the Noise/Data Ratio for n - dimensional (nD) data is:

$$\frac{N}{D} = \frac{|\Sigma|}{\prod_{i=1}^{n} \sigma_{ii}}$$

$$= \frac{\prod_{i=1}^{n} \lambda_i}{\prod_{i=1}^{n} \sigma_{ii}} \tag{5.24}$$

where $\prod_{i=1}^{n} \lambda_i$ is the product of the eigenvalues $\lambda_i, i = 1, ..., n$ of the data covariance matrix Σ resulting from the spectral decomposition $\Sigma = \mathbf{V}\Lambda\mathbf{V}'$, where the orthonormal matrix of eigenvectors $\mathbf{V}$ is such that $\mathbf{V}'\mathbf{V} = \mathbf{V}\mathbf{V}' = \mathbf{I}_n$, the $(n \times n)$ identity matrix . (Los, 1989a, 1997; *Cf.* also Chapter 8).

5.4.4 Modeling 3-Dimensional Uncertainty and Inexactness

Using the nD Noise/Data Ratio , we have again the following equivalent ways of presenting modeling certainty and uncertainty:

(1) Trivariate modeling uncertainty

(i) $|\Sigma| > 0$, the data covariance matrix is positive definite , i.e. its determinant is positive;

(ii) $0 < \rho_{ij}^2 < 1$, for some $i, j = 1, 2, 3, i \neq j$, i.e., some bivariate coefficient of determination shows less than complete explanation or inexactness ;

(iii) $\widehat{\mathbf{P}}_i^{CLS} \neq \widehat{\mathbf{P}}_j^{CLS}$ (after normalization), for all $i, j = 1, 2, 3, i \neq j$, the CLS projectors don't coincide;

(iv) $0 < \left|\widehat{\mathbf{P}}_1^{CLS} + \widehat{\mathbf{P}}_2^{CLS} + \widehat{\mathbf{P}}_3^{CLS}\right| < 1$, there exists an uncertainty gap within the orthant of the data frame of data reference ;

(v) $3D \ N/S > 0$, the noise/signal ratio is positive, since the inexact data contain some noise together with the signal.

(2A) Trivariate modeling certainty for $q = 2$

(i) $|\Sigma| = 0$, the data covariance matrix is singular , i.e., its determinant equals zero;

(ii) $\rho_{ij}^2 = 1$, for *all* $i, j = 1, 2, 3, i \neq j$, i.e., *all* bivariate coefficients of determination show exactness ;

(iii) $\widehat{\mathbf{P}}_i^{CLS} = \widehat{\mathbf{P}}_j^{CLS}$ (after normalization), for all $i, j = 1, 2, 3, i \neq j$, all CLS projectors coincide;

(iv) $\left|\widehat{\mathbf{P}}_1^{CLS} + \widehat{\mathbf{P}}_2^{CLS} + \widehat{\mathbf{P}}_3^{CLS}\right| = 0$, there exists no uncertainty gap within the orthant of the frame of data reference ;

(v) $3D \ N/S = 0$, the Noise/Signal Ratio is zero, since the (exact) data contain only the signal.

(2B) Trivariate modeling certainty for $q = 1$

(i) $|\Sigma| > 0$, the data covariance matrix is positive definite , i.e., its determinant is positive;

(ii) $\rho_{ij}^2 = 0$, for some $i, j = 1, 2, 3, i \neq j$, i.e., at least one bivariate coefficient of determination shows no explanation;

(iii) $\widehat{\mathbf{P}}_i^{CLS} \perp \widehat{\mathbf{P}}_j^{CLS}$ and $\widehat{\mathbf{P}}_i^{CLS} \neq \widehat{\mathbf{P}}_k^{CLS} = \widehat{\mathbf{P}}_j^{CLS}$ (after normalization), for some $i, j, k = 1, 2, 3, i \neq j, k$, at least one CLS projectors is orthogonal to another while the other two coincide;

(iv) $0 < \left|\widehat{\mathbf{P}}_1^{CLS} + \widehat{\mathbf{P}}_2^{CLS} + \widehat{\mathbf{P}}_3^{CLS}\right| << 1$, there exists an uncertainty gap within the orthant of the frame of data reference ;

(v) $3D \ N/S = 0$, the $3D$ Noise/Signal Ratio is positive, since the inexact data contain some noise together with the signal.

5.5 Stationarity Tests

5.5.1 Stationarity Windowing

For the results of our empirical analysis to hold, the observed covariances need to be stationary, *i.e.*, to be not subject to changes. One approach to check such data stationarity is to break a data set of T observations into a series of subsets of observations. For each data subset a covariance matrix is computed and each subset covariance matrix is subjected to the aforementioned identification analysis. The results of the analysis are then compared. When the differences are small, and the computed results overlap, stationarity is observed. An efficient way of checking for stationarity is to compute all possible data subset covariance matrices using *smoothers* , *i.e.*, combinations of Kalman filters (*Cf.* Anderson and Moore, 1979). When the computed structural invariant q in one or more of the subsets differs from the computed invariant in the remaining subsets, one must conclude that the data is non-homogeneous .

5.5.2 Inertia-based Prediction

Once we have identified the CLS model $\mathbf{A}^{CLS}\widehat{\mathbf{x}}' = 0$, using all possible LS projections, one can use this model for *prediction based upon extrapolation* of the past. Prediction is based upon the *inertia* and *homogeneity* assumptions that the future data set will have the same informational structure as the past, *i.e.*, that it will remain homogeneous with respect to the past. The number of variables that can be effectively forecasted is $q = rank(A)$. The number of required data inputs is $n - q$.

Example 35 *The $(n, q) = (3, 2)$ model, with $q = 2$ independent simultaneous equations, is identified from $n = 3$ data series. In this case, one needs only one data series as input to forecast the other two data series. For the model*

$$\widehat{x}_1 = b_2\widehat{x}_2 \ and, \ simultaneously, \ \widehat{x}_1 = b_3\widehat{x}_3 \tag{5.25}$$

one needs only one input series, say, x_3 to forecast both x_1 and x_2, since

$$\widehat{x}_2 = \frac{\widehat{x}_1}{b_2}$$

$$= \frac{b_3\widehat{x}_3}{b_2} \qquad (5.26)$$

Assuming the inertia assumption is valid for extrapolation, the uncertainty in the prediction results then from two sources:

(1) the uncertainty, or indeterminateness, in the CLS identified linear coefficients $\mathbf{A}^{CLS}$, which result from the inexactness of the historical data used in the identification. When the data are inexact, the resulting model must be also inexact, since one particular model result is a unique projection of the data, but there are infinitely many projections possible with the data, within finite ranges.

(2) the uncertainty of the future input series, in our example, say, $x_3 = \widehat{x}_3 + \widetilde{x}_3$, since empirical data series always contain some fundamental noise.

5.6 Exercises

5.6.1 Basic Understanding of CLS

Exercise 36 *Suppose we have the following data covariance matrix Σ of rates of return on three stocks and its inverse, the information matrix Σ^{-1}:*

$$\Sigma = \begin{bmatrix} 2.0596 & 0.3752 & 1.0775 \\ 0.3752 & 0.7903 & 0.3547 \\ 1.0775 & 0.3547 & 0.8673 \end{bmatrix}^{-1} \qquad (5.27)$$

and

$$\Sigma^{-1} = \begin{bmatrix} 1.3999 & .14204 & -1.7973 \\ .14204 & 1.5642 & -.81618 \\ -1.7973 & -.81618 & 3.7197 \end{bmatrix} \qquad (5.28)$$

1. How many systematic relationships exist among the three stock returns?

2. Why? Write out all data-allowed orthogonal projection matrices, or projectors, based on the given information matrix.

3. Choose only the first projection matrix and compute the corresponding unsystematic $\widetilde{\Sigma}$ and systematic covariance matrices $\widehat{\Sigma}$, using for the unsystematic covariance matrix the Complete Least Squares (CLS) noise projection formula:

$$\widetilde{\Sigma}^{CLS} = \Sigma A(A'\Sigma A)^{-1}A'\Sigma \qquad (5.29)$$

4. How would a series x of T observations on the three rates of return be decomposed into their systematic (modeled) parts and unsystematic parts using the matrices you've computed in 3.? (Write the expressions only in their compact matrix notation!).

5.6.2   Bank Performance Identification From Inexact Data - Trivariate Data Set

Exercise 37 *The following data are from 32 bank holding companies followed regularly by Salomon Brothers, Inc. , in their published statistical report for the year 1985. In accordance with Salomon Brothers, Inc.'s Yearbook, variable x_1 is the net interest margin of each bank holding company, which is total interest income (fully tax equivalent) less total interest expense in percent of total assets. Variable x_2 and x_3 are obtained from the quarterly report on the 50 largest bank holding companies in the U.S., prepared by the staff of the Board of Governors of the Federal Reserve System . Variable x_2 is the consumer loans in percent of total loans to the U.S. addresses. Variable x_3 is the net purchased funds in percent of total assets. The Economic Advisor of the Banking Studies and Analysis Function of the Federal Reserve Bank of New York proposed in 1986 a simple single equation model to relate this three data series to each other to create a trivariate model. He used this model for future screening and monitoring of the performance of these bank holding companies. As discussed in Chapter 1, similar models had been introduced by Altman in the early 1970s to monitor and to provide early warnings for possible bankruptcies of (bank) corporations, e.g., Altman's Zeta - model of 1977. (Cf. the Exercise on Credit-Scoring of Chapter 1). The Federal Reserve used such early warning models until at least 1992, despite its clearly observed unreliability and other deficiencies. New data - analytic technology has raised the following questions. Is such a $(n, q) = (3, 1)$ model consistent with the data? What happens if the model structure is inconsistent with the data structure ? Are the data too "noisy" to do any analysis at all? To answer these questions you will perform a few simple computations.*

1. First, compute the trivariate (3×3) data covariance matrix .

2. Plot the 3 bivariate correlation pictures based on the data covariance matrix. Determine the corresponding bivariate projection, or "regression" slope, coefficients and compute the 3 corresponding bivariate Noise/Signal Ratios .

3. From the trivariate information matrix, determine if the proposed $(n, q) = (3, 1)$ model is consistent with the data, using Complete Least Squares (CLS) analysis and explain your data analysis.

4. If you find that the geometry of the $(n, q) = (3, 1)$ model is inconsistent with geometry of the data , then the $(n, q) = (3, 2)$ model is the only alternative (Why?). Compute the noise and signal matrices of the three orthogonal $(n, q) = (3, 2)$ CLS model projections and compute the three corresponding signals and noise series. (These series can be plotted in 3-dimensional data space.

5. If you have access to a 3-dimensional graphing capability (*e.g.*, in Matlab or Mathematica), try to plot them, together with the original data, as shown in this Chapter).

Remark 38 *The foregoing problem was the topic of a fierce academic debate between financial economist Cornelis Los , now Associate Professor at the University of Adelaide, and two prestigious Bayesian Probabilists : physicist Professor E. T. Jaynes of Washington University in St. Louis, Missouri, U.S.A. and econometrician Professor Arnold Zellner of the University of Chicago, Illinois, U.S.A. The debate was won on scientific points by Cornelis Los, according to Professor R. E. Kalman of the ETH in Zurich, Switzerland, and Winner of the 1985 Kyoto Prize for High Technology. The debate is documented in Benzing and Dunleavy (1992), (Los (1989a & b, 1992), Jaynes (1992) and Zellner (1992). For recent examples of applications of algebraic - geometric, multi-dimensional-multi-variate analysis by Complete Least Squares, see Los (1997, 1999).*

ANALYSIS OF BANK DATA
(T x n) = (32 x 3) Matrix

T	y1	y2	y3
1	3.56	11.50	4.30
2	2.06	1.70	61.00
3	3.47	14.60	48.00
4	3.27	11.30	48.00
5	3.49	26.50	49.00
6	2.64	9.90	45.00
7	2.98	11.30	52.00
8	2.75	1.20	67.00
9	3.38	27.60	37.00
10	2.38	8.40	31.00
11	3.72	9.40	44.00
12	2.89	15.30	54.00
13	5.18	34.30	9.00
14	4.93	18.20	23.00
15	3.24	10.50	44.00
16	3.73	21.20	36.00
17	5.48	39.40	15.00
18	4.17	32.40	11.00
19	3.48	17.70	25.00
20	3.26	12.70	42.00
21	4.15	28.70	22.00
22	3.83	21.00	31.00
23	4.33	28.80	24.00
24	5.32	38.10	5.00
25	4.95	28.10	13.00
26	3.25	10.70	38.00
27	3.17	8.50	42.00
28	3.26	7.10	42.00
29	3.46	15.30	34.00
30	4.59	23.50	19.00
31	3.61	16.50	40.00
32	4.44	17.00	20.00

5.6.3   Identification of 1928 Cobb - Douglas Production Model - Trivariate Data Set

Exercise 39 *In 1928 Cobb and Douglas presented a system analysis of some macroeconomic data, which established the first empirically identified production model. Cobb and Douglas called the resulting equation a production "function", although* *they did not establish that fact. However their production model formed the founda-tion for Solow 's growth theory and the research into productivity growth factors, such as "technological progress " and "human capital development ". Cobb and Douglas claimed that their production model showed neutral economies of scale , i.e., constant returns to scale , with a labor production elasticity of 3/4 and a capital production elasticity of 1/4. A simple CLS analysis shows that Cobb and Douglas were correct in asserting that their logarithmically transformed data were to be described by an $(n, q) = (3, 1)$ linear model (and not a $(n, q) = (3, 2)$ linear model), but incorrect in claiming that their neutral "constant returns of scale " was the inevitable scientific conclusion . Their numerical conclusion. regarding the production elasticities of the labor and capital inputs, was strictly dependent on their subjectively chosen projection direction . In fact, the data shows that constant, increasing and diminishing returns to scale are all three compatible with the very uncertain data , depending on the pro-jection directions and that their elasticities are too uncertain for a definite conclusion. Indeed, many empirical researchers have found their $(n, q) = (3, 1)$ model "regression "coefficients highly unstable, because of the non - stationarity and non - homogeneity of the data.*

1. Compute the logarithms of the following original data set of Cobb and Douglas (1928) and completely analyze the information matrix . Identify the scientific prejudices of Cobb and Douglas empirical economic analysis.

2. Demonstrate that constant, increasing and diminishing returns to scale are all three compatible with the very uncertain data, depending on the projection directions

3. Find out why Cobb and Douglas determined labor and capital elasticities to be 3/4 and 1/4 respectively.

Original Cobb & Douglas data

output	labor	capital
100	100	100
101	105	107
112	110	114
122	118	122
124	123	131
122	116	138
143	125	149
152	133	163
151	138	176
126	121	185
155	140	198
159	144	208
153	145	216
177	152	226
184	154	236
169	149	244
189	154	266
225	182	298
227	196	335
223	200	366
218	193	387
231	193	407
179	147	417
240	161	431

The data are taken from Capital Table II, p.145; Labor Table III, p.148; Production Output Table IV, p.149 in Cobb and Douglas (1928).

5.7 Bibliography

Alexander, C. (1999) "Volatility and Correlation: Measurement, Models and Applications," Chapter 4 in Alexander, C. (Ed.) *Risk Management and Analysis, Volume 1: Measuring and Modelling Financial Risk*, John Wiley & Sons, New York, NY, 125 - 171.

Anderson, B. D. O. and Moore, J. B. (1979) *Optimal Filtering*, Prentice-Hll, Inc., Englewood Cliffs, NJ.

Bekker, P.A. (1986) *Essays on Identification in Linear Models with Latent Variables*, Ph.D. Thesis, Catholic University Tilburg.

Benzing, C. and Dunleavy, K. (1992) "A Comment on "Scientific" Economic Analysis," *Eastern Economic Journal*, **7**, 523 - 525.

Cobb, C. W. and Douglas, P. H. (1928) " Theory of Production," *American Economic Review*, **18** (1), Supplement, pp. 139 - 165.

Dhrymes, P. (1978) *Introductory Econometrics*, Springer - Verlag, New York, NY.

Frisch, R. (1934) *Statistical Confluence Analysis by Means of Complete Regression Systems*, Publication No. 5, University of Oslo Economic Institute, Oslo, Norway.

Haavelmo, T. (1944) "The Probability Approach in Econometrics," *Econometrica*, **12**, Supplement.

Hannah, J. (1996) "A Geometric Approach to Determinants," *The American Mathematical Monthly*, **103**, 401 - 409.

Herr, D. G. (1980) "On the History of the Use of Geometry in the General Linear Model," *The American Statistician*, **34**, 43 - 47.

Hooks, L. (1992) "A Test of the Stability of Early Warning Models of Bank Failures," Financial Industry Studies Working Paper, Federal Reserve Bank of Dallas, September 1992, No. 2-92, 25 pages.

Jaynes, E. T. (1992) "Commentary on Two Articles by C. A. Los," *Computers & Mathematics With Applications*, " **17** (8/9), 267 - 273.

Kalman, R. E. (1991) "A Theory for the Identification of Linear Relations," in R. Dautray, ed., *Frontiers in Pure and Applied Mathematics*, **13**, North - Holland Publishers, Amsterdam, pp. 117 - 132.

Kalman, R. E. (1991b) *Nine Chapters on Identification*, Center for Mathematical System Theory, University of Florida, Gainesville, FL, m.s., October 28, 97 pages.

Kalman, R. E. (1994) "Randomness Reexamined," *Modeling, Identification and Control*, **15** (3), 141 - 151.

Kalman, R. E. (1995) "Randomness and Probability," *Mathematica Japonica*, **41** (1), 41 - 58 & " Addendum," **41** (2), 463.

Kell, C. McM. and Los, C. A. (1988) "How to Determine the Corank and Noise Level of a System?", in *Identification and Parameter Estimation*, International Federation of Automatic Control, Pergamon Press, Oxford, pp. 599 - 606.

Laidler, E. (1977) *The Demand for Money: Theories and Evidence*, Dun-Donnelley, New York, NY.

Los, C. A. (1986a) "Quality Control of Empirical Econometrics: A Status Report," Research Paper No. 8606, Federal Reserve Bank of New York, New York, NY, April, 67 pages.

Los, C. A. (1986b) "Why There Is Still No Empirical Evidence For A Money Equation! Comments on "An historical perspective to the econometrics of money and income"," Research Paper, No. 8614, Federal Reserve Bank of New York, New York, NY, December, 18 pages.

Los, C. A. (1987a) "The Frobenius - Kalman and Reiersøl Procedures to Identify a System's Corank," Research Report, Nomura Research Institute (America),

Inc., New York, NY, August, 37 pages.

Los, C. A. (1987b) "Why Least Squares Always Works But Never Identifies," Research Report, Nomura Research Institute (America), Inc., New York, NY, October, 20 pages.

Los, C. A. (1989a) "The Prejudices of Least Squares, Principal Components and Common Factor Schemes," *Computers & Mathematics With Applications*, **17** (8/9), 1269 - 1283.

Los, C. A. (1989b) "Identification of a Linear System From Inexact Data: A Three-Variable Example," *Computers & Mathematics With Applications*, **17** (8/9), 1285 - 1304.

Los, C. A. (1992a) "Reply to Benzing's and Dunleavy's Comments on "A Scientific View of Economic Data Analysis"," *Eastern Economic Journal*, **17**, 526 -531.

Los, C. A. (1992b) "Reply to E. T. Jaynes' and A. Zellner's Comments On My Two Articles," *Computers and Mathematics With Applications*, **24** (8/9), 277 - 288.

Los, C. A. (1994a) "The Measurement of Complex Empirical Systems," in Accardi, L. (Ed.), *The Interpretation of Quantum Theory: Where Do We Stand?*, Instituto della Enciclopedia Italiana Fondata Da G. Treccani, Fordham University Press, United States of America, November, pp. 243 - 256.

Los, C. A. (1994b) "The Accuracy of Social Science Observations: Kepler and Galton Compared," Research Report, EMEPS Associates, Inc., Jersey City, NJ, July, 19 pages.

Los, C. A. (1995) "A Scientific View of Economic and Financial Data Analysis," in Janssen, J. C., Skiadas, H. and Zopounidis, C. (Editors), *Advances in Stochastic Modelling and Data Analysis*, Kluwer Academic Publishers, The Netherlands, pp. 111-127.

Los, C. A. (1997) "Valuation of Six Asian Stock Markets: Financial System Identification in Noisy Environments," *Econometric Society Australasian Meeting*, Vol. 4, 2 - 4 July, Melbourne, Australia, pp. 589 - 621.

Los, C. A. (1999) "Galton's Error and the Under-Representation of Systematic Risk," *Journal of Banking and Finance*, **23** (12), November, 1793 - 1828.

Nielson, G. M., Hagen, H. and Müller, H. (1997) *Scientific Visualization: Overviews, Methodologies and Techniques*, IEEE Computer Society, Los Alamitos, CA, pp. 495 - 500.

Oliver, D. (1995) *The Shaggy Steed of Physics: Mathematical Beauty in the Physical World*, Springer - Verlag, New York, NY.

Reilly, F. K. and Brown, K. C. (1997) *Investment Analysis and Portfolio Management*, The Dryden Press, Harcourt Brace College Publishers, New York, NY.

Rodgers, J. L., Nicewander, W. A. and Toothaker, L. (1984) "Linearly Independent, Orthogonal and Uncorrelated Variables," *The American Statistician*, **38**, 133 - 134.

Solnik, B., Boucrelle, C. and Le Fur, Y. (1996) "International Market Correlation and Volatility," *Financial Analysts Journal*, September - October, 17 - 34.

Zellner, A. (1992) "Brief Comment on C. A. Los' Papers," *Computers and Mathematics With Applications*, **24** (8/9), 275.

chapter:6,page:1

Chapter 6
OPTIMAL PORTFOLIO FORMATION

6.1 Introduction

In Chapter 4, we showed how to compute a data covariance matrix from the inexact rates of return series of the various assets, using simple matrix algebra. In this and the next Chapter, we will use this data covariance matrix in three different ways:

(1) We will use it to compose optimal investment portfolios in a rational fashion by computing Markowitz' (1952, 1987, 1991, 1999) Efficient Portfolio Frontier .*

(2) We will combine the efficient portfolios with "risk free" cash to customize the amount of risk according to the risk preferences of the portfolio manager , *c.q.*, his client, the (global) investor.

(3) We will discuss the difference between systematic and unsystematic risks, using the decomposition of the data covariance matrix into a systematic covariance matrix and a noise covariance matrix.

6.2 Mean - Variance Analysis

Financial assets , such as common stocks, small company stocks, long-term corporate bonds, long-term and intermediate government bonds and Treasury Bills, have many different characteristics . But for Markowitz' *Mean-Variance Analysis* we only focus on the first two moments - the means and the covariance matrix - of the distributions of their economic *rates of return (RoR)*, in nominal, or in real terms, *i.e.*, after inflation adjustment (Markowitz, 1952, 1991, 1992, 1999). The mean provides a measure of the average level of the RoR. The variance, or the standard deviation, provides a measure of the RoR's overall volatility or risk. But, most importantly, the RoR's covariances provide information about the systematic risks.

The *mean portfolio RoR* , $\overline{x}_p$, is the weighted linear combination of the average RoRs of the assets, $\overline{x}$, contained in the portfolio

$$\overline{x}_p = \mathbf{w}'\overline{\mathbf{x}}' \tag{6.1}$$

---

*Harry M. Markowitz was the 1990 (jointly with Merton M. Miller and William F. Sharpe) winner of the Nobel Memorial Prize in Economics for pioneering work in the theory of financial economics.

where $\overline{x}_p$ is a scalar, $\overline{\mathbf{x}}$ is a $n \times 1$ vector of average asset RoRs

$$\overline{\mathbf{x}}' = \overline{y}' \iota_T'$$
$$= \begin{bmatrix} \overline{x}_1 \\ \overline{x}_2 \\ ... \\ \overline{x}_n \end{bmatrix} \tag{6.2}$$

and $\mathbf{w}$ is a $n \times 1$ vector of *portfolio allocation weights* ,

$$\mathbf{w}' = \begin{bmatrix} w_1 & w_2 & ... & w_n \end{bmatrix} \tag{6.3}$$

such that the sum of the weights equals unity. Thus $\mathbf{w}'\iota = 1$, where ι is the $n \times 1$ unit vector .

The portfolio risk, σ_{pp} is the variance of the portfolio rate of return, which is the weighted covariance matrix

$$\sigma_{pp} = \mathbf{w}'\Sigma\mathbf{w} \tag{6.4}$$

where Σ is the covariance matrix of the assets' RoRs. Often the portfolio risk as standard deviation

$$\sigma_p = \sqrt{\mathbf{w}'\Sigma\mathbf{w}} \tag{6.5}$$

is presented instead.

6.3   Efficient Frontier With Two Assets

Tracing Markowitz' *Efficient Portfolio Frontier* consists of varying the n asset allocation weights w_i in such a fashion that, for a given level of $\overline{x}_p$, the portfolio risk σ_{pp} is minimized. Suppose we have a portfolio with two assets, a bond and shares in a common stock, with mean RoRs of $\overline{r}_1$ and $\overline{x}_2$, respectively, so that

$$\overline{\mathbf{x}} = \begin{bmatrix} \overline{x}_1 \\ \overline{x}_2 \end{bmatrix} \tag{6.6}$$

with a covariance matrix

$$\Sigma = \begin{bmatrix} \sigma_{11} & \sigma_{12} \\ \sigma_{12} & \sigma_{22} \end{bmatrix} \tag{6.7}$$

The mean portfolio RoR is

$$\begin{aligned} \overline{x}_p &= \mathbf{w}'\overline{\mathbf{x}}' \\ &= w_1\overline{x}_1 + w_2\overline{x}_2 \\ &= w_1\overline{x}_1 + (1 - w_1)\overline{x}_2 \end{aligned} \tag{6.8}$$

since $w_1 + w_2 = 1$. Furthermore, its variance is

$$
\begin{aligned}
\sigma_{pp} &= \mathbf{w}'\Sigma\mathbf{w} \\
&= w_1^2\sigma_{11} + w_2^2\sigma_{22} + 2w_1w_2\sigma_{12} \\
&= w_1^2\sigma_{11} + (1-w_1)^2\sigma_{22} + 2w_1(1-w_1)\sigma_{12} \qquad (6.9)
\end{aligned}
$$

Notice that both the mean $\bar{x}_p$ and the risk σ_{pp} of the portfolio RoRs are continuous functions of the asset weight w_1. Therefore, we can determine the asset weight w_1 (respectively, $w_2 = 1 - w_1$), by setting the first derivative of σ_{pp} with respect to w_1 equal to zero

$$
\frac{\partial\sigma_{pp}}{\partial w_1} = 2w_1\sigma_{11} - 2(1-w_1)\sigma_{22} + 2(1-2w_1)\sigma_{12} = 0 \qquad (6.10)
$$

or

$$
w_1(\sigma_{11} + \sigma_{22} - 2\sigma_{12}) = \sigma_{22} - \sigma_{12} \qquad (6.11)
$$

so that the optimal asset allocation is

$$
\begin{aligned}
w_1^{opt} &= \frac{\sigma_{22} - \sigma_{12}}{\sigma_{11} + \sigma_{22} - 2\sigma_{12}} \\
&= \frac{\sigma_{22} - \sigma_{12}}{\sigma_{11} + \sigma_{22} - 2\rho_{12}\sqrt{\sigma_{11}\sigma_{22}}} \qquad (6.12)
\end{aligned}
$$

when we substitute the bivariate correlation coefficient between the bond and stock RoRs, $\rho_{12} = \frac{\sigma_{12}}{\sqrt{\sigma_{11}\sigma_{22}}}$ for the covariance σ_{12}. This produces always the *minimum* portfolio risk, since the second derivative

$$
\frac{\partial^2}{\partial w_1^2}\sigma_{pp} = \sigma_{11} + \sigma_{22} - 2\sigma_{12} > 0 \qquad (6.13)
$$

When percentage w_1^{opt} of the available capital is invested in the bond and the remainder $1 - w_1^{opt}$ in the stock, the optimal mean RoR and the optimal (= minimum) risk of the portfolio are, respectively

$$
\begin{aligned}
\bar{x}_p^{opt} &= \mathbf{w}^{opt\prime}\bar{\mathbf{x}}' \\
&= w_1^{opt}\bar{x}_1 + (1 - w_1^{opt})\bar{x}_2 \qquad (6.14)
\end{aligned}
$$

and

$$
\begin{aligned}
\sigma_{pp}^{opt} &= (\mathbf{w}^{opt})'\Sigma\mathbf{w}^{opt} \\
&= (w_1^{opt})^2\sigma_{11} + (1 - w_1^{opt})^2\sigma_{22} + 2w_1^{opt}(1 - w_1^{opt})\rho_{12}\sqrt{\sigma_{11}\sigma_{22}} \qquad (6.15)
\end{aligned}
$$

This pair of equations describe Markowitz' Efficient Portfolio Frontier , which can be graphed in a bivariate (2-dimensional) space , since for each optimal portfolio mean $\overline{x}_p^{opt}$ there is a corresponding minimal portfolio variance σ_{pp}^{opt}. Notice that the minimum variance of the portfolio depends very strongly on the correlation between the assets in the portfolio, since the allocation weights directly depend on it according to the preceding formulas (See Fig. 1). Notice that for the two extreme situations:

(1) when $\rho_{12} = 1$ (perfect positive correlation), there is no advantage from diversification , since the portfolio risk (measured as standard deviation) is the weighted average of the assets' standard deviations (Try the exercise!);

(2) when $\rho_{12} = -1$ (perfect negative correlation), there is *perfect hedge* potential by diversification, since there is a unique allocation,

$$w_1^{opt} = \frac{\sqrt{\sigma_{22}}}{\sqrt{\sigma_{11}} + \sqrt{\sigma_{22}}} \tag{6.16}$$

eliminating the portfolio risk, $\sigma_{pp}^{opt} = 0$ (Try the exercise!)

6.4 Efficient Frontier With Multiple Assets

We will now generalize the bivariate portfolio to the n-variate case, by applying some results of the powerful *Kuhn-Tucker Theorem* for non-linear optimization under constraints (*Cf.* Baumol, 1972, pp. 151 - 170). First, we form the so-called *Lagrangian function* $L(\mathbf{w}, \lambda_1, \lambda_2)$, which is a function of the n elements of the *asset allocation vector* $\mathbf{w}$ and of the two scalar *Lagrangian multipliers* λ_1 and λ_2.[†] These multipliers are the *shadow prices* for the two generic portfolio constraints , *i.e.*, for the *additivity constraint* that the allocation weights must add up to unity, $\mathbf{w}'\boldsymbol{\iota}_n = 1$, and for the *definitional constraint* that the weighted average of the average RoRs equals a particular average portfolio RoR, $\mathbf{w}'\overline{\mathbf{x}} = \overline{x}_p$. Thus, first, we form the Lagrangian function

$$L(\mathbf{w}, \lambda_1, \lambda_2) = \mathbf{w}'\Sigma\mathbf{w} + \lambda_1(1 - \mathbf{w}'\boldsymbol{\iota}_n) + \lambda_2(\overline{x}_p - \mathbf{w}'\overline{\mathbf{x}}) \tag{6.17}$$

Next, to find the optimum of this Lagrangian function, we set the $n + 2$ partial first derivatives equal to zero, *i.e.*, the derivatives with respect to the n elements of the allocation vector $\mathbf{w}$, and the derivatives with respect to the two scalar Lagrangian

---

[†]The French physicist Joseph Louis, comte de Lagrange (1736 - 1813), was one of the most important mathematical and physical scientists of the late 18th century. He invented and brought to maturity the calculus of variations and later applied the new discipline to celestial mechanics, especially to finding improved solutions to the three-body problem. He also contributed significantly to the numerical and algebraic solution of equations and to number theory. In his classic *Mecanique Analytique* (*Analytical Mechanics*, 1788), he transformed mechanics into a branch of mathematical analysis. The treatise is notable for its use of the theory of differential equations. Another central concern of Lagrange was the foundations of calculus. In a 1797 book he stressed the importance of Taylor series and the concept of function. Lagrange served as professor of geometry at the Royal Artillery School in Turin (1755-66). Because of overwork and poor pay, his health suffered, leaving him with a weakened constitution for life.

multipliers λ_1 and λ_2:

$$\frac{\partial L}{\partial \mathbf{w}} = 2\mathbf{w}'\Sigma - \lambda_1 \iota_n' - \lambda_2 \overline{\mathbf{x}}' = 0 \qquad (6.18)$$

$$\frac{\partial L}{\partial \lambda_1} = 1 - \mathbf{w}' \iota_n = 0 \qquad (6.19)$$

$$\frac{\partial L}{\partial \lambda_2} = \overline{x}_p - \mathbf{w}'\overline{\mathbf{x}} = 0 \qquad (6.20)$$

Remark 40 *It is an excellent exercise to show that the $(n+2) \times (n+2)$ matrix of partial second derivatives is positive definite, so that the optimum is, indeed, a - constrained - minimum. When additional constraints are imposed, e.g., no short sales are allowed, this conclusion doesn't hold true in general, since the matrix of second derivatives may be positive semi-definite and singular , so that it can't be inverted. This situation is apparently in practice quite common, when portfolio managers impose (too) many constraints . It explains why Markowitz experienced so many problems with practical implementations (Cf. Markowitz, 1987). Only a very select set of constraints is mathematically (logically) allowed. Some restrictions are mathematically not allowed: they are either inconsistent with each other or illogical. This is something which many practicing fund managers fail to understand when they insist on imposing such constraints on their portfolio management !*

By post-multiplying the first n equations, resulting from taking the n derivatives with respect to $\mathbf{w}$, by the information matrix Σ^{-1} (which empirically always exists, since $\Sigma > 0$), we find that

$$\mathbf{w}' = \frac{(\lambda_1 \iota_n' + \lambda_2 \overline{\mathbf{x}}')\Sigma^{-1}}{2} \qquad (6.21)$$

Substitute this expression into the derivatives with respect to λ_1 and λ_2 to get the two equations

$$\frac{(\lambda_1 \iota_n' + \lambda_2 \overline{\mathbf{x}}')\Sigma^{-1} \iota_n}{2} = 1 \text{ (a scalar)} \qquad (6.22)$$

$$\frac{(\lambda_1 \iota_n' + \lambda_2 \overline{\mathbf{x}}')\Sigma^{-1}\overline{\mathbf{x}}}{2} = \overline{x}_p \text{ (a scalar)} \qquad (6.23)$$

By expanding these two equations (Good exercise!) one finds that in matrix form this is equivalent to

$$\frac{\Delta}{2} \cdot \begin{bmatrix} \lambda_1 \\ \lambda_2 \end{bmatrix} = \begin{bmatrix} 1 \\ \overline{x}_p \end{bmatrix} \qquad (6.24)$$

or

$$\begin{bmatrix} \lambda_1^{opt} \\ \lambda_2^{opt} \end{bmatrix} = 2.\Delta^{-1}. \begin{bmatrix} 1 \\ \overline{x}_p \end{bmatrix} \tag{6.25}$$

where the 2×2 symmetric and positive definite matrix Δ is such that

$$\Delta = \begin{bmatrix} \iota_n' \Sigma^{-1} \iota_n & \overline{x}' \Sigma^{-1} \iota_n \\ \iota_n' \Sigma^{-1} \overline{x} & \overline{x}' \Sigma^{-1} \overline{x} \end{bmatrix} \tag{6.26}$$

Then the two optimal Lagrangian multipliers are

$$\begin{bmatrix} \lambda_1^{opt} \\ \lambda_2^{opt} \end{bmatrix} = 2.\Delta^{-1}. \begin{bmatrix} 1 \\ \overline{x}_p \end{bmatrix} \tag{6.27}$$

Of course, once we have thus computed the optimal values for the Lagrangian multipliers λ_1^{opt} and λ_2^{opt}, we can find the n Markowitz' optimal portfolio allocation weights from the optimization condition

$$\mathbf{w}^{opt} = \frac{\Sigma^{-1}(\lambda_1^{opt}\iota_n + \lambda_2^{opt}\overline{x})}{2} \tag{6.28}$$

Again, we have the two equations for Markowitz' Efficient Portfolio Frontier, but this time for n assets, which can be plotted in a 2-dimensional graph :

$$\overline{x}_p^{opt} = \mathbf{w}^{opt\prime}\overline{x} \tag{6.29}$$

$$\sigma_{pp}^{opt} = (\mathbf{w}^{opt})'\Sigma\mathbf{w}^{opt} \tag{6.30}$$

or, more often, with the volatility or risk measure

$$\sigma_p^{opt} = \sqrt{\sigma_{pp}^{opt}} \tag{6.31}$$

See Fig. 1. for an example of the efficient frontiers for multi-currency investments in nine stock indices in Asia, Germany and the U.S., in different portfolio combinations. The computation of the international capital allocation weights for these combinations, which requires tensor (Kronecker) algebra to deal with all accounting identities, is discussed in Chapter 14.

Remark 41 *Markowitz 'Mean-Variance analysis assumes that the first and second moments of the rates of return of the portfolio assets exist as finite entities. That may not be the case. Mandelbrot and Wallis (1968) researched such fractal phenomena of infinite mean and variance. More recently, Peters (1994, pp. 200 - 205) uses 8,000 samples from the Cauchy distribution, which has infinite mean and variance, to demonstrate that the sample sequential mean and variance never converge.*

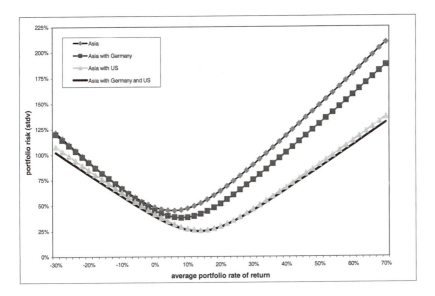

Figure 1   Efficient frontiers of strategic multi-currency investments, July 1992 - October 1997

Empirically, Peters also shows that the sequential mean of the five-day Dow Jones Industrials Index (DJIA) does converge only after about 1,000 days, but that its sequential variance does not converge. This suggests that the DJIA has a finite mean, but an infinite variance. Thus in the long run, the DJIA is characterized by a stable mean and infinite memory, in the manner of a stable Lévy or fractal distribution. Our own research indicates that the S&P500 Index has similar characteristics as the DJIA. More research about these long term dependence characteristics of asset rates of return is required. Samuelson (1967) proofs that when stable distributions do not satisfy Markowitz 'assumptions, the expected portfolio risk diversification does not necessarily not occur. In some extreme cases, the portfolio risk is even amplified, when particular assets are added to the portfolio.

6.5   Value-at-Risk and *RiskMetrics*^{TM}

6.5.1   *Value-at-Risk*

Hedging based on Markowitz Efficiency Frontier Analysis (Markowitz, 1952) combined with Complete Capital Market Pricing , like J. P. Morgan's *RiskMetrics*^{TM} (J. P. Morgan, 1995a & b) and *CreditMetrics*^{TM} (J. P. Morgan, 1997a & b) is potentially a much more sophisticated form of portfolio hedging than single asset hedging . All assets and liabilities are simultaneously and mutually hedged by each other, in addition to hedging against special systematic factors . Unfortunately, that story is not so easy.

The original 1988 risk-based Capital Guidelines of the Bank of International Settlements (B.I.S., 1994) (*Cf.* Jorion, 1996; Wilson, 1998; Butler, 1999), computed the variance of the portfolio by summing up the variances of the assets , not taking account of the covariances between the assets and the liabilities

$$VaR(B.I.S.)_{old} = \alpha \times \sqrt{\sum_i \sigma_{A_i A_i}} \times E$$

$$= \text{risk aversion constant} \times \sqrt{\sum_i variance(Asset_i)} \times \text{Net Capital}$$

(6.32)

The concept of VaR is based on the essential risk management question: How much money might the bank lose over the next period of time?[‡] The risk aversion constant is based on the assumption of a normal distribution of the VaR and is usually set at $\alpha = 1.96$ times (for 95% confidence). However, this assumption of a normally distributed VaR is scientifically uncorroborated as recent research has shown. The empirical distribution of the VaR is asymmetric . It is skewed to the right. The normal (or Gaussian) distribution is symmetric . Empirical rates of return distributions exhibit also much more or less kurtosis than the distributions, *i.a.*, because of long term dependence phenomena of persistence and anti-persistence .

But by ignoring the offsetting covariances, these original VaR base Capital Guidelines required too much capital. *RiskMetrics*[TM] attempted to introduce a Grand Unification Theory (GUT) of Finance. *RiskMetrics*[TM] tries to reduce the required amount of capital by taking account of the covariances, together with exact pricing of the fundamental and derivative financial instruments by Complete Capital Market Pricing theory (*Cf.* Chapter 8), and by accounting for systematic factors. Following the 1994 recommendations by a Working Group of the Euro-currency Standing Committee of the Central Banks of the Group of Ten Countries , in January 1996, the B.I.S. conceded the superiority of the Markowitz approach, and, *a fortiori*, the portfolio optimization part of the J. P. Morgan's *RiskMetrics*[TM] approach, in a Supplement to the 1988 Basle Capital Accord . It accepted that covariances can reduce total portfolio risk, so that less risk-based capital is required. These improvements were implemented in 1998. Thus, currently, for international banks, because of the Basle Accord (of 1988, plus its later amendments in 1992 and 1998) the currently

---

[‡]Originally the time horizon was 10 working days, but now it is often one day. This question was asked from the commercial banks by Jerry Corrigan , former President of the Federal Reserve Bank of New York , former Chairman of the B.I.S. and now Managing Director of Goldman Sachs , and from the staff at J. P. Morgan by Dennis Weatherstone , Chairman and CEO of J. P. Morgan, Inc. Mr. Weatherstone received his answer each day at 4 : 15pm. in terms of daily revenue loss with 5% probability.

computed VaR is:

$$VaR(B.I.S.)_{new} = \alpha \times \sigma_p(E) \times E \qquad (6.33)$$

where the existing portfolio risk is:

$$\sigma_p(E) = \sqrt{\sigma_{pp}(A - L)}$$
$$= \sqrt{\sigma_{pp}(A) + \sigma_{pp}(L) + 2Cov(A, L)} \qquad (6.34)$$

without any optimization. The optimal VaR can be found simply by implementation of Markowitz' portfolio optimization

$$VaR^{opt} = \alpha \times \sigma_p^{opt}(E) \times E^{opt} \qquad (6.35)$$

But such an optimization is left at the discretion of the individual banks. Currently the B.I.S. Capital Accord does not prescribe such an optimization. Both the optimal portfolio wealth or equity

$$E^{opt} = A^{opt} - L^{opt} \qquad (6.36)$$

which results from the optimized balance sheet, and the optimal portfolio risk

$$\sigma_p^{opt}(E) = \sqrt{\sigma_{pp}(A^{opt}) + \sigma_{pp}(L^{opt}) + 2Cov(A^{opt}, L^{opt})} \qquad (6.37)$$

result from this optimization procedure.

Example 42 *These procedures can be used both for incremental asset/liability management and for complete corporate balance sheet restructuring. In 1993, as Chief Economist in New York, I optimized the balance sheet of ING Bank in New York. On the basis of the departmental revenues and expenses and existing capital allocations monthly rates of return were computed for the various departments and divisions, e.g., for Treasury, Corporate Finance, Corporate Restructuring, Emerging Markets, Domestic Asset Management, Dutch Real Estate, Chicago Branch, Atlanta Branch, Los Angeles Branch, etc. Some of these departments had high return-high risk and others low return-low risk profiles . But several had deleterious low return-high risk profiles . Using mean-variance analysis both the return/risk profile of each department was computed and the optimal efficiency frontier. Both were plotted in a return/risk graph. Based on this graph management took decisions regarding the required reduction of the risk in some departments and increase of return in others, relative to the efficiency frontier. These management decisions changed the balance sheet structure of ING Bank (later ING Capital) in New York and made it more efficient. In 1993 I computed ING Bank's optimal monthly VaR, long before J. P. Morgan published its RiskMetrics^{TM} manual.*

6.5.2   Singularity Problem of RiskMetrics^{TM} and CreditMetrics^{TM}

J. P. Morgan's *RiskMetrics*^{TM} and *CreditMetrics*^{TM} attempt to create a *Grand Universal Theory (GUT) synthesis* between Markowitz ' Mean - Variance Portfolio Selection and the Complete Capital Market Pricing (CCMP) theory (*Cf.* Chapter 8). The original motivation for using Markowitz' portfolio optimization approach was to create a viable alternative for the simplistic first order Capital Guidelines (1988) of the Bank of International Settlements (B.I.S.) .

Unfortunately, by definition, the *RiskMetrics*^{TM} and *CreditMetrics*^{TM} approaches suffer from the *singularity problem* and cannot produce exact hedging results. Already in December 1990 at the ETH in Zürich, Switzerland, I demonstrated this in detail, by a simple application of mathematical system identification theory to a portfolio of only four stocks.[§] The argument is, in a nutshell, as follows, applying the system identification concepts of Chapters 4 and 5.

The data covariance matrix Σ of all financial instruments is always positive definite and will thus always produce an efficient portfolio frontier. In *RiskMetrics*^{TM} this matrix Σ is decomposed into two parts, the systematic covariance matrix $\widehat{\Sigma}$ and the unsystematic covariance matrix $\widetilde{\Sigma}$, so that $\Sigma = \widehat{\Sigma} + \widetilde{\Sigma}$. The systematic variation is explained by an exact model $A\widehat{\Sigma} = \mathbf{0}$, the unsystematic variation remains unexplained. However, the systematic covariance matrix $\widehat{\Sigma}$ is *singular* , by definition, since $A\widehat{\Sigma} = \mathbf{0}$: the rows, respectively columns, of Σ are linear combinations of each other. This implies that $\widehat{\Sigma}$ cannot be inverted and no exact efficient portfolio frontier can be formed from the systematic covariance matrix $\widehat{\Sigma}$ (Check the derivation of the efficient frontier above, which requires the inversion of the positive definite Σ!).

The *RiskMetrics*^{TM} and *RiskMetrics*^{TM} methodology induces this singularity of $\widehat{\Sigma}$ by their systematic cash flow shredding and allocation following the CCMP theory. *Cash flow shredding* is the process of determining the best set of cash flows, irrespective of the cash flow timing, to represent the risks of holding a particular financial instrument. The *cash flow allocation* involves allocating the individually shredded cash flow to surrounding temporal (and exposure and credit) vertices of $n = 300$ *primitive securities* .[¶] Thus the order of $\widehat{\Sigma}$ in *RiskMetrics*^{TM} is at least 300×300.

Since $\widehat{\Sigma}$ cannot be identified with certainty from the available data Σ (an infinite number of linear combinations of the n orthogonal CLS projections are possible), the resulting portfolio efficiency set must be inexact - it is an open set - and no continuous exact efficient frontier exists for the systematic efficiency set! This implies that

---

[§]In my lecture on "Some Data Analytic Problems in Modern Portfolio Theory," by invitation of the Institute for Empirical Economic Research at the University of Zürich , Switzerland, December 21, 1990. This lecture was again presented in Professor Phoebus Dhrymes ' Workshop in Econometrics at Columbia University in New York City, February 1991. These specific conclusions were also part of Los' Lecture "A Scientific View of Economic Data Analysis" before The New York Academy of Sciences , March 21, 1992 and finally published in Los (1995 and 1999).

[¶]Chapter 8 explains the abstract concept of a primitive security.

there are no exact continuous hedges possible for whole portfolios against systematic influences, like interest rate shifts, and no unique exact value can be computed for the Value-at-Risk (VaR) on the basis of the systematic portfolio data. Simply put, *the VaR has to remain uncertain, since the data are uncertain.* Consequently, any Capital Guidelines based on the VaR concept must remain indicative and cannot be exactly computed from the empirical data. This is to the dismay of financial accountants , who prefer to deal with exact accounting identities , but even more so to the dismay of the regulatory authorities of central banks !

Remark 43 *In the context of CreditMetrics^{TM}, Morgan (1997b, p.4) stated, correctly and, cautiously: "CreditMetrics is neither a credit rating tool nor a pricing model,* **nor does it provide, in its current version, a portfolio optimization methodology"** *(Our emphasis). J. P. Morgan (1997b, p. 7) clarified the empirical application of CreditMetrics^{TM} to determine individual credit value distributions as follows: "To compute the volatility of portfolio value from the volatility of individual asset values requires estimates of correlation in credit quality changes. Since credit quality correlations cannot easily be directly observed from historical data many different approach (sic!) to estimating correlations, including a simple constant correlation, can be used within CreditMetrics^{TM}." (Our emphasis). We disagree with J. P. Morgan's 1997 assessment. It is J. P. Morgan's CCMP approach,[‖] which resulted in a singular systematic covariance matrix $\widehat{\Sigma}$ which prevented Markowitz' portfolio optimization. On the other hand, credit quality correlations can be directly observed from historical data and result in a non-singular data covariance matrix Σ which allows Markowitz' portfolio optimization. J. P. Morgan clearly did not recognize that the data covariance matrix contains unsystematic variation $\Sigma = \widehat{\Sigma} + \widetilde{\Sigma}$, despite the fact that RiskMetrics^{TM} "takes account of volatility of recovery rates, which are notoriously uncertain." (J. P. Morgan, 1997, p.8).*

In a recent seminar in June 1996 at the Nanyang Business School of the Nanyang Technological University in Singapore , Professor Emeritus Mark Garman of Berkeley University (Director of the firm Financial Engineering Associates, Inc.) confirmed that the systematic matrices of *RiskMetrics^{TM}* are, indeed, very close to being singular - and sometimes actually are - producing considerable problems with the required (explicit or implicit) inversion of $\widehat{\Sigma}$! However, Los (1998, 1999) demonstrates, as discussed in Chapter 14, that the management of a multi-currency strategic portfolio proceeds independently of CCMP, that the nonsingular 300×300 covariance matrix $\widehat{\Sigma}$ does not have to be used, since the exact accounting identities can be separated from the risk elements by simple tensor algebra, and that a measured positive definite data covariance Σ is sufficient for Markowitz 'portfolio optimization. In other words, the solution of the singularity problem of RiskMetrics^{TM} and CreditMetrics^{TM} is available in Chapter 14!

[‖] The Complete Capital Market Pricing (CCMP) theory is discussed in Chapter 8.

6.6   Exercises

Exercise 44 *Data covariance matrices form essential inputs in Markowitz' portfolio optimizing mean-variance analysis and in systematic risk analysis , as, for example, used for hedging. Given a (T × n) raw data matrix* y *with T observations on n variables, how do you compute its data covariance matrix* Σ*? Give your answer in matrix notation, in EXCEL formula commands and in keyboard sequences .*

Exercise 45 *The following data consist of the annual rates of return of three stocks listed on the New York Stock Exchange in 1974 - 1983. Create an EXCEL spreadsheet that will compute Markowitz' Efficient Portfolio Frontier of this Singapore stock portfolio. Determine the Global Minimum Variance (GMV) portfolio . For the GMV portfolio, find the allocation weights of all three stocks, the GMV portfolio's average return and its volatility or risk.*

(10x3) matrix of RoRs

Year	AMR	BS	GE
1974	-35.05%	-11.54%	-42.46%
1975	70.83%	24.72%	37.19%
1976	73.29%	36.65%	25.50%
1977	-20.34%	-42.71%	-4.90%
1978	16.63%	-4.52%	-5.73%
1979	-26.59%	1.58%	8.98%
1980	1.24%	47.51%	33.50%
1981	-2.64%	-20.42%	-2.75%
1982	106.42%	-14.93%	69.68%
1983	19.42%	36.80%	31.10%

Exercise 46 *Plot this stock portfolio's Efficient Portfolio Frontier for the available data period.*

Exercise 47 *In this exercise we allow for short selling . What does that mean in terms of the allocation weights? What would (graphically) happen with the Efficient Portfolio Frontier when short selling is not allowed? Why (in terms of efficiency)? How would you go about (algebraically) implementing the constraint of no short selling? (Think in terms of the Kuhn-Tucker Theorem).*

Exercise 48 *One of the presumptions of this Markowitz' mean-variance analysis is that the stock price generating processes are stationary . What does this mean in terms of the Efficient Portfolio Frontier? How would you test for such stationarity ?*

6.7   Bibliography

Bank for International Settlements (1994) "A Discussion Paper on Public Disclosure of Market and Credit Risks by Financial Intermediaries," Basle, September.

Baumol, W. J. (1972) *Economic Theory and Operations Analysis*, 3rd ed., Prentice/Hall International, Inc., Englewood Cliffs, N.J.

Butler, C. (1999) *Mastering Value at Risk: A Step-by-step Guide to Understanding and Applying VaR*, Financial Times/Pitman Publishing, New York, NY.

CreditMetrics^{TM} - *Technical Document* (1997a), J. P. Morgan, New York, NY, 2 April.

Introduction to CreditMetrics^{TM} (1997b) J.P. Morgan, New York, NY, pp. 1 - 36

Introduction to RiskMetrics^{TM} (1995a), 3rd ed., J.P. Morgan, New York, NY, pp. 1 - 8.

Jorion, P. (1996) *Value at Risk: The New Benchmark for Controlling Market Risk*, Irwin Professional, New York, NY.

Los, C. A. (1995) "A Scientific View of Economic and Financial Data Analysis," in Janssen, J. C., Skiadas, H. and Zopounidis, C. (Editors), *Advances in Stochastic Modelling and Data Analysis*, Kluwer Academic Publishers, Dordrecht, The Netherlands, pp. 111-127.

Los, C. A. (1998) "Optimal Multi-Currency Investment Strategies With Exact Attribution in Three Asian Countries," *Journal of Multinational Financial Management*, **8** (2/3), September, 169 - 198.

Los, C. A. (1999) "Comment on "Combining Attribution Effects Over Time"," *The Journal of Performance Measurement*, **4** (1), Fall 1999, 5 - 6.

Markowitz, H. M. (1952) "Portfolio Selection," *Journal of Finance*, **7** (1), 77 - 91.

Markowitz, H. M. (1992) *Mean-Variance Analysis in Portfolio Choice and Capital Markets*, Blackwell, Oxford, UK (original 1987).

Markowitz, H. M. (1991) "Foundations of Portfolio Theory," *The Journal of Finance*, **46** (2), June, 469 - 477.

Markowitz, H. M. (1999) "The Early History of Portfolio Theory: 1600 - 1960," *Financial Analysts Journal*, **55** (4), July/August, 5 - 16.

Reilly, F. K. and Brown, K. C. (1997) *Investment Analysis and Portfolio Management*, The Dryden Press, New York, NY.

RiskMetrics^{TM} - *Technical Document* (1995b), 3rd ed., J. P. Morgan, New York, NY.

Samuelson, P. A. (1967) "Efficient Portfolio Selection for Pareto-Lévy Investments," *Journal of Financial and Quantitative Analysis*, **2** (2), June, 107 - 122.

Saunders, A. (1999) *Credit Risk Measurement: New Approaches to Value at Risk and Other Paradigms*, John Wiley and Sons, New York, NY.

Wilson, T. C. (1998) "Value at Risk," Chapter 3 in Alexander, C. (Ed.) (1999), *Risk Management and Analysis, Volume 1: Measuring and Modelling Financial Risk*, John Wiley & Sons, New York, NY, pp. 61 - 124.

chapter:7,page:1

Chapter 7
SYSTEMATIC FINANCIAL RISK ANALYSIS

7.1 Introduction

In this Chapter we return to the discussion of Chapter 5, but in the context of the portfolio selection analysis of Chapter 6. We will:

(1) price the relative risk taken by portfolio manager using Sharpe's (1964) bivariate Capital Asset Pricing Model (CAPM) and illustrate it with real world mutual fund examples (*Cf.* also Lintner, 1965; Black, 1993). We will also discuss a very serious shortcoming of this bivariate model , in particular its bias towards apparently reduced systematic risk (*Cf.* Los, 1999).

(2) compute how the portfolio manager can find "risk-free" profits from systematic investments by financial arbitrage , using Ross' (1976) Arbitrage Pricing Theory (APT) . The APT model is a multivariate model identified from n inexact economic and financial market data series. The CAPM can be viewed as the simplest, bivariate version of the APT.

At the end of this Chapter we will go beyond portfolio selection and the determination of systematic market risks to the quantitative determination of the *risk preferences* of the investors. Investors prefer to avoid risk and require a reward for engaging in risky investments. We will model the investor's trade-off between portfolio risk and expected return and define precisely and quantitatively what is meant by *speculation* , *risk aversion* , *risk neutrality* and *gambling* . We will find that speculation is a fundamental characteristic of well-functioning markets (and not a moral vice!) and that the quantitative determination of the risk preferences of the investors is a necessary ingredient for the strategic asset allocation policies of effective fund managers .

7.2 Fundamental Market Model

Financial markets can be viewed as huge portfolios, which exhibit systematic and unsystematic characteristics. For simplicity sake, a market is often represented by a weighted index , similar to the (weighted) mean price $\overline{P}_p$ or (weighted) mean RoR $\overline{x}_p$ of a portfolio.

Example 49 *The S&P500 Index represents a market portfolio of 500 stocks, where these stock market indices represents an indexed value of the average market price of* *these stocks.*

7.2.1 Systematic and Unsystematic Risk

Systematic risk is risk, *i.e.*, price or RoR variation, that can be explained, or modeled. *Unsystematic risk* , or epistemic uncertainty , cannot be explained or modeled . In terms of Chapter 3, the data covariation can always be decomposed into systematic and unsystematic covariation

$$\Sigma = \widehat{\Sigma} + \widetilde{\Sigma} \tag{7.1}$$

For a portfolio, the portfolio variance can be decomposed also into systematic variation $\widehat{\sigma}_{pp}$ and unsystematic variation $\widetilde{\sigma}_{pp}$ since

$$\begin{aligned} \sigma_{pp} &= \mathbf{w}'\Sigma\mathbf{w} \\ &= \mathbf{w}'\widehat{\Sigma}\mathbf{w} + \mathbf{w}'\widetilde{\Sigma}\mathbf{w} \\ &= \widehat{\sigma}_{pp} + \widetilde{\sigma}_{pp} \end{aligned} \tag{7.2}$$

It is empirically found that when the number of assets n in a portfolio increases, the unsystematic risk $\widetilde{\sigma}_{pp} \simeq \eta$ (small) declines, but that a certain level of systematic risk $\widehat{\sigma}_{pp} > \epsilon$ (substantial) remains, that is related to the structure of the market . The more efficient a market is, *i.e.*, the less systematic structure due to inefficiencies it exhibits, the smaller the systematic risk. The less efficient a market is, the larger the systematic risk. Most of the unsystematic risk can be diversified away by appropriate portfolio selection.

7.2.2 Absolute and Relative Risk

We can measure our *absolute risk* performance σ_{pp} *relative* to the risk of cash , σ_{cc}, or relative to the risk inherent in investing in a market index , σ_{mm}. First, we discuss measuring portfolio risk relative to the risk of cash. Suppose we have a risky asset (or portfolio), $\overline{x}_a > 0$, $\sigma_{aa} > 0$. Our portfolio risk can be reduced by combining the risky asset with "risk-free" cash, $\overline{x}_c > 0$, $\sigma_{cc} = 0$, into a new portfolio.

Remark 50 *Risk-free cash is an abstract concept, since no empirically measured economic asset is completely risk-free, i.e., without variation in its real value . For example, the real value of consumer cash is the "inverse" of the consumer price index , which always shows variation = (inflation or deflation), in particular in an international growth context. In the Finance literature often risk free = default-risk free . Furthermore, when a default-risk free cash bill is held until maturity, the nominal value is, indeed, risk free, i.e., without variation, but not its real value , due to inflation.*

The mean RoR of the new portfolio is

$$\begin{aligned} \overline{x}_p &= w_1\overline{x}_a + (1 - w_1)\overline{x}_c \\ &= \overline{x}_c + w_1(\overline{x}_a - \overline{x}_c) \end{aligned} \tag{7.3}$$

where $(\overline{x}_a - \overline{x}_c)$ is the average *premium* earned by the asset $\overline{x}_a$ above the average cash return $\overline{x}_c$. Since the bivariate portfolio covariance matrix is

$$\Sigma = \begin{bmatrix} \sigma_{aa} & 0 \\ 0 & 0 \end{bmatrix} \tag{7.4}$$

the minimal portfolio risk for this two asset portfolio is simply

$$\sigma_{pp}^{opt} = \mathbf{w}'\Sigma\mathbf{w}$$
$$= w_1^2 \sigma_{aa} \tag{7.5}$$

Notice that, consequently, by substitution for the optimal portfolio weight, the optimal portfolio return is

$$\overline{x}_p^{opt} = \overline{x}_c + w_1(\overline{x}_a - \overline{x}_c)$$
$$= \overline{x}_c + \sqrt{\frac{\sigma_{pp}^{opt}}{\sigma_{aa}}}(\overline{x}_a - \overline{x}_c) \tag{7.6}$$

This means that, inversely, we can also state that

$$(\overline{x}_a - \overline{x}_c) = \sqrt{\frac{\sigma_{aa}}{\sigma_{pp}^{opt}}} \cdot (\overline{x}_p^{opt} - \overline{x}_c) \tag{7.7}$$

When the portfolio consists of the whole market, including the risk-free cash, and the market is efficient and operates optimally in Markowitz' sense, one can thus state that the *premium of an individual asset* $(\overline{x}_a - \overline{x}_c)$ is related to the *market premium* $(\overline{x}_p^{opt} - \overline{x}_c)$ via its *relative risk* $\sqrt{\frac{\sigma_{aa}}{\sigma_{pp}^{opt}}}$.

7.2.3 Sharpe Ratio

The more familiar *Sharpe Ratio* is the simple (discounted) measure of the portfolio performance relative to that of cash

$$SR = \frac{(\overline{x}_p - \overline{x}_c)}{\sigma_p} \tag{7.8}$$

The Sharpe Ratio measures the price of portfolio performance, since it provides a portfolio's *premium per unit of risk* (Sharpe, *1966*). Comparable ratios can be found in Jensen (1968) and Treynor (1965).

7.3 CAPM, Beta and Epistemic Risk

We can extend the portfolio selection choice of the fund manager as follows. The fund manager can choose to invest in the individual asset with average premium RoR $\overline{x}_p - \overline{x}_c > 0$, in the market index with average premium RoR $\overline{x}_m - \overline{x}_c > 0$, or in a combination of these two. Fund managers try to beat the market, but, at worst, they should not do worse than the market, both in terms of their portfolio's mean RoR $\bar{x}_p > 0$ and in terms of their own portfolio risk σ_{pp}, as measured by, say, the Sharpe Ratio. In practice, this isn't true, since more than 85% of fund managers are outperformed by the market. There are only a select few fund managers who consistently beat the market. So, let the purchasers of mutual funds and unit trusts be aware!. Indeed, since 1973 Malkiel (1980) has consistently recommended to invest in market neutral index funds, for that very reason.

If we measure the rates of return as deviations from the means, we again encounter the bivariate model situation, familiar from Chapter 4. Thus, we begin again with the first two moments:

$$\mathbf{x} = \begin{bmatrix} x_p - x_c \\ x_m - x_c \end{bmatrix} \tag{7.9}$$

and

$$\Sigma = \begin{bmatrix} \sigma_{pp} & \sigma_{pm} \\ \sigma_{pm} & \sigma_{mm} \end{bmatrix} \tag{7.10}$$

There are two extreme Least Squares projections, with an infinite number of linear combinations in between. First, the LS projection of the asset's RoR on the RoR of the market index produces one extreme model solution

$$\widehat{(x_p - x_c)} = \beta_m \widehat{(x_m - x_c)}$$
$$= \frac{\sigma_{pm}}{\sigma_{mm}} \widehat{(x_m - x_c)} \tag{7.11}$$

This is the conventional *Capital Asset Pricing Model* (CAPM), as conventionally presented in the financial literature (Sharpe, 1963, 1964). Second, following the prescriptions of Chapter 3, we also have the unconventional reverse projection

$$\widehat{(x_m - x_c)} = \frac{\sigma_{pm}}{\sigma_{pp}} \widehat{(x_p - x_c)} \tag{7.12}$$

Thus in this second projection the market premium is a multiple of the *asset's current price of risk*. Here we look at the systematic part of the premium, $\widehat{(x_p - x_c)}$.

Remark 51 *This additional, unconventional view leads to the interesting conclusion that the CAPM implies that all portfolios are simply linear multiples of the market portfolio and vice versa. This is, perhaps, a rather unrealistic conclusion, but one implied by the CAPM. This is the unrealistic, so-called centroid solution of Sharpe for Markowitz' (considerably) more complex and complete solution of the portfolio selection problem.* *Sharpe suggested his practical centroid solution in the early 1960s*

---

*Harry Markowitz and William Sharpe shared the Nobel Memorial Prize for Economics in 1990, together with Merton Miller.

to enable the computation of a portfolio selection in a time when computing power was still very limited. At that time Markowitz' solution, which centers on the inversion of an $n \times n$ covariance matrix , could not be implemented by practicing mutual fund managers for a realistic number n of stocks . (Cf. Markowitz own remarks in the "Appendix: Personal Notes" of Markowitz, 1991, pp. 381 - 384). Currently, we can implement Markowitz ' complete portfolio optimization solution for a realistic number $(n \geqslant 25)$ of stocks in an EXCEL spreadsheet . That's technological progress!

Actually, an infinite number of model solutions and thus the empirically measured relative risk , or beta β lies between these two "best," LS projections:

$$\frac{\sigma_{pm}}{\sigma_{mm}} = \beta_m \leq \beta \leq \beta_p = \frac{\sigma_{pp}}{\sigma_{pm}} \tag{7.13}$$

Recall that with the help of the bivariate coefficient of determination ρ_{pm}^2 one can easily find the coefficient of the reverse LS projection, since

$$\beta_p = \frac{\beta_m}{\rho_{pm}^2} \tag{7.14}$$

Remark 52 *Empirically, it has been observed that these two LS extreme projections approach each other when the portfolio contains an increasing number of assets from the market index, because the correlation of the portfolio with the market then, of course, tends to improve, or $\rho_{pm} \to 1$. One finds that in most modern markets, e.g., the S&P500, already ca. 20 of the available assets provide most of the market direction. This is the basis for the formation of so-called simulated "market-neutral" index portfolio which can track the market index closely, with considerably fewer assets included in the simulated index portfolio than the original index. This reduces the transaction costs of accurately tracking the market .*

7.3.1 Mutual Funds Selection Based on Beta

We call *Galton's Error* to exclusively report the lower projection slope β_m and the bivariate coefficient of determination ρ_{pm}^2, but not the upper projection slope β_p.[†] The conventional statistical literature , including the economic and the financial literature , does not only commit Galton's Error, it also doesn't report the Noise/Signal Ratios , *i.e.*, ratio of the unsystematic risk to the systematic risk . In other words, it reports only the downward biased computational result of β_m, often, but not always, together with an indication of the model uncertainty ρ_{pm}^2 ,but it does not provide the complete picture. This consistent but erroneous deficiency in scientific reporting is even more pronounced for the cases with more than two variables, where it is never reported how the model invariant q is determined, otherwise than *a priori* from "theory. " In

---

[†]This section is based on Los (1999a). It was Galton's Error to take his regression towards the mean as complete and objective scientific evidence , while it was incomplete and biased evidence.

almost all cases, it is (incorrectly) assumed that $q = 1$, *i.e.*, that the model consists of a single linear equation .

This selective and biased modeling of the data has led to persistent and expensive misunderstanding of the concepts of epistemic uncertainty and risk in the financial industry , as the following simple empirical example illustrates.

Current financial industry performance presentation standards recommend to select mutual funds by their return/risk profile. The market risk is measured by the relative rate of return volatility , *i.e.*, as measured relative to that of a benchmark market index , and the return by some average return over a appropriate period (Black, 1993). This relative risk measure is called Sharpe's "beta" (Sharpe, 1963, 1964).[‡]

Extending the conventional use of Sharpe's β, we suggest the following, more precise, definitions for the available portfolios and assets (*Cf.* Los, 1999a):

(i) *defensive* , when $\beta_m \leq \beta \leq \beta_p < 1$, where unity is the beta of the market itself. The relative risk of the portfolio, as measured by the beta β, is lower than the market's.

(ii) *market–neutral* , when $\beta_m = \beta = \beta_p = 1$. This exact situation cannot empirically occur, but some funds, with considerably fewer assets than the particular market index, track that index sufficiently close, with very little "slippage." Consequently, such a small "tracking "portfolio can be considered (almost) equivalent to the market index.

(iii) *aggressive* , when $1 < \beta_m \leq \beta \leq \beta_p$. The relative risk of the portfolio, as measured by the beta β is higher than the market's.

(iv) *undecided* , when $\beta_m \leq \beta \leq \beta_p$ *and* $\beta_m < 1 < \beta_p$.

Notice that these new definitions are more precise than the ones originally provided by Sharpe (1966), or the ones available in the conventional financial literature , because these new definitions take explicit account of the epistemic uncertainty . The conventional financial literature does not contain the last category of "undecided," since it doesn't account for epistemic uncertainty.

Regrettably, Sharpe's beta is still computed and presented by the financial industry as the lower projection β_m, as recommended, for example, by *The AIMR Performance Presentation Standards (Cf.* AIMR, 1993, pp. 34 - 35, and AIMR, 1996a, pp. 92 - 95), which are adopted as part of the (new) AIMR's Standard of Professional Conduct V.B concerning Performance Presentation (AIMR, 1996b, p.

[‡]William Sharpe shared the 1990 Nobel Prize in Economics for his contribution to financial economics, in particular for his "beta "concept, which allowed the unique pricing of capital assets . Unfortunately, this section and Los (1999a) make clear that inexact empirical data cannot provide such model uniqueness . The CAPM controversy is not new, although our explanation for the beta's uncertainty is.

9). The deficient, but official recommendation concerning the computation and presentation of the beta β is now promoted to become a global investment performance standard.[§]

But these simple computations have led to a severe under-representation of the empirically observed systematic risks of the selected funds by the financial industry. Therefore the question can be rased if the current recommendations by the AIMR are consistent with its own Standard of Professional Conduct IV, the Relationships with and Responsibilities to Clients and Prospects, in particular, with Standard IV.A.2 concerning Research Reports and Standard IV.A.3 concerning Independence and Objectivity.[¶]

This under-representation of systematic investment risk can be demonstrated by looking at how many mutual funds are ranked aggressive , defensive , or market neutral by Sharpe's beta, and how many funds are truly aggressive defensive or neutral, when taking account of all the epistemic uncertainty implied by the data.

For the data we use the computed betas and bivariate coefficients of determination in Morningstar's convenient (Windows based) *Principia for Mutual Funds* of July 1995, as released on computer diskettes to the general public on December 31, 1995.[‖]

First, we notice in Table 1. that only $3,227$ out of a total universe of $7,051$ funds have measurable risk, as indicated by a computed coefficient of determination larger than zero, or 45.8% of the total universe. The other funds are younger than 3 years and don't have a 3-year record to base such computations on. However, for 12 of these $3,227$ funds the lower beta β_m equals zero in the two published digits beyond the decimal point. Thus only $3,215$ funds have measured systematic market risk as defined by the CAPM, or 45.6% of the total universe.

[§]The original AIMR Performance Presentation Standards (AIMR, 1993), which took effect on January 1, 1993, were amended and restated on September 13, 1996 to include some international concerns (AIMR, 1996a). This restatement did not amend the incomplete computation of Sharpe's beta. The AIMR Performance Presentation Standards form part of the AIMR's Code of Ethics and Standards of Professional Conduct (AIMR, 1996b). These latest standards are now the model for the Global Investment Persformance Standards (GIPS) Committee (1998).

[¶]New knowledge is not always appreciated. When the author, who is a member of the AIMR, raised these difficult issues in personal letters of August 2, 1994 and January 3, 1995, respectively, to two successive Directors of Research of the AIMR, his proposals for amendments were twice officially and firmly rejected in writing. In some cases, rectification of similar erroneous rejections of scientific conclusions has arrived only 350 years later.

[‖]These data diskettes are available, at cost, from Morningstar, Inc. , 225 West Wacker Drive, Chicago, Illinois 60606, and are updated quarterly. Morningstar is a respected mutual funds monitor , with an excellent reputation, that computes the betas and corresponding coefficients of determination of the mutual funds strictly according to the accepted industry standards . According to Morningstar's *OnFloppy User's Guide* (p.22): "Morningstar bases alpha, beta, and R-squared on a least squares regression of the fund's excess return over T-bills compared with the excess returns of the fund's benchmark index. These calculations are computed for the trailing 36-month period."

TABLE 1.: SYSTEMATIC RISK OF MUTUAL FUNDS		#	%
1.	Morningstar's Principia for Mutual Funds universe, 12/31/95	7,051	
2.	Together with the condition $0 < \rho^2_{pm} \leq 1$	3,227	
3.	And with 3-year (Sharpe's) beta $0 < \beta_m$	3,215	
4.	**AIMR Performance Presentation Standards, 1993:**		
	(i) Defensive funds: $0 < \beta_m < 1$	2,047	63.7
	(ii) Neutral, market index funds: $\beta_m = 1$	67	2.1
	(iii) Aggressive funds: $1 < \beta_m$	1,101	34.2
	Total funds with measurable systematic market risk	3,215	100.0
5.	**Complete Least Squares (CLS) analysis:**		
	(i) Defensive funds: $0 < \beta_m \leq \beta_p < 1$	608	18.9
	(ii) Neutral, market index funds: $\beta_m = \beta_p = 1$	18	0.6
	(iii) Aggressive funds: $1 < \beta_m \leq \beta_p$	1,101	34.2
	(iv) Undecided: $0 < \beta_m < 1 < \beta_p$	1,488	46.3
	Total funds with measurable systematic market risk	3,215	100.0

If we accept Sharpe's beta criterion for selecting funds by their relative volatility or systematic market risk characteristic, then the number of defensive funds selected by correctly implementing Sharpe's beta is 25.6% of the 2,047 claimed to be defensive by the current industry standards. In addition, the number of actual market index funds is only 26.9% of the 67 funds claimed to be market index funds in this representative data universe . Finally, of the 3,215 funds for which the appropriate data were available 954, or 45%, could not be categorized as defensive, aggressive or market index, in spite of the claims of the financial industry.

In addition, we may want to apply the criterion of accuracy of the measurement of this systematic risk as in Table 2.

TABLE 2.: SYSTEMATIC RISK AND	ACCURACY			
Complete Least Squares (CLS) analysis:	$\frac{N}{S} \leq 10.56\%$	%	$\frac{N}{S} \leq 2.51\%$	%
(i) Defensive funds: $0 < \beta_m \leq \beta_p < 1$	182	40.4	23	28.4
(ii) Neutral, market index funds: $\beta_m = \beta_p = 1$	18	4.0	18	22.2
(iii) Aggressive funds: $1 < \beta_m \leq \beta_p$	171	38.0	27	33.3
(iv) Undecided: $0 < \beta_m < 1 < \beta_p$	79	17.6	12	14.8
Funds with measurable systematic market risk	450	100.0	81	100.0

Table 2. shows that accuracy of measurement of the systematic market risk is an important criterion when one insists on "truth in advertising." Based on the reasonable criterion of a Noise/Signal Ratio of less or equal to 10.56% - corresponding with $\rho^2_{pm} = 0.90$, i.e., "90% confidence " in the parlance of conventional statistics -

only 450 out of a total universe of 3, 215 funds with measurable market risk pass the test. That is an astonishingly low 14.0% of the total fund universe! When we increase the measurement accuracy only a bit further to a Noise/Signal Ratio of less or equal to 2.51% - corresponding with $\rho_{12}^2 = 0.975$, or "97.5% confidence" - only 81 funds, or 2.5% of our universe, pass this simple accuracy test . Based on these nontrivial results of the exceedingly low risk measurement accuracy , professional financial economists should express a note of concern about the exaggerated advertising claims of the mutual funds industry.

To gain an impression of some of the investment magnitudes involved, have look at the following numbers. The mutual fund industry in the U.S.A. grew from US95$ billion in assets in 1979, to nearly US2$ trillion by the end of 1994; an increase of over 20 times. Even after taking account of consumer price inflation and the resulting loss of purchasing power in the U.S.A. of more than 90% over the same period, the increase in real assets is still a very sizeable eleven times in fourteen years.

Most of this increase in real assets has actually occurred in the last three years. American investors poured a net US377$ billion into equity mutual funds alone in $1993 - 95$. Since the end of 1994 until the middle of 1996, the Dow Jones Industrial Average climbed by nearly 50% and the broader $S\&P500$ index by 46%, increasing the financial wealth of the U.S.A. by US2.4$ trillion, more than the entire annual output of Germany .**

Compare now these market sizes with the magnitudes of the fund universes we've analyzed. By September 1993 there existed 4, 347 open-ended mutual funds . The following year Morningstar monitored about 79% of them. Its *Mutual Funds OnFloppy* data universe contained 3, 434 funds with an average median market capitalization of US0.5$ billion in net assets by the end 1994. Its updated successor universe, Morningstar's *Principia for Mutual Funds,* used in our analysis, contained already more than double this number at the end of 1995: 7, 051 funds.

Because of the fast growth in the number of new mutual funds, there were now many more smaller funds include , since the average median market capitalization of this universe is US264.9$ million in net assets. But the more restricted universe of 3, 215 funds, on which the conclusions of Table 1. are based, has an comparable average median capitalization of US514.6$ million in net assets, while the universes of 450 funds and of 81 funds have an average median market capitalizations of US510.5$ million, respectively US510.4$ million in net assets.

Since this increasingly massive process of mutual fund selection and pricing is biased by the under-representation of market risk, as our analysis suggests, very serious misallocation between the investment alternatives could result, based on their currently presented biased relative return/risk profiles . Also, since a substantial amount of this investment capital may consist of "hot money" these market allocations are not likely to be patient or secure. Indeed, *The Economist* refers to the argument "that many mutual-fund investors do not understand what they are doing;

**According to *The Economist*, July 6, 1996, pp. 18 and 21.

and that, when they realize what the risks are, they will flee."[††]

There is no reason for panic, however, according to the same article in *The Economist*, because of the apparent maturity of the modern investors . The younger investors: "not only say they accept the risk involved - in a recent survey by American financial regulators, 94% of investors said they knew they could lose money in share dealings as well as gain it - they also seem, in practice, to respond calmly when prices fall."

The biased published betas do not only raise macro concerns relevant for national policy makers , or global asset allocators , but also micro concerns relevant for individual portfolio managers . Since the downward biased beta's β_m are used in the computation of cross hedging ratios , when portfolio positions are hedged by derivatives , like futures, to reduce the systematic risk exposure of these positions, serious doubts should be raised about the effectiveness of such hedges . In our opinion, there is more uncertainty about the systematic risk than current portfolio managers , regulators and the educators of financial analysts recognize..

A scientific debate on the issue of the adequacy of a single risk measure for mutual funds, like the beta, is therefore timely. The Securities and Exchange Commission (S.E.C.) , in reaction to recent sharp price drops for several supposedly low-risk mutual funds , has asked fund managers to look more carefully at their risk management controls that track derivative positions. The S.E.C. is trying to condense the myriad risks of mutual funds into a single measure that would convey these risks to investors. In 1995, the S.E.C. floated a Concept Release (= White Paper) on the issue, requesting comments on or before July 7, 1995 (SEC, 1995). Our comments in the current Chapter should forewarn the S.E.C. that its quest for a single measure for multi - faceted investment risk is likely to be just as quixotic and fruitless as the quest for a single I.Q. measure when fundamental principles of science are ignored (*Cf.* Gould, 1981).

A complete representation of the empirical systematic uncertainty is required. Thus, for the bivariate CAPM, at least two measures must be published: the correlation coefficient ρ_{pm} (or, equivalently in the bivariate case, the coefficient of determination ρ_{pm}^2) together with the β_m, since all other bivariate measurements can be derived from these two. Next, one must educate the investors about the uncertainty gap for β, about $\beta_m \leq \beta \leq \beta_p = \frac{\beta_m}{\rho_{pm}^2}$. It was this recommendable practice of Morningstar to publish both β_m and ρ_{pm}^2 that enabled us to scientifically, *i.e.*, completely, categorize the mutual funds, while still using the CAPM categorization as currently accepted by the financial industry.[‡‡]

[††] *The Economist*, July 6, 1996, p. 18.

[‡‡]I'm *not* recommending the CAPM bivariate presentation of systematic market risk practice as the only or the best presentation of systematic risk. Here, I only state that the current investment performance standards and practice are biased and misleading to investors. Of course, an investor can reduce the risks of his portfolio by appropriate portfolio diversification , when the rate of return data satisfy particular stationarity and independence conditions (*Cf.* Chapter 6). In the next section,

7.4 Related Topics

7.4.1 Multi-Factor Models

The CAPM of Sharpe (1964) has been generalized by Ross (1976) to include many variables instead of a single market index (*Cf.* Burmeister, Roll and Ross, 1994). Confusingly, Ross calls his multivariate model a "Factor Model," whereby his "factors" are actually economic or financial market variables, usually measured as deviations from their means. However, the term factor model has in statistics the very different meaning of "bundled-variable model ," whereby the "factor-bundles " are determined by procedures variously called "factor analysis " (when performed on a correlation matrix) and "principal component analysis " (when performed on a covariance matrix) (Los, 1989).

In fact, Ross' own "Factor Model" is a single equation linear model of the form

$$\mathbf{A}\widehat{\mathbf{x}}' = a_1\widehat{x}_1 + a_2\widehat{x}_2 + ... + a_n\widehat{x}_n = 0 \tag{7.15}$$

This amounts to a form of simple "regression" model ($q = 1$), although the actual implementation is that of a principal components model ($q = n - x$, with x the number of factors).

Ross' motivation was to find the many components of $\widehat{\mathbf{x}} = \mathbf{x} - \widetilde{\mathbf{x}}$ producing systematic portfolio risk $\widehat{\sigma}_{pp} = \mathbf{w}'\widehat{\Sigma}\mathbf{w}$, such that $\mathbf{A}\widehat{\mathbf{x}}' = 0$, or, equivalently, $\mathbf{A}\widehat{\Sigma} = \mathbf{0}$, instead of the amorphous single "market," as measured by the single market index of the CAPM. These systematic components could then be used for risk free arbitrage , or so Ross argued.

Los' (1989) critique of Ross' implementation of APT does not imply that an improved version of Ross' theoretical effort cannot be implemented. Instead of assuming that $q = 1$, as Ross did, one must first determine the model invariant q from the information matrix Σ^{-1}, before one computes the many possible CLS projections. When the epistemic uncertainty in the data $\widetilde{\Sigma} = \Sigma - \widehat{\Sigma}$ is relatively small, and the many CLS projections produce roughly similar results for the various extreme (Grassmanian) CLS projection coefficients $\mathbf{A}^{CLS}$, arbitrage pricing based on systematic influences $\widehat{\mathbf{x}}$, $\mathbf{A}\widehat{\mathbf{x}}' = 0$, is still possibly, although never completely risk-free.

Remark 53 *The fact that the systematic covariance matrix $\widehat{\Sigma}$ is singular , by definition, since $\mathbf{A}\widehat{\Sigma} = \mathbf{0}$, has serious consequences for the desired reconciliation of Markowitz Mean-Variance Analysis and Ross' Arbitrage Pricing Theory (Cf. also Chapter 6). Mathematically such a reconciliation is not possible, since Markowitz' theory is based*

I add that, while Sharpe's erroneous beta compares with *Galton's Error* of regressing towards the mean, the current practice of factor, or principal components analysis of investment portfolios, based on Asset Pricing Theory (APT) compares more closely to the erroneous practice of I.Q. testing (*Cf.* Gould, 1981).

Compare the models of Burmeister, Roll and Ross (1994) and Elton and Gruber (1995) with the principal components analysis "procedure " used by Barr Rosenberg's commercial consulting firm BARRA, Inc. to implement Ross' APT.

upon positive definite covariance matrices , which can be inverted, while Ross' theory is based upon singular systematic covariance matrices subjectively selected from the positive definite data covariance matrix. (Cf. Los, 1989). An infinite number of model selections is possible within a restricted range set of empirically allowable models, and thus any particular selection must be subjective and "prejudiced." Ross' theory, and by implication Sharpe's Capital Asset Pricing Theory (CAPM), which is a special bivariate case of the n-variate APT, doesn't properly account for such epistemic uncertainty . Since there is thus an infinity of possible systematic efficiency frontiers (Cf. Los, 1994), empirical portfolio managers, like Fidelity International, Inc. , do show in their marketing literature an uncertainty range of possible efficiency frontiers.

7.4.2   Mdmv Model Comparison Between CAPM and APT

Given particular conditions of stationarity and time independence of the rates of investment return, the *exact CAPM* is true when all investment portfolios in the market are completely diversified . Then there is no unsystematic portfolio variation, the portfolios are centroid, and thus the portfolios are valued only for their exposure to systematic risk. We speak of a *centroid portfolio*, when all (systematic) variation in the (required) expected rates of return of the portfolios can be explained by only one factor.

Mathematically, this exact CAPM requires that the determinant of the data covariance matrix of the rates of return of all assets in this portfolio, which equals the product of its eigenvalues, is zero:

$$|\Sigma| = \prod_{i}^{n} \lambda_i = 0 \qquad (7.16)$$

since the ordered eigenvalues are such that $\lambda_1 > 0$, and $\lambda_i = 0$ for $i = 2, ..., n$.

The exact CAPM is thus an exact one-factor model and has, therefore, $q = n - 1$ exact linear relationships among the rates of return of the assets in a portfolio. Fig. 1. illustrates what is meant by such multi-dimensional modeling *certainty* , when $n = 3$ and $q = 2$, by plotting an exact CAPM in the $3D$ data space . The exact CAPM is represented by the single ray model in the center, which is the result of the crossing of $q = 2$ planes (= the two independent exact relationships = the two independent linear equations).

The black dots in the center of Fig. 1. are again the observations in the $3D$ frame of data reference (Cf. Fig. 1. in Chapter 5). The origin of this $3D$ frame of data reference is in the center of Fig. 1.. The observations lie on the ray, *i.e.*, they are exactly explained by a ray model . Such an exact ray model must be described by $q = 2$ linearly independent equations . Notice the projections of the

---

This section is based on Los (1999a)
This is Fig. 2. in Los (1999a).

3 - Dim Data Space (32 obs.)
Exact Model (n,q) = (3,2)

Model:
x1 + 0.0602.x3 = 0
x1 - 0.0931.x2 = 0

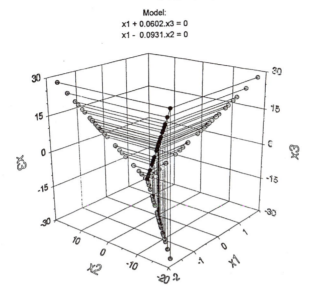

Figure 1   Exact CAPM $(n, q) = (3, 2)$

exact observations and the ray model on the $2D$ frames of data reference on the three sides of Fig. 2. There, in each of the three 2D frames $\rho_{ij}^2 = 1$. Thus, in the exact case there is complete model certainty . The model invariant $q = 2$ is easily identified from exact data, but note that in this exact case $|\Sigma| = 0$ and the information matrix doesn't exist .

What is found in case of the empirical *inexact CAPM* ? Empirically, the determinant of the data covariance matrix of the rates of return of a (fully diversified) portfolio is (almost always) positive:

$$|\Sigma| = \prod_{i}^{n} \lambda_i > 0 \qquad (7.17)$$

This implies that empirically all eigenvalues $\lambda_i \neq 0$, $i = 1, 2, ..., n$. Thus, empirically, the inexact CAPM is *necessarily and always* a multifactor model! Therefore, debate in the financial literature has necessarily centered on the statistical game of deciding which of those factors are "significant" and which are considered "insignificant".

Not coincidentally, the debate about the two main valuation models in modern asset valuation

The proponents of the (exact) CAPM decide to accept the first of the ranked eigenvalues as representing the amplitude of the one-factor (systematic) variation, $\lambda_1 > 0$. By implication, the remaining $n - 1$ eigenvalues are considered amplitudes of unsystematic risk (noise) variation and set equal to zero: $\lambda_i = 0$ for $i = 2, ..., n$. Consequently, in the $n-$dimensional data space there must be $q = n - 1$ exact linear relationships or "planes" (Los, 1989, 1999).

This inexact CAPM is illustrated in Fig. 2. with three assets, which clearly illustrates what is meant with mdmv modeling of uncertain linear relationships , when $n = 3$ and $q = 2$.

Fig. 2. does not show the exact one-factor ray model, which goes through the center as in Fig. 1.. But the three vertices , $LS1$, $LS2$ and $LS3$, are the three elementary CLS projections, which map the data in three different projection directions , depending on where the model uncertainty (= unsystematic risk) is allocated by the projector . The cone-shaped area between these three vertices represents the complete $3D$ model uncertainty inherent in the data and is computed from the adjoint of the data covariance matrix (Cf. Sinkhorn, 1993). Although the true Grassmanian model coordinates within this cone are uncertain, they are clearly bound by finite projection boundaries formed by the three vertices, as in the bivariate case.

The ratio of the volume of this cone spanned by the three CLS vertices relative to the volume of the orthant of the frame of data reference is given by the $3D$ Noise/Data Ratio presented in Chapter 5:

$$\frac{N}{D} = \frac{|\Sigma|}{\sigma_{11}\sigma_{22}\sigma_{33}}$$
$$= (1 - \rho_{12}^2 - \rho_{13}^2 - \rho_{23}^2 + 2\rho_{12}\rho_{13}\rho_{23}) \tag{7.18}$$

Notice again the projections of the observations and the three boundary projections in the $2D$ frames of data reference on the three side panels of the orthant. There we find illustrated in each of the three $2D$ frames the 2D Noise/Signal Ratio

$$0 < (1 - \rho_{ij}^2)/\rho_{ij}^2 < 1 \tag{7.19}$$

---

and portfolio management - (CAPM) and the APT - has now been raging in the financial literature for more than 25 years. This debate heated further up after the severe critique of the CAPM by French and Fama (1992) and no obvious resolution is in sight, considering the erroneous assumptions on which the debate is based. Reilly and Brown (1997) devote their whole Chapter 10, pp. 305 - 332, plus parts of other Chapters of their AIMR/CFA endorsed textbook, to a complete and fully referenced survey of this debate. Besides a survey of the CAPM controversies, Reilly and Brown (1997) also include a detailed discussion of the APT debate between Roll and Ross on one side and Dhrymes, Friend, the Gultekins and Shanken on the other side, regarding the testability of the APT. Why that debate is without merit is readily explained in the current section within the context of CLS modeling (Cf. Los, 1989): because the selection of the number of factors has to remain subjective.

This is Fig. 3. in Los (1999a)

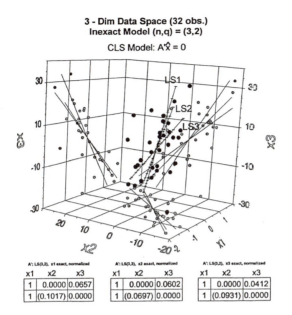

3 - Dim Data Space (32 obs.)
Inexact Model (n,q) = (3,2)

CLS Model: A'x̂ = 0

A': LS(3,2), x1 exact, normalized			A': LS(3,2), x2 exact, normalized			A': LS(3,2), x3 exact, normalized		
x1	x2	x3	x1	x2	x3	x1	x2	x3
1	0.0000	0.0657	1	0.0000	0.0602	1	0.0000	0.0412
1	(0.1017)	0.0000	1	(0.0697)	0.0000	1	(0.0931)	0.0000

Figure 2   Inexact CAPM $(n, q) = (3, 2)$ with three exact CLS$(3, 2)$ projections

Thus, there is complete, but limited model uncertainty. The extension to still higher dimensional data sets is straightforward, as we already noticed in Chapter 5.

In contrast, the proponents of what, perhaps, can be called the "strong" version of the empirical APT , decide that the last of the ranked eigenvalues should be set equal to zero, $\lambda_n = 0$, because it is considered the amplitude of insignificant unsystematic risk or noise variation, and that there are $n-1$ "significant" amplitudes of systematic variation $\lambda_i \neq 0$ for $i = 1, 2, ..., n-1$. The result is the very simple APT model of Roll and Ross with one exact linear relationship, $q = 1$ (= one single equation = one plane).

My critique of the strong version of APT is not that empirically always more than one eigenvalue is "significantly" non-zero, but that it cannot be objectively decided how many eigenvalues should be retained as representing the amplitudes of "significant" systematic variation ; or, equivalently, that it cannot be objectively decided how many eigenvalues should be set equal to zero, as representing the amplitudes of "insignificant" unsystematic risk, or noise variation. Indeed, mathematically,

---

For example, Los(1991) analyzed a simple economicprediction model with $(n, q) = (5, 4)$. Since $r = n - q = 1$, there was only one major economic factor in the presented $n = 5$ variable economy , commonly known as the business cycle .

that choice has to necessarily remain a subjective choice , as Los (1989) proves.

One consequence of this mathematical necessity of epistemic uncertainty, when confronted with empirical data, is that in the financial literature of the past 25 years, there has been a proliferation of APT models with various - four, five, and up to twenty-five, etc. - numbers of factors considered "significant" enough to represent the systematic variation in the rates of return data from larger investment portfolios. But mathematically, no objective choice can be made between these models qua their scientific veracity .

Since the problem is not unique to finance, but can be found in any discipline where mdmv modeling takes place, the only useful recommendation that can be given is that financial analysts can learn from signal processing engineers what are "acceptable" and "unacceptable" levels of unsystematic risk, or noise, and implement particular noise filter criteria. Multiresolution theory based on wavelets and bandwidth filtering provides some criteria for the what can be considered unacceptable levels of noise and risk (*Cf.* Chapter 2 and Ogden, 1997, pp. 131 - 132) Thus, financial analysts can learn from the signal processing literature for their investigation of the efficiency of markets.

How important is this epistemological issue for finance? It concerns the fundamental capital valuation models of CAPM, the APT and the Multi-Index models used in post-CAPM modern portfolio analysis, and it also concerns several credit valuation models. Such finance models use mdmv methodology , with a subjective choice of number of "factors" $(= n - q)$, or of number of "linear equations" $(= q)$.

For example, Fama and French' (1992) model for $n \geq 3$ includes three variables: the average return of a firm, its book value/market value ration and the size of its market capitalization, has one linear relationship, $q = 1$ and thus retains $n - q = 2$ factors. The question is, is this model really producing acceptable levels of unsystematic risk when $n > 3$ and still only $n - q = 2$ factors are retained? Mathematically it means that French and Fama claim that there are $q = n - 2$ (with $n > 3$) linear relationships in the data. As shown in Reilly and Brown (1997), Chapter 10, this is contradicted by most empirical results.

Another example of an mdmv model is Elton and Gruber's (1995) simplest Industry Index Model , which includes also three variables: the rates of return of a firm, a market index and one industry index , *e.g.*, for the steel industry. Their model is mathematically similar to French and Fama's.

Finally, the credit scoring model of Altman, Haldeman and Narayanan used in the commercial pricing of distressed sovereign and bank debt is an mdmv model, since it includes many correlated factors, represented by accounting ratios (*Cf.* Chapter 1, Exercise 2). The correct pricing of such distressed debt has become an important global phenomenon, after the banking crises in the U.S.A. , Japan , Indonesia , Thailand , etc.

Cf. Reilly and Brown, 1997, Chapters 9 & 10, for a survey of the published empirical evidence , in particular pp. 326 - 329.

Whatever unsystematic risk is left, after filtering of the systematic risk represented by such financial mdmv model will be valued by the market. One cannot know directly from the data where the unsystematic risk resides, since its allocation depends on the projection direction (*Cf.* Chapter 5). Thus it cannot be objectively decided which factor contributes most to the mispricing of capital .

Such uncertainty about the pricing of systematic risk and the potential for serious mispricing caused by the subjective choice of the projection direction (in which factoral direction, as represented by the eigenvectors, should one hedge or do arbitrage?) constitutes a fundamental empirical market inefficiency . In a nutshell: empirical markets can be shown to be Arrow - Debreu incomplete (*Cf.* Chapter 8), since for any empirical portfolio of any (finite) size, the data covariance matrix of the rates of return is positive definite, $\Sigma > 0$.

7.5 Risk Aversion, Neutrality and Gambling

Let's now look closely at some useful definitions of investment behavior :

(1) *Speculation* is the assumption of risk in obtaining a return on a risky investment above the risk-free return, *i.e.* in obtaining a *risk-premium.*

(2) *Gambling* is the assumption of risk, no matter what the return on the investment is. While speculation is a rational trade-off activity, which prices the odds, or discounts the risks, gambling isn't, since there is no trade-off and thus no pricing of the odds and no discounting of the risks.

(3) A *fair game* is an investment with a zero risk premium. There is no arbitrage opportunity and no risk taking.

Currently, the academic debate about the role of uncertainty and risk in economic decision making is heating up in the context of the (in-)completeness of the financial markets. Chichilnisky (1996, p. 101) claims that *scientific uncertainty* , "the uncertainty derived from the fact that scientists do not know exactly how industrial activity alters the risks we face," can, in principle be hedged fully with the use of CAT (or "catastrophe") futures . These financial instruments were theoretically introduced by Chichilnisky and Heal (1992) and have recently started trading on the Chicago Board of Trade (CBOT) . These CAT futures are still very illiquid and it is still to be seen if they can and will be used for hedging against the consequences of all human follies described by Bernstein (1996), for example, against the consequences of the Southeast Asian "haze." However, Chichilnisky emphasizes that there is "a more pervasive and complex type of endogenous uncertainty in the markets: ignorance about the output of the economy in equilibrium ," which she calls "strict endogenous uncertainty."(Chichilnisky, 1996, p. 102). This implies uncertainty about expected earnings, ergo about the expected rates of return , be it "required" or "estimated" expected returns. She proves in a Theorem that such "strict endogenous uncertainty cannot be hedged fully, no matter how many securities are introduced to make the market complete." Thus, there remains unhedgeable epistemic risk because of *fundamental market incompleteness* . We discuss fundamental market incompleteness and the role it plays in global portfolio management in Chapter 14.

A *portfolio's utility* or *preference value* can be modeled by a simple relationship between the expected return and the expected portfolio variance. Thus an investor derives from his portfolio investment the following utility

$$U_p = \overline{x}_p - \frac{\alpha}{2}\sigma_{pp} \qquad (7.20)$$

Notice that the utility is positively related to the portfolio's average RoR $\overline{x}_p$ and negatively related to its risk measured by the portfolio variance σ_{pp}. The coefficient α is called the *risk aversion*, or *preference factor*. An investor is:

(1) *risk-averse*, when $\alpha > 0$. Such an investor engages in rational speculation.

(2) *risk-seeking*, when $\alpha < 0$. Such an investor engages in irrational gambling.

(3) *risk-neutral*, when $\alpha = 0$, since risk does not enter his preferences. *Risk-neutral pricing* is based on fair games and plays a crucial role in arbitrage-free options pricing.

For example, for the bivariate portfolio with one risk-free (cash) and one risky asset, we found that the mean RoR of the expected portfolio

$$\begin{aligned} \overline{x}_p &= \mathbf{w'}\overline{\mathbf{x}} \\ &= \overline{x}_c + w_1(\overline{x}_a - \overline{x}_c) \end{aligned} \qquad (7.21)$$

and the minimal expected portfolio variance

$$\begin{aligned} \sigma_{pp}^{opt} &= \mathbf{w'}\Sigma\mathbf{w} \\ &= w_1^2\sigma_{aa} \end{aligned} \qquad (7.22)$$

Thus the portfolio's utility may be written

$$U_p = \overline{x}_c + w_1(\overline{x}_a - \overline{x}_c) - \frac{\alpha}{2}w_1^2\sigma_{aa} \qquad (7.23)$$

An investor will try to maximize the utility of his portfolio. By setting the first derivative of U_p with respect to the portfolio allocation weight w_1 equal to zero, we find

$$\frac{\partial U_p}{\partial w_1} = (\overline{x}_a - \overline{x}_c) - \alpha w_1\sigma_{aa} = 0 \qquad (7.24)$$

Other trade-off models are possible. This one is based on the economists' Marginal Value of Money theory, with a quadratic utility function .

or

$$\alpha = \frac{(\overline{x}_a - \overline{x}_c)}{w_1 \sigma_{aa}} \tag{7.25}$$

(Notice, that the second derivative , $\frac{\partial^2 U_p}{\partial w_1^2} = -\alpha \sigma_{aa}$, is negative for a rational risk-aversive investor. Thus the investor *maximizes* the utility of his portfolio). By confronting an investor with a particular portfolio, with given risk premium $(\overline{x}_a - \overline{x}_c)$ and risky variance σ_{aa}, and by letting him choose the allocation w_1 between the risky and the risk-free investment, one can quantify his personal risk preference α, using this simple exact speculative model.

One can also measure the average risk preference of a financial market as follows. By definition, the collective of market participants is 100% invested in the market portfolio (as measured by, for example, the S&P500 Index). Therefore the market risk aversion factor is

$$\overline{\alpha}_m = \frac{(\overline{x}_m - \overline{x}_c)}{\sigma_{mm}} \tag{7.26}$$

This is the average market price of risk, because it measures the average premium return $(\overline{x}_m - \overline{x}_c)$ required on average to compensate for the market risk σ_{mm}.

Example 54 *Over the past 50 years the market risk premium in the USA has been ca. 4%, while the market portfolio returns had a standard deviation of ca. 10%. Thus the average market risk aversion in the USA, which has very efficient financial markets, has been*

$$\overline{\alpha}_m = \frac{0.04}{(0.10)^2} = 4 \tag{7.27}$$

Since this coefficient is a non-dimensional scalar , it is possible to compare the risk aversion of markets over time and with each other, by using the efficient markets of the USA as a standard for comparison. For example, it is possible in the inefficient markets of South-east Asia , which probably show a much higher market risk σ_{mm} because of substantial systematic distortions, that the risk aversion is lower than in the USA, i.e., $\overline{\alpha}_m < 4$. But our final empirical conclusion will depend on the average market premiums paid out, which is the subject of current empirical investigation.

7.6 Exercises

Exercise 55 *Plot a Price-Yield curve and, separately, a Security Characteristic Line . Which of the two plots represents an exact model and which one an inexact model ? Why? How can you indicate this in the two plots?*

See Chapter 14 for some empirical examples for average Asian stock market risk premia.

Exercise 56 *Imagine that you are a financial analyst for PanAgora Asset Management, Inc. , a firm headquartered in Boston, Massachusetts, USA, which manages US\$16 billion in assets for pension plans , endowments ; foundations , unions , and financial services providers around the globe. E. P., its Chief Investment Officer , and author of the path-breaking book* **Fractal Market Analysis** *, asks you to analyze the following, abstract, data covariance matrix* Σ *of continuous rates of returns (RoRs) of the S&P 500 Index and Microsoft stock, respectively, using Complete Least Squares projections :*

$$\Sigma = \begin{bmatrix} \sigma_{11} & \sigma_{12} \\ \sigma_{12} & \sigma_{22} \end{bmatrix} \tag{7.28}$$

1. What are the adjoint (or adjugate matrix), the determinant and the inverse of this symmetric (2×2) data covariance matrix Σ? Write the bivariate coefficient of determination and the corresponding Noise/Signal ratio of these two variables.

2. The contour plot of the concentric isometric information ellipses is algebraically given by the expression

$$\widehat{\mathbf{x}}\prime\Sigma^{-1}\widehat{\mathbf{x}} = d \tag{7.29}$$

where d is a parametric scalar (which can take different, but constant values) and $\mathbf{x}$ is the (2×1) vector of possible deviations from the means of the RoRs. Write out this expression algebraically and optimize it with respect to each of the two variables. Which exact linear projection models result and why? Plot one isometric ellipse with the resulting two linear models. What does it tell you about the inexactness of the relationship between the two variables?

3. How can you relate the analysis of the concentric information ellipses in question 3(b) to the decomposition of the data covariance matrix Σ into a systematic $\widehat{\Sigma}$ and an unsystematic CLS covariance matrix $\widetilde{\Sigma}^{CLS}$, where

$$\widetilde{\Sigma}_i^{CLS} = \Sigma \mathbf{A}_i'(\mathbf{A}_i\Sigma\mathbf{A}_i')^{-1}\mathbf{A}_i\Sigma \tag{7.30}$$

and $\mathbf{A}_i \equiv \mathbf{A}_i^{CLS}$ is the ith (Grassmanian) Least Squares projection coefficient matrix ?

4. How would you implement the formula for the unsystematic covariance matrix of question 3(c) in an EXCEL spreadsheet ? Write out sequentially all the necessary EXCEL formula commands and keyboard sequences , similar to what you used in your term assignment.

7.7 Bibliography

AIMR (1993) "Performance Presentation Standards, Association for Investment Management and Research, Charlottesville, NC.

AIMR (1996a) "Performance Presentation Standards Handbook 1997, Association for Investment Management and Research, Charlottesville, NC.

AIMR (1996b) "Standards of Practice Handbook, Association for Investment Management and Research, Charlottesville, NC.

Altman, E. I., Haldeman, R. G., and Narayanan, P. (1977) "Zeta Analysis: A New Model to Identify Bankruptcy Risk of Corporations," *The Journal of Banking and Finance*, 1, 29 - 54.

Bernstein, P. L. (1996) *Against the Gods: The Remarkable Story of Risk*, John Wiley and Sons, New York, NY.

Black, F. (1993) "Return and Beta, " *The Journal of Portfolio Management*, 45, 8 - 18.

Burmeister, E., Roll, R. and Ross, S. A. (1994) *A Practitioner's Guide to Arbitrage Pricing Theory*, The Research Foundation of The Institute of Chartered Financial Analysts, Charlottesville, VA.

Chichilnisky, G. (1996) "Markets with Endogenous Uncertainty: Theory and Policy," *Theory and Decision*, 41, 99 - 131.

Chichilnisky, G. and Heal, G. M. (1992) "Global Environmental Risks," *Journal of Economic Perspectives*, 7, 65 - 86.

Elton, J. and Gruber, M. J. (1995) "The Correlation Structure of Security Returns: Multi-index Models and Grouping Techniques," in *Modern Portfolio Theory and Investment Analysis*, 5th ed., John Wiley and Sons, New York, NY, pp. 160 - 180.

Fama, E. F. and French, K. (1992) "The Cross Section of Expected Stock Returns," *The Journal of Finance*, 42, 427 - 465.

GISP Committee (1998) *Global Investment Performance Standards*, Association for Investment Management and Research, Charlottesville, NC, February 6.

Gould, J. (1981) *The Mismeasure of Man*, W. W. Norton and Co., New York, NY.

Jensen, M. (1968) "The Performance of Mutual Funds in the Period 1945 - 1964," Journal of Finance, 23 (2), May, 389 - 416.

Lintner, J. (1965) "The Valuation of Risk Assets and the Selection of Risky Investments in Stock Portfolios and Capital Budgets," *Review of Economics and Statistics*, 47, 13 - 37.

Los, C. A. (1986a) "Collinearity Analysis of a Simple Money Demand Equation," Research Paper No. 8604, Federal Reserve Bank of New York, NY, March, 36 pages.

Los, C. A. (1989) "The Prejudices of Least Squares, Principal Components and Common Factor Schemes," *Computers & Mathematics With Applications*, 17 (8/9), 1269 - 1283.

Los, C. A. (1991) "A Scientific View of Economic Data Analysis," *Eastern Economic Journal*, 17, 61 - 71.

Los, C. A. (1994) "The Measurement of Complex Empirical Systems," in Accardi, L. (Ed.), *The Interpretation of Quantum Theory: Where Do We Stand?*, Instituto della Enciclopedia Italiana Fondata Da G. Treccani, Fordham University Press, United States of America, November, pp. 243 - 256.

Los, C. A. (1998/1999) "Risk Management Practices of Unit Trusts in Singapore," *The Journal of Performance Measurement*, **3** (2), Winter, 6 - 21.

Los, C. A. (1999a) "Galton's Error and the Under-Representation of Systematic Risk," *Journal of Banking and Finance*, **23** (12), November, 1793 - 1828.

Los, C. A. (1999b) "The 1998 Third Annual Survey of Risk Management Practices of Unit Trusts in Singapore," *The Journal of Performance Measurement*, **3** (4), Summer 1999, 15 - 34.

Malkiel, B. G. (1980) *A Random Walk Down Wall Street*, 5th ed., W. W. Norton & Co., New York, NY.

Ogden, R. T. (1997) *Essential Wavelets for Statistical Applications and Data Analysis*, Birkhäuser, Boston, MA.

Reilly, F. K. and Brown, K. C. (1997) *Investment Analysis and Portfolio Management*, The Dryden Press, New York, NY.

Ross, S. A. (1976) "Arbitrage Theory of Capital Asset Pricing," *Journal of Economic Theory*, **13**, 341 - 360.

SEC (1995) "Improving Descriptions of Risk by Mutual Funds and Other Investment Companies," CFR Parts 239, 270 and 274 [Release Nos. 33-7153; 34-35546; IC-20974; File No. S7-10-95]. Securities and Exchange Commission, New York, NY, March 29.

Sharpe, W.F. (1963) "A Simplified Model for Portfolio Analysis," *Management Science*, **9**, 277 - 293.

Sharpe, W. F. (1964) "Capital Asset Prices: a Theory of Market Equilibrium Under Conditions of Risk," *Journal of Finance*, **19**, 425 - 442.

Sharpe, W. F. (1966) "Mutual Fund Performance," *Journal of Business*, **39** (1), January, Supplement, 119 - 139.

Sinkhorn, R. (1993) "The Range of the Adjugate Map, *Mathematics Magazine*, **66**, 109 - 113.

Treynor, J. L. (1965) "How to Rate Management of Investment Funds," *Harvard Business Review*, **43** (1), January - February, 63 - 75.

chapter:8,page:1

Chapter 8
COMPLETE VALUATION AND DYNAMIC RISK THEORY

8.1 Introduction

In the previous Chapter, we discussed how to select a Markowitz'- mean - variance - optimal portfolio of assets and how to identify some of its inherent systematic risks. We used *inexact* historical data as inputs for the model identification. In contrast, in this Chapter we discuss *exact* theoretical models of speculative valuation of future investment outcomes, similar to the exact speculative DDM valuation of common shares (*Cf.* Chapter 3). Thus we first encounter the so-called *Complete Capital Market Pricing (CCMP)* of Arrow and Debreu. In the 1950s, Kenneth Arrow and Gerard Debreu showed how individuals and companies can eliminate their particular risk profile if there exist as many independent securities as there are future states of the world.[*]

Similar to the abstract axiomatic assumptions of Kolmogorov's (1933) *probability theory*,[†] Complete Capital Market Pricing theory is based on the following three assumptions:

(1) we have, a priori, *exhaustive* knowledge of all possible investment

---

[*]Kenneth J. Arrow, b.1921, developed the "impossibility theorem," which states that a perfect system of democratic choice-making is impossible in principle. He received the Nobel Memorial Prize in Economics jointly with Sir John R. Hicks in 1972. Gerard Debreu, also b.1921, was awarded the 1983 Nobel Memorial Prize in Economics for having incorporated new analytical methods into economic theory and for his rigorous reformulation of the theory of general equilibrium. Debreu constructed mathematical economic models for analyzing the equilibrium of free-market economies based on the independent actions of consumers and producers. His book *Theory of Value: An Axiomatic Analysis of Economic Equilibrium* (1959) is considered a modern classic of economics.

[†]Russian mathematician Andrei Nikolaevich Kolmogorov, 1903 - 1987, made fundamental contributions to mathematical logic, the theory of functions, differential equations, topology, and other branches of mathematics. He is most renowned, however, for his work in the field of probability. Kolmogorov published his first paper on probability in 1929. He then expanded it into his landmark book (Kolmogorov, 1933). His book presented the first full axiomatic treatment of the subject, and its rigorous mathematics is still in use. Kolmogorov's (1933) three axioms for the probability P of an event are:

I. $P(A) \geqslant 0$, the probability a an event A is *non-negative*;

II. When S is the universe of all events, $P(S) = 1$, the probability of a *certain* event equals unity;

III. If $AB = 0$ then $P(A + B) = P(A) + P(B)$, the probability of two *disjoint* events is *additive*.

outcomes, *i.e.*, we know the whole *universe* $\mathbb{S}$, or set of possible outcomes with perfect 100% certainty;

(2) all the uncertain investment outcomes are *probabilistic*, *i.e.*, they occur with a particular probability P, a fraction of unity, but, in contrast to Kolmogorov's axiomatic probability, this is not necessarily a positive probability, or a probability smaller than unity. We deal in CCMP with *pseudo-probabilities*, *i.e.*, fractions that only add up to unity.

(3) we have *perfect* knowledge of all the probabilities with which each investment outcome will occur, *i.e.*, the probabilities are *mutually exclusive, mutually independent,* or *disjoint,* and they are *additive.*

Notice that the first and third of these assumptions are the same as Kolmogorov's, but that the second assumption differs because of the assumed time symmetry in finance.[‡]

Of course, these *omniscient* or *complete* knowledge assumptions about the probability distribution of investment outcomes is rather unrealistic. Furthermore, uncertainty, or randomness, cannot be empirically corroborated, even though the , randomness, or irregularity can be measured. In fact, it has recently become very doubtful that a key probability assumption like disjointedness, or independence, can hold true in a finite reality (*Cf.* Kalman, 1994, 1995 and 1996).

However, this abstract and empirically uncorroborated CCMP theory, forms the foundation of modern option pricing theory and the accompanying financial engineering, as these disciplines developed in the 1970s -1980s. Therefore a current professional quantitative financial analyst (a "quant") must familiarize him/her self with CCMP theory[§]. Some examples of non-corroboration will be shown in the com-

---

[‡]It is hard to imagine what negative probability means in the empirical world, except that does occur mathematically in finance, because of the time symmetry implied in financial compounding (from the present to the future) and its inverse of financial discounting (from the present to the present. *Cf* Chapter 2).

[§]CCMP theory, and its application in the form of option pricing are, epistemologically speaking, teleological theories and therefore suspect in the eyes of empirical scientists. *Teleology* is the study of things or events in terms of their purposes or ends (Greek *telos* = purpose). For example, options are exactly priced from the ensemble of the assumed possible future outcomes of the random walk pricing processes of the underlying assets. From ancient times to the present, many philosophers and scientists have thought that various natural processes could be explained only in terms of the purposes that they were achieving, or in terms of the ends, or goals, that they were reaching for. However, in modern empirical science since Galileo Gallilei, we explain events by referring to their historical and current observations (data), not by referring to their purpose, as was done in pre-scientific times. Galileo Gallilei (1564 - 1642) was an Italian astronomer and mathematician, who was condemned and imprisoned by Pope Urban VIII in 1633 for his correct identification, from inexact telescopic observations, that the earth is a planet in the Copernican heliocentric planetary system. Only in 1992, 350 years after his death, Pope John Paul II acknowledged the error of the Catholic Church in condemning Gallilei's work. According to Gallilei and René Descartes (1596 - 1650), teleological purposes could neither be known nor discovered and empirical sensory evidence

ing Chapters on options. Indeed, mispricing. is endemic in the financial markets and market arbitrage can pay off handsomely.

We find that one of the reason for the profitability of market arbitrage is that markets are inefficient, *i.e.*, their pricing processes don't follow random walks, nor even martingales[¶]. Long term dependencies exist, the so called global dependencies, which cause important non-periodic cyclicities (Mandelbrot and Wallis, 1968) and differ from conventional serial dependencies. CCMP theory doesn't completely capture and price these systematic, and thus predictable, empirical covariance risks (*Cf.* Chapters 4, 6, and 7).

In the second half of this Chapter, we'll study Markov state transition theory, which is intimately related to CCMP, to extend our understanding of the systematic dynamics involved in securities markets pricing processes, which follow random walks, or at least martingales, when they are efficient, according to the Efficient Market Hypothesis (EMH) of Fama (1970). Only when a securities market process is efficient, and follows a martingale, is it a suitable underlying spot market for the derivatives market. When a securities market is inefficient and follows a serially dependent Markov process, technical trading, based on "trading rules", is possible and profitable. Then there exists "predictability" in the pricing process and thus arbitrage opportunities. Thus before one engages in technical trading, it's useful to test at least if the underlying pricing process is Markov.

A second area where Markov transition theory is implemented is in *credit migration*. Credit migration is the dynamic process of the up-and downgrading of credit quality over time. Since the credit quality of bonds, for example, is one of the discrete variables in the bond pricing model (*Cf.* Chapter 3), this credit migration process is an important determinant of securities pricing. Credit migration is observably an inefficient Markov process. Thus it contains predictability and considerable opportunities for arbitrage. Since the current Southeast Asian region has been experiencing considerable credit problems, in particular in its banking system, the process of the

---

combined with mathematical logic should not be subjectively interpreted. By systematic doubt and empirical data based research, scientists have progressively removed teleological inquiry from one branch of the study of nature after another. There is no longer doubt that teleological explanation is unnecessary, or even misleading, to account for the behavior of living, conscious beings. The recently identified model of the human genome, explaining the development of the DNA helix and the chemical development of the brain in a human embryo, are modern day examples of empirical research thought to be impossible less than half a century ago. I'm sure that even option pricing will eventually become empirically explained, instead of teleologically, as it still is. Eventually, the teleological tradition of (Bayesian) probability theory will yield to factual empirical observation and measurement. However, some financial scholars beg to differ, like Price (1996) at the Maharishi University, who still thinks that the mathematics of option theory is not optional and that it is logically necessary.

[¶]For the sequence $\{X(t) : t = 1, 2, ...\}$, if

$$E\{X(t+1) \mid X(1), X(2), ..., X(t)\} = X(t)$$

then the sequence$\{X(t)\}$ is called a martingale.

downgrading and, occasionally, upgrading of credit, has considerably gained in financial, and political, importance, as it provides opportunities for a profitable trade in,
for example, nonperforming bank loans.

8.2   Expected Return and Risk

When there is risk, there is, per definition, more than one payoff possible on an
investment, depending on the state of the market. Therefore let's look at the following
payoff example. Suppose we encounter a *one-period* investment opportunity and the
investor has a choice between investing $100,000 in a risk-free ($\sigma_c = 0$) Treasury bill
to receive a $y_c = 6\%$ return of $6,000 with certainty, and a risky ($\sigma_a > 0$) investment
with three possible *payoffs*. For this risky investment it is *expected* with a *priori*
known probability $p_1 = 0.5$ that the *a priori* known return will be $\hat{y}_1 = 40\%$ or
$40,000, with a probability $p_2 = 0.3$ that the *a priori* known return will be $\hat{y}_2 = 10\%$
or $10,000, and with $p_3 = 0.2$ that the *a priori* known return will be $\hat{y}_3 = -20\%$, or
$-$20,000. Thus, in matrix notation, the 1×3 row row vector $\hat{\mathbf{y}}'$ of three disjoint *a
priori* payoff states is:

$$\begin{aligned} \hat{\mathbf{y}}' &= \begin{bmatrix} \hat{y}_1 & \hat{y}_2 & \hat{y}_3 \end{bmatrix} \\ &= \begin{bmatrix} 0.40 & 0.10 & -0.20 \end{bmatrix} \end{aligned} \tag{8.1}$$

The 3×1 column vector $\mathbf{p}$ is the vector of corresponding *a priori* known state probabilities:

$$\begin{aligned} \mathbf{p} &= \begin{bmatrix} p_1 \\ p_2 \\ p_3 \end{bmatrix} \\ &= \Phi \iota_3 \\ &= \begin{bmatrix} p_1 & 0 & 0 \\ 0 & p_2 & 0 \\ 0 & 0 & p_3 \end{bmatrix} \begin{bmatrix} 1 \\ 1 \\ 1 \end{bmatrix} \\ &= \begin{bmatrix} 0.5 & 0 & 0 \\ 0 & 0.3 & 0 \\ 0 & 0 & 0.2 \end{bmatrix} \begin{bmatrix} 1 \\ 1 \\ 1 \end{bmatrix} \\ &= \begin{bmatrix} 0.5 \\ 0.3 \\ 0.2 \end{bmatrix} \end{aligned} \tag{8.2}$$

and the matrix

$$\Phi = \begin{bmatrix} p_1 & 0 & 0 \\ 0 & p_2 & 0 \\ 0 & 0 & p_3 \end{bmatrix} \tag{8.3}$$

is the diagonal matrix ($\Phi = \Phi'$) with the *a priori* known probabilities on the diagonal axis. According to Kolmogorov's unit additivity constraint, these positive probabilities must add up to unity

$$
\begin{aligned}
\mathbf{p}'\iota_3 &= \iota_3'\Phi\iota_3 \\
&= \begin{bmatrix} 1 & 1 & 1 \end{bmatrix} \begin{bmatrix} p_1 & 0 & 0 \\ 0 & p_2 & 0 \\ 0 & 0 & p_3 \end{bmatrix} \begin{bmatrix} 1 \\ 1 \\ 1 \end{bmatrix} \qquad (8.4) \\
&= \sum_{i=1}^{3} p_i \\
&= 1 \qquad\qquad\qquad\qquad\qquad\qquad (8.5)
\end{aligned}
$$

The *expected return* of the risky investment is the weighted return:

$$
\begin{aligned}
\overline{y}_p = \mathbf{p}'\widehat{\mathbf{y}} \,(&= \iota_3'\Phi\widehat{\mathbf{y}} = \widehat{\mathbf{y}}\Phi\iota_3 = \widehat{\mathbf{y}}'\mathbf{p}) \\
&= \begin{bmatrix} p_1 & p_2 & p_2 \end{bmatrix} \begin{bmatrix} \widehat{y}_1 \\ \widehat{y}_2 \\ \widehat{y}_3 \end{bmatrix} \\
&= p_1\widehat{y}_1 + p_2\widehat{y}_2 + p_3\widehat{y}_3 \\
&= 0.5 \times 0.4 + 0.3 \times 0.1 + 0.2 \times -0.2 \\
&= 0.19 \qquad\qquad\qquad\qquad\qquad\qquad (8.6)
\end{aligned}
$$

Remark 57 *Note that the probability weights function like portfolio allocation weights. The difference is that allocation weights are under the control of the portfolio manager, while a priori known probabilities are "allocation weights" given by the Deus Ex Machina (e.g., Adam Smith's[||] Invisible Hand).*

[||]Often called the Founder of Modern Economics, Adam Smith (1723 - 1790), was a wide-ranging social philosopher and economist whose masterwork, *An Inquiry into the Nature and Causes of the Wealth of Nations* (1776), is one of the most influential studies of Western civilization. Smith was well versed in science and history. Smith's major (*laissez-faire*) thesis in *The Wealth of Nations* was that, except for limited functions (defense, justice, certain public works), the state should refrain from interfering with the economic life of a nation. He suggested that businessmen seeking their own interest are led "as if by an invisible hand" to promote the well-being of society. He sharply criticized the mercantilist writers of his day, who advocated state intervention in international trade to achieve an inflow of foreign treasure. Smith claimed that mercantilism confused money and wealth, ignoring the fact that the only real purpose of money is to purchase goods and services. He maintained that free trade increased the wealth of nations, while restrictions on trade diminished their wealth.

Now, $\widehat{\mathbf{x}}$ is the 3×1 column vector of the deviations from the mean of the probability weighted expected return $\overline{y_p}$:

$$
\begin{aligned}
\widehat{\mathbf{x}} &= \begin{bmatrix} \widehat{x}_1 \\ \widehat{x}_2 \\ \widehat{x}_3 \end{bmatrix} \\
&= \widehat{\mathbf{y}} - \iota_3 \overline{y_p} \\
&= \begin{bmatrix} 0.40 \\ 0.10 \\ -0.20 \end{bmatrix} - \begin{bmatrix} 1 \\ 1 \\ 1 \end{bmatrix} 0.19 \\
&= \begin{bmatrix} 0.21 \\ -0.09 \\ -0.39 \end{bmatrix}
\end{aligned}
\tag{8.7}
$$

A probability weighted deviation from the mean is:

$$
\begin{aligned}
\Phi \widehat{\mathbf{x}} &= \begin{bmatrix} p_1 & 0 & 0 \\ 0 & p_2 & 0 \\ 0 & 0 & p_3 \end{bmatrix} \begin{bmatrix} \widehat{x}_1 \\ \widehat{x}_2 \\ \widehat{x}_3 \end{bmatrix} \\
&= \begin{bmatrix} 0.5 & 0 & 0 \\ 0 & 0.3 & 0 \\ 0 & 0 & 0.2 \end{bmatrix} \begin{bmatrix} 0.21 \\ -0.09 \\ -0.39 \end{bmatrix} \\
&= \begin{bmatrix} .105 \\ -.027 \\ -.078 \end{bmatrix}
\end{aligned}
\tag{8.8}
$$

Remark 58 *Indeed, the sum of the probability weighted deviations from the mean equals zero:*

$$
\iota_3' \Phi \widehat{\mathbf{x}} = \mathbf{p}' \widehat{\mathbf{x}}
\tag{8.9}
$$

$$
= \iota_3' \Phi \left(\widehat{\mathbf{y}} - \iota_3 \overline{y_p} \right)
\tag{8.10}
$$

$$
= \begin{bmatrix} 1 & 1 & 1 \end{bmatrix} \begin{bmatrix} 0.5 & 0 & 0 \\ 0 & 0.3 & 0 \\ 0 & 0 & 0.2 \end{bmatrix} \begin{bmatrix} 0.21 \\ -0.09 \\ -0.39 \end{bmatrix}
$$

$$
= \iota_3' \Phi \widehat{\mathbf{y}} - \iota_3' \Phi \iota_3 \overline{y_p}
$$

$$
= \overline{y_p} - 1.\overline{y_p}
$$

$$
= 0
\tag{8.11}
$$

The probability weighted, or *expected variance* of the risky investment's return is *correctly* computed as the matrix product of the probability weighted deviations from the probability weighted mean:

$$
\begin{aligned}
\sigma_{\widetilde{y}\widetilde{y}} &= \widehat{\mathbf{x}}'\Phi'\Phi\widehat{\mathbf{x}} \\
&= \widehat{\mathbf{x}}'\Phi^2\widehat{\mathbf{x}} \quad\quad\quad\quad\quad\quad\quad\quad\quad\quad\quad\quad (8.12) \\
&= \begin{bmatrix} \widehat{x}_1 & \widehat{x}_2 & \widehat{x}_3 \end{bmatrix}
\begin{bmatrix} p_1^2 & 0 & 0 \\ 0 & p_2^2 & 0 \\ 0 & 0 & p_3^2 \end{bmatrix}
\begin{bmatrix} \widehat{x}_1 \\ \widehat{x}_2 \\ \widehat{x}_3 \end{bmatrix} \\
&= \begin{bmatrix} p_1^2\widehat{x}_1^2 & 0 & 0 \\ 0 & p_2^2\widehat{x}_2^2 & 0 \\ 0 & 0 & p_3^2\widehat{x}_3^2 \end{bmatrix} \\
&= p_1^2\widehat{x}_1^2 + p_2^2\widehat{x}_1^2 + p_3^2\widehat{x}_3^2 \\
&= 0.5^2 \times (0.4 - 0.19)^2 + 0.3^2 \times (0.1 - 0.19)^2 + 0.2^2 \times (-0.2 - 0.19)^2 (8.13) \\
&= 1.783\,8 \times 10^{-2} \quad\quad\quad\quad\quad\quad\quad\quad\quad\quad (8.14)
\end{aligned}
$$

Thus the standard deviation of the expected risky portfolio is

$$
\begin{aligned}
\sqrt{\sigma_{\widetilde{y}\widetilde{y}}} &= \sqrt{1.783\,8 \times 10^{-2}} \quad\quad\quad\quad (8.15) \\
&= 0.133\,56 \quad\quad\quad\quad\quad\quad (8.16) \\
&= 13.356\% \quad\quad\quad\quad\quad\quad (8.17)
\end{aligned}
$$

or, in percentage of the investment capital, $13,356, which is smaller than the expected profit of 19% or $19,000. Still, this investment opportunity is clearly risky. The 100% secure investment delivers 6% or $6,000 with certainty. Thus the *expected risk premium* of $13.356\% - 6\% = 7.356\%$, or $7,356 compensates for $13,000, or one standard deviation of uncertainty, as compensation for investing $100,000 in the risky investment.

Remark 59 *Bodie, Kane and Marcus (1993), p. 151, compute*

$$
\sigma_{\widetilde{y}\widetilde{y}} = \widehat{\mathbf{x}}'\Phi\widehat{\mathbf{x}} \quad\quad (8.18)
$$

$$
= \begin{bmatrix} \widehat{x}_1 & \widehat{x}_2 & \widehat{x}_3 \end{bmatrix}
\begin{bmatrix} p_1 & 0 & 0 \\ 0 & p_2 & 0 \\ 0 & 0 & p_3 \end{bmatrix}
\begin{bmatrix} \widehat{x}_1 \\ \widehat{x}_2 \\ \widehat{x}_3 \end{bmatrix}
$$

$$
= p_1\widehat{x}_1^2 + p_2\widehat{x}_1^2 + p_3\widehat{x}_3^3
$$

$$
= 0.5 \times (0.4 - 0.19)^2 + 0.3 \times (0.1 - 0.19)^2 + 0.2 \times (-0.2 - 0.19)^2
$$

$$
= 0.549 \quad\quad (8.19)
$$

Their too high expected risk, is mathematically incorrect, since their computation does not take account of the squaring of the "probability weights."

Remark 60 *We call the diagonality assumption, the Frisch assumption of CCMP theory. This designation follows Ragnar Frisch's (1934) seminal covariance analysis,* *in which he presumed such a diagonal covariance matrix. The Frisch presumption is also found in econometrics, where it plays a role in the modeling of the weighted residuals and the computation of the Generalized Least Squares (GLS) projection.***

8.3 Complete Capital Market Pricing

This simple example of *expected* portfolio returns and variances can be extended to all possible expected investment opportunities by introducing the abstract concept of a primitive security. A *state-i primitive security* pays \$1 if state i occurs with probability p_i and nothing if any other state occurs. Examples of states of the market are the following: expected state 1 of the market could be that the economy is expected to exhibit GDP growth of 10% a year, while state 2 could be GDP growth of 3% a year and state 3 GDP growth of -5%.

A primitive security is thus like a lottery ticket, with an all or nothing payout. The states are *exhaustive* and *mutually exclusive*, *i.e.*, they are *complete*. They comprise all possible states expected and that these states don't overlap. *In theoria*, there can be assumed an *infinite number of states of the market*, thus an infinite number of end-of-period payoff states for a risky asset, $n \to \infty$, and a corresponding infinite number of primitive securities. But since empirical markets are finite, we usually expect only a finite number of $n < \infty$ states of the market.

This abstract concept of a primitive security allows the exact decomposition of market securities into portfolios of primitive securities, because no covariances are expected to exist between them. They are *additive* and *disjoint*. *In abstracto*, because of the exact decomposition implied by the completeness assumptions, every market security may be considered an exact linear combination, or , of various primitive securities. Thus, according to CCMP theory, the observed empirical covariances between the returns of the empirical market securities result from only the linear combinations of these presumed primitive securities and not from any possible inexactness or noise resulting from market imperfections. In CCMP theory, the market data covariance matrix of market RoRs is only systematic: $\Sigma = \widehat{\Sigma}$. CCMP theory assumes that the empirical markets are truly complete and unique, i.e. exact. It assumes that there is no epistemic uncertainty and thus the determinant of the data covariance matrix $|\Sigma| = |\widehat{\Sigma}| = 0$.[††]

Remark 61 *In the exact analysis of the yield curve, we decomposed the exact normal bond into a whole series of zero-coupon bonds, to create the term structure (Cf. Chapters 3 and 13). Thus the terms of the term structure are strictly independent.*

**Our Complete Least Squares (CLS) projections should not be confused with the Generalized Least Squares (GLS) projection. There is a world of difference between the two concepts (*Cf.* Los, 1989a). The term "Complete " in CLS means: "from all directions", and is multi-lateral. The GLS projection is a unilateral projection.

[††]Chapter 14 will empirically demonstrate that this assumption of CCMP is empirically not true, since it can be demonstrated that, empirically, $\Sigma \neq \widehat{\Sigma}$ or, equivalently, that $|\Sigma| > 0$.

*Thus the theoretical term structure has a segmented "bucket" structure. The logarithmic transformation of the theoretical term structure is an exact linear combination of these independent, segmented buckets. But, in empirio, it is found that the neighboring zero-coupon rates actually show substantial unsystematic covariance. The zero-coupon "buckets" are thus empirically not independent, but show uncertain collinearity. This is the problem of the model identification (and **not** realization) of the empirical term structure dynamics. This scientific problem has recently produced an increased output in the theoretical financial literature, but it is still empirically uncorroborated. Many advanced fixed-income securities dealers, in particular on Wall Street, who are interested in fixed-income risk management based on the covariant term structure theory, are now computing term structure covariance matrices based on empirical observations, trying to account for this epistemic uncertainty, or market inefficiency, by liquidity premiums.*

To emphasize, the heroic assumptions underlying the CCMP theory are that the payoff states are *complete*, i.e., *mutually exclusive and exhaustive*. Thus their uncertain outcome is assumed to be *probabilistic* according to Kolmogorov's (1933) axiomatic definition. Payoff states are *mutually exclusive* when they are independent and don't show expected covariance, so that their expected relative occurrence, or probabilities, are independent and the expected covariance matrix is diagonal. payoff states are *exhaustive* when their probabilities sum up to unity, $\sum_{i=1}^{\infty} p_i = 1$. This assertion assumes that it is possible to have *perfect knowledge* of all the possible payoff states that may occur, like in the case of a roulette wheel, a card game, or a lottery ticket, *i.e.*, like casino games. The financial markets don't sufficiently recognize that **only** under these abstract, omniscient and scientifically uncorroborated assumptions, one can price speculative securities, like stocks and options, using the CCMP.

Ironically, would the CCMP theory be scientifically corroborated, the financial markets would be true casinos and their invariant odds could be easily established by model realization, *i.e.*, via the model realization $A\Sigma = A\widehat{\Sigma} = 0$, by anybody and the markets would cease to function! But thus far nobody has succeeded to establish such immutable odds, say, in the stock markets in New York, Tokyo, Hong Kong, Singapore, Frankfurt, or London. Therefore, the research question if empirical capital markets actually function as casinos is a research hypothesis, which can be empirically falsified. It is a scientific identification problem involving model identification, *i.e.* both the decomposition of the data covariance matrix $\Sigma = \widehat{\Sigma} + \widetilde{\Sigma}$ *and* the model realization $A\widehat{\Sigma} = 0$. The empirical evidence thus far gathered points to falsification: the empirical financial markets are not casinos, because they contain considerable epistemic uncertainty, *i.e.*, inexactness, and thus they are incomplete.[‡‡]. Incomplete

---

[‡‡]As in Chapter 5. Some related research we recently performed at the Nanyang Technological University in Singapore is:

[i] to test if the transaction pricing in the Asian stock and FX markets follow random walks, *i.e.*, if the changes in prices are independent stationary, and random. Such Markov tests were originally

financial markets are inefficient and they harbor opportunities for profitable arbitrage trading.

8.4   Risk - Neutral Pricing

8.4.1   Single Price Law of Efficient Markets

Following the CCMP theory, an investor's opportunity set of *state-contingent portfolio payoffs* consists of linear combinations of the state-contingent primitive security payoffs, under two assumptions. First, we assume that the capital market is *perfect* (*e.g.*, short selling is allowed and the market is perfectly liquid). This means that there is *no opportunity for arbitrage*. In other words, the market is assumed to be in *perfect equilibrium* and any two securities or portfolios with the same state-contingent payoff vectors must be priced identically. This no-arbitrage equilibrium condition is known as the **Single Price Law of Efficient Markets**.

Second, when the number of unique linearly independent securities n equals the total number of alternative future payoff states T, the market is said to be *complete* $n = T$. All possible future states are priced by the values of the so-called primitive securities. Let the $n \times 1$ vector π_0 of the *current values of primitive securities* be

$$
\begin{aligned}
\pi_0 \; &= \; \begin{bmatrix} \pi_{01} \\ \pi_{02} \\ \ldots \\ \pi_{0n} \end{bmatrix} \\[4pt]
&= \; \left(\frac{1}{1+r} \right) \mathbf{p} \\[4pt]
&= \; \left(\frac{1}{1+r} \right) \Phi \iota_n
\end{aligned} \tag{8.20}
$$

where π_0 = vector of current values of state-i primitive securities = the one-period discounted values of the vector of future probabilities $\mathbf{p}$ that states $i, i = 1, 2, ..., n$ are expected to occur. A state-i primitive security pays \$1 in state i and \$0 in all other states. Let $\widehat{\mathbf{y}}$ be the matrix containing the n expected payoff vectors of the n securities, where

$$
\widehat{\mathbf{y}}_i' = \begin{bmatrix} \widehat{y}_{i1} & \widehat{y}_{i2} & \cdots & \widehat{y}_{iT} \end{bmatrix} \tag{8.21}
$$

developed to study the information processing of nervous systems (Cf. Sherry, 1992). The financial markets can be viewed as the nervous system of the capitalist market system. The preliminary results in Los (1999, 2000) falsify all three fundamental assumptions.

[ii] if the "up and down ticks" of a financial market form a truly binomial distribution, following the research lead by Kalman (1996). The results there are also negative for the financial markets, which show long term dependence with Hurst exponents often close to 0.3 for developed FX markets, indicating antipersistence, and close to 0.65 for developed stock markets, indicating persistence (Cf. similar results collected in Peters, 1994).

is the *expected payoff vector* of security i. Then, for $T = n$, the square *state contingent payoff matrix*

$$\hat{\mathbf{y}}' = \begin{bmatrix} \hat{\mathbf{y}}_1' \\ \hat{\mathbf{y}}_2' \\ \cdots \\ \hat{\mathbf{y}}_n' \end{bmatrix}$$

$$= [\hat{y}_{it}]$$

$$= \begin{bmatrix} \hat{y}_{11} & \hat{y}_{12} & \cdots & \hat{y}_{1T} \\ \hat{y}_{21} & \hat{y}_{22} & \cdots & \hat{y}_{2T} \\ \cdots & \cdots & \cdots & \cdots \\ \hat{y}_{n1} & \hat{y}_{n2} & \cdots & \hat{y}_{nT} \end{bmatrix}$$

$$= \begin{bmatrix} \hat{y}_{11} & \hat{y}_{12} & \cdots & \hat{y}_{1n} \\ \hat{y}_{21} & \hat{y}_{22} & \cdots & \hat{y}_{2n} \\ \cdots & \cdots & \cdots & \cdots \\ \hat{y}_{n1} & \hat{y}_{n2} & \cdots & \hat{y}_{nn} \end{bmatrix} \qquad (8.22)$$

The $n \times n = T \times T$ expected payoff ("expected observation") matrix $\hat{\mathbf{y}}'$ is generically *asymmetric*. But, because of the assumed *completeness of the market, i.e.,* (i) the assumption of linearly independence of its payoff vector rows (= independent securities) and (ii) the assumption of linearly independence of its state columns (= independence of the states), $\hat{\mathbf{y}}'$ is a square positive definite matrix, $|\hat{\mathbf{y}}'| > 0$, and thus invertible: $(\hat{\mathbf{y}}')^{-1}$ exists.

Remark 62 *When $n = T$ and $|\hat{\mathbf{y}}'| > 0$, we have complete markets and we can apply the exact realization analysis of this Chapter and the following Chapters 9, 10, 12 and 13, as follows: $\mathbf{p}'\hat{\mathbf{y}} = \overline{\mathbf{y}}_p$, where $\overline{\mathbf{y}}_p$ is an $n \times 1$ vector. Or, by taking deviations from the means, we have $\mathbf{p}'\hat{\mathbf{x}} = \mathbf{A}\hat{\mathbf{x}} = \mathbf{0}$, an $n \times 1$ vector of zeros. But, when $T > n$, we have incomplete markets and $\hat{\mathbf{x}}'\hat{\mathbf{x}} = \hat{\Sigma} \neq \Sigma = \mathbf{x}'\mathbf{x}$ and $|\Sigma| = |\mathbf{x}'\mathbf{x}| > 0$, so that the information matrix Σ^{-1} exists, and we must apply inexact identification analysis (as in Chapters 4, 5, and 7), with $\Sigma = \hat{\Sigma} + \tilde{\Sigma}$ and $\mathbf{A}\hat{\mathbf{x}} = \mathbf{0}$.*

The *vector of market equilibrium prices* of the n securities is

$$\mathbf{P}_0 = \begin{bmatrix} P_{1,0} \\ P_{2,0} \\ \cdots \\ P_{n,0} \end{bmatrix} \qquad (8.23)$$

The current equilibrium market prices $\mathbf{P}_0$ are related to the present values of the primitive states π_0 (or the "discounted odds") and the expected payoff vectors $\hat{\mathbf{y}}_i'$ as follows:

$$\mathbf{P}_0 = \hat{\mathbf{y}}'\pi_0 \qquad (8.24)$$

Next, we can compute the *arbitrage-free equilibrium values* of the state-i primitive securities π_0 ($=$ "the current prices of lottery tickets in i future lotteries") by inverting this relationship:

$$\pi_0 = (\widehat{\mathbf{y}}')^{-1} \mathbf{P}_0 \qquad (8.25)$$

Thus the ith row of the inverted payoff matrix, $(\widehat{\mathbf{y}}')^{-1}$, provides us a recipe how to retrieve the values of the primitive securities π_0 from the current prices of n market securities, under the assumption of perfect, complete markets. The elements of each row of the $(\widehat{\mathbf{y}}')^{-1}$ matrix will tell us exactly how many units of each of the n market securities to hold long or short to create the primitive securities.

Example 63 *Suppose there are $n = 3$ market securities $\mathbf{P}_0$ and $n = 3$ states for the expected payoffs, then the three market securities prices are related to the values of the $n = 3$ primitive securities π_0 via the matrix of expected payoffs $\widehat{\mathbf{y}}'$, as follows*

$$\mathbf{P}_0 = \begin{bmatrix} P_{1,0} \\ P_{2,0} \\ P_{3,0} \end{bmatrix}$$

$$= \begin{bmatrix} \widehat{y}_{11} & \widehat{y}_{12} & \widehat{y}_{13} \\ \widehat{y}_{21} & \widehat{y}_{22} & \widehat{y}_{23} \\ \widehat{y}_{31} & \widehat{y}_{32} & \widehat{y}_{33} \end{bmatrix} \begin{bmatrix} \pi_{01} \\ \pi_{02} \\ \pi_{03} \end{bmatrix}$$

$$= \begin{bmatrix} \widehat{y}_{11}\pi_{01} + \widehat{y}_{12}\pi_{02} + \widehat{y}_{13}\pi_{03} \\ \widehat{y}_{21}\pi_{01} + \widehat{y}_{22}\pi_{02} + \widehat{y}_{23}\pi_{03} \\ \widehat{y}_{31}\pi_{01} + \widehat{y}_{32}\pi_{02} + \widehat{y}_{33}\pi_{03} \end{bmatrix}$$

$$= \widehat{\mathbf{y}}' \pi_0 \qquad (8.26)$$

This equation makes clear that the equilibrium values of the current market prices equal the value - weighted, expected payoffs.

Arbitrage-Free Equilibrium

When the current market prices would be lower than the respective value weighted expected payoffs, there would be a market disequilibrium. The market securities would be undervalued and the ensuing arbitrage buying of these securities would drive their current prices up to restore equilibrium. *Vice versa*, when the current market prices would be higher than the value weighted expected payoffs, the market securities would be overvalued. The ensuing arbitrage selling of these securities would drive their prices down and restore equilibrium. Thus the equality $\mathbf{P}_0 = \widehat{\mathbf{y}}' \pi_0$ is an *arbitrage-free equilibrium equality*.

With this fundamental pricing information, which provides the "present value of the future odds", we can now price any market security, existing or to be engineered.

The payoff of any financial asset can be duplicated by the portfolio of primitive securities that consists of w_j, $j = 1, 2, ..., n$, units of state-j primitive securities.

The complete term structure of the U.S. Treasury yield curve is often assumed to be truly exact and independent (perfectly segmented), so that one can, in principle, price any fundamental security (including stocks) from this term structure. The market volatility, or market risk, part of each maturity's value is then priced by independent options, each with their own corresponding maturity. As we will see in Chapter 9, options can be viewed as simple portfolios of one risky and one risk-free asset.

Risk-Neutrality

Risk-neutrality requires that the "sum of the discounted future odds " equals the discount factor, or

$$
\iota'_n \pi_0 = \left(\frac{1}{1+r} \right) \iota'_n \Phi \iota_n
$$

$$
= \left(\frac{1}{1+r} \right) \leq 1, \text{ a scalar} \tag{8.27}
$$

where r is the risk-free interest rate of a T-bill, say, with the same maturity as the investment horizon of the investor. Another way of phrasing this is that the future pseudo-probabilities, which are the future odds, have to add up to unity, or

$$
(1+r)\iota'_n \pi_0 = \iota'_n \Phi \iota_n
$$
$$
= \iota'_n \mathbf{p}
$$
$$
= 1 \tag{8.28}
$$

Accounting Identity

The value of a *portfolio of market securities* is

$$
P_p = \mathbf{w}' \mathbf{P}_0 \tag{8.29}
$$

and the portfolio allocation weights must add up to unity, according to the *accounting identity*

$$
\mathbf{w}' \iota_n = 1 \tag{8.30}
$$

One talks about "maturity buckets," as if these segments of the term structure don't commute with each other. However, rational expectations theory, which is based on the single price law of valuation, clearly argues against such a perfectly, segmented term structure. After all, these "maturity buckets " communicate continuously with each other via market arbitrage! Thus, there exist exact relationships, when the arbitrage is perfect, but inexact relationships when it is imperfect, *e.g.*, because of commission fees. Arguing for independent term structure segments is, first, the observation that the intra-segment cash flows, within each maturity bucket, are likely to be much larger than the inter-segment, communicating cash flows; second, the degrees of risk and uncertainty of the various term structure segments are different.

8.4.2   Arbitrage-Free Securities Design

How can we design new securities using this fundamental pricing mechanism? Suppose we want to create a portfolio with n market securities, with given current market prices $\mathbf{P}_0$, with the following desired payoff vector:

$$\widehat{\mathbf{z}}' = \begin{bmatrix} \widehat{z}_1 & \widehat{z}_2 & \dots & \widehat{z}_n \end{bmatrix} \tag{8.31}$$

which gives the desired payoffs depending on the n various states of the market. We create a new portfolio with portfolio allocations

$$\mathbf{w}' = \begin{bmatrix} w_1 & w_2 & \dots & w_n \end{bmatrix} \tag{8.32}$$

that consists of w_i, $i = 1, 2, \dots n$ units of each security i for the given $n \times n$ expected payoff matrix $\widehat{\mathbf{y}}'$ and desired payoff $\widehat{\mathbf{z}}'$ from

$$\mathbf{w}'\widehat{\mathbf{y}}' = \widehat{\mathbf{z}}' \tag{8.33}$$

so that the payoff of the portfolio in state 1 will be given by

$$\mathbf{w}'\widehat{\mathbf{y}}_1 = \widehat{z}_1, \text{ a scalar} \tag{8.34}$$

where $\widehat{\mathbf{y}}_1$ is the first column of the expected payoff matrix $\widehat{\mathbf{y}}'$. In state 2, the payoff will be:

$$\mathbf{u}'\widehat{\mathbf{x}}_2 = \widehat{z}_2, \text{ a scalar} \tag{8.35}$$

where $\mathbf{y}_2$ is the second column of the expected payoff matrix $\widehat{\mathbf{y}}'$, and so on. Thus, we find for the whole portfolio allocation vector:

$$\mathbf{w}' = \widehat{\mathbf{z}}'(\widehat{\mathbf{y}}')^{-1} \tag{8.36}$$

It is easy to check that this transformation leads to the desired payoff, since the currently observed market prices $\mathbf{P}_0$ give the portfolio value

$$\begin{aligned} P_p &= \mathbf{w}'\mathbf{P}_0 \\ &= \widehat{\mathbf{z}}'(\widehat{\mathbf{y}}')^{-1}\mathbf{P}_0 \\ &= \widehat{\mathbf{z}}'\boldsymbol{\pi} \end{aligned} \tag{8.37}$$

i.e., the value of the desired payout equals the cost of the purchase of the portfolio

$$\widehat{\mathbf{z}}'\boldsymbol{\pi} = \mathbf{w}'\mathbf{P}_0 \tag{8.38}$$

so that there is no further opportunity for an arbitrage profit. Notice that elements of the currently desired payoff vector $\widehat{\mathbf{z}}'$ can be negative, zero or positive payoffs, and also elements of the allocation vector $\mathbf{w}'$ can be negative (short), zero (neutral) or positive (long) allocations. We will implement this CCMP theory in Chapter 9 to binomially price options and in Chapter 10 to price options via the Black - Scholes formula.

8.5 Markov State Transition Theory

8.5.1 Exact Markov Dynamics

In this section we introduce the theory of finite Markov state transition dynamics (*Cf.* Graham, 1987, Chapter 6). An exact finite *Markov chain* is a $n \times 1$ vector of n state valuations $\boldsymbol{\pi}$, which evolves in discrete time periods as follows:

$$\boldsymbol{\pi}(t) = \mathbf{A}(t)\boldsymbol{\pi}(t-1) \tag{8.39}$$

where $\mathbf{A}(t)$ is the time dependent $n \times n$ *state transition matrix* at time t. Notice that the n states at time t are only directly dependent on the states at time $t-1$. A *homogeneous* Markov chain has a time independent (constant) state transition matrix

$$\boldsymbol{\pi}(t) = \mathbf{A}\boldsymbol{\pi}(t-1) \tag{8.40}$$

where the $n \times n$ matrix $\mathbf{A} = [a_{ij}]$, with $i, j = 1, 2, ..., n$. For a homogeneous Markov chain

$$\begin{aligned}
\boldsymbol{\pi}(t) &= \mathbf{A}\boldsymbol{\pi}(t-1) \\
&= \mathbf{A}^2\boldsymbol{\pi}(t-2) \\
&= \mathbf{A}^3\boldsymbol{\pi}(t-3) \\
&= ... \\
&= \mathbf{A}^t\boldsymbol{\pi}(0)
\end{aligned} \tag{8.41}$$

Example 64 *This is an example of how to compute the value of migrating credit, which is of particular importance in markets of distressed debt and emerging markets debt. Suppose we have one risky market security, e.g., a rated corporate bond P_0, which can be in three different payoff states of grade quality - excellent, good and bad -, but this time we assume that the valuation of the payoff states of this security evolves over time. Thus the present value of this bond at time t is*

$$\begin{aligned}
P_0(t) &= \widehat{\mathbf{y}}'\boldsymbol{\pi}(t) \\
&= \boldsymbol{\pi}(t)'\widehat{\mathbf{y}} \\
&= \widehat{y}_1\pi_1(t) + \widehat{y}_2\pi_2(t) + \widehat{y}_3\pi_3(t)
\end{aligned} \tag{8.42}$$

Here the 3×1 vector $\boldsymbol{\pi}(t)$ provides the "one-period odds," or present values of the bond's quality states. These values change over time. Thus the value of the bond evolves over time too, even though the contracted payoff vector $\widehat{\mathbf{y}}$ remains unchanged:

$$\begin{aligned}
P_{1,0}(t) &= \widehat{\mathbf{y}}'\boldsymbol{\pi}(t) \\
&= \widehat{\mathbf{y}}'\mathbf{A}(t)\boldsymbol{\pi}(t-1) \\
&= .... \\
&= \widehat{\mathbf{y}}'\mathbf{A}^t\boldsymbol{\pi}(0)
\end{aligned} \tag{8.43}$$

The exact contracted payoff vector $\hat{\mathbf{y}}$ of a rated corporate bond consist of the regular coupon (cash) payments plus the principal (cash) payment at maturity. But the odds vector $\boldsymbol{\pi}(t)$ provides a time dependent valuation of these contracted cash flow payments, according to the rating of the bond, which changes over time. The default payoff vector depends on a particular identification from historically observed, uncertain recovery rates.

8.5.2 Limiting Markov Chain Distribution

Often one would like to know if and how such a Markov process converges. A matrix $\mathbf{A}$ is called *row stochastic*, if its elements are such that

$$a_{ij} \geqslant 0, \; i, j = 1, 2, ..., n, \text{ and} \tag{8.44}$$

$$\sum_{j=1}^{n} a_{ij} = 1, \; i - 1, 2, ..., n \tag{8.45}$$

i.e., the rows of A form stochastic "distributions." A matrix $\mathbf{A}$ is called *column stochastic*, if its elements are such that

$$a_{ij} \geqslant 0, \; i, j = 1, 2, ..., n \tag{8.46}$$

$$\sum_{i=1}^{n} a_{ij} = 1, \; j - 1, 2, ..., n \tag{8.47}$$

When a matrix A is both row and column stochastic, it is called *doubly stochastic*. A special case of a stochastic matrix is a *stochastic vector*, *i.e.*, a vector for which the sum of its components is 1. A particular notion we will encounter in *credit migration*, i.e., in the transition to states of different bond quality grades, is that of an absorbing state. When the ith row of $\mathbf{A}$ consists of only zeros with one 1 in the jth position, the ith state is called an *absorbing state*. This means that when a transition is made to the absorbing state, no further transitions, and "no escape" to another state, is possible.

According to Graham (1987, p. 200):

"The elegance of the theory of finite Markov chains depends partly on the fact that the nature of the chain can be determined, when the eigenvalues of the associated transition matrix $\mathbf{A}$ are known."

What are eigenvalues? *Eigenvalues λ_i, $i = 1, 2, ..., n$ are determined by the spectral decomposition*

$$\mathbf{V'AV} = \Lambda$$

$$= \begin{bmatrix} \lambda_1 & 0 & ... & 0 \\ 0 & \lambda_2 & ... & 0 \\ ... & ... & ... & ... \\ 0 & 0 & ... & \lambda_n \end{bmatrix} \tag{8.48}$$

Thus Λ is a diagonal matrix of eigenvalues, and $\mathbf{V}$ is an *orthonormal matrix (i.e.,* $\mathbf{VV}' = \mathbf{I} = \mathbf{V}'\mathbf{V})$, consisting of all the corresponding *eigenvectors*. Consequently,

$$\mathbf{VV}'\mathbf{AV} = \mathbf{AV}$$
$$= \mathbf{V}\Lambda \qquad (8.49)$$

or

$$\mathbf{A}\widehat{\mathbf{v}}_j = \lambda_j \widehat{\mathbf{v}}_j \qquad (8.50)$$

for each j, *i.e.*, the *characteristic equation* of $\mathbf{A}$. If $\mathbf{A}$ is a stochastic matrix, then we have the following characteristic equation for $\mathbf{A}$

$$\mathbf{A}\iota_n = \begin{bmatrix} a_{11} & a_{12} & \dots & a_{1n} \\ a_{21} & a_{22} & \dots & a_{2n} \\ \dots & \dots & \dots & \dots \\ a_{n1} & a_{n2} & \dots & a_{nn} \end{bmatrix} \begin{bmatrix} 1 \\ 1 \\ \dots \\ 1 \end{bmatrix}$$

$$= 1. \begin{bmatrix} 1 \\ 1 \\ \dots \\ 1 \end{bmatrix}$$

$$= 1.\iota_n \qquad (8.51)$$

where $\iota_n = [1, 1, ..., 1]'$ the usual $n \times 1$ unit vector. Hence 1 is an eigenvalue of $\mathbf{A}$ and ι_n the corresponding eigenvector. Consequently, the *spectral radius* $\rho(\mathbf{A})$ of a stochastic matrix $\mathbf{A}$, *i.e.*, its largest eigenvalue, equals unity:

$$\rho(\mathbf{A}) = \max_i |\lambda_i(\mathbf{A})| \text{ for } i = 1, 2, ..., n$$
$$= 1 \qquad (8.52)$$

Next, if $\mathbf{A}$ is a stochastic matrix, then so is $\mathbf{A}^t$, $t = 1, 2, ...$ Since $\mathbf{A}$ is stochastic, we have

$$\mathbf{A}\iota_n = 1.\iota_n = \iota_n \qquad (8.53)$$

so that also

$$\mathbf{A}^2\iota_n = \mathbf{A}(\mathbf{A}\iota_n)$$
$$= \mathbf{A}\iota_n$$
$$= \iota_n \qquad (8.54)$$

and, by induction

$$\mathbf{A}^t\iota_n = \iota_n, t = 1, 2, ... \qquad (8.55)$$

Since the eigenvalues of $\mathbf{A}$ are $|\lambda_i(\mathbf{A})| \leq 1$, $\mathbf{A}$ is *power convergent*. That means that

$$\mathbf{A}^t = \mathbf{V}\Lambda\mathbf{V}'\mathbf{V}\Lambda\mathbf{V}'....\mathbf{V}\Lambda\mathbf{V}'$$
$$= \mathbf{V}\Lambda^t\mathbf{V}' \tag{8.56}$$

converges in the limit to an $n \times n$ finite constant nonnegative matrix $\mathbf{Q}$

$$\lim_{t\to\infty} \mathbf{A}^t = \lim_{t\to\infty} \mathbf{V}\Lambda^t\mathbf{V}'$$
$$= \mathbf{Q}$$
$$= [\widehat{\mathbf{q}}_1, \widehat{\mathbf{q}}_2, ..., \widehat{\mathbf{q}}_n] \geqslant 0 \tag{8.57}$$

where $\widehat{\mathbf{q}}_j, j = 1, 2, ..., n$ are the nonnegative columns of $\mathbf{Q}$. This succeeds, since all other eigenvalues of a stochastic matrix than its spectral radius are smaller than 1 in absolute value: $|\lambda_i(\mathbf{A})| < 1$.

We will now develop an elegant method to compute $\mathbf{Q}$, once we know the transition matrix $\mathbf{A}$. We have

$$\mathbf{Q} = \lim_{t\to\infty} \mathbf{A}^{t+1}$$
$$= \mathbf{A} \lim_{t\to\infty} \mathbf{A}^t$$
$$= \mathbf{A}\mathbf{Q} \tag{8.58}$$

so that we have the exact relationship

$$\mathbf{A}\widehat{\mathbf{q}}_j = 1.\widehat{\mathbf{q}}_j, \;\; j = 1, 2, ..., n \tag{8.59}$$

But since $\mathbf{A}$ is a row stochastic matrix, we also have again

$$\mathbf{A}\boldsymbol{\iota}_n = 1.\boldsymbol{\iota}_n \tag{8.60}$$

so that each column of $\mathbf{Q}$ is a multiple of the unit vector $\boldsymbol{\iota}_n$,

$$\widehat{\mathbf{q}}_j = r_j\boldsymbol{\iota}_n \tag{8.61}$$

where r_j is a scalar. Hence

$$\mathbf{Q} = [\widehat{\mathbf{q}}_1, \widehat{\mathbf{q}}_2, ..., \widehat{\mathbf{q}}_n]$$
$$= [r_1\boldsymbol{\iota}_n, r_2\boldsymbol{\iota}_n, ..., r_n\boldsymbol{\iota}_n]$$
$$= \boldsymbol{\iota}_n\mathbf{r}' \tag{8.62}$$

Similarly, there is a characteristic equation for the transpose of the transition matrix

$$\mathbf{A}'\widehat{\mathbf{z}} = 1.\widehat{\mathbf{z}} \tag{8.63}$$

with $\widehat{\mathbf{z}}$ the exact eigenvector corresponding with the spectral radius

$$\rho(\mathbf{A}) = \rho(\mathbf{A}') = 1 \tag{8.64}$$

so that

$$(\mathbf{A}')^t\widehat{\mathbf{z}} = 1.\widehat{\mathbf{z}}, \, t = 1, 2, ... \tag{8.65}$$

Thus, by substitution, we have

$$\begin{aligned} \widehat{\mathbf{z}}'\mathbf{Q} &= \widehat{\mathbf{z}}' \lim_{t \to \infty} \mathbf{A}^t \\ &= \lim_{t \to \infty} \mathbf{z}'\mathbf{A}^t \\ &= \widehat{\mathbf{z}}' \end{aligned} \tag{8.66}$$

or

$$\begin{aligned} \widehat{\mathbf{z}}'\mathbf{Q} &= \widehat{\mathbf{z}}'\iota_n\mathbf{r}' \\ &= \widehat{\mathbf{z}}' \end{aligned} \tag{8.67}$$

But this means that the scalar product $\widehat{\mathbf{z}}'\iota_n \neq 0$. Hence we can compute

$$\mathbf{r}' = (\widehat{\mathbf{z}}'\iota_n)^{-1}\widehat{\mathbf{z}}' \tag{8.68}$$

and

$$\begin{aligned} \mathbf{Q} &= \iota_n\mathbf{r}' \\ &= \iota_n(\widehat{\mathbf{z}}'\iota_n)^{-1}\widehat{\mathbf{z}}' \end{aligned} \tag{8.69}$$

which is our desired result: a recipe for computing $\mathbf{Q}$. Notice that

$$\mathbf{r}' = (\mathbf{z}'\iota_n)^{-1}\mathbf{z}' \tag{8.70}$$

is a stochastic vector since the summation of the row elements of $\mathbf{r}'$ add up to unity:

$$\begin{aligned} \mathbf{r}'\iota_n &= (\widehat{\mathbf{z}}'\iota_n)^{-1}\widehat{\mathbf{z}}'\iota_n \\ &= 1 \end{aligned} \tag{8.71}$$

Then, $\mathbf{Q}$ is also a row stochastic matrix, since

$$\begin{aligned} \mathbf{Q}\iota_n &= \iota_n\mathbf{r}'\iota_n \\ &= \iota_n \end{aligned} \tag{8.72}$$

8.5.3   Ehrenfest's Heat Exchange Example

To illustrate these theoretical concepts and procedures with a simple $n = 4$ example, we first turn to an early exact model of heat exchange (*Cf.* Graham, 1987, pp. 235 - 237). The modern option pricing model is founded on a similar model of heat diffusion, as we will see in Chapter 10. In 1907 Paul Ehrenfest proposed the following exact model to explain, in terms of molecular displacement, the exchange of heat between two *isolated* bodies at different temperatures. There are two urns containing a total of N balls labeled $1, 2, ..., N$. At each time point $t = 1, 2, ...$ and integer between 1 and N is selected at random. The corresponding ball is removed from its urn and replaced in the other one. It is assumed that this process can be repeated in such a way that all selections are *independent* from each other. We want to determine the limiting relative frequency distribution of this process: how will the balls eventually be distributed in the first urn whatever the initial distribution?

Conceptually, when $\pi(t)$ represents the number of balls in the urn at time t, then $\{\pi(t)\}$ is a Markov chain on the set of states $\{0, 1, 2, ..., N\}$, *i.e.*, $n = 4$. The time independent transition matrix is $\mathbf{A} = [a_{ij}]$, where a_{ij} is the probability that the process in state i (i balls in the first urn) at time $t - 1$ is in state j at the consecutive time point t. Given that the process is in state i at time $t - 1$, the probability that the selected random integer corresponds to a number on a ball in the first urn is $\frac{i}{N}$. Then there will be $j = i - 1$ balls in the urn at time t. Similarly, the probability that the selected integer corresponds to a number on a ball in the second urn is $\frac{N-i}{N} = 1 - \frac{i}{N}$ at time $t - 1$, in which case there will be $j = i + 1$ balls in the first urn at time t. Thus,

$$a_{ij} = \frac{i}{N} \text{ for } j = i - 1 \qquad (8.73)$$

$$= 1 - \frac{i}{N}, \text{ for } j = i + 1 \qquad (8.74)$$

$$= 0, \text{ otherwise} \qquad (8.75)$$

For example, for $N = 3$ there are $n = N + 1 = 4$ states, $\{0, 1, 2, 3\}$, and for $i, j = 0, 1, 2, 3$, the state transition matrix looks like

$$\mathbf{A} = [a_{ij}] = \begin{bmatrix} 0 & 1 & 0 & 0 \\ \frac{1}{3} & 0 & \frac{2}{3} & 0 \\ 0 & \frac{2}{3} & 0 & \frac{1}{3} \\ 0 & 0 & 1 & 0 \end{bmatrix} \qquad (8.76)$$

Paul Ehrenfest (1880 - 1933) was one of Germany's greatest theoretical physicists of the early 20th century. Ehrenfest quickly picked up the quantum concept of Max Planck and gave it a strong basis with his *adiabatic* principle, which long guided early quantum theory. An adiabatic process is any process that occurs without heat transfer. In finance, the adiabatic condition = no arbitrage condition.

In finance, "heat exchange" would be equivalent to mutual cash flows due to market arbitrage.

Notice that state 0 and state 3 are absorbing states since the first and the fourth rows of $\mathbf{A}$ contain only one state with probability 1. Using the preceding procedure, we will now determine the limiting distribution of this homogeneous Markov chain, using the preceding theory of a limiting Markov chain distribution. First, the 4 eigenvalues of A are $\lambda_i(\mathbf{A}) = 1, \frac{1}{3}, -\frac{1}{3}, -1$. The matrix $\mathbf{A}$ is clearly row stochastic. Thus its spectral radius

$$\rho(\mathbf{A}) = 1 \tag{8.77}$$

with the corresponding eigenvector $\iota'_4 = [1, 1, 1, 1]$. The eigenvector of $\mathbf{A}'$ corresponding to the spectral radius $\rho(\mathbf{A}) = 1$ is $\mathbf{z}' = [1, 3, 3, 1]$, so that the sum of its elements is

$$\widehat{\mathbf{z}}' \iota_4 = 8 \tag{8.78}$$

Thus

$$\lim_{t \to \infty} \mathbf{A}^t = \mathbf{Q}$$
$$= \iota_4 (\widehat{\mathbf{z}}' \iota_4)^{-1} \widehat{\mathbf{z}}'$$
$$= \begin{bmatrix} 1 \\ 1 \\ 1 \\ 1 \end{bmatrix} \frac{1}{8} [1, 3, 3, 1]$$
$$= \begin{bmatrix} \frac{1}{8} & \frac{3}{8} & \frac{3}{8} & \frac{1}{8} \\ \frac{1}{8} & \frac{3}{8} & \frac{3}{8} & \frac{1}{8} \\ \frac{1}{8} & \frac{3}{8} & \frac{3}{8} & \frac{1}{8} \\ \frac{1}{8} & \frac{3}{8} & \frac{3}{8} & \frac{1}{8} \end{bmatrix} \tag{8.79}$$

So in the long run, when $t \to \infty$, the probabilities of $0, 1, 2, 3$ balls in the first urn converge to $\frac{1}{8}, \frac{3}{8}, \frac{3}{8}, \frac{1}{8}$, respectively, whatever the initial distribution. The determinant of the limiting distribution matrix is zero: $|\mathbf{Q}| = 0$: no energy for further transition is left.

8.6 Default and Credit Migration Frequencies

We will now implement Ehrenfest's theoretical procedure to compute the final credit distribution, taking account of historically observed credit migration and of the preceding theory of limiting Markov chain distributions.

From historical records, relative transition frequencies are computed for each possible credit event, including upgrades and downgrades and defaults. The probability that an debt obligor will migrate over a given time horizon to another credit rating, *i.e.*, another credit state, can then be derived from the resulting transition matrix, under the assumption of a homogeneous transition process.

Table 1. provides an example of such a historical record for credit migration based on Standard & Poors credit ratings. This table can be used for one period ahead predictions. Each migration results in a predicted change in asset value, derived from credit spread data and, in default, from possible recovery rates. Each value outcome is then weighted by its relative frequency of occurrence, to create a distribution of value across each credit state. From the resulting frequency distribution one can then compute each asset's return/risk profile (Morgan, 1997a & b).

TABLE 1.	ONE-	YEAR	TRANSITION	MATRIX				
Initial	Ratings	at	year-	end	(%)			
Rating	AAA	AA	A	BBB	BB	B	CCC	Default
AAA	90.81	8.33	0.68	0.06	0.12	0	0	0
AA	0.70	90.65	7.79	0.64	0.06	0.14	0.02	0
A	0.09	2.27	91.05	5.52	0.74	0.26	0.01	0.06
BBB	0.02	0.33	5.95	86.93	5.30	1.17	0.12	0.18
BB	0.03	0.14	0.67	7.73	80.53	8.84	1.00	1.06
B	0	0.11	0.24	0.43	6.48	83.46	4.07	5.21
CCC	0.22	0	0.22	1.30	2.38	11.24	64.86	19.78
Source:	Standard	&	Poor's	CreditWeek	(15	April	1996)	

Notice that we can add one extra row to make Table 1 a square matrix , since there should be one absorbing state, the default state, from where "no escape" = no upgrading is possible. Suppose that this one-year $n \times n = 8 \times 8$ transition matrix Λ is time-independent (a very strong assumption!) and the credit migration forms a homogeneous Markov chain. Then we can again implement the preceding procedure

---

Table 1. is an average record of many historical measurements. This exact average record $\widehat{\mathbf{A}}$ is identified from inexact data $\mathbf{A}$: $\widehat{\mathbf{A}} = \mathbf{A} - \widetilde{\mathbf{A}}$. The degree of uncertainty $\widetilde{\mathbf{A}}$ of the transition records in this particular Table 1., and therefore the reliability of this exact transition matrix $\widehat{\mathbf{A}}$ is not known. Professor Altman and his students in the Stern Graduate School of School of New York University has devoted enormous effort to identifying such transition matrices, for the general benefit of the global debt trading and management industry (Cf. Altman, 1989; Altman and Kishore, 1996; Altman and Suggitt, 2000). Recently, there has been more interest in the (lack of) stability of these transition matrices, i.e., in the reliability of their identification (Cf. Nickell, Perraudin and Varetto, 2000).

to determine the final credit distribution, as follows.

$$
\mathbf{A} = \begin{bmatrix}
.9081 & .0833 & .0068 & .0006 & .0012 & 0 & 0 & 0 \\
.0070 & .9065 & .0779 & .0064 & .0006 & .0014 & .0002 & 0 \\
.0009 & .0227 & .9105 & .0552 & .0074 & .0026 & .0001 & .0006 \\
.0002 & .0033 & .0595 & .8693 & .0530 & .0117 & .0012 & .0018 \\
.0003 & .0014 & .0067 & .0773 & .8053 & .0884 & .0100 & .0106 \\
0 & .0011 & .0024 & .0043 & .0648 & .8346 & .0407 & .0521 \\
.0022 & 0 & .0022 & .01300 & .0238 & .1124 & .6486 & .1978 \\
0 & 0 & 0 & 0 & 0 & 0 & 0 & 1
\end{bmatrix} \tag{8.80}
$$

Matrix $\mathbf{A}$ is row stochastic and thus its spectral radius

$$
\rho(\mathbf{A}) = \max_i |\lambda_i(\mathbf{A})|
$$
$$
= 1 \tag{8.81}
$$

with the corresponding eigenvector

$$
\widehat{\mathbf{z}}' = [0, 0, 0, 0, 0, 0, 0, 1] \tag{8.82}
$$

so that the sum of its elements is

$$
\widehat{\mathbf{z}}' \iota_8 = 1 \tag{8.83}
$$

Thus, the limiting distribution of this Standard & Poors based credit migration is

$$
\lim_{t \to \infty} \mathbf{A}^t = \mathbf{Q}
$$
$$
= \iota_8 (\widehat{\mathbf{z}}' \iota_8)^{-1} \widehat{\mathbf{z}}'
$$

$$
= \begin{bmatrix} 1 \\ 1 \\ 1 \\ 1 \\ 1 \\ 1 \\ 1 \\ 1 \end{bmatrix} .1. [\, 0 \ 0 \ 0 \ 0 \ 0 \ 0 \ 0 \ 1 \,]
$$

$$
= \begin{bmatrix}
0 & 0 & 0 & 0 & 0 & 0 & 0 & 1 \\
0 & 0 & 0 & 0 & 0 & 0 & 0 & 1 \\
0 & 0 & 0 & 0 & 0 & 0 & 0 & 1 \\
0 & 0 & 0 & 0 & 0 & 0 & 0 & 1 \\
0 & 0 & 0 & 0 & 0 & 0 & 0 & 1 \\
0 & 0 & 0 & 0 & 0 & 0 & 0 & 1 \\
0 & 0 & 0 & 0 & 0 & 0 & 0 & 1 \\
0 & 0 & 0 & 0 & 0 & 0 & 0 & 1
\end{bmatrix} \tag{8.84}
$$

So, in the long run, when $t \to \infty$, all credit measured by Standard & Poors ratings ends up in default with certainty, whatever the initial distribution. This is a rather unrealistic , (perhaps) disturbing and absurd, but perfectly logical conclusion of the strong assumptions of this model, in particular of the time independence of $\mathbf{A}(t) = \mathbf{A}$, *i.e.*, of the assumed Markovian homogeneity, on which such computations are based.

As the economist John Maynard Keynes, who was concerned about the risks of the instability of money value and of credit, stated:

> "*In the long run*, we are all dead. Economists set themselves too easy, too useless a task if in tempestuous seasons they can only tell us that when the storm is long past the ocean is flat again." (Keynes, 1923, p. 80).

Despite the inadequacy of economists and real world economies what they are, the historical record shows that it likely that hard-nosed solutions for a structural economic collapse will be found, before such a blanket default of all Standard and Poors rated credit is reached.

8.7   Exercises

Exercise 65 *Complete Capital Market Pricing (CCMP) Theory. Consider the following 3-state economy, i.e., there are three different expected states of the market during the coming year. Suppose there are three different market securities - security A, security B and security C and that the state contingent payoff table with the expected payoff values for each market security in each state is as follows.*

Security	Price $	Recession	State of the Economy Moderate Growth	Boom
A	$10.00	-$15.00	$15.00	$25.00
B	$15.00	$25.00	$10.00	-$15.00
C	$12.00	$13.00	$15.00	$12.00

John Maynard Keynes (1883 - 1946) was one of the most influential economists in the 20th century. He became first known because of his critique of the peace treaty of Versailles, which imposed debilitating war repair payments on Germany after the First World War, in his book *The Economic Consequences of the Peace* (1919). Next he wrote *A Treatise on Probability* (1921) and a *Tract on Monetary Reform* (1923). But he is best known for his classic, difficult to read, and still controversial, work on economic theory, *The General Theory of Employment, Interest and Money* (1936). He played an important role at the Bretton Woods Conference of 1944, which established the basis of the postwar international monetary system of fixed exchange rates. That system of fixed exchange rates was abandoned by the Smithsonian Agreement of 1971 and replaced by the current system of volatile exchange rates (*Cf.* Chapter 14)

Cf. the resolution of the Japanese financial crisis of 1989, the European financial crisis of 1992/93, the Mexican financial crisis in 1994 and the resolution of the Indonesian financial crisis in 1997/98. The political-economic outcome of a financial crisis depends on how many credit issuing firms go into default and how much nominal credit is at stake.

Set up an EXCEL spreadsheet to perform the following computations:

1. Given the observed equilibrium market prices of the three securities and their expected payoff vectors, compute the vector of primitive security prices (the state "odds" implicit in the current market prices and the contingent payoff table).

2. Suppose one of the payoff rows in this contingent payoff table is the one for a custom designed SECURITY. What is the market price of that SECURITY?

3. Construct an arbitrage-free (risk neutral) portfolio using the three securities.

Example 66 *Dynamic Credit Risk Theory. We will now investigate the effects of default risk on the returns from holding corporate bonds to maturity and value such risky bonds. A bond's promised return = its yield to maturity, i.e., the internal rate of return calculated from the bond's current market price and its contracted coupon payments and contracted principal payment in the future. But a bond's expected return takes into account both the bond's probability of future default and the percentage of its principal, which holders can expect to recover in case of default. The expected rate of return of a bond = [(Sum of expected series of discounted year - end cash flows)/(price of bond)] - 1. We'll use a Markov chain model to solve for the expected return on a risky bond, taking account of the probability of default, the transition of the issuer between states of credit worthiness, and the recovery rate of the principal when the bond defaults. Suppose there are four corporate credit grades: A, B, C and D (= default). The bond under review is currently rated B, has an annual coupon rate of 7%, has still 5 more years until maturity, is priced at 97 cents to the dollar and we expect that only 45% of the bond's principal value can be recovered out of bankruptcy, once the bond's issuer goes into default. Standard & Poor's Research Department provides us with the following simple credit migration matrix:*

Credit Migration (State Transition) Matrix A:
Credit Grades

	A	B	C	D
A	0.90	0.09	0.01	0.00
B	0.06	0.86	0.07	0.01
C	0.03	0.11	0.70	0.16
D	0.00	0.00	0.00	1.00

1. Explain what the various credit grades and credit transition probabilities in this matrix mean.

2. Compute the series of expected bond payoffs in the coming 5 years.

3. Compute this corporate bond's expected rate or return.

Exercise 67 *Imagine that you are a financial analyst for ING Bank, Inc. in New York, which specializes in the "vulture" business, i.e.; this bank makes a market in distressed debt, in particular, of emerging markets. The Head Trader P. G. asks you to value the bond of a distressed company in Indonesia using the option-theoretic method. The bond under review is in dollar terms and is currently still rated B. It has an annual coupon rate of 8%, has still two more years until maturity and is currently priced in the market at 80 cents to the dollar. ING's Corporate Department expects that only 40% of the bond's principal value will be recoverable, once the company under review goes into bankruptcy. Based on some rough analysis of a sample of bonds in similar distressed circumstances, the Corporate Department also provides you with the same very simple credit migration matrix of the preceding question:*

1. Compute the series of expected cash flows in the coming two years, if P. G. decides to purchase the bond.

2. Can you determine what the expected yield of this distressed corporate bond is? How?

3. Is this an attractive bond to purchase or not? Would you buy it? Why or why not?

8.8   Bibliography

Altman, E. I. (1989) "Measuring Corporate Bond Mortality and Performance," *Journal of Finance*, **44** (4), December, 909 - 922.

Altman, E. I. and Kishore, V. M. (1996) "Almost Everything You Wanted to Know about Recoveries on Defaulted Bonds," *Financial Analysts Journal*, November - December, 57 - 64.

Altman, E. I. and Suggitt, H. J. (2000) "Default Rates in the Syndicated Bank Loan Market: A Mortality Analysis," *Journal of Banking and Finance*, **24** (1,2), January, 229 - 253.

Bodie, Z., Kane, A. and Marcus, A. J. (1993) *Investments*, Irwin, Homewood, IL, 2nd ed.

CreditMetrics[TM] - *Technical Document* (1997), J. P. Morgan, New York, NY, April, 193 pages.

Introduction to CreditMetrics[TM] : *The benchmark for understanding credit risk* (1997), J. P. Morgan, New York, NY, April 2, 36 pages.

Fama, E. F. (1970) "Efficient Capital Markets: A Review of Theory and Empirical Work," *Journal of Finance*, **25** (3), 383 - 417.

Frisch, R. (1934) *Statistical Confluence Analysis by Means of Complete Regression Systems*, Publication No. 5, University of Oslo Economic Institute, Oslo, Norway.

Graham, A. (1987) *Nonnegative Matrices and Applicable Topics in Linear Algebra*, Halsted Press/John Wiley & Sons, New York, NY.

Kalman, R. E. (1994) "Randomness Reexamined," *Modeling, Identification and Control*, **15** (3), 141 - 151.

Kalman, R. E. (1995) "Randomness and Probability," *Mathematica Japonica*, **41** (1), 41 - 58 & " Addendum," **41** (2), 463.

Kalman, R. E. (1996) "Probability in the Real World as a System Attribute," *CWI Quarterly*, **9** (3), 181 - 204.

Keynes, J. M. (1923) *A Tract on Monetary Reform*, MacMillan and Co., Ltd, London, UK.

Kolmogorov, A. N. (1933) *Grundbegriffe der Wahrscheinlichkeitsrechnung*, Springer Verlag, Berlin. (Translated by Nathan Morrison: *Foundations of Probability*, Chelsea, New York, NY, 1950).

Mandelbrot, B. B. and Wallis, J. R. (1969) "Some Long-run Properties of Geophysical Records," *Water Resources Research*, **5**, 321 - 340.

Nickell, P., Perraudin, W. and Varotto, S. (2000) "Stability of Rating Transitions," *Journal of Banking and Finance*, **24** (1), January, 203 - 207.

Peters, E. E. (1994) *Fractal Market Analysis*, John Wiley & Sons, Inc., New York, NY.

Ross, S. A. (1976) "Options and Efficiency," *Quarterly Journal of Economics*, **90** (1), February, 75 - 89.

Saunders, A. (1999) *Credit Risk Measurement: New Approaches to Value at Risk and Other Paradigms*, John Wiley and Sons, New York, NY.

Sherry, C.J. (1992) *The Mathematics of Technical Analysis*, Probus Publishing Company, Chicago, IL.

Treacy, W. F. and Carey, M. (2000) "Credit Risk Rating Systems at Large US Banks," *Journal of Banking & Finance*, **24** (1-2), January-February, 167 - 201.

chapter:9,page:1

Chapter 9
OPTION PRICING I

9.1 Introduction

In the preceding Chapter, we learned about the exact, speculative Complete Capital Market Pricing (CCMP) theory. This theory is based on the unrealistic assumptions of *a priori* perfect knowledge of all possible investment outcomes and of the independent probabilities with which they occur (either explicitly, or implicitly in a expected payoff matrix). The exact CCMP theory presumes that the capital market is *perfect and complete* : there is *no opportunity for arbitrage* . The market is always in equilibrium : it is perfectly liquid and has one price per asset, *i.e.*, there is no friction caused by transaction costs or other entry barriers . Consequently, the expected covariances between the primitive investment outcomes are presumed to be zero. The primitive securities are presumed to be independent .

Remark 68 *This theoretical ideal is clearly contradicted by the empirical evidence of the ample (Internet) demand for J. P. Morgan's RiskMetrics^{TM} (300 × 300) data covariances matrices of 300 ideal market securities, based on CCMP .* *Apparently many fund managers think the markets are imperfect . There is epistemic uncertainty and thus many opportunities for arbitrage, since*

$$A\Sigma = A(\widehat{\Sigma} + \widetilde{\Sigma})$$
$$= A\widetilde{\Sigma} \neq 0 \qquad (9.1)$$

(Recall that $A\widehat{\Sigma} = 0$). *In contrast, if the markets would be perfect , we would have exact linear combinations of all empirical market securities :*

$$A\Sigma = A\widehat{\Sigma} = 0 \qquad (9.2)$$

Consequently, there would exist no opportunity for further arbitrage. In addition, in Chapter 14 we will see, first, that there are observed market risk covariances Σ between not only the various asset markets and cash markets within a country, but also between the asset markets of various countries, their respective cash markets and the various foreign exchange markets; and, second, that these observed covariances cannot be attributed exclusively to systematic covariances $\widehat{\Sigma}$.

---

*The rights to *Riskmetrics^{TM}* and *CreditMetrics^{TM}* were recently sold to Reuters, Inc. , possibly because of the empirical problems clients encountered with this idealized model.

However, the simple CCMP theory, which ignores epistemic uncertainty and observed unsystematic risk covariances, still forms the foundation for current option pricing . In this Chapter we will learn how to price options accordingly, using binomial pricing. Binomial option pricing is the most widely used form of option pricing. Its limit produces, under a very strict idealized theoretical assumption, *i.e.*, of strict independence , the prize-winning valuation formula of Black - Scholes option pricing.

9.2 Pricing By Arbitrage

In Chapter 3, we learned how to value the fundamental securities of cash, bonds and stocks based on the discounting of cash flows. In Chapter 8 we learned about risk-neutral pricing based on fair games. Now we synthesize this knowledge and we will learn how to *derive* the value of *derivatives* , like options, futures and swaps, from the fundamental valuations by *arbitrage pricing* , based on *risk-neutrality* . To demonstrate the principles, we first consider the following simple scenario:

- There are only two dates: today and this date exactly one year from now.

- There are two fundamental assets : a stock (= risky asset) S and a one year Treasury bill or T-bill (= risk-free cash) B.

The price of a T-bill $B = \$1$. The T-bill's one-year interest rate $r = 6\%$.

- Today the stock price $S_0 = \$50$ and we *know* that a year from now it will be either up by $u = 10\%$ ($\Rightarrow \$55$), or down by $d = -4\%$ ($\Rightarrow \$48$). Thus the future stock market situation is completely described by only two possible future outcomes, *i.e.*, only two future states completely describe the outcome of this experiment.

- There is one derivative: a *European call option* written on the stock with payoff $\max(S_0 - X, 0)$, which we want to price today at c_0. The call option matures a year from now and has exercise price $X = \$50$, so it pays $\$55 - \$50 = \$5$ when the stock goes up and $\$0$ otherwise.

Pricing by arbitrage is based on the logic of the *Single Price Law of Efficient Markets* we met in Chapter 8: *if two assets have the same payoffs , they must have the same market price*. Thus, there is a portfolio of stocks and T-bills which exactly replicates the call option's future payoffs, represented by the following two simultaneous equations :

$$55w_1 + 1.06w_2 = 5 \tag{9.3}$$
$$48w_1 + 1.06w_2 = 0 \tag{9.4}$$

with the portfolio allocation weights summing to unity, $w_1 + w_2 = 1$. This can be written in matrix notation as

$$\widehat{\mathbf{y}}\mathbf{w} = \begin{bmatrix} 55 & 1.06 \\ 48 & 1.06 \end{bmatrix} \begin{bmatrix} w_1 \\ w_2 \end{bmatrix}$$

$$= \begin{bmatrix} 5 \\ 0 \end{bmatrix}$$

$$= \begin{bmatrix} c_{u1} \\ c_{d1} \end{bmatrix}$$

$$= \mathbf{c}_1 \qquad (9.5)$$

Here the

$$\widehat{\mathbf{y}} = \begin{bmatrix} 55 & 1.06 \\ 48 & 1.06 \end{bmatrix} \qquad (9.6)$$

is the 2×2 nonsingular matrix $\widehat{\mathbf{y}}$ of two exact future outcomes on two variables, being a stock and cash. Their portfolio combination $\widehat{\mathbf{y}}\mathbf{w}$ produces two new securities with two future outcomes

$$\mathbf{c}_1 = \begin{bmatrix} c_{u1} \\ c_{d1} \end{bmatrix}$$

$$= \begin{bmatrix} 5 \\ 0 \end{bmatrix} \qquad (9.7)$$

Solving for the 2×1 vector of portfolio allocation weights $\mathbf{w}$ we find:

$$\mathbf{w}^{opt} = \widehat{\mathbf{y}}^{-1}\mathbf{c}_1$$

$$= \begin{bmatrix} 55 & 1.06 \\ 48 & 1.06 \end{bmatrix}^{-1} \begin{bmatrix} 5 \\ 0 \end{bmatrix}$$

$$= \begin{bmatrix} 0.71429 \\ -32.345 \end{bmatrix} \qquad (9.8)$$

Thus purchasing 71.429 % of a share of the stock for $50 \times .71429 = \$35.72$ and borrowing $\$1 \times 32.345 = \$32.35$ at 6% for a year, will give payoffs of $5 if the stock price goes up and $0 if the stock price goes down, *i.e.*, the payoffs of the call option. It follows that the current price of the call option, c_0, must be equal to the cost of replicating its payoffs

$$c_0 = \mathbf{w}^{opt\prime}\mathbf{P}_0$$

$$= \mathbf{c}_1'\left(\widehat{\mathbf{y}}'\right)^{-1}\mathbf{P}_0 \quad (= \mathbf{c}_1'\boldsymbol{\pi})$$

$$= \begin{bmatrix} 0.71429 & -32.345 \end{bmatrix} \begin{bmatrix} 50 \\ 1 \end{bmatrix}$$

$$= \$35.72 - \$32.35$$

$$= \$3.37 \qquad (9.9)$$

Notice how this is a straightforward implementation of the CCMP of Chapter 8: the current price of the call option c_0 is derived from the current market prices $\mathbf{P}_0$ of the fundamental securities - stock and T-bill -, the expected payoff matrix of the fundamental securities $\widehat{\mathbf{y}}$, and the desired future payoff of the call option $\mathbf{c}_1$. The implied portfolio allocation weights are

$$\mathbf{w}^{opt\prime} = \mathbf{c}_1'(\widehat{\mathbf{y}}')^{-1} \tag{9.10}$$

On the other hand, the "odds"

$$\boldsymbol{\pi} = (\widehat{\mathbf{y}}')^{-1}\mathbf{P}_0 \tag{9.11}$$

are implied by the pay-off matrix $\widehat{\mathbf{y}}$ and the current securities prices $\mathbf{P}_0$. As we will see, this simple arbitrage argument can be easily extended to multiple periods.

Remark 69 *While the portfolio optimization results of Markowitz can be extended to real, inefficient - imperfect and incomplete - markets , by allowing for non-zero noise covariances and more states than primitive securities $(\widetilde{\Sigma} \neq \mathbf{0},\ T > n)$, the CCMP theory result cannot be so easily extended, by definition (since, by assumption of perfect and complete arbitrage , $\widetilde{\Sigma} = 0$ and $T = n$). When the payoff matrix $\mathbf{v}$ is no longer square and is of order $T \times n$, with $T > n$, so that we can no longer compute the direct inverse $\mathbf{y}'^{-1}$, we need to use the Penrose inverse*

$$(\mathbf{x}'\mathbf{x})^{-1} = \Sigma^{-1} \tag{9.12}$$

i.e., the information matrix , when $\mathbf{x} = \mathbf{y} - \iota_3\overline{y_p}$.[†] Because of the epistemic uncertainty $\widetilde{\Sigma} \neq \mathbf{0}$, we need to use CLS projections, as in Chapters 4, 5 and 7.

9.3   Single - Period Binomial Option Pricing

We will now generalize the logic of our simple example and show the intimate connection between portfolio selection theory and CCMP theory . Fig. 1 provides a graphical presentation of our numerical example of simple single - period binomial option pricing, using the state prices.[‡] The following discussion refers to this Fig. 1.

For *efficient* - perfect and complete - markets the results are equivalent, *i.e.,* the price of the portfolios is the same equilibrium price. Recall from Chapter 7: the expected payoff $\mathbf{c}_1'\boldsymbol{\pi}$ equals the cost of the portfolio security $\mathbf{w}'\mathbf{P}_0$:

$$\mathbf{c}_1'\boldsymbol{\pi} = \mathbf{w}'\mathbf{P}_0 \tag{9.13}$$

so that *there is no further opportunity for an arbitrage profit* .

[†]The English mathematical physicist Roger Penrose, b. 1931, has made important contributions to relativity theory and the study of the hypothetical celestial objects called black holes , or "space singularities." In the 1960s and 1970s, Penrose worked with Stephen Hawking on the nature of black holes – theorized points of infinite density in space. He worked out a system for mapping the 4-dimensional space - time surrounding a black hole. This kind of map is now called a *Penrose map*
.

[‡]In the box of Fig. 1, piu $= \pi_u$ and pid $= \pi_d$.

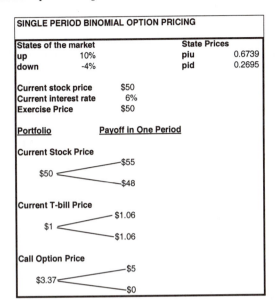

Figure 1

9.3.1 Using Portfolio Theory

Let's first generalize the two asset example. For the application of arbitrage pricing , we must solve the two simultaneous equations

$$S_0(1+u)w_1 + (1+r)w_2 = \max(S_0(1+u) - X, 0) \tag{9.14}$$
$$S_0(1+d)w_1 + (1+r)w_2 = \max(S_0(1+d) - X, 0) \tag{9.15}$$

or, in matrix notation

$$
\begin{aligned}
\widehat{\mathbf{y}}\mathbf{w} &= \begin{bmatrix} S_0(1+u) & (1+r) \\ S_0(1+d) & (1+r) \end{bmatrix} \begin{bmatrix} w_1 \\ w_2 \end{bmatrix} \\
&= \begin{bmatrix} \max(S_0(1+u) - X, 0) \\ \max(S_0(1+d) - X, 0) \end{bmatrix} \\
&= \begin{bmatrix} c_{u1} \\ c_{d1} \end{bmatrix} \\
&= \mathbf{c}_1 \tag{9.16}
\end{aligned}
$$

The determinant of the expected payoff matrix is

$$
\begin{aligned}
|\widehat{\mathbf{y}}| &= (1+r)S_0(1+u) - (1+r)S_0(1+d) \\
&= S_0(1+r)(u-d) \tag{9.17}
\end{aligned}
$$

Notice that, for $\widehat{\mathbf{y}}$ to be positive definite , we need, generically, that $u > d$. The percentage price change in the "up" state is larger than the percentage change in the "down" state . This will be satisfied when $u > 0$ and $d < 0$. The adjoint of the expected payoff matrix $\widehat{\mathbf{y}}$ is

$$Adj\widehat{\mathbf{y}} = \begin{bmatrix} (1+r) & -(1+r) \\ -S_0(1+d) & S_0(1+u) \end{bmatrix} \tag{9.18}$$

By using the definition of the inverse matrix , we find for the implied, or "optimal " portfolio allocation weights $\mathbf{w}^{opt}$:

$$\begin{aligned} \mathbf{w}^{opt} &= \widehat{\mathbf{y}}^{-1}\mathbf{c}_1 \\ &= \frac{Adj\widehat{\mathbf{y}}}{|\widehat{\mathbf{y}}|}\mathbf{c}_1 \end{aligned} \tag{9.19}$$

Thus, for the two variable case, these allocation weights are:

$$\begin{aligned} \mathbf{w}^{opt} &= \frac{Adj\widehat{\mathbf{y}}}{|\widehat{\mathbf{y}}|}\begin{bmatrix} c_{u1} \\ c_{d1} \end{bmatrix} \\ &= \frac{\begin{bmatrix} (1+r)\left[c_{u1} - c_{d1}\right] \\ S_0(1+u)c_{d1} - S_0(1+d)c_{u1} \end{bmatrix}}{[S_0(1+r)(u-d)]} \end{aligned} \tag{9.20}$$

The resulting current call price is

$$\begin{aligned} c_0 &= \mathbf{P}'_0\mathbf{w}^{opt} \\ &= \begin{bmatrix} S_0 & 1 \end{bmatrix}\mathbf{w}^{opt} \end{aligned} \tag{9.21}$$

or

$$c_0 = \frac{(1+r)S_0\left[c_{u1} - c_{d1}\right] + S_0(1+u)c_{d1} - S_0(1+d)c_{u1}}{[S_0(1+r)(u-d)]} \tag{9.22}$$

Simplifying this expression gives the current call option price

$$c_0 = c_{u1}\frac{(r-d)}{(1+r)(u-d)} + c_{d1}\frac{(u-r)}{(1+r)(u-d)} \tag{9.23}$$

Thus the current price of the one-period binomial call option , c_0, is determined by multiplying the call's payoff in the future "up" state, c_{u1}, by the "up" *state price*

$$\pi_u = \frac{(r-d)}{(1+r)(u-d)} \tag{9.24}$$

and by multiplying the call's payoff in the future "down" state, c_{d1}, by the "down" state price

$$\pi_d = \frac{(u - r)}{(1 + r)(u - d)}. \tag{9.25}$$

Notice that the sum of the state prices equals the one-period discount factor :

$$
\begin{aligned}
(\pi_u + \pi_d) &= \left[\frac{(r - d)}{(1 + r)(u - d)} + \frac{(u - r)}{(1 + r)(u - d)} \right] \\
&= \frac{1}{1 + r}
\end{aligned} \tag{9.26}
$$

Thus the sum of the state prices, which value the uncertain future states, is a **certain** *discounted future \$1 payoff* over one period, which is provided by the (risk-free) T-bill! This is the essence of *risk-neutral valuation* by way of arbitrage and the valuation of primitive securities . The products

$$(1 + r)\pi_u = \frac{(r - d)}{(u - d)} \tag{9.27}$$

$$(1 + r)\pi_d = \frac{(u - r)}{(u - d)} \tag{9.28}$$

are called the *risk-neutral pseudo-probabilities* . The one-period risk-neutral probabilities are thus essentially one-period forward state prices .

9.3.2 Pseudo - Probabilities

As probabilities do, these pseudo-probabilities add up to unity:

$$(1 + r)(\pi_u + \pi_d) = \frac{(1 + r)}{(1 + r)} = 1 \tag{9.29}$$

But, these pseudo-probabilities are not necessarily positive. Of course, when $i > 0$, $u > 0$ and $d < 0$, the first risk-neutral pseudo-probability is necessarily positive

$$(1 + r)\pi_u = \frac{(r - d)}{(u - d)} > 0 \tag{9.30}$$

However, the second risk-neutral pseudo-probability is NOT necessarily positive. There are two mathematically possible situations:

$$(1 + r)\pi_d = \frac{(u - r)}{(u - d)} > 0, \text{ if } u > r \tag{9.31}$$

and

$$(1 + r)\pi_d = \frac{(u - r)}{(u - d)} < 0, \text{ if } u < r \tag{9.32}$$

Of course, when we have perfect knowledge about u (and d), as is assumed in CCMP, we can guarantee that the potential positive return on the risky premium u is higher than the risk-free cash rate r, to compensate for the risk of investing in a risky asset: $(u - r) > 0$. But when we have imperfect knowledge , as in the real world, when we deal with uncertain predictions, there can be no such guarantee.

Remark 70 *Risk-neutral valuation does not imply that the true expected return on the option is equal to the risk-free rate of interest r. The **actual** expected return on the option is evaluated with respect to the true historical, ex post, outcomes , not with respect to the a priori risk-neutral probabilities (= **theoretical** a priori relative frequencies) implied by the subjective expectations expressed by the expected payoff matrix .*

Summary 71 *If in one period the stock price (= risky asset) can move up by a fraction u and down by a fraction d, and if the one-period interest rate is r, then any other asset can be priced by valuing its payoff in the "up" state by π_u and by valuing its payoff in the "down" state by π_d, where π_u and π_d are defined as above.*

9.3.3   Using CCMP Theory

The risk neutrality result derived from a simple portfolio leads directly to the use of CCMP theory for the general case of *one-period binomial option pricing* by way of state prices. Think about the market determining a state price π_u for the opportunity to receive a certain \$1 in the "up" state of the market and a state price of π_d for the opportunity to receive \$1 in the "down" state of the market. Then, both the stock and the T-bill have to also be valued using these *state prices* $\pi' = \begin{bmatrix} \pi_u & \pi_d \end{bmatrix}$ by satisfying the two simultaneous equations :

$$S_0(1 + u)\pi_u + S_0(1 + d)\pi_d = S_0 \tag{9.33}$$

$$(1 + r)\pi_u + (1 + r)\pi_d = 1 \tag{9.34}$$

This can be rewritten as the following exact one-period *state price equation* in matrix form

$$\begin{bmatrix} (1+u) & (1+d) \\ (1+r) & (1+r) \end{bmatrix} \begin{bmatrix} \pi_u \\ \pi_d \end{bmatrix} = \begin{bmatrix} 1 \\ 1 \end{bmatrix} \tag{9.35}$$

which we can solve for the state prices

$$
\begin{aligned}
\pi &= \begin{bmatrix} \pi_u \\ \pi_d \end{bmatrix} \\
&= \begin{bmatrix} (1+u) & (1+d) \\ (1+r) & (1+r) \end{bmatrix}^{-1} \begin{bmatrix} 1 \\ 1 \end{bmatrix} \\
&= \begin{bmatrix} \left(\frac{(r-d)}{(1+r)(u-d)} \right) \\ \left(\frac{(u-r)}{(1+r)(u-d)} \right) \end{bmatrix}
\end{aligned}
\tag{9.36}
$$

Remark 72 *For this solution to be possible, the determinant* $|\widehat{\mathbf{y}}|$ *must be positive:* $(1+r)(u-d) > 0$. *This is true in the perfect knowledge world of CCMP, since we know that* $u > 0$ *and* $d < 0$. *Theoretically, there must be a positive risk premium* $(u-r) > 0$ *for the risk-aversive investor to be interested to borrow at the risk-free rate* r *and to invest in a risky stock. Because, if it were known that the risk premium would be negative and* $(u-r) < 0$, *a risk-aversive investor would prefer to invest completely in T-bills.*[§]

Just like for the valuation stock and the T-bill, these state prices can be used for the valuation of the binomial call option in the state price equation :

$$c_0 = \mathbf{c}_1' \boldsymbol{\pi}$$
$$= c_{u1}\pi_u + c_{d1}\pi_d$$
$$= \left[\ \max(S_0(1+u) - X, 0) \quad \max(S_0(1+d) - X, 0) \ \right] \begin{bmatrix} \pi_u \\ \pi_d \end{bmatrix} \qquad (9.37)$$

Summary 73 *By pricing the two future states of the markets based on fundamental securities valuation (in particular, the one-period ahead "certain" earnings prediction of the stock market combined with the available one-period interest rate), we can derive the binomially priced value of* any other *one-period financial instrument. This is the financial engineering power of the CCMP theory derived from its (unrealistic and a-historical) theoretical assumptions .*

9.4 Multi - Period Binomial Option Pricing

The binomial one-period option pricing model based on the CCMP theory can easily be extended to more periods. Consider a two-period binomial pricing model situation, in which, in each of the two subsequent periods:

- the stock price goes up by 10% or down by 4%, and

- in each period the interest rate remains an unchanged 6%.

Fig. 2 provides a graphical presentation of this numerical example of two-period binomial option pricing, using the state prices.

[§]On the other hand, a risk - taking speculator may still prefer to invest in the risky stock instead of in T - bills! Chapter 14 provides examples of historical, *ex post*, positive and negative risk premia.

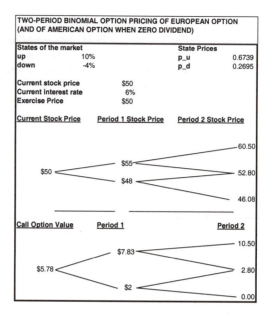

Figure 2

Then each period has the same state prices

$$\boldsymbol{\pi} = \begin{bmatrix} \pi_u \\ \pi_d \end{bmatrix}$$

$$= \begin{bmatrix} \left(\frac{(r-d)}{(1+r)(u-d)} \right) \\ \left(\frac{(u-r)}{(1+r)(u-d)} \right) \end{bmatrix}$$

$$= \begin{bmatrix} \frac{(0.06+0.04)}{(1.06)(0.10+0.04)} \\ \frac{(0.10-0.06)}{(1.06)(0.10+0.04)} \end{bmatrix}$$

$$= \begin{bmatrix} 0.67385 \\ 0.26954 \end{bmatrix} \tag{9.38}$$

Following our numerical example, after two periods the stock price is either

$$S_0(1+u)(1+u) = \$50 \times 1.1 \times 1.1 = \$60.50 \text{ (after two upticks), or} \tag{9.39}$$

$S_0(1+u)(1+d) = \$50 \times 1.1 \times 0.96 = \$52.80$ (after an up-and a downtick, or *vice versa*), or

$$\tag{9.40}$$

$$S_0(1+d)(1+d) = \$50 \times 0.96 \times 0.96 = \$46.08 \text{ (after two downticks)} \tag{9.41}$$

Given the unchanged exercise price of $X = \$50$, this implies that the terminal option payoff is either $10.50, $2.80, or $0. (See Fig. 2) So at the beginning of the second period (= end of the first period) the option price in the "up" state is

$$
\begin{aligned}
c_{u1} &= \$10.50\pi_u + \$2.80\pi_d \\
&= \$10.50 \times 0.67385 + \$2.80 \times 0.26954 \\
&= \$7.83
\end{aligned}
\tag{9.42}
$$

and in the "down" state

$$
\begin{aligned}
c_{d1} &= \$2.80\pi_u + \$0\pi_d \\
&= \$2.80 \times 0.67385 + \$0 \times 0.26954 \\
&= \$2.00
\end{aligned}
\tag{9.43}
$$

Thus, currently, at the beginning of the first period, the call option is worth

$$
\begin{aligned}
c_0 &= \$7.83\pi_u + \$2.00\pi_d \\
&= \$7.83 \times 0.67385 + \$2.00 \times 0.26954 \\
&= \$5.78
\end{aligned}
\tag{9.44}
$$

This logic of *"backwardation ,"* i.e., *backward pricing* - starting from the stock market's valuations of future states combined with corresponding expected interest rates - can be extended to many periods, since, for each period, the beginning value of the (derivative) security must be equal to a state price valuation of the end-of-period values

$$
c_0 = c_{u1}\pi_u + c_{d1}\pi_d
\tag{9.45}
$$

Of course, the expectations may be different for each period and so may the expected interest rate in each period. Therefore, different state prices may need to be computed for each period

Remark 74 *Multi-period binomial option pricing provides an open-form solution for the pricing of options, in particular for American options , which can be exercised before their maturity . The only remaining issue is thus how many periods to include in the pricing. That practical problem can be resolved pragmatically by adopting a stopping rule based on the required accuracy of the pricing, e.g., to two digits (= cents). Based on such a stopping rule the computations can be considerably accelerated by rational pruning of the rapidly branching binomial pricing tree (Cf. Fig. 2).*¶

¶Price (1996) even writes about the "horticulture for binomial trees ," when considering the speed of American option pricing..

9.5   Put - Call Parity

Once the value of a *European call option* is computed, the corresponding *put option* value can be computed using the following fundamental put-call relation. The *Put - Call Parity* relation (for European options) states that owning one share of stock S_0, plus a put on one share p_0, and being short a call on one share c_0 (with the strike price X and expiration dates t of the options being the same), will guarantee a terminal wealth at the expiration date of the options equal to the present value of the strike price of the options:[||]

$$S_0 + p_0 - c_0 = \frac{X}{(1+r)^t} \tag{9.46}$$

The proof of this important proposition (*Cf.* Benninga, 1997) follows the logic of the *cash flows* in arbitrage pricing in the following self-explanatory Table 1:

TABLE 1.: AT CURRENT	DATE AND	FUTURE	DATE
Action	Current cash flow	$S_t < X$	$S_t \geq X$
Buy a call	$-c_0$	0	$S_t - X$
Buy discount bond with payoff X at time t	$\frac{-X}{(1+r)^t}$	X	X
Write a put	$+p_0$	$S_t - X$	0
Short one share of the stock	$+S_0$	$-S_t$	$-S_t$
TOTAL	$S_0 + p_0 - c_0 - \frac{X}{(1+r)^t}$	0	0

The strategy of buying a call, buying a discount bond, writing a put and shorting one share of stock has future payoffs equal to zero, no matter what happens with the price of the stock. Thus the initial cash flow of this strategy must be also zero. It is a fundamental fact of finance that if a financial strategy has future payoffs which are identically zero, then its current cost must also be zero!

If the value of a call option is determined from binomial (or Black - Scholes) valuation, the *value of a put option*, with the same strike price and expiration date as the call option, can be determined from this put - call parity , since

$$p_0 = c_0 - S_0 + \frac{X}{(1+r)^t} \tag{9.47}$$

Example 75 *For the preceding binomially valued call option, which expires after two periods, $t = 2$, an $S_0 = \$50$ stock which pays no dividend , $D_1 = 0$, and an interest rate $x = 6\%$, the value of a two year put with a strike price $X = \$50$ is*

$$p_0 = 5.60 - 50 + \frac{50}{(1.06)^2}$$

$$= \$0.10 \tag{9.48}$$

[||]This ignores the possible dividend earned on the stock.

Another application of the put-call parity relation is the creation of a long position of *synthetic stocks* by way of selling a discount bond (= borrow money), and then to buy a call and sell a put, since

$$S_0 = c_0 - p_0 + \frac{X}{(1+r)^t} \tag{9.49}$$

Example 76 *For our example,*

$$S_0 = 50 = 5.60 - 0.10 + \frac{50}{(1.06)^2} \tag{9.50}$$

The advantage of creating long positions of synthetic stocks is the considerable reduction of transaction costs and ease of execution, since no ownership changes hands when trading synthetic stocks. But the resulting total portfolio risk of owning synthetic stock remains the same as with a long position in the stock self!

Remark 77 *The continuous version of the Put-Call Parity, often used in combination with swap computations, is:*

$$c_0 - p_0 = S_0 - Xe^{-rT} \tag{9.51}$$

9.6 European, American and Asian Options

We will now compare the pricing of an European, an American and an Asian call option, using the risk-neutral valuation approach of the CCMP theory.

The one- and two-period *European call options* that we valued before, can be exercised only at maturity T and has as payoff $\max(S_T - X, 0)$.

An *American call option* can be exercised at any time between moment of purchase and maturity and has as payoff $\max(S_t - X, 0)$, with $0 < t \le T$. So, in principle, an American option should be worth more than an European option. But this is only true if the underlying stock pays a dividend during the life of the option. When there is zero dividend, the American and European call options have the same value, since it is easy to prove that the right to exercise prior to maturity has zero value, as follows (modified from O'Brien and Srivastava, 1995).

In one-period valuation we found that the current value of an option is always

$$\begin{aligned} c_0 &= \mathbf{c}_1' \boldsymbol{\pi} \\ &= c_{u1}\pi_u + c_{d1}\pi_d \end{aligned} \tag{9.52}$$

with

$$c_{u1} = \max(S_0(1+u) - X, 0) \tag{9.53}$$
$$c_{d1} = \max(S_0(1+d) - X, 0) \tag{9.54}$$

and

$$\pi_u + \pi_d = \frac{1}{1+r} \tag{9.55}$$

Adding and subtracting the strike price X, we get

$$c_0 = \max(S_0(1+u), X)\pi_u + \max(S_0(1+d), X)\pi_d - X \tag{9.56}$$

This implies that

$$c_0 \geq S_0(1+u)\pi_u + S_0(1+d)\pi_d - X \tag{9.57}$$

However, we noted that under perfect knowledge risky stocks need to receive a premium over risk-free bills, $(u - r) > 0$, otherwise no risk-aversive investor would be persuaded to invest in risky stock. Thus, it must be true that, with perfect knowledge, the expected value of the return

$$u\pi_u + d\pi_d > r \tag{9.58}$$

and

$$c_0 \geq S_0(1+r) - X \tag{9.59}$$

which implies, for a positive risk-free cash rate r, that

$$c_0 > S_0 - X \tag{9.60}$$

This demonstrates that, under conditions of perfect knowledge, the value of a call is always greater than what can be obtained by exercising the call ($= S_0 - X$). Thus the call option should never be exercised before maturity and, for non-dividend cases, European and American call options have the same value.

Remark 78 *This result is not true, however, for European and American put options!*

An *Asian call option* has a payoff at maturity T of $\max(S_a - X, 0)$, where S_a is the average stock price over the life of the option. This complicates the option valuation problem considerably, since now the value of the call option depends on the actual path followed by the underlying stock price. The Asian call option is therefore a *path-dependent call option* . Fig. 3. provides a two-period example of an Asian call option.

First we look at the binomial tree for the expected stock price payoffs to compute the state prices π. We start with an initial stock price of $10, which can

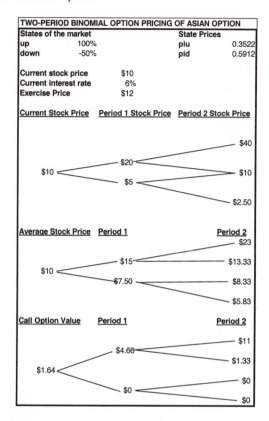

TWO-PERIOD BINOMIAL OPTION PRICING OF ASIAN OPTION				
States of the market			**State Prices**	
up	100%		piu	0.3522
down	-50%		pid	0.5912
Current stock price		$10		
Current interest rate		6%		
Exercise Price		$12		

Current Stock Price   **Period 1 Stock Price**   **Period 2 Stock Price**

$40

$20

$10 $10

$5

$2.50

Average Stock Price   **Period 1**   **Period 2**

$23

$15 $13.33

$10

$7.50 $8.33

$5.83

Call Option Value   **Period 1**   **Period 2**

$11

$4.66

$1.33

$1.64

$0 $0

$0

Figure 3

show an up tick of 100% in each (annual) period and a down tick of 50%, with an annual interest rate of 6%. This gives us the following state prices:

$$\boldsymbol{\pi} = \begin{bmatrix} \pi_u \\ \pi_d \end{bmatrix}$$

$$= \begin{bmatrix} \left(\frac{(r-d)}{(1+r)(u-d)} \right) \\ \left(\frac{(u-r)}{(1+r)(u-d)} \right) \end{bmatrix}$$

$$= \begin{bmatrix} \frac{(0.06+0.50)}{(1.06)(1.00+0.50)} \\ \frac{(1.00-0.06)}{(1.06)(1.00+0.50)} \end{bmatrix}$$

$$= \begin{bmatrix} 0.3522 \\ 0.59119 \end{bmatrix} \tag{9.61}$$

Next, we compute the binomial pricing tree for the average stock prices (Notice that because of the path dependence, the symmetry of the payoffs is lost). With a strike price of $12, we can compute the option payoffs for each period. Finally, we compute the call option value, using the state prices implied by the expected stock price payoffs in each period and the option payoffs for each period, by *backward valuation* , using for each period the state price equation :

$$c_0 = \mathbf{c}_1' \boldsymbol{\pi}$$
$$= c_{u1}\pi_u + c_{d1}\pi_d \qquad (9.62)$$

Applying this backward state pricing procedure, we find that this Asian option is worth $1.64.

Surprisingly, perhaps, the style of the option - European, American or Asian - affects the computed option payoffs, but it doesn't affect the computed state prices! The state prices are immutable and can be used independently of the styles of option pricing, since they are computed exactly from the expected state payoffs of the market. These expected state payoffs are based on the assumption that the prices are produced by efficient markets that follow random walks. What are random walks?

9.7   Random Walks and Brownian Motion

A *random walk* is a *discrete* process such that the *innovation* , or shock, ε_t in each period t is *independent* from the innovation in each other period and has a constant variance. The independence and stationarity (= identical distributiveness) of such a stochastic process is often just assumed, although one can test for both (*Cf.* Los, 1999, 2000a & b). Formally, a *random walk* pricing process X_t is such that

$$X_t = X_{t-1} + \varepsilon_t \qquad (9.63)$$

with ε_t *independent* from $\varepsilon_{t-\tau}$, with integer $\tau > 0$ and $Var(\varepsilon_t) = \sigma_{\varepsilon\varepsilon}$ (a constant). A *Wiener process* is the *continuous* version of the discrete random walk process.** A random walk is thus a $n = 1$ homogeneous Markov chain (*Cf.* Chapter 8), of which the state transition matrix is given by a unity scalar, together with an additive, independent shock or "innovation."

Remark 79 *Both mathematically precisely defined stochastic processes - random walks and Wiener processes - have as their intellectual predecessor the empirically*

**The American mathematician Norbert Wiener (1894 - 1964), is best known for his development of an interdisciplinary approach to the study of communication and control processes in living organisms and machines. His interest in this approach, for which he coined the word cybernetics, arose from work he was doing on automated control systems for antiaircraft guns during World War II.

Wiener also contributed to the theory of stochastic processes and the theory of Brownian motion, constructing a rigorous mathematical description of a physical process that is subject to random change. He taught at M.I.T. from 1919 to 1960.

observed microscopic Brownian motion . Brownian motion is the randomly agitated behavior of colloidal particles suspended in a fluid. The random agitation is caused by the atomic vibrations.[††]

On March 29, 1900, a Ph.D. thesis by Louis Bachelier entitled "Theory of Speculation" was accepted by the Faculty of Sciences of the Academy of Paris , the Sorbonne (*Cf*. Dimand, 1993; Osborne, 1959).[‡‡] In his thesis, Bachelier developed the theory of price fluctuations in a market, answering the question, "Does the recent history of a stock or bond market give any information about its future performance?" with a resounding *No*. His thesis contained the first mathematical presentation of a random walk, including the basic increment equation . Bachelier's thesis advisor was Henri Poincaré , one of the most celebrated mathematicians of all time, who lectured on Brownian motion in 1900 at the International Congress of Physics in Paris.

In a series of papers published from 1905 to 1908, Albert Einstein successfully incorporated the suspended particles into the mathematical molecular-kinetic theory of heat. It was Einstein's exact Boltzmanian heat-diffusion model (*Cf*. Chapter 8 for the Ehrenfest model), which went all the way back to Fourier (*Cf*. Chapter 2), together with Bachelier's 1900 model of the Brownian motion of stock prices, which inspired Paul Samuelson to come up with his "randomization" proof. Samuelson's (1965) proof that rationally expected prices fluctuate "randomly," forms the core of the option pricing theory developed by Fischer Black and Myron Scholes in 1973, to be discussed in Chapter 10.

We can empirically test if a particular market pricing process is random walk efficient, *i.e.*, if it follows a random walk, by implementing non-parametric tests for

---

[††]*Brownian motion*, the motion of microscopic particles suspended in a liquid, was discovered in 1827 by the Scottish botanist Robert Brown , 1773 - 1858. The first to observe, in 1831, the nucleus of a living cell, Brown contributed to plant classification techniques and pioneered in fossil-plant studies.

[‡‡]In 1997 the Bachelier Finance Society was founded by financial engineers to honor Bachelier's pathbreaking work.

Thus, perhaps Poincaré should be credited with inventing the theory of Brownian motion, instead of the economist Bachelier, or the mathematical physicist Einstein. Jules Henri Poincaré, 1854 - 1912, was one of France's greatest theoretical scientists and a Professor at the Sorbonne (University of Paris) since 1881. His contributions to mathematics, mathematical physics, and, in particular, celestial mechanics and the philosophy of science were often basic, profound, and highly original (Cf. his *New Methods of Celestial Mechanics*, 1892 - 99, *Lessons of Celestial Mechanics*, 1905-10, *Science and Hypothesis*, 1901, *Science and Method*, 1908 and *The Value of Science*, 1904). Poincaré was the originator of algebraic topology and of the theory of analytic functions of several complex variables. He made fundamental advances in algebraic geometry and he was interested in number theory.

Einstein extended Boltzmann's work and calculated the average trajectory of a microscopic particle buffeted by random collisions with molecules in a fluid or in a gas. and observed that his calculations could account for Brownian motion, the apparently erratic movement of pollen in fluids.

The Austrian physicist Ludwig Boltzmann (1844 - 1906), developed, with J. W. Gibbs, the branch of physics known as statistical mechanics , which uses the laws of probability to describe how the properties of atoms determine the visible properties of matter .

stationarity and independence.

Example 80 *Using some tests developed for the study of information processes by nervous systems , Sherry (1992) demonstrates that the S&P500 Index follows a random walk process, but that the Dow Jones Industrial Index (DJIA) of the New York Stock Exchange doesn't. Recently, we applied Sherry's nonparametric tests to monthly and weekly stock price index data to study the relative efficiency of the stock markets of Hong Kong, Indonesia, Malaysia, Singapore, Taiwan, and Thailand in 1995 - 1996 (Los, 2000a). We did this also for minute-by-minute currency quotations to study the relative efficiency of the currency markets of Hong Kong , Indonesia , Malaysia , the Philippines , Singapore , Taiwan and Thailand (Los, 1999, 2000b). The results of these nonparametric tests have already led to more intensive research on long term time dependence in the financial markets (Los, 2000c).*

9.8   Exercises

Exercise 81 *Suppose we observe the following current data for this stock call option: stock price = \$40.00; cash interest rate = 3.75%; maturity = 3 months; strike price = \$36.00; stock price volatility = 35% on an annual basis. Set up EXCEL spreadsheets that will calculate the value of the European, American and Asian call options, using three-period binomial call option pricing . First, translate the data from continuous to discrete time (Cf. Chapter 2). In particular, translate first the annual stock price volatility back to possible discrete stock price up-and down ticks for the maturity of the options. Then compute the state prices and do backward valuation for all three cases.*

Exercise 82 *Why is an Asian call option less expensive than an American or European call option?*

Exercise 83 *Using the data of question 1, set up an EXCEL spreadsheet that will calculate the value of the European call option using 30-period binomial pricing.*

Exercise 84 *Determine the boundary period of the in-the-money-calls .*

Exercise 85 *The Treasurer of an international bank in Hong Kong believes that the stock market in Taiwan is expected to remain very volatile in the coming quarter, now that the Taiwan dollar remains under downward pressure. Owning a call option on a non-dividend paying stock , of which the current price is \$100/share, he would like to purchase a synthetic put , while not losing his opportunity to gain on the call. Thus he asks you to compute the price for the put. You obtain the following information from the Bloomberg : the annual interest rate is 10%, and the call's strike price is \$106. The volatility, as measured by the standard deviation of the underlying stock, you currently compute to be 60%/year. You may have forgotten the Black-Scholes pricing formula* *(to be discussed in the next Chapter!), but you recall that binomial option pricing can provide a good approximation and, of course, you'll use the (discrete) put-call parity to compute the put from the call. Calculate the value of the call and the put using two-period binomial option pricing . Set up a two-period binomial option pricing tree and do backward valuation using the additional computational finance formulas (Hint: first determine how long the discrete pricing period ΔT is!). Again, show your answers both in EXCEL keyboard sequences and numerically.*

1. For the up tick u, you use the first order approximation

$$(1 + u) = exp[\sigma_s * \Delta T^{0.5}] \qquad (9.64)$$

2. From CCMP theory you know that the one-period state price for the up tick is

$$\pi_u = \frac{(r - d)}{(1 + r)(u - d)} \qquad (9.65)$$

9.9 Bibliography

Bachelier, L. (1900) "Théorie de la Spéculation," (Doctoral dissertation in Mathematical Sciences, Faculté des Sciences de Paris, defended March 29, 1900), *Annales de l' École Normale Supérieure*, **3** (17), 21 - 86. Translated, with permission of Gauthier-Villars, Paris, France, as Chapter 2 in Cootner, P. H. (Ed.) (1964) *The Random Character of Stock Market Prices*, M.I.T. Press, Cambridge, MA, pp. 17 - 78.

Benninga, S. (1997) *Financial Modeling*, The M.I.T. Press, Cambridge, MA.

Benninga, S., Steinmetz, R. and Stroughair, J. (1993) "Implementing Numerical Option Pricing Models," *The Mathematica Journal*, **3** (4), 66 - 73.

Dimand, R. W. (1993) "The Case of Brownian Motion: a Note on Bachelier's Contribution," *British Journal of the History of Science*, **26**, 233 - 234.

Fama, E. F. (1970) "Efficient Capital Markets: A Review of Theory and Empirical Work," *Journal of Finance*, **25**, 383 - 417.

Los, C. A. (1999) "Nonparametric Testing of the High-Frequency Efficiency of the 1997 Asian Foreign Exchange Markets," *Journal of Multinational Financial Management*, **9** (3-4), October, 265 - 289.

Los, C. A. (2000a) "Nonparametric Efficiency Testing of Asian Stock Markets, Using Weekly Data," in Fomby, T., B. and Carter Hill, R. (Eds.), *Advances in Econometrics: Applying Kernel and Nonparametric Estimation to Economic Topics*, Vol. 14, JAI Press, Inc., Stamford, CT, 329 - 363.

Los, C. A. (2000b) "Nonparametric Efficiency Testing of Asian Foreign Exchange Markets," in Abu - Mostafa, Y. S., LeBaron, B., Lo, A. W., and Weigend, A. S. (Eds.), *Computational Finance 1999 – Proceedings of the Sixth International Conference, Leonard N. Stern School of Business, New York University, January 6-8, 1999*, M.I.T. Press, Cambridge, MA.

Los, C. A. (2000c) "Frequency and Time Dependence of Financial Risk," *The Journal of Performance Measurement*, **5** (4), Summer 2000.

Merton, R. C. (1973) "Theory of Rational Options Pricing," *Bell Journal of Economics and Management Science*, **4**, Spring, 141 - 183.

O'Brien, J. and Srivastava, S. (1996) *Investments, A Visual Approach: Options Tutor,* South-Western College Publishing, New York, NY.

Osborne, M. F. M. (1959) "Brownian Motion in the Stock Market," *Operations Research*, **7**, March-April, 145 - 173. Reprinted as Chapter 4 in Cootner, P. H. (Ed.) (1964), *The Random Character of Stock Market Prices*, M.I.T. Press, Cambridge, MA, pp. 100 - 128.

Price, J. F. (1996) "Optional Mathematics Is Not Optional," *Notices of the American Mathematical Society*, **43** (9), 964 - 971.

Samuelson, P. A. (1965) "Proof That Properly Anticipated Prices Fluctuate Randomly," *Industrial Management Review*, **6**, Spring, 41 - 49.

chapter:10,page:1

Chapter 10
OPTION PRICING II

10.1 Introduction

In this Chapter we continue our financial discourse in terms of the exact speculative Complete Capital Market Pricing (CCMP) theory, using the risk-neutral valuation principle, to explain Black - Scholes option pricing (*Cf.* Merton, 1995, 1998). The CCMP theory of Chapter 8 assumes an artificial "parallel," or "complementary," risk-neutral world, in which the actual *stylized uncertainty*, together with the risk-free cash rate, is translated into state prices, *i.e.*, into discounted pseudo-probabilities, which are then used to value the various state payoffs of the securities with.

In the parallel world of a risk-neutral world, all assets have the same expected return equal to the risk-free rate of interest, because risk-neutral investors do not require any premium for bearing risk. Thus, in this parallel world, the rate of return on an asset, *i.e.*, the growth rate of its price, equals the risk-free rate of interest of a zero-coupon discount bond. If not, risk-free arbitrage profits could still be obtained in this risk-neutral world. This would be in contradiction with the assumption that the market in this parallel valuation world is always in efficient equilibrium.

In 1973, three professors of Finance, Fischer Black (Fig. 1), Myron Scholes and Robert Merton, derived a formula to price European call options on non-dividend paying stocks by similar abstracting arguments.* The Black - Scholes pricing model is an speculative exact model. It can be derived from the binomial pricing model by the usual limiting convergence argument (*Cf.* Chapter 1), based on the strict independence of the states, combined with the assumption that stock prices follow a *continuous (= differentiable), stationary,* geometric Brownian (= Wiener) motion.

A discontinuity in the stock prices is not accommodated by Black and Scholes' original model, but Merton (1975) derived a formula, which allows stock price movements to be discontinuous. However, the Brownian motion requires *complete independence* of the innovations, or shocks, a condition which, as Kalman demonstrated (1996), cannot satisfied by the finite empirical world, and which more recently is corroborated not to exist empirically. Given these, necessarily unrealistic, assumptions it should not surprise us that the Black - Scholes model delivers a closed-form solution,

---

*In 1997 Myron S. Scholes received (jointly with Robert C. Merton) the Nobel Memorial Prize in Economics for this new method to determine the value of derivatives. Fischer Black had died two years earlier. The Nobel Prize is only awarded to living scientists.

Figure 1   In Memoriam: Fischer Black, 1938 - 1995

not unlike the DDM of chapter 3, but at the cost of introducing a variable which is only indirectly observable and which has to be estimated: the volatility of the stock price.

All variables in the Black - Scholes model are independent of the risk preferences of the investors and the model is thus risk-neutral. This speculative, exact pricing model, and its various extensions and derivations, is widely used by financial analysts, traders, financial engineers, etc., to price stock options, stock index options, currency options, commodity price options, *et cetera*. This occurs, despite the fact that the model is not scientifically corroborated by empirical market pricing. In fact, it tends to provide biased pricing, open for arbitrage, because it does not properly allow asymmetrics and for epistemic (model) uncertainty.[†]

The continuing popularity of the speculative exact Black - Scholes model derives from the fact that, given the abstract assumption of perfect markets, it computes a rational price for options independent of any views of market direction. The Black - Scholes price is independent of the market's (expected) direction, since it prices

---

[†]Notwithstanding these scientific shortcomings, Robert C. Merton (Harvard) and Myron S. Scholes (Stanford) received in 1997 the "Bank of Sweden Prize in Economic Sciences in Memory of Alfred Nobel "for a new method to determine the value of derivatives," published in 1973. Fischer Black died in 1996 and Nobel Prizes aren't awarded posthumously, but his contribution was acknowledged in the Prize's citation. Additional reasons cited are: "Their methodology has paved the way for economic valuations in many areas. It has also generated new types of financial instruments and facilitated more efficient risk management in society." The Chicago Board of Options Exchange introduced trade in options in April 1973, one month before publication of the Black-Scholes option-pricing formula.

risk measured by the *symmetric* standard deviation σ_s which measures the volatility of the underlying asset price. However, *in empiria*, it is found that empirical price distributions are skewed and not symmetric.

10.2 Black - Scholes Option Pricing

In this Section, we'll discuss both the Black-Scholes pricing of non-dividend-paying stock and of continuous dividend-paying stock.

10.2.1 Non-Dividend-Paying Stock

Under Certainty

Recall from the preceding Chapter 9 the continuous version of the Put-Call Parity

$$c_0 - p_0 = S_0 - Xe^{-rT} \tag{10.1}$$

This implies that, under the abstract conditions of *model certainty*, an *in-the-money* European call option $c_0 > 0$ (when the put value is zero, $p_0 = 0$) is valued by the portfolio of purchasing (= long) a non-dividend-paying stock S_0 and paying for it by selling (= short) a bond with discounted value equivalent to the strike price r, so that for maturity) T, strike price X, and constant (= "flat ") risk-free interest rate r. Thus its (theoretical) *intrinsic value* is:

$$c_0 = S_0 - Xe^{-rT} \tag{10.2}$$

Under Stylized Uncertainty

Of course, the empirical world exhibits uncertainty. But instead of scientifically measuring this empirical uncertainty, randomness, or irregularity, as suggested by Kalman and Pincus (Kalman, 1996; Pincus and Singer, 1996; Pincus and Kalman, 1997) to model the option pricing, the Merton-Black - Scholes paradigm has been to postulate the *stylized uncertainty* of independent, identically distributed rate of return increments. Then it prices a call option under the conditions of this stylized uncertainty. We will show how the Black - Scholes model results from applying a limiting convergence argument to the binomial option pricing model discussed in Chapter 9, which prices options under the conditions of this stationary probabilistic uncertainty, *i.e.*, a very peculiar form of stylized uncertainty.[‡] Thus the Black - Scholes model is also a speculative exact model, like the DDM of Chapter 3.

Generalizing Binomial Option Pricing Recall from Chapter 9 that with discrete time periods, under conditions of stylized uncertainty, we found that the exact

---

[‡]There exist now **two** speculative theories of stylized stationary probability, Kolmogorov's original axiomatic definition (1933; *cf.* Chapter 8), and non-Kolmogorov axiomatic probability, which is currently researched by mathematics Professor Luigi Accardi in Rome, Italy (Accardi, 1988).

one-period binomial option pricing model produces the call option value

$$c_0 = \mathbf{c}_1' \boldsymbol{\pi}$$
$$= \pi_u c_u + \pi_d c_d$$
$$= p_u \frac{c_u}{(1+r)} + p_d \frac{c_d}{(1+r)} \tag{10.3}$$

where

$$c_u = \max(S_0(1+u) - X, 0) \text{ and} \tag{10.4}$$
$$c_d = \max(S_0(1+d) - X, 0) \tag{10.5}$$

with *state prices*

$$\pi_u = \frac{(r-d)}{(1+r)(u-d)} \text{ and} \tag{10.6}$$

$$\pi_d = \frac{(u-r)}{(1+r)(u-d)} \tag{10.7}$$

where u is an up tick and d a down tick in the stock price, or, equivalently, with *risk-neutral pseudo-probabilities*

$$p_u = (1+r)\pi_u = \frac{(r-d)}{(u-d)} \text{ and} \tag{10.8}$$

$$p_d = (1+r)\pi_d = \frac{(u-r)}{(u-d)} \tag{10.9}$$

Note again that these pseudo-probabilities do add up to unity $p_u + p_d = 1$.

Remark 86 *These up and down ticks are derived from the standard deviation of the stock price σ_{ss} by the following two first-order approximating formulas[§]*

$$1 + u = e^{+\sigma_s \sqrt{\Delta t}} \tag{10.10}$$

$$1 + d = e^{-\sigma_s \sqrt{\Delta t}} \tag{10.11}$$

where the fundamental time unit for pricing $\Delta t = \frac{T}{m}$, i.e., T is the maturity of the option and m is the frequency of pricing. In the following exposition, we set $m = T$, so that we normalize $\Delta t = 1$.

Similarly, the exact two-period binomial option pricing model produces the call option value

$$c_0 = p_u^2 \frac{c_{uu}}{(1+r)^2} + 2p_u p_d \frac{c_{ud}}{(1+r)^2} + p_d^2 \frac{c_{dd}}{(1+r)^2} \tag{10.12}$$

[§]These approximating formulas come out of the $\widehat{I}$to calculus of geometric random walk theory.(*Cf.* Gibson, 1991) where

$$c_{uu} = \max\left[S_0(1+u)^2 - X, 0\right] \tag{10.13}$$

$$c_{ud} = \max\left[S_0(1+u)(1+d) - X, 0\right] = c_{du} \text{ and} \tag{10.14}$$

$$c_{dd} = \max\left[S_0(1+d)^2 - X, 0\right] \tag{10.15}$$

with the same risk-neutral probabilities. This two-period form can be rearranged, so that the general structure of binomial pricing can be deduced

$$
\begin{aligned}
c_0 &= \frac{1}{(1+r)^2} \sum_{j=0}^{2} \binom{2}{j} p_u^j p_d^{2-j} \max\left[S_0(1+u)^j(1+d)^{2-j} - X, 0\right] \\
&= \frac{1}{(1+r)^2} \sum_{j=0}^{2} \frac{2!}{j!(2-j)!} p_u^j p_d^{2-j} \max\left[S_0(1+u)^j(1+d)^{2-j} - X, 0\right]
\end{aligned} \tag{10.16}
$$

Here

$$
\binom{2}{j} = \frac{2!}{2!(2-j)!} \tag{10.17}
$$

$$
= \frac{1}{(2-j)!} \tag{10.18}
$$

is the binomial coefficient = the number of combinations for two trials (= the number of up ticks in a total of two trials). By induction, the generalized exact multi-period binomial option pricing model provides the call option value

$$c_0 = \frac{1}{(1+r)^T} \sum_{j=0}^{T} \binom{T}{j} \left(p_u^j p_d^{T-j}\right) \max\left[S_0(1+u)^j(1+d)^{T-j} - X, 0\right] \tag{10.19}$$

where

$$
\binom{T}{j} = \frac{T!}{j!(T-j)!} \tag{10.20}
$$

is the binomial coefficient for a total of T trials.[¶] Since we know that the option will finish *in-the-money* on all these paths, it is no longer necessary to take the maximum. Thus, in expanded form

$$c_0 = S_0 \left[\sum_{j=0}^{T} \binom{T}{j} \frac{(p_u(1+u))^j (p_d(1+d))^{T-j}}{(1+r)^j(1+r)^{T-j}}\right] - \frac{X}{(1+r)^T} \left[\sum_{j=a}^{T} \binom{T}{j} p_u^j p_d^{T-j}\right] \tag{10.21}$$

[¶]Suppose you want to form a three-person team from fifteen candidates and you want to know how many possible teams can be formed: $\binom{15}{3} \equiv \frac{15!}{3!(15-3)!} = \frac{15!}{3!12!} = \frac{15.14.13}{3.2.1} = 455$ teams. Here $n! = n*(n-1)!$ and $0! = 1$.

When we define the new risk-neutral pseudo-probabilities

$$
\begin{aligned}
\frac{p_u(1+u)}{(1+r)} &= (1+u)\pi_u \\
&= \frac{(r-d)(1+u)}{(u-d)(1+r)} \\
&= b
\end{aligned}
\tag{10.22}
$$

we find that

$$
\begin{aligned}
\frac{p_d(1+d)}{(1+r)} &= (1+d)\pi_d \\
&= \frac{(u-r)(1+d)}{(u-d)(1+r)} \\
&= (1-b)
\end{aligned}
\tag{10.23}
$$

Notice that these new risk-neutral pseudo probabilities consist of the original risk-neutral probabilities, multiplied by one additional discounted up, or down tick, which is the same as the original state prices with one more up, or down tick.

With these substitutions, we can finally write the general exact binomial option pricing model in a somewhat simpler form as

$$
\begin{aligned}
c_0 &= S_0 \left[\sum_{j=0}^{T} \binom{T}{j} b^j (1-b)^{T-j} \right] - \frac{X}{(1+r)^T} \left[\sum_{j=a}^{T} \binom{T}{j} p_u^j (1-p_u)^{T-j} \right] \\
&= S_0 B\,[T,b] - \frac{X}{(1+r)^T} B\,[T,p_u]
\end{aligned}
\tag{10.24}
$$

where B stands for "binomial distribution." Thus the call option's price is equal to the discounted expected future value of the stock, given that the stock will end up in-the-money: $S_0 B\,[T,b]$ less the present value of the expected cost incurred by exercising the call (*i.e.*, for which we pay cash) $-\frac{X}{(1+r)^T} B\,[T,p_u]$.

We now apply the conventional limiting convergence argument combined with the continuity and complete independence assumptions to these two binomial distributions. These two binomial distributions form the new, rather convoluted state prices by which we value the stock price and the discounted strike price in the risk-neutral world. When the number of unit periods $\Delta t = \frac{T}{m}$, into which we divide the maturity T, increases, the strictly up-and down ticks become smaller and smaller. So, arguably, we switch from discretely compounded rates of return to continuously compounded rates of return, since

$$
\lim_{m \to \infty} m(1 + \frac{rT}{m}) = e^{rT}
\tag{10.25}
$$

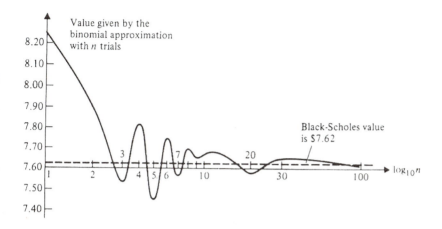

Figure 2 Limiting binomial option pricing of an American call with no dividend payments

and the two binomial distributions transform into two standard normal cumulative distributions.$^{\parallel}$

This limiting convergence process of the binomial option pricing towards the Black - Scholes price is not smooth, as can be seen in Fig. 2.

Remark 87 *We emphasize that this limiting convergence transformation is only true under the abstract theoretical assumptions of continuity and complete independence. In empirical reality, which is fractally discrete, discontinuous, finite and, most importantly, (time) dependent, these assumptions don't hold true and the abstract limiting process does not apply. Consequently, at this moment we have to conclude that the following Black - Scholes pricing is a speculative exact valuation model and not a scientific empirical inexact valuation model, of which we know the degree of epistemic uncertainty.*

Black - Scholes Option Pricing In the limit, under the abstract assumptions of *stylized uncertainty, continuity* and *complete independence*, the limiting process converges to the exact Black - Scholes option pricing model, which incorporates the risk-neutral pseudo-probabilities in the form of two *standard normal cumulative distributions* $N(d_1)$ and $N(d_2)$, such that the European call option price is

$$c_0 = S_0 N(d_1) - X e^{-rT} N(d_2) \tag{10.26}$$

$^{\parallel}$For a complete explanation of this limiting convergence process, *Cf.* Gibson (1991, Chapter 4); also Black and Scholes (1973).

Here $N(d_i)$ is the probability that a standard normally distributed variable with mean 0 and variance 1 is less than $d_i, i = 1, 2$, where

$$d_1 = \frac{\ln(\frac{S_0}{X}) + (r + \frac{\sigma_{ss}}{2})T}{\sigma_s \sqrt{T}} \qquad (10.27)$$

and

$$d_2 = \frac{\ln(\frac{S_0}{X}) + (r - \frac{\sigma_{ss}}{2})T}{\sigma_s \sqrt{T}}$$
$$= d_1 - \sigma_s \sqrt{T} \qquad (10.28)$$

where σ_{ss} is the variance, and $\sigma_s = \sqrt{\sigma_{ss}}$ the volatility, of the stock price (which is assumed to move as a *Wiener process*), and r is the constant risk-free interest rate.

Applying the Put-Call Parity, one finds that the Black - Scholes value of an *in-the-money* European *put option* p_0 (when the intrinsic call value is zero) is

$$p_0 = -S_0 N(-d_1) + Xe^{-rT} N(-d_2) \qquad (10.29)$$

10.2.2   Continuous-Dividend-Paying Stock

If the stock pays continuous dividend (*e.g.*, a stock index), with a certain dividend yield equal to g, the Black - Scholes pricing model is modified in the following way: we discount the stock price for the accumulated dividend. Thus, the Black - Scholes value of an in-the-money European call option c_0, with exercise price X, on stock S_0 is

$$c_0 = S_0 e^{-gT} N(d_1) - Xe^{-rT} N(d_2) \qquad (10.30)$$

$N(d_i)$ is the probability that a standard normally distributed variable with mean 0 and variance 1 is less than $d_i, i = 1, 2$, where

$$d_1 = \frac{\ln(\frac{S_0}{X}) + (r - g + \frac{\sigma_{ss}}{2})T}{\sqrt{\sigma_{ss}T}} \qquad (10.31)$$

σ_{ss} is the variance of the stock price and r is the constant risk-free interest rate and

$$d_2 = \frac{\ln(\frac{S_0}{X}) + (r - g - \frac{\sigma_{ss}}{2})T}{\sigma_s \sqrt{T}}$$
$$= d_1 - \sigma_s \sqrt{T} \qquad (10.32)$$

Applying the put-call parity, one finds that the Black - Scholes value of an in-the-money European put option p_0 is

$$p_0 = c_0 - S_0 e^{-gT} + Xe^{-rT}$$
$$= S_0 e^{-gT} N(d_1) - Xe^{-rT} N(d_2) - S_0 e^{-gT} + Xe^{-rT} \qquad (10.33)$$

so that

$$p_0 = S_0 e^{-gT} [N(d_1) - 1] - X e^{-rT} [N(d_2) - 1] \qquad (10.34)$$

or, equivalently,

$$p_0 = -S_0 e^{-gT} N(-d_1) + X e^{-rT} N(-d_2) \qquad (10.35)$$

10.3 Historical and Implied Volatility

10.3.1 Volatility Computation by "Trial and Error"

O'Brien and Srivastava (1997) provide the following example of IBM stock options. The stock price less the present value of the dividend was $44.26, and the risk-free rate was 2.867%, while the published strike prices were 35, 40, 45 and 50. The date of the information was October 15, 1993 and the maturity date of the option was November 20, 1993. Furthermore, the historical volatility or risk of the return of the IBM stock price had been estimated at 30% (*i.e.*, $\sigma_s = 0.3$) so we have the five data inputs

$$S_0 = 44.26, \, r = 0.02867, \, \sigma_{ss} = 0.09, \, T = 0.0986$$

The value of T is calculated by counting the number of days to maturity and dividing by 365 days. Typically, the variance of the stock returns is calculated on a monthly or weekly basis; this then is annualized. Thus the standard deviation or volatility of this stock price is 30%/*year*.

Empirical real world volatility estimates are often not stationary or independent. This contradicts the essential assumptions of the Black - Scholes model that the stock prices follow a geometric Brownian motion

$$\Delta S_t = \ln S_t - \ln S_{t-1} = \varepsilon_t, \, \varepsilon_t \sim i.i.d(0, \sigma_{ss}) \qquad (10.36)$$

Therefore in practice sensitivity analysis is applied, by varying the size of the variance a bit. This led to the following Black - Scholes option prices in Table 1, compared with the actual bid and ask prices (whereby, for convenience, the usual quotes in "eights" have been converted into decimals).

TABLE 1:	Prices		Volatility		
Strike	Bid	Ask	0.30	0.35	0.40
35	9.375	9.875	9.37	9.38	9.42
40	4.875	5.000	4.64	4.79	4.98
45	1.437	1.875	1.39	1.66	1.94
50	0.5	0.375	0.28	0.36	0.54

Remark 88 *The fact that there are bid - ask spreads is a indication that these markets are not perfectly liquid, as the theory assumes, since the bid and ask prices differ by, at least, the transaction costs. Since the bid and ask prices differ from each other, the Single Price Law of Efficient Markets is empirically violated. In a perfectly efficient market there are no transaction costs (since information is gratis!) and the bid and ask prices are the same.*

Only when the volatility is a higher 35%, the Black - Scholes model yielded prices within the observed bid - ask spreads, while the option values obtained from the historically estimated volatility of 30% were slightly lower than the observed market prices. This suggests that the measured volatility doesn't capture all the pricing uncertainty, *e.g.*, pricing uncertainty includes epistemic uncertainty.

The essential problem here is that one parameter in the Black - Scholes pricing model cannot be observed directly: the volatility of the stock σ_s. But using the pricing model, one can infer from the observed option price the *implied volatility*.

Example 89 *Suppose the value of a call on a non-dividend-paying stock is 1.875 when $S_0 = 21$, $X = 20$, $r = 0.10$, and $T = 0.25$. The unique implied volatility is the value of σ_s, which when substituted into the Black - Scholes model gives $c_0 = 1.875$. This implied value can then found by a bit of trial - and - error.*

Remark 90 *Implied volatilities can be used to monitor the market's subjective opinion about the volatility, or market risk of a particular stock. In many empirical markets this subjective market risk changes over time. In fact, one can conclude from this perspective that the option market prices the stock price risk! One can also use it to compute the Black - Scholes price of one option from the price of another option. Even so, one should remain aware that the implied volatility σ_s consists of two parts: the systematic stock price risk $\widehat{\sigma}_s$ and the epistemic uncertainty or unsystematic risk $\widetilde{\sigma}_s$ about the Black - Scholes pricing model. Thus $\sigma_s = \widehat{\sigma}_s + \widetilde{\sigma}_s$. When viewed in this fashion, the Black - Scholes model can be viewed as an imperfect measurement model to observe the systematic stock price risk.*

10.3.2 Volatility Computation by At-the-Money Formula

Bharadia, Christofides and Salkin (1995 and 1996) presented a new closed form formula for computing the implied volatility for at-the-money call options, *i.e.*, when the stock price equals the strike price, $S_t = X$. Recently, we made a comparison between the implied volatility as computed by the conventional open-ended "trial and error" method and new closed-form solution of Bharadia *et al.* (1995; *cf.* Los, 1997). In both cases one can plot the *volatility smile*, *i.e.*, the relationship between the volatility and the level of the strike price.

We empirically falsify their claims that their at-the-money formula produces a more moderate implied volatility than the conventional trial-and-error method and therefore leads to a more efficient empirical fit. This can be easily demonstrated in

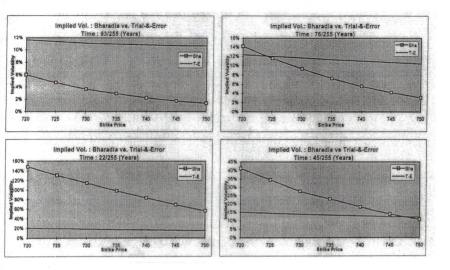

Figure 3   Comparison of volatility smiles: Bharadia et al. at-the-money formula (Bha) versus trial-and-error (T-E)

Fig. 3. First, Bharadia's formula produces too much curvature in the volatility smile, so that their volatility is quickly too large for relatively low strike prices. Second, on some days, their volatility smile can be shown to be empirically larger or lower than the trial-and-error volatility at all available strike prices. This unpredictable inconsistency between the two available methods is a reflection of the fundamental epistemic uncertainty inherent in the application of the exact speculative Black - Scholes to empirical market data. Both methods can lead, and often do lead, to serious mispricing of options, providing considerable arbitrage opportunities.[**]

10.4   Options' Greek Alphabet

Similar to the theoretical world of quantum mechanics (from where the original CCMP theory emerged. *Cf.* Risk.FINEX, 1992), the world of options has produced a variety of expressions describing the various option sensitivities. These sensitivities are used for fine tuning and arbitrage of option prices, and for specialized hedging (*Cf.* Walmsley, 1992). Most of these option sensitivities are derived from the following simple multi-dimensional, extended, second - order *Taylor expansion,* describing the change in the option price under the influence of the various independent factors

---

[**]So much so, for example, that in 1993 ING Bank, Inc. in New York employed one full trader to exploit these option arbitrage opportunities.

(*Cf.* Chapter 2):

$$\Delta c_0 = \delta.\Delta S_0 + \frac{\gamma.(\Delta S_0)^2}{2} + \rho.\Delta r + v.\Delta \sigma_s + \theta.\Delta T \tag{10.37}$$

and

$$\Delta p_0 = \delta_p.\Delta S_0 + \frac{\gamma_p.(\Delta S_0)^2}{2} + \rho_p.\Delta r + v_p.\Delta \sigma_s + \theta_p.\Delta T \tag{10.38}$$

Here $\Delta =$ "change in" *ceteris paribus, i.e.*, when keeping all other factors constant.

$\delta = \frac{\Delta c_0}{\Delta S_0} = delta$, the sensitivity of the call option price c_0 to a change in the market price S_0 of the underlying stock. For the Black - Scholes option pricing model $\delta = N(d_1)$

$\gamma = \frac{\Delta c_0}{(\Delta S_0)^2} = \frac{\delta}{\Delta S_0} = gamma$, the sensitivity of delta to a change in the market price S_0 of the underlying stock;

$\rho = \frac{\Delta c_0}{\Delta r} = rho$, the sensitivity of the call option price c_0 to a change in the risk-free rate of interest;

$v = \frac{\Delta c_0}{\Delta \sigma_s} = vega$, the sensitivity of the call option price c_0 to a change in the stock price's volatility $\sigma_s = \sqrt{\sigma_{ss}}$.

$\theta = \frac{\Delta c_0}{\Delta T} = theta$, the sensitivity of the call option price c_0 to a change in the maturity of the option T.

Example 91 *At a given price the (empirically measured) sensitivities of a call option are as follows:* $\delta = 0.45/point$, $\gamma = 0.05/point$, $\rho = 0.05/\%$, $v = 0.12/\%$, $\theta = 0.05/day$. *If* $\Delta S_0 = 2 points$, $\Delta \sigma_s = 6\%/year$, $\Delta r = 0.15\%$, $\Delta T = -1 day$ *then the price of the call option can be calculated to change by* $\Delta c_0 = \$1.68$.

Remark 92 *It is important to emphasize that this theoretical option price sensitivity - un extended second-order Taylor expansion - holds only true when it is assumed that the changes are linearly independent or orthogonal, i.e., show no correlations. However, both theory and empiry suggest a much more complex nonlinear system of relationships, with correlations due to both systematic and unsystematic influences. For example, in the Black - Scholes pricing model, the delta $\delta = N(d_1)$ is already a function of five variables r, σ_s, T, S_0 and X. The raw data set of the Black - Scholes model contains six variables $[c_0, S_0, r, X, \sigma_s, T]$. It has been suggested that these six variables can be modeled by an inexact linear model of several independent simultaneous equations, which should be identified from the complete data covariance matrix. These raw data may be subjected to exact nonlinear transformations before covariance analysis is applied. The usual Taylor expansion approximation of the Black - Scholes model restricts itself to only one unilateral projection $c_0 = c_0[S_0, r, X, \sigma_s, T]$, but, in principle, other projections are possible. For example, $S_0 = S_0[c_0, r, X, \sigma_s, T]$,*

$r = r\,[S_0, c_0, X, \sigma_s, T]$, *or the implied volatility projection* $\sigma_s = [c_0, S_0, r, X, T]$ *are all allowable projections. Current research is precisely focusing on this multidirectional projection issue, since it may generate some additional arbitrage profits, if it helps the dynamic hedging.*

Example 93 *In Fig. 4. we have visualized the empirical November option on Hong Kong's Hang Seng Index, as priced on October 3, 1996, in four dimensions. (Cf. Derman, Kani and Zou, 1996, for a similar, but theoretical surface). The data are from The Asian Wall Street Journal of October 4, 1996. We find on the two horizontal reference ordinates the available strike prices* X *and times to maturity* T, *respectively, and on the vertical ordinate the call prices* c_0. *The two variables that were fixed by the end of trading day time are the stock index* S_0 *and the risk-free rate* r. *The volatility is indicated by coloring or shading. This 4D visualization immediately reveals which option contracts show high volatility (likely to be expensive) or low volatility (likely to be cheap). This is important information for option traders, who are searching for arbitrage opportunities. Similar visualizations will assist scientific financial analysis in a way that was unthinkable even a decade ago (Cf. Galagher, 1994; Nielson, Hagen and Müller, 1997; Wolff and Yaeger,1993)*

By simple derivation, we can find from the Black - Scholes models for the call c_0 and the put p_0 the following explicit sensitivity relationships for calls c_0 and puts p_0. First, the sensitivity of the call and the put to the underlying stock price, as expressed by

Delta

$$\delta_c = \frac{\Delta c_0}{\Delta S_0} = e^{-gT} N(d_1) \tag{10.39}$$

and

$$\delta_p = \frac{\Delta p_0}{\Delta S_0} = e^{-qT}\,[N(d_1) - 1] \tag{10.40}$$

Gamma

$$\gamma_c = \frac{\Delta\Delta c_0}{(\Delta S_0)^2} = \frac{\Delta \delta_c}{\Delta S_0} = \frac{e^{-qT} N'(d_1)}{S_0 \sqrt{\sigma_{ss} T}} = \frac{\Delta \delta_p}{\Delta P} = \frac{\Delta\Delta p_0}{(\Delta S_0)^2} = \gamma_p > 0 \tag{10.41}$$

where the first derivative of the standard normal cumulative distribution is:

$$N'(d1) = \frac{1}{\sqrt{2\pi}} e^{-\frac{d_1^2}{2}} \tag{10.42}$$

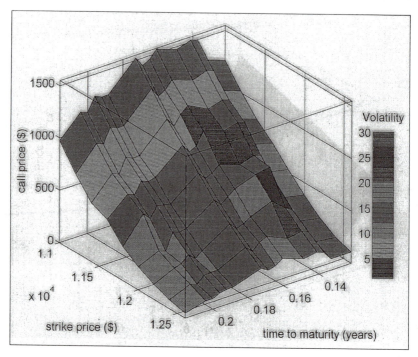

Figure 4   Hang Seng Index November Option, 3 Oct 1996, value in four dimensions

Next, we look at the interest rate sensitivity of the call and put, or the
Rho

$$\rho_c = \frac{\Delta c_0}{\Delta r} = XTe^{-rT}N(d_2) > 0 \qquad (10.43)$$

and

$$\rho_p = \frac{\Delta p_0}{\Delta r} = -XTe^{-rT}N(-d_2) < 0 \qquad (10.44)$$

Then, the very important sensitivity of the call and the put to the volatility:
Vega

$$\upsilon_c = \frac{\Delta c_0}{\Delta \sigma_s} = S_0 e^{-qT}N'(d_1)\sqrt{T} = \frac{\Delta p_0}{\Delta \sigma_s} = \upsilon_p > 0 \qquad (10.45)$$

Finally, the sensitivity of the call and the put with respect to the maturity of each:

Theta

$$\theta_c = \frac{\Delta c_0}{\Delta T} = \frac{-S_0 e^{-qT} N'(d_1)\sigma_s}{2\sqrt{T}} - q S_0 e^{-qT} N(d_1) + r X e^{-rT} N(d_2) \qquad (10.46)$$

and

$$\theta_p = \frac{\Delta p_0}{\Delta T} = \frac{+S_0 e^{-qT} N'(d_1)\sigma_s}{2\sqrt{T}} + q S_0 e^{-qT} N(-d_1) - r X e^{-rT} N(-d_2) \qquad (10.47)$$

Remark 94 *Notice that for the Gamma and the Vega the expressions for the call and the put options are the same, but that the Delta, Rho and Theta derivatives differ between the call and the put options.*

10.5 Dynamic Hedging Strategies

The previous single equation sensitivity relationships are used for hedging. For example, to temporarily offset an disadvantageous change in a strategic long position of a common stock, one can short options. The delta provides information on how many options to buy, since, *ceteris paribus*, there is no impact on the net portfolio position, when

$$\Delta c_0 - \delta \Delta S_0 = 0 \qquad (10.48)$$

$$\text{or } \Delta S_0 = \frac{1}{\delta} \Delta c_0 \left(= \frac{1}{\delta} \text{ when } \Delta c_0 = 1 \right) \qquad (10.49)$$

In other words, the change in the long stock position can be hedged by shorting $\frac{1}{\delta}$ options. This is called *delta hedging*. For the Black - Scholes European option pricing model for non-dividend-paying stock, the *hedge ratio* for a call option is

$$h = \frac{1}{\delta} = \frac{1}{N(d_1)} \qquad (10.50)$$

and for a put option

$$h = \frac{1}{\delta} = \frac{1}{N(d_1) - 1} \qquad (10.51)$$

Looking at the definition of δ, for continuous-dividend-paying stock the hedge ratios are for a call option

$$h = \frac{1}{\delta} = \frac{1}{e^{-qT} N(d_1)} \qquad (10.52)$$

and for a put option

$$h = \frac{1}{\delta} = \frac{1}{e^{-qT}[N(d_1) - 1]} \quad (10.53)$$

But since the hedge ratios depend on variables r, σ_s, T, S_0 and r and these variables change over time, the hedge ratios change too. Thus, in delta hedging the option portfolio must be dynamically rebalanced over time. One must continuously buy and sell options. This may lead to extra transaction costs, which should be accounted for in total optimal portfolio management.

10.6   Exercises

Exercise 95 *The Black - Scholes pricing model for a European call option with an annual continuous dividend yield g on the underlying asset is*

$$c_0 = S_0 e^{gt} N(d_1) - X e^{-rT} N(d) \quad (10.54)$$

where

$$d = \frac{\ln(S_0/X) + (r - g - \sigma_s^2/2)T}{\sigma_s \sqrt{T}} \quad (10.55)$$

and

$$d_1 = d + \sigma_s \sqrt{T} \quad (10.56)$$

Given the usual values of the standard normal cumulative distribution $N(d)$ for $0 \leq d \leq 3.99$ (to be found in a statistical table, or in EXCEL as the function NORMS-DIST), assume a stock with an annual dividend yield of 5%. The annual interest rate is 10%, time to maturity is six months (= 0.5 years), the strike price is \$102, the current stock price is \$100 and the volatility, measured by the standard deviation, of the underlying stock price is 6%. What is the call option price?

Exercise 96 *The Put-Call Parity in continuous time, which incorporates a continuous dividend yield on the underlying asset is*

$$c_0 = p_0 + S_0 e^{-gT} - X e^{-rT} \quad (10.57)$$

Assume all the data inputs to be the same as in the preceding question. What is the price of the corresponding European put option?

Exercise 97 *Set up an EXCEL spreadsheet for the Black - Scholes pricing of a European option. Suppose we observe the following current data for this stock call option: stock price = \$40.00; cash interest rate = 3.75%; maturity = 3 months; strike price = \$38.00; stock price volatility = 50% on an annual basis. What is the Black - Scholes price of this European call option?*

Exercise 98 *Assuming that the current Nikkei–225 Index is at ¥14500, the annual dividend of the Nikkei Index 2.5%, the Japanese annual interest rate is 2.75%, time to maturity is three months and the volatility of the return of the underlying asset is 25%/year, what is the price of the call option with a strike price of ¥15500?*

Exercise 99 *Consider a stock that pays continuous dividend with a dividend yield of 2%. The stock currently sells for $50. The volatility of the stock is 40% and the risk-free rate is 6%/year. You have in your portfolio different European options with exactly three months to maturity. Compute the delta, gamma and vega of the following options: Call options with exercise price of 45, 50 and 55 and put options with exercise price 45,50 and 55*

Exercise 100 *Compute the delta, gamma and vega of a portfolio consisting of 150 units of the 45 call, 400 units of the 45 put and 200 units of the 55 call of the preceding question.*

Exercise 101 *Design a delta - neutral hedging strategy for this last portfolio, using a 50 call.*

10.7   Bibliography

Black, F. and Scholes, M. (1973) "The Pricing of Options and Corporate Liabilities," *Journal of Political Economy*, **81**, May - June, 637 - 659.

   Bharadia, M. A. J., Christofides, N. and Salkin, G. R. (1995) "Computing the Black-Scholes Implied Volatility: Generalization of a Simple Formula," *Advances in Futures and Options Research*, **8**, 15-29.

   Bharadia, M. A. J., Christofides, N. and Salkin, G. R. (1996), "A Quadratic Method for the Calculation of Implied Volatility Using the Garman-Kohlhagen Model, " *Financial Analysts Journal*, **52** (2), 61 - 64.

   Bodie, Z. and Merton, R. C. (1995) "The Informational Role of Asset Prices: The Case of Implied Volatility," Chapter 6 in Crane, D. B. *et. al.* (Eds.), *The Global Financial System: A Functional Perspective*, Harvard Business School Press, Boston, MA, pp. 197 - 224.

   Clarke, R. G. (1992) "Short-Term Behavior of Option Prices: Hedging Relationships," Chapter 6 in *Options and Futures: A Exercise*, The Research Foundation of The Institute of Chartered Financial Analysts, Charlottesville, VA, pp. 57 - 68.

   Derman, E., Kani, I. and Zou, J. Z. (1996) "The Local Volatility Surface: Unlocking the Information in Index Option Prices," *Financial Analysts Journal*, July - August, 25 - 36.

   Gallagher, R. S. (Ed.) (1994) *Computer Visualization: Graphis Techniques for Scientific and Engineering Analysis*, CRC Press, Boca Raton, FL.

   Gibson, R. (1991) *Option Valuation: Analyzing and Pricing Standardized Option Contracts*, McGraw-Hill, Inc., New York, NY.

Hull, J. C. (1996) *Options, Futures and Other Derivatives,* (3rd ed.), Prentice Hall International, Inc., New York, NY.

Kalman, R. E. (1996) "Probability in the Real World as a System Attribute," *CWI Quarterly,* **9** (3), 181 - 204.

Kolmogorov, A. N. (1933) *Grundbegriffe der Wahrscheinlichkeitsrechnung,* Sprir Verlag, Berlin. (Translated by Nathan Morrison: *Foundations of Probability,* Chelsea, New York, NY, 1950).

Los, C. A. (1997) "Visualization of Call Options and Implied Volatility," *MOD-SIM97 - International Congress on Modelling and Simulation Proceedings,* **3,** 8 - 11 December, Hobart, Tasmania, pp. 1311 - 1316.

Merton, R. C. (1975) "Theory of Finance from the Perspective of Continuous Time," *Journal of Financial and Quantitative Analysis,* **10** (4), November, 659 - 674.

Merton, R. C. (1995) "Influence of Mathematical Models in Finance on Practice: Past, Present and Future," Chapter 1 in Howison, S. D., Kelly, F. P. and Wilmott, P. (Eds.), *Mathematical Models in Finance,* Chapman & Hall, London, pp. 1 - 13.

Merton, R. C. (1998) "Applications of Option-Pricing Theory: Twenty-Five Years Later," *American Economic Review,* 323 - 349.

Nielson, G. M., Hagen, H. and Müller, H. (1997) *Scientific Visualization: Overviews, Methodologies and Techniques,* IEEE Computer Society, Los Alamitos, CA.

Pincus, S. and R. E. Kalman (1997) "Not All (Possibly) "Random" Sequences Are Created Equal," *Proceedings of the National Academy of Sciences (USA),* **94,** April, 3513 - 3518.

Pincus, S. and B. H. Singer (1996) "Randomness and Degrees of Irregularity," *Proceedings of the National Academy of Sciences (USA),* **93,** 2083 - 2088.

Risk/FINEX (1992) *From Black - Scholes to Black Holes,* Risk Magazine, Ltd, London.

Walmsley, J. (1992) "Options Applications," Chapter 17 in his book *The Foreign Exchange and Money Markets Guide,* John Wiley & Sons, Inc., New York, NY, pp. 363 - 403.

Wolff, R. S. and Yaeger, L. (1993) *Visualization of Natural Phenomena,* Telos/Springer Verlag, Boston, MA.

chapter:11,page:1

Chapter 11
BOND PORTFOLIO VALUATION AND MANAGEMENT

11.1 Introduction

A fixed income security may appear to be a secure asset, since its valuation model appears exact and certain. Still, there are many other risks inherent in such a security, since there is more than one volatile variable which systematically influences the price of a bond. Not all of these influences are exact, since they are discontinuous.

For example, Chapter 3 showed that a Treasury bond is an multivariate exact model, when viewed as a simple five-variable instrument, with four continuously changing variables: its price PB_0, principal B_T, maturity T, coupon rate CF and interest rate r. However, a sixth variable may be related to it in an inexact fashion: the credit risk quality of the bond. This *credit grade* of a corporate bond ξ is a discontinuous variable and its relationship to the bond's value is uncertain.

That's why international rating agencies exist, like Moody's Investors Service, Standard & Poors Corporation, Duff and Phelps, , and Fitch Investors Service to identify and classify the grades of bonds, bank deposits, commercial paper, etc. (*Cf.* Altman, 1996, 1968; and Altman, Haldeman, Narayanan, 1977). A corporate bond may even migrate from one credit grade to other grades, as we saw in Chapter 8.

11.2 Bond Price Volatility

11.2.1 Risks in Fixed Income Securities

According to the various discernible systematic variables and identification models, we can discern the following risks inherent in corporate bonds:

1. *Interest rate risk* is the most common risk of fixed-income securities. The first and second order Taylor expansion approximations, *i.e.*, duration and convexity, are exact and continuous. However, total interest rate risk is essentially inexact, because higher-order effects have an impact beyond the first and second order, in particular, because the empirical option model surface (*Cf.* Chapter 10) is nonlinear and time-varying.

2. *Reinvestment risk* is speculative, inexact, discontinuous. One doesn't know at what level of the interest rates the coupon yield can be reinvested.

3. *Credit risk*, or *default risk* is inexact and discontinuous. It is essentially subjectively rated by specialized rating agencies, despite their impressive arsenal of quantification techniques.

4. *Volatility risk* of the market price, as a comprehensive measure, includes both the systematic risks and unsystematic risks.

5. *Call risk*, is inexact, per definition, as we saw in the open-ended binomial pricing and closed-form Black - Scholes models of Chapters 9 and 10, mainly because nobody can uniquely ascertain the underlying asset volatility, implicitly or explicitly.

6. *Liquidity risk* is inexact. The width of the bid-ask spread depends on the kind of market, in particular on the transaction costs and the costs of entry barriers.

7. *Yield-curve risk* is inexact. The first-order effects of a purely parallel shift in the yield curve can be modeled exactly, but the tilting of the yield curve, or its relative curvature, can not. Liquidity premiums make an exact term structure based on unbiased expectations practically impossible. Most fixed income markets exhibit some illiquid segmentation (= "bucket structure") because of institutional specialization of the investors with their different investment horizons and resulting cash flow (il-)liquidities*.

8. *Inflation, or purchasing power risk* is inexact, for the simple reason that there is not one agreed index for measuring overall price inflation and the measurement of the loss of purchasing power. Usually some fixed-weight consumer price index is used, although a chain price index would provide more consistent and accurate inflation measurement (Los, 1985). In addition, inflation prediction models can only be inexactly identified and not exactly realized.

9. *Currency risk* is inexact, but can also be split into exact systematic and inexact unsystematic risks

10. *Event risk* is, per definition, discontinuous and inexact.

11. *Sector risk* is inexact, *e.g.*, oil price risk for the bonds issued by an oil refinery caused by the discretionary, unsystematic and thus unidentifiable political decisions of the OPEC Cartel.

11.2.2 Measures of Interest-Rate Risk

The most common risk for bonds is interest rate risk, because a change in the interest rate exactly changes a bond's market value via its price - yield curve relationship.

---

*In one of my recent lectures I demonstrated that it even possible to design a cash flow viscosity coefficient, which measures the degrees of cash flow illiquidity of the segmented term structure caused by the different investment horizons.

Since each type of bond has its own price - yield curve, each bond has its own interest rate sensitivity. The slope and curvature of its exact price - yield curve determines how much its intrinsic value changes under the impact of a change in yield (Fig. 1.). The relative slope of the price - yield curve is measured by *modified duration* and its curvature by *convexity*.

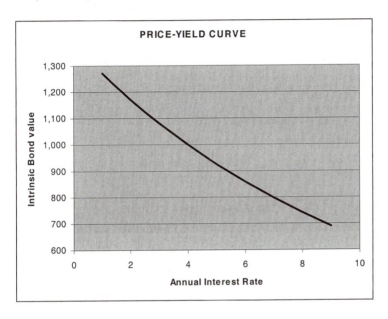

Figure 1   Price-yield curve of a coupon bond

Recall from Chapter 3 that the (present) value of a annual bond is the sum of an annuity and a discounted zero:

$$PB_0 = PVA_0 + PV_0$$
$$= \left[\sum_{t=1}^{T} \frac{CF}{(1+r)^t}\right] + \left[\frac{B_T}{(1+r)^T}\right] \tag{11.1}$$

The marginal change in the price of a bond caused by a marginal change in its yield r can be approximated by the following one factor, second-order Taylor expansion *approximation* (*Cf.* Chapter 2)

$$\Delta PB_0 = -\delta.\Delta r + \frac{\gamma.(\Delta r)^2}{2} \tag{11.2}$$

where, as before, Δ = "marginal change in," *ceteris paribus*, *i.e.*, keeping all other factors unchanged. Here

$$-\delta = \frac{\partial PB_0}{\partial r} \tag{11.3}$$

is the first derivative of the current bond value with respect to yield and a negative number (since $\delta > 0$), and

$$\gamma = \frac{\partial^2 PB_0}{\partial r^2} \tag{11.4}$$

its second derivative (usually, but not always, $\gamma > 0$).

11.3 Macauley and modified durations

11.3.1 Modified duration

*Modified duration D_{Mod} is the *relative* first order marginal (percentage) change in the (present) value of the bond caused by a marginal change in its yield r*

$$\begin{aligned} D_{Mod} &= \frac{\delta}{PB_0} \\ &= -\frac{1}{PB_0}\frac{\partial PB_0}{\partial r} \end{aligned} \tag{11.5}$$

The relationship between PB_0 and r is negative and the slope of this price - yield curve is given by $\frac{\partial PB_0}{\partial r}$, but (modified) duration δ is usually presented as a positive number (therefore the minus sign in the second equation). Duration is used in hedging of fixed-income securities, *e.g.*, bond portfolio immunization. But how does one compute D_{Mod}?

11.3.2 Interpretation and Various Definitions

There are actually many useful ways of computing duration based on its various definitions, each with its own purpose and interpretation. Historically, the first duration concept developed for fixed-income securities was Macauley duration. It was proposed in 1938 by Frederick Macauley of the U.S.' National Bureau of Economic Research (NBER). But already in 1945 it was understood by M.I.T. Professor Paul Samuelson that Macauley duration was related to the interest rate sensitivity measured by modified duration.[†] In the 1980s the concept of modified duration was popularized, and effectively used to generate arbitrage profits, by Dr. Martin Leibowitz, the Director of Research of Salomon Brothers, Inc.

[†]Paul Anthony Samuelson, b. 1915, is the author of *Economics* (15th ed. in 1995, with W. D. Nordhaus), the largest-selling college economics textbook in the world. His published Ph.D. dissertation, *Foundations of Economic Analysis* (1947), was one of the earliest attempts to apply mathematical principles to economic problems. Samuelson won the Nobel Memorial Prize in Economics in 1970.

11.3.3 Macauley duration

Macauley duration, D_{Mac} is the *weighted average time* of the receipt of the total value of the bond. It answers the question "how long does it take, on average, to get all your money back?", or "what is the average time that a bond investment is outstanding." Thus Macauley duration is defined as

$$D_{Mac} = \frac{\left[\sum_{t=1}^{T} \frac{t.CF}{(1+r)^t}\right] + \left[\frac{T.B_T}{(1+r)^T}\right]}{PB_0} \tag{11.6}$$

The various time periods of the bond are weighted by its constituent discounted cash flows, relative to the (present) value of the bond.

How are Macauley duration and modified duration related? By taking the first derivative of the bond with respect to its yield r, we find that

$$\frac{\partial PB_0}{\partial r} = \sum_{t=1}^{T} \frac{-t.CF}{(1+r)^{t+1}} + \frac{-T.B_T}{(1+r)^{T+1}}$$

$$= \frac{-1}{(1+r)}\left[\sum_{t=1}^{T} \frac{t.CF}{(1+r)^t} + \frac{T.B_T}{(1+r)^T}\right] \tag{11.7}$$

But then

$$D_{Mod} = -\frac{1}{PB_0}\frac{\partial PB_0}{\partial r}$$

$$= \frac{1}{(1+r)}\frac{\left[\sum_{t=1}^{T} \frac{t.CF}{(1+r)^t} + \frac{T.B_T}{(1+r)^T}\right]}{PB_0} \tag{11.8}$$

or

$$D_{Mod} = \frac{D_{Mac}}{(1+r)} \tag{11.9}$$

Since modified duration is the percentage change in price for a given change in yield, one can approximate the first-order relative sensitivity of the bond price to a change in its yield by

$$\frac{\Delta PB_0}{PB_0} = -D_{Mod} \times \Delta r \tag{11.10}$$

or

$$D_{Mod} = -\frac{1}{PB_0}\frac{\Delta PB_0}{\Delta r} \tag{11.11}$$

Example 102 *Let the coupon be $CF\% = 10\%$, the maturity $T = 10$ years, the current price $PB_0 = 100$ and the Macauley duration $D_{Mac} = 6.543$ years. The bond is semi-annual. modified duration is $D_{Mod} = \frac{6.543}{1+\frac{0.10}{2}} = 6.23$. This implies that if the yield changes by 100 basis points, the price of the bond changes approximately by 6.23%. So, if the yield increases by 100 basis points, the new price is 93.77 using only this first order change approximation (the exact new price = 94.03). If the yield decreases by 100 basis points, the new price is approximately 106.23 (the exact new price is 106.50).*

How are the various factors T, CF, and r related to duration? As *maturity* T increases, duration D_{Mod} increases, except for very long, deep-discount bonds, for which duration eventually flattens and then even can decrease, as can be seen in Fig. 2..[‡] But for zero coupon bonds, Macauley duration $D_{Mac} = T$ the bond's maturity,

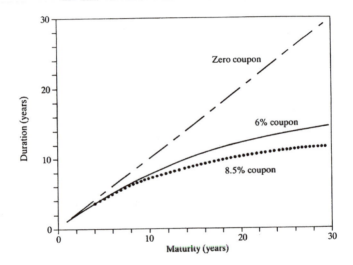

Figure 2   Duration versus maturity of fixed interest bonds

since

$$D_{Mac} = \frac{\frac{T.B_T}{(1+r)^T}}{PB_0}$$
$$= \frac{T.PB_0}{PB_0}$$
$$= T \qquad (11.12)$$

[‡]From Bostock, Wooley and Duffy, 1989, p. 31.

As the *coupon CF* increases, duration decreases and as the *yield r* increases, duration decreases.

11.3.4 Dollar duration

Dollar duration is the actual dollar change in the total market value of a bond due to a 100 basis point change in yield. Thus *Dollar duration* = *modified duration* × *(Accrued Price)*/100 = 100 × *dollar bond value of a basis point change* =

$$\frac{\Delta PB_0}{\Delta r} = \frac{-D_{Mod} \times PB_0}{100} \tag{11.13}$$

Dollar duration is in dollars and it is additive. Thus, it is useful for measuring effects on complete portfolios, in contrast to modified duration, which isn't additive, since the number depends on the magnitude of the value of the underlying bond.

Recall from the preceding Chapters that financial instruments can be sliced up into those with *realizable exact cash flows*, and those that have *state-contingent exact cash flows* (*i.e.*, measured by derivatives). For the ones with realizable exact cash flows, we can use exact discounting for backward valuation (*Cf.* Chapter 3). For the ones with state contingent (= speculative) exact cash flows, we use state prices (= combinations of discounting and risk-neutral pseudo-probabilities) for backward valuation (*Cf.* Chapter 8, 9 and 10).

While Macauley duration, modified duration, and Dollar duration are exact, certain models[§], the next one, effective duration is exact and speculative, because it is based on a combination of *a bond and an option.*

11.3.5 Effective duration

Effective (option-adjusted) duration measures the first-order interest-rate sensitivity of bonds with imbedded options (*Cf.* Babbel, Merrill and Panning, 1997). Examples of bonds with imbedded options are callable bonds and put bonds.

11.4 Option-Adjusted Spreads and Imbedded Options

Callable bond (or *call bond*) value B_C = value of noncallable bond held to maturity B_{NC} minus value of call option C:

$$B_C = B_{NC} - C \tag{11.14}$$

The call option reduces the value of the bond, since the investor has effectively sold an option to the issuer to call the bond. Fig. 3. provides the price yield curve of a generic callable bond. Notice the call option value $C = B_{NC} - B_C$. Callable bonds are priced at a discount to non-callable bonds. In return for the higher risk, investors receive higher yields by selling those options.

[§]To be precise, they are the exact, systematic, part of a Taylor expansion of first and second roder. The remainder term of a Taylor expansion is the inexact, unsystematic part.

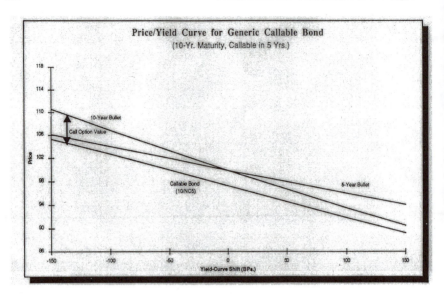

Figure 3   Price/yield curve for callable bond, compared with a 10-year bullet (zero) and a 5-year bullet (zero)

Putable bond (or *put bond*) value B_P = value of nonputable bond held to maturity B_{NP} plus value of put option P:

$$B_P = B_{NP} + P \qquad (11.15)$$

The put option increases the value of a bond, since the investor has effectively bought an option from the issuer to return the bond to the issuer, when its value drops to a certain level. Putable bonds are priced at a premium to non-callable bonds (Fig. 4.). In return for the lower risk, investors receive lower yields by buying these options.[¶]

While we value zero bonds usually by using the yield-to-maturity (YTM) spread (See Chapter 3), the option-adjusted spread is used for bonds with imbedded options.

Option-adjusted spread (OAS) of a callable bond = yield-to-maturity spread (YTMS) of the corresponding callable bond (= zero bond - call option):

$$OAS_{callable} = YTMS_{callable} - YTMS_{zero} \qquad (11.16)$$

[¶]An option-adjusted bond differs from a *convertible bond*, which converts from a bond (a liability) into equity, when the imbedded option is exercised. The "exercise" price of the bond depends on the underlying equity share price, according to a particular contracted formula. (Cf. Ho and Pfeffer,1996). An option-adjusted bond converts into cash when the imbedded option is exercised.

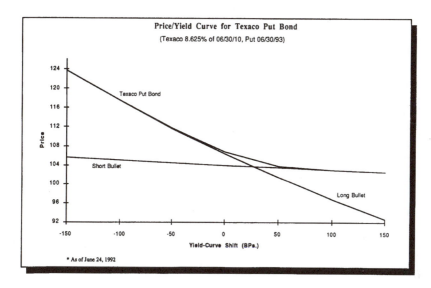

Figure 4   Price/yield curve for Texaco putable bond, compared with a short and a long bullet

OAS requires the use of an option-valuation model to value the call option C subtracted from the noncallable zero bond. But more often than not the value of the call C is derived from the market prices of the zero and the callable bond (via so-called "back-door valuation"). Usually $OAS_{callable} > 0$.

Option-adjusted spread (OAS) of a putable bond = yield-to-maturity (YTM) spread of the corresponding putable bond (= zero bond + put option):

$$OAS_{putable} = YTMS_{putable} - YTMS_{zero} \qquad (11.17)$$

Usually $OAS_{putable} < 0$. Thus one approach to value the imbedded option is by computing its *replacement cost*, that is, the cost of synthesizing the risk and reward of the option features (over some expiration horizon), using traded instruments, where value is readily apparent.

Remark 103 *In Chapter 3 we defined the term structure of interest rates as the relationship between the spot interest rates r and the term-to-maturity T. The term structure provides the unbiased, rational expectation of forward rates and is used for actual value calculations (Cf. Heath, Jarrow and Morton, 1992). However, practitioners in the investment community often monitor the yield curve, which is the relationship between the yield-to-maturity YTM and the term-to-maturity T. This is because the yield curve is easier to observe than the derived term structure of interest rates and because the shifts in the yield curve are closely related to the shifts* *in the term structure of interest rates. Of course, because of (il-)liquidity premiums, i.e., premiums for lack of liquidity, the yield curve is not exact, but somewhat uncertain and "fuzzy." Usually several yield curves from different fixed-income markets are spliced together to obtain a complete maturity spectrum. The resulting curve is inexact. (The yield curve of the U.S. government securities is the most detailed and complete and therefore used as basis for many global investment valuations). But for the pricing of bonds, swaps and other decomposable securities, one must use the spot interest rates of the term structure rather than the yield-to-maturity of the yield curve to discount the cash flows (unless the term structure is flat). We return to the issue of engineering a complete discounting function from several different yield curves in greater detail in Chapter 13 (Cf. Fons, 1994)*

Remark 104 *Option-adjusted bonds (OAB) are speculative exact valuation models with six data dimensions, when they are priced off Treasury zeros. Thus*

$$POAB_0 - POAB_0(B_T, T, r, X, \sigma_{BB}) = 0 \qquad (11.18)$$

The six variables are: (1) the present value of the option-adjusted bond $POAB_0$, (2) its principal B_T, (3) the maturity T, (4) the yield r of the underlying zero bond, (5) the strike price X, and (6) the volatility of the bond σ_{BB}. However, often they are priced off quality-graded corporate bonds. In that case, they are inexact valuation models, because of (7) the discontinuous quality grade ξ (Cf. Chapter 3). Corporate bonds are often coupon bonds, adding (8) an extra coupon variable Cf. Thus, the usual inexact option-adjusted bond valuation model is a 8-dimensional inexact model:

$$POAB_0 - POAB_0(B_T, T, r, CF, X, \sigma_{BB}, \xi) \approx 0 \qquad (11.19)$$

There is no easy way to visualize this 8-dimensional empirical interaction surface, since we can only visualize four dimensions at a time. The following solution appears acceptable: standardize the principal $B_T = 1,000$ and strip its coupon, $CF = 0$, fix the time of observation and thus r, and provide the market information by grade quality ξ. This still leaves four dimensions $(POAB_0, T, X, \sigma_{BB})$ to visualize for market information display in the media and for arbitrage pricing, as the visualization in Chapter 10 for the empirical Hang Seng Index option.

11.5   Convexity

Duration is not constant, but changes along the price - yield curve (*Cf.* Figs. 1., 3. and 4.). The change in duration given a change in yield is called *convexity*. It is the second derivative with respect to the yield and measures the curvature of the price - yield relationship.

11.5.1 Definition of Convexity

γ is the second derivative of the price - yield relationship:

$$\gamma = \frac{\partial^2 PB_0}{\partial r^2}$$
$$= \left[\sum_{t=1}^{T} \frac{t.(t+1).CF}{(1+r)^{t+2}} \right] + \left[\frac{T.(T+1).B_T}{(1+r)^{T+2}} \right] \tag{11.20}$$

(Modified) Convexity $=$ dollar convexity/price:

$$Con_{Mod} = \frac{\gamma}{PB_0}$$
$$= \frac{1}{PB_0} \frac{\partial^2 PB_0}{\partial r^2} \tag{11.21}$$

while the percentage change *due to convexity* is

$$\frac{\Delta PB_0}{PB_0} = \frac{1}{2} Con_{Mod}.(\Delta r)^2$$
$$= \frac{1}{2} \frac{\gamma}{PB_0} (\Delta r)^2 \tag{11.22}$$

Convexity generally changes the same way as duration with changes in maturity T, coupon CF and yield r. In the Exercises you will encounter several examples.

11.5.2 Positive and Negative Convexity

Most bonds exhibit *positive convexity*, so when the yield drops, the rate of the price increases becomes larger, *i.e.*, duration increases. *Vice versa*, when yields rise, the duration decreases.

Example 105 *Noncallable bonds and putable bonds have positive convexity. A putable bond has a higher convexity than the corresponding zero (Cf. Fig. 4.).*

Some bonds exhibit *negative convexity* (= *concavity*), so when the yield drops, the duration drops too. *Vice versa*, when the yield rises, duration increases. A callable bond has lower convexity than the corresponding zero (*Cf.* Fig. 3.). In fact, bonds with imbedded call options sometimes exhibit drastic negative convexity. They exhibit *price compression* when their yield drops, causing a sharp drop in the economic rate of return on the bond investment when interest rates decline.

11.6 Default Risk and Effective Duration of Bonds

How do we compute the effective, or option-adjusted, duration of callable bonds using what we already know about non-callable bonds from Chapter 3? The following two formulas provide some insight, based as they are on first and second order Taylor approximations:

$$\text{Option-Adjusted Duration} = \frac{B_{NC}}{B_C}.D_{ModNC}.(1 - \delta_c) \qquad (11.23)$$

and

$$\text{Option-Adjusted Convexity} = \frac{B_{NC}}{B_C}.[Con_{ModNC}.(1 - \delta_c) - B_{NC}.\gamma_c.D^2_{ModNC}] \qquad (11.24)$$

where:

B_{NC} = value of noncallable bond

B_C = value of a callable bond

D_{ModNC} = modified duration of equivalent noncallable bond

Con_{ModNC} = (modified) convexity of equivalent noncallable bond

$\delta_c = \frac{\Delta C}{\Delta B}$ = marginal change in value of imbedded call option relative to the marginal change in the value of the bond

$\gamma_c = \frac{\Delta \Delta C}{(\Delta B)^2} = \frac{\Delta \delta_c}{\Delta B}$ = convexity of the callable bond.

When interest rates are high and bond prices are low, $\delta_c = 0 = \gamma_c$, because the call will be far out-of-the-money and the value of the call will also be near zero. In this case, $B_C = B_{BC} - C$ and $C = 0$, $\frac{B_{NC}}{B_C} = 1.0$, and the Option-Adjusted Duration = D_{ModNC} and the Option-Adjusted Convexity = Con_{ModNC}. Thus, when the interest rates are very high, the duration and convexity of a callable bond will be about the same as of a noncallable bond.

In contrast, when the interest rates are very low, and bond prices are very high, $\delta_c = 1.0$ and the duration of a callable bond will approach zero, since the price - yield curve flattens. Furthermore, the option-adjusted convexity becomes negative at these very low interest rates. The price - yield curve becomes negatively convex.

Remark 106 *Securitized real estate loans, e.g., home mortgages, are typically such long term bonds, which were held by the Savings & Loans (S&L's) and commercial banks in the U.S. in the 1980s. When U.S. interest rates dropped in the second half of the 1980s, many home owners saw an opportunity to refinance their mortgages at the lower interest rates. Thus, they returned their mortgages prematurely, compressing their prices in the process. Consequently, the S&L's and many commercial banks saw the economic return on their mortgage portfolios, i.e., their assets, sharply drop, and some of these S&Ls and commercial banks went bankrupt. When interest rates rose in the first half of the 1980sAdjustable rate mortgages (ARMs) helped the S&Ls to protect their rates of return on their assets (ROAs), and thus their rates of return on their* *equity (ROEs)*. It did not protect the ones, which were unable to substitute ARMs for fixed rates mortgages fast enough. However, the S&L's were insufficiently immunized to the price compression in the second half of the 1980s in the U.S.' competitive home mortgage market, when homeowners took the initiative to refinance. Thus, bond portfolio immunization suddenly became a very important bank risk management issue, and the banks started to include convexity figures on their bond portfolio risk management systems (See Box below).

Coupon	Maturity	Price	Yield	M Dur	Yv32	Hedge Ratio	Issuer	Call/Put Info Date / Price	Par Val	ExtSDn	Typ4Dn	RefSEq	Typ4Up	Ext4Up	Age
8.125	02/15/98	110-13+	5.718	4.034	0.879	0.856	TREAS NOTE		-33000	433	36	-21645	-61	-433	20
8.000	05/15/98	114-14	5.792	4.211	0.636	0.698	TREAS NOTE		-8000	112	9	-5592	-16	-112	7
8.250	07/15/98	111-04	5.842	4.423	0.634	0.702	TREAS NOTE		108000	-1517	-126	75858	212	1517	10
9.250	08/15/98	115-27	5.863	4.269	0.610	0.730	TREAS NOTE		-60000	876	73	-43806	-123	-876	8
6.375	01/15/99	101-29+	5.986	4.906	0.624	0.714	TREAS NOTE		13500	-193	-16	9642	27	193	12
7.000	04/15/99	104-29+	6.036	4.928	0.593	0.751	TREAS NOTE		18615	-282	-20	14131	40	282	5
6.375	07/15/99	101-30+	6.054	5.237	0.586	0.760	TREAS NOTE		-2000	30	3	-1520	-4	-30	1
6.375	01/15/00	101-18	6.096	5.560	0.552	0.807	TREAS NOTE		-10000	161	13	-8066	-23	-161	1
8.500	02/15/00	113-01	6.190	5.211	0.513	0.868	TREAS NOTE		-15000	260	22	-13018	-36	-260	7
8.875	05/15/00	115-07+	6.241	5.407	0.494	0.902	TREAS NOTE		-35400	639	53	-31928	-89	-639	4
8.750	08/15/00	114-20+	6.284	5.455	0.483	0.922	TREAS NOTE		36000	-663	-55	33191	93	663	9
7.750	02/15/01	108-17+	6.375	5.844	0.477	0.933	TREAS NOTE		-10000	187	15	-9031	-28	-187	5
13.125	05/15/01	142-31+	6.370	5.530	0.388	1.148	TREAS BOND		-20000	459	38	-22960	-64	-459	21
7.875	08/15/01	109-10	6.441	6.087	0.455	0.979	TREAS NOTE		-30000	587	49	-29374	-82	-587	13
7.500	11/15/01	106-27+	6.463	6.379	0.452	0.965	TREAS NOTE		-7250	143	12	-7144	-20	-143	13
14.250	02/15/02	153-05+	6.413	5.656	0.346	1.267	TREAS BOND		37000	-852	-79	47800	133	952	20
7.500	05/15/02	107-02	6.475	6.639	0.433	1.028	TREAS NOTE		-30000	617	51	-30825	-86	-617	17
10.750	02/15/03	130-22	6.535	6.414	0.359	1.239	TREAS BOND		33000	-966	-80	48314	135	966	18

Sample fixed-income trading risk analysis report, supplied by Prudential Securities Analysis in 1988

11.7 Bond Portfolio Immunization

Portfolio immunization is the immunization of the net equity position on the balance sheet against interest rate risk. It is a form of duration hedging against first order interest rate risk. *First-order interest rate risk* is concerned only with parallel shifts in the yield curve and not with tilting, *i.e.*, the changing curvature, of the yield curve.

As we just learned, the first order or marginal interest rate sensitivity of assets and liabilities is measured by (modified) duration. On the basis of the accounting identity (*Cf.* Chapter 1) that Equity is the difference between Assets and Liabilities,

$$E = A - L \tag{11.25}$$

we have, after taking first derivatives and by compensating substitution:

$$\frac{1}{E}\frac{\Delta E}{\Delta r}.E = \frac{1}{A}\frac{\Delta A}{\Delta r}.A - \frac{1}{L}\frac{\Delta L}{\Delta r}.L \tag{11.26}$$

Thus, substituting for terms by (Modified) Duration, we find

$$D_{Mod}^E.E = D_{Mod}^A.A - D_{Mod}^L.L \tag{11.27}$$

By substituting for and dividing through by equity E, we get

$$D_{Mod}^E = \frac{D_{Mod}^A.A - D_{Mod}^L.(A - E)}{E} \tag{11.28}$$

so that the duration of the Equity is expressed in terms of Assets and of the Liabilities only:

$$D_{Mod}^E = D_{Mod}^L + \frac{A}{E}.(D_{Mod}^A - D_{Mod}^L) \tag{11.29}$$

Thus, the duration of the net equity E equals the duration of the liabilities, corrected by the product of the *leverage factor*:

$$\frac{A}{E} = \frac{E + L}{E}$$
$$= 1 + \frac{L}{E} \tag{11.30}$$

and the balance sheet's *duration mismatch* $(D_{Mod}^A - D_{Mod}^L)$. Fig. 5. provides a graphical presentation of this balance sheet immunization relationship.

How can the balance sheet be immunized against first order interest rate risk? Answer: when the equity' duration equals zero, $D_{Mod}^E = 0$. This is true only when the *immunizing duration mismatch* is

$$(D_{Mod}^A - D_{Mod}^L) = -\frac{E}{A}.D_{Mod}^L \tag{11.31}$$

or

$$D_{Mod}^A = (1 - \frac{E}{A}).D_{Mod}^L \tag{11.32}$$

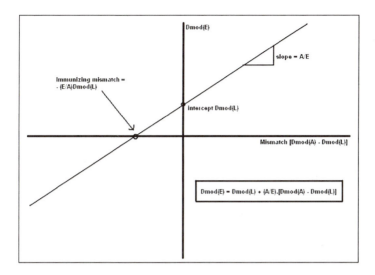

Figure 5   Portfolio immunization: the immunizing mismatch $\neq 0$

Example 107 *When equity is 8% of total (default risk adjusted) assets (as was recommended in 1988 by the B.I.S. Capital Guidelines for commercial banks), the portfolio is only immunized against first order interest rate risk when $D_{Mod}^A = 92\%.D_{Mod}^L$. (And NOT when $D_{Mod}^A = D_{Mod}^L$ as, apparently, many bond portfolio managers still think).*

Portfolio immunization emerged from the management of bond portfolios, in particular by (global) insurance firms. But, it has now become accepted by more diversified portfolios, including bonds, stocks, real estate, once it was realized that other types of assets and liabilities also exhibited interest rate risk.

11.8   Duration of Common Stocks

The duration measure is valid not only for bonds, but also for equity to the extent that payments from equities are predictable or stable. We found from the Dividend Discount Model (DDM) in Chapter 3 that, when a stock pays a constant dividend D and its cost of capital is q, the present value of the stock is $S_0 = \frac{D}{q}$. Thus the

Duration of Equity is

$$
\begin{aligned}
D_{Mod} &= -\frac{1}{S_0}\frac{\Delta S_0}{\Delta q} \\
&= -\left(\frac{q}{D}\right)\cdot\left(-\frac{D}{q^2}\right) \\
&= \frac{1}{q}
\end{aligned}
\tag{11.33}
$$

For a stock which pays dividend at a constant growth rate g and the cost of capital q, the present value is $S_0 = \frac{D}{q-g}$. Thus its duration is

$$
\begin{aligned}
D_{Mod} &= -\frac{1}{S_0}\frac{\Delta S_0}{\Delta q} \\
&= \frac{1}{q-g}
\end{aligned}
\tag{11.34}
$$

In general, since the value of an asset is:

$$
A_0 = \frac{E_1}{r}
\tag{11.35}
$$

where E_1 is the expected economic earnings of the asset in the next period, we find that the duration of an asset A_0 is

$$
D_{Mod} = \frac{1}{r} - \frac{1}{E_1}\frac{\Delta E_1}{\Delta r}
\tag{11.36}
$$

Thus, approximately, the marginal interest rate sensitivity of *any* asset is $\frac{1}{r}$, plus the marginal interest rate sensitivity of its expected economic earnings in the coming period $\frac{1}{E_1}\frac{\Delta E_1}{\Delta r}$. When these economic earnings remain constant, as is the case in the DDM, the second term equals zero and the duration of an asset is:

$$
D_{Mod} = \frac{1}{r}
\tag{11.37}
$$

11.9   Interest Rate Risk Management

Conventional interest rate risk management relies on hedging against first and second order interest rate risk by *duration hedging* and *convexity hedging*, respectively. Slightly more sophisticated approaches use combinations of futures and options as first and second order interest risk management hedges, in particular for horizon hedging.

11.9.1 Horizon Hedging

Horizon hedging is a form of interest rate risk management which hedges against second order interest rate risk, *i.e.*, against convexity risk. While traditional risk measures (*e.g.*, delta, or dollar-duration) apply to static market conditions, *i.e.*, a particular point in time and a certain price level, horizon hedging hedges risk across a spectrum of prices and yields. Convexity identifies the potential divergence of the static hedge from the portfolio as the interest rate shifts. Convexity is, by definition, asymmetrical with respect to the market price level. Otherwise a simple hedge position could simultaneously offset both price and convexity risks.

Options and zero coupon bonds are highly convex financial instruments. They can provide hedges against portfolio convexity, when added to a conventional duration hedge of bonds with imbedded options. While the imbedded option may enhance the yield of the bond, it also adds to the interest rate risk. When no convexity hedge is applied, duration hedges of such convex bonds must be constantly monitored and adjusted when market prices change, resulting in *volatility exposure* and increased transaction costs.

Combination hedges are synthetic hedges that include options as an *automatic hedge adjustment* of the conventional duration hedge. This is true at least over a particular horizon of possible interest rate shifts, respectively shifts in bond prices, within a particular period of time, which often is the expiration date of the option. Combination hedges help to reduce minimize the monitoring and adjustment costs of managing a large bond portfolio.

Often a combination hedge uses interest rate (bond) futures to hedge the duration risk and options to hedge the negative convexity that leads to phenomena like price compression. Exchange-traded futures and options are useful hedges since they are liquid and can be put on and taken off quickly and they are relatively cheap because of their leverage. Thus combination hedges can overcome some of the difficulties of hedging an imbedded option bond, like a Mortgage Backed Security (MBS), with a conventional Treasury bond: they are considerably cheaper and provide better insurance over a particular horizon of interest rate outcomes.

For example, Fig. 6. shows, for a particular expected interest rate horizon, the price - yield curves for a GNMA ("Ginnie Mae") 9.5% coupon bond (indicated by the solid line) compared with that of a non-callable long bond (indicated by the interrupted line), as of March 1, 1991. GNMA bonds are backed by the mortgages guaranteed by the U.S. Government National Mortgage Association (GNMA). Notice that the callable GNMA bond shows negative convexity and price compression at low interest rate levels, compared with the positive convexity of the non-callable long bond. The risk management problem is: how does one value or hedge this element of interest rate horizon risk?

The first step to solve this problem is to apply a simple futures hedge by selling an interest rate futures, which eliminates the first - order risk, i.e., the "slope" risk of the price - yield curve of the GNMA bond. Fig. 7. shows the resulting net

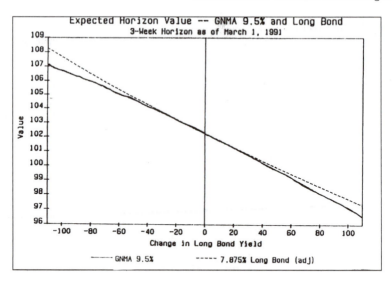

Figure 6   Comparison of the MBS profile of the GNMA bond to a non-callable bond clearly identifies the embedded option feature

interest rate risk profile after applying the futures hedge. Next, the *horizon strategy* attempts to lessen the residual risk by selling a few put options. These put options can be selected from the *library* of put options available to the portfolio manager by an optimizing "fitting" program, e.g., a minimum vector norm or Least Squares program, which minimizes the squared residual risk over the interest rate horizon. Such an optimizing library program tries to match the curvature of the net risk profile in Fig. 7. with a combination of the curvatures of the time profiles of the sold puts.

Fig. 8. shows the optimized hedge residual, or net risk, profile over the expected interest rate horizon, after applying the optimized combination hedge of a futures plus two put options. Notice that sharp drop-offs remain at the extremes, since this application of horizon strategy chooses to ignore extreme interest rate (yield) changes larger than ±70 basis points. Also drawn in Fig. 8. is the expected Gaussian probability distribution of the interest rate changes.

Remark 108 *Recently, financial analysts, economists and engineers have become more concerned about extreme interest rate changes and their severe impact on bond prices, since (1) they occur more frequently than predicted by Gaussian distributions, (2) they occur asymmetrically and (3) they show non-periodic cyclicity, i.e., they recur in cycles with variable periodicity. Consequently, there is now more research interest in (a) stable probability distributions, since they can exhibit different degrees*

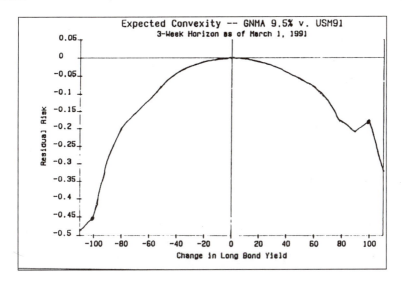

Figure 7   Expected convexity: net risk profile after applying a simple futures hedge

of kurtosis, e.g., exhibit heavy tails and peakedness, and of skewedness, and in (b) long term dependence phenomena.

11.10   Exercises

Exercise 109 *Compute the Macauley duration, modified duration, (modified) convexity and dollar convexity for a 6%, 5-year, semi-annual bond selling to yield 9%, with a current price of 92.5209. (design an EXCEL spreadsheet table)*

Exercise 110 *Consider the preceding bond. If the required yield increases by 200 basis points, from 9% to 11%, what is the approximate percentage change in the price of the bond using the duration and convexity measures you've computed? And what if the required yield decreases by 200 basis points? How does this differ from the actual change in price?*

Exercise 111 *Explain what happens with the value of a putable bond when the interest rate rises and when it drops. Do the same with the value of a callable bond? Explain also which party benefits in each of these cases: the buyer or the seller?*

Exercise 112 *When the equity of a commercial bank is 10% of its assets, how should its balance sheet be immunized against interest rate shocks? Does the size and the direction of these interest rate shocks matter for your conclusion and why?*

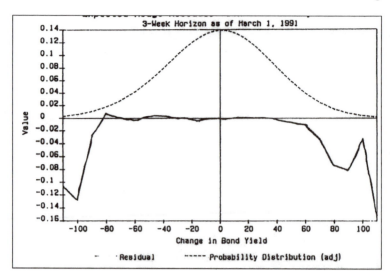

Figure 8   Net optimized horizon hedge risk profile of a GNMA bond, with expected Gaussian
probability distribution

11.11   Bibliography

Altman, E. I. (1996) "Credit-Scoring Models and the Valuation of Fixed-Income Securities and Commercial Loans," CREFS Seminar presentation at SAB/NBS/NTU, 21 June, Singapore, 17 pages.

Babbel, D. F., Merrill, C., and Panning, W. (1997) "Default Risk and the Effective Duration of Bonds," *Financial Analysts Journal*, January - February, 35 - 44.

Bostock, P , Woolley, P., and Duffy, M. (1989) "Duration Based Asset Allocation, " in Stoakes, C. and Freeman, A., *Managing Global Portfolios*, Euromoney Publications, London, pp. 27 - 49.

Dybvig, P. H. and Marshall, W. J. (1996) "Pricing Long Bonds: Pitfalls and Opportunities," *Financial Analysts Journal*, January - February, 32 - 39.

Fabozzi, F. J. (1993) *Bond Markets, Analysis and Strategies*, Prentice - Hall, Englewood Cliffs, NJ.

Fons, J. S. (1994) "Using Default Rates to Model the Term Structure of Credit Risk," *Financial Analysts Journal*, September - October, 25 - 32.

Heath, D., Jarrow, R. and Morton, A. (1992) "Bond Pricing and the Term Structure of the Interest Rates: A New Methodology," *Econometrica*, **60** (1), 77 - 105.

Ho, T. S. Y. and Pfeffer, D. M. (1996) "Convertible Bonds: Model, Value

Attribution, and Analytics," *Financial Analysts Journal*, September - October, 35 - 44.

Los, C. A. (1985) "Measurement Problems of Inflation Disaggregation," *Journal of Business and Economic Statistics*, **3** (3), July, 244 - 253.

O'Brien, J. and Srivastava, S. (1996) *Investments, A Visual Approach: Bond Valuation and Bond Tutor*, South-Western College Publishing, New York, NY.
chapter:12,page:1

Chapter 12

FORWARDS AND FUTURES

12.1 Introduction

In this Chapter we return from the *speculative exact* option models based on the assumption of stylized uncertainty, as in Chapters 9 and 10, and as imbedded in bonds in Chapter 11, to pure *exact* models. These models are similar to the continuous Treasury bond models we discussed in Chapter 3. In particular, we will discuss forwards and futures, which are based on the exact risk-free *term structure* . which incorporates the *rational expectations* hypothesis .

Similar to risk-free cash, these contracts are used for *hedging* , *i.e.*, altering and shifting the financial risks associated with holding and trading assets. In addition, these contracts are used to modify the risk/return profile of whole portfolios . In the Exercises we will encounter some visualization of such portfolio risk modification. In particular, at the end of this Chapter, we will discuss the risks involved in portfolio insurance , using these hedging instruments. Portfolio insurance is not based on an exact model, but is based on a Taylor series approximation , as discussed in Chapters 2 and 10.

12.2 Forwards and Futures Valuation

A *forward contract* is an agreement between two parties , in which one party is obliged to deliver a stated amount (contract size) of a stated asset at the *settlement date T* in the future, and the other party is obligated to pay a specified *invoice amount* F_0 for the assets at the time of *delivery* and settlement. Forward contracts are *not* investments in the strict sense; they are agreements to engage in a trade at a future date and at a fixed price F_0. Thus, in principle, it costs nothing to enter into such a forward contract, except the *broker's commission* . No money has to be borrowed for investment and no money changes hands between the two contracting parties at the time of the deal. The trade will take place at the settlement date T of the contract. However, forward contracts suffer from:

   (a) possible illiquidity (when there is gapping, *i.e.*, no market is made and no bid and ask prices available, or when the bid/ask spread is very wide) and

   (b) possible lack of ; one of the parties may negate on the contract.

Therefore, the markets have designed futures contacts instead. A *futures contract* is a standardized forward contract that has been securitized and is traded in a public market place. Futures contracts are traded on *futures exchanges* which provide clearing houses , to ensure greater *liquidity* (= efficiency of pricing) and to guarantee *contract integrity* .

To insure the integrity of futures contracts, parties entering into futures contracts are required to put up *margin* , *i.e.*, a good faith deposit, and to mark-to-market their futures prices on a daily basis. *Marking-to-market* is the settling in cash of any outstanding $margin_t = F_0 - S_t$ between the *contracted futures price* F_0 and the *current spot price* S_t of the underlying asset. Thus, the daily changes in the spot price S_t determine the mark-to-market cash flows in and out the *margin accounts* . The *underlying asset* can be a physical entity (gold, copper, oil, grains, sugar, pork bellies, orange juice, etc.), a cash equivalent (T-bonds, T-bills, foreign exchange), or a stock index (S&P500 Index).

Futures are used for speculation , hedging (long and short) , and arbitrage . The following market agents participate in the financial markets , each with their own specific function:

1. *Speculators* use "naked" positions in the futures market to accept the price risk in the hopes of earning a profit. Recall that speculators are not gamblers , although they purchase the financial risk. Futures allow a speculator to build a potential long portfolio with very little cash investment (only for the "margin" $F_0 - S_t$ and the broker's commission costs), thus the potential leverage of their cash investment is very high. The shortcoming is that when the futures aren't sold just before, or on settlement day, the market participant risks the substantial amount of cash S_T required to buy the underlying asset as valued on settlement day. This *settlement risk* can be avoided and the leverage can be further enhanced (= enlarged or reduced) by buying or writing (selling) *options on futures* . In contrast to futures, which are obligations, options give the right to exercise , not the obligation (Ross, 1976a).

2. *Hedgers* use the futures market in conjunction with counter positions in the spot market to pass price risk on to speculators. Hedgers alter and shift financial risk . They sell the financial risk to the speculators.

3. *Arbitragers* benefit from any misalignment between the prices of futures and the spot prices of their underlying assets to earn risk-free profits. Arbitragers are involved in fair games . They make the markets liquid and thus efficient , since they help to reduce the bid/ask spreads by their arbitrage trades (Ross, 1976b).

12.2.1 *Forwards and Futures Pricing*

Forwards F_0 are valued by arbitrage-free pricing , *i.e.*, the equilibrium "no free lunch" pricing, or implementation of the **Single Price Law of Efficient Markets** . *Cf.*

Chapter 8). With spot price S_0 and, in an efficient market, the risk free rate r and settlement date T, the exact valuation model of a forward is as follows, in discrete time:

$$F_0 = S_0(1+r)^T \tag{12.1}$$

and in continuous time:

$$F_0 = S_0 e^{rT} \tag{12.2}$$

These two equations are exact models of an equilibrium relationship and the correlation between the spot and futures market is $\rho_{sf} = 1.0$. But markets are not always in perfect equilibrium, because of market inefficiencies. Consequently, this futures valuation model is not always exact.

Example 113 *Fig. 1. shows the correlation between the S&P500 spot market in New York and the S&P500 futures market in Chicago. Although most of the time the bivariate correlation between these two markets $0.9 < \rho_{sf} < 1.0$, it clearly is not perfect. In fact, quite frequently during these nine years the correlation is $0.8 < \rho_{sf} < 0.7$. Fig. 1. shows that in the period of 1982 - 1991 there were at least*

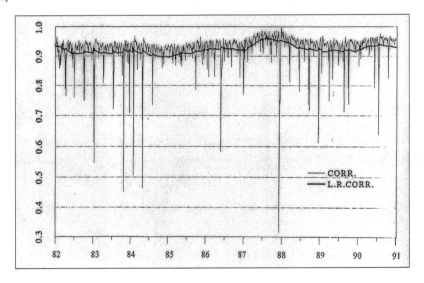

Figure 1   Correlation between the S&P500 spot and futures market, 1982 - 1991

eleven instances when $\rho_{sf} < 0.7$, when the coefficient of determination $\rho_{sf}^2 < 0.5$. The almost breakdown between the spot and futures markets of Black Monday, 19 November 1987, when the correlation $\rho_{sf} < 0.3$, is clearly visible. This breakdown *is discussed in greater detail in the section on portfolio insurance at the end of this Chapter.*

Some of the market inefficiency is caused by market fees and commissions. For example, in the futures market, when there are *carrying* (= storage and insurance) *costs* charged at rate c and an annualized yield q is earned (which reduces the carrying costs), the value of the forward or futures contract is given by the following discrete time *Futures - Spot Parity Theorem* , or *Cost-of-Carry Relationship* :

$$F_0 = S_0(1 + r + c - q)^T \qquad (12.3)$$

This can be rewritten as

$$\frac{F_0}{S_0} = (1 + r + c - q)^T \qquad (12.4)$$

and in continuous time (*Cf.* Chapter 2) as

$$\frac{F_0}{S_0} = e^{(r+c-q)T} \qquad (12.5)$$

These models are strictly speaking inexact, since the carrying costs c are often discontinuous step functions, while the annualized yield q cannot always be ascertained in advance and remains uncertain.

Remark 114 *The current price of a futures contract F_0 is not the market's expectation of what the spot price of the underlying asset will be on settlement day S_T. But the futures-spot parity does tell us that the ratio of the current futures price F_0 to the current spot price S_0 incorporates a expectation about the risk-free interest rate r, for given cost-of-carry c and yield q.*

12.2.2   Foreign Exchange Futures

By arbitrage arguments, we find that the following *Foreign Exchange Parity Relationship* holds, since the cost-of-carry of foreign exchange $c = 0$, while the yield on foreign exchange is the foreign interest rate , $q = r_f$:

$$\frac{F_0}{S_0} = e^{(r_d - r_f)T} \qquad (12.6)$$

Here F_0 and S_0 stand for the current futures and spot prices of a *domestic* currency per unit of *foreign* currency , respectively (*e.g.*, *S\$/US\$*), r_d and r_f for domestic and foreign cash interest rates, respectively, and T for the time to expiration of the forward contract in number or fraction of year(s).

Example 115 *Suppose the US interest rate $r_f = 6.25\%$, the Singapore interest rate is $r_d = 4.75\%$ and the current exchange rate is $S_0 = 1.58S\$/1.00US\$$. What should be the 6-months forward exchange rate ? Answer:*

$$F_0 = S_0 e^{(r_d - r_f)T}$$
$$= 1.58 e^{(0.0475-0.0625)\times\frac{6}{12}}$$
$$= 1.5565S\$/US\$ \tag{12.7}$$

The financial-economic raison d'etre for this result is that, since less Singapore dollars are earned in these six months than US dollars, the Singapore dollar becomes relatively more scarce and thus appreciates versus the US dollar!

Remark 116 *The foreign exchange parity does tell us that the ratio of the current futures price F_0 to the current spot price S_0 incorporates a expectation about the interest rate differential $(r_d - r_f)$ between the two countries. It does not predict where the exchange rate will go!*

12.3 Risks in the Futures Markets

There are two important financial risk characteristics of the futures markets , which are often misunderstood: *basis risk* and *calendar spread risk* .

12.3.1 Basis risk

The futures *basis* is the spread between the current spot market price and the current futures price. Thus, the current $t = 0$ basis is:

$$basis_0 = S_0 - F_0$$
$$= S_0 - S_0 e^{(r_0+c_0-q_0)T}$$
$$= S_0(1 - e^{(r_0+c_0-q_0)T}) \tag{12.8}$$

while later on, for $t > 0$, the basis between time t and the settlement date is

$$basis_t = S_t - F_t$$
$$= S_t - S_t e^{(r_t+c_t-q_t)(T-t)}$$
$$= S_t(1 - e^{(r_t+c_t-q_t)(T-t)}) \tag{12.9}$$

Since, in practice, neither the borrowing cash rate r, nor the cost-of-carry c, nor the yield q are constants, but from day-to-day fluctuating variables r_t, c_t and q_t, respectively, the basis fluctuates also in an unpredictable manner! Therefore, it is difficult to predict the spread that will exist between the spot and futures market over time, even though these markets tend to move closely together. They are highly correlated due to continuous arbitrage between the spot and futures markets.

Of course, the price of a futures contract will converge toward the price of the underlying asset in the spot market as the settlement date T approaches. On settlement day, when the expiration date $T = 0$, the price of a futures contract equals the price of the underlying asset in the spot market and the futures basis is zero :

$$
\begin{aligned}
basis_T &= S_T - F_T \\
&= S_T - S_T e^{(r_T + c_T - q_T)0} \\
&= S_T(1 - e^{(r_T + c_T - q_T)0}) \\
&= S_T(1 - 1) \\
&= 0
\end{aligned}
\tag{12.10}
$$

Remark 117 *Don't confuse the futures $basis_t = S_t - F_t$ with the $margin_t = F_0 - S_t$!*

12.3.2 Calendar spread risk

The *calendar spread* is the difference between two futures contracts with different expiration dates T_1 and T_2

$$
\begin{aligned}
\frac{F_0(T_2)}{F_0(T_1)} &= \frac{S_0 e^{r_2 T_2}}{S_0 e^{r_1 T_1}} \\
&= e^{r_2 T_2 - r_1 T_1} \\
&= e^{1 f_2 (T_2 - T_1)}
\end{aligned}
\tag{12.11}
$$

Thus, the calendar spread between two futures contracts on the same underlying asset with different settlement dates, $T_1 \neq T_2$, implies a *forward rate* (*Cf.* Chapter 3):

$$
\begin{aligned}
_1 f_2 &= \frac{\ln\left(\frac{F_0(T_2)}{F_0(T_1)}\right)}{T_2 - T_1} \\
&= \frac{r_2 T_2 - r_1 T_1}{T_2 - T_1}
\end{aligned}
\tag{12.12}
$$

Since this forward rate $_1 f_2$ tends to stay fairly constant over time, calendar spreads tend to remain fairly constant, while the basis tends to converge to zero over time. However, it is important to understand that such combinations of futures can be used to engineer these *synthetic forward rates* .

12.4   Hedging with Futures

The purpose of hedging is to immunize the value of a portfolio insensitive to changes in some underlying risk factor, like the spot price of the assets included in the portfolio. Thus, in its simplest form, the long position of the asset(s) to be hedged is combined with a short position in a hedging instrument , like cash, a cash equivalent index

, or a futures (= risk-free instruments), or an option (= risky instrument). In this fashion, a change in the value of the asset(s) and a change in the hedging instrument are mutually offsetting .

As we discussed in Chapter 10, the simplest form of hedging is *delta hedging* , which is only hedging the first derivative of the changing value. For example, let the change in the value of the long stock portfolio ΔV_S and the change in the value of shortened futures ΔV_F be offsetting

$$\Delta V_S - \Delta V_F = \Delta(Q_S S_0) - \Delta(Q_F F_0) = 0 \tag{12.13}$$

where Q_S is the number of units of the asset to be hedged and Q_F is the number of futures contracts with which we hedge. Since value V = quantity × price = $Q \times P$ and the quantities remain unchanged

$$Q_S \Delta S_0 - Q_F \Delta F_0 = 0 \tag{12.14}$$

But then the required number of futures contracts for marginal hedging is

$$Q_F = Q_S \frac{\Delta S_0}{\Delta F_0}$$
$$= Q_S.h \tag{12.15}$$

where $h = \frac{\Delta S_0}{\Delta F_0}$ is the *hedge ratio* . The hedge ratio informs how much change in futures is needed to offset a change in the value of the stocks

$$\Delta F_0 = \frac{\Delta S_0}{h} \tag{12.16}$$

Since we have the futures value in discrete time

$$F_0 = S_0(1 + r + c - q)^T \tag{12.17}$$

we find that the exact futures hedge ratio in discrete time is:

$$h = \frac{\Delta S_0}{\Delta F_0}$$
$$= \frac{1}{(1 + r + c - q)^T} \tag{12.18}$$

In continuous time this is:

$$h = \frac{\Delta S_0}{\Delta F_0}$$
$$= \frac{1}{e^{(r+c-q)T}} \tag{12.19}$$

Often the asset to be hedged, and certainly the futures contract, comes in fixed *contract sizes* s. Therefore the number of contracts to be sold is $\frac{Q_F}{s}$.

Remark 118 *Compare this exact hedge ratio of the risk-free futures with the inexact hedge ratio of delta hedging of risky options in the Chapter 7. The hedge ratio is the inverse of the delta. But there is another difference: since this futures hedge ratio depends on the variables r_t and T (c and q do not change so often), it changes in an exact fashion with changes in r_t and T. In contrast, the hedge ratios for options also contain the exact normal distribution $N(d_1)$, which is dependent on the identified inexact volatility σ_s of the underlying asset S_0. As we noticed in Chapter 10, σ_s is an identified inexact parameter, which in practice is often not constant, because the pricing process of S_0 is often not stationary. There are even pricing processes for which the variance does not even exist, in the sense that it never converges to a constant.*

A change in a long position of an asset can be hedged by shorting cash , a cash equivalent index, futures (= risk-free hedges) or options (= risky hedges). In preceding Chapters we already discussed how a change in a long position of an asset can be hedged by shorting cash (*e.g.*, cash hedging in Chapter 7), or by options (*e.g.*, Black-Scholes delta hedging in Chapter 10), or even by shorting synthetic options. A *synthetic option* is created from actual stocks and bonds, or from futures, using the put-call parity (*Cf.* Chapter 9).

12.4.1 Imperfect Insurance

According to Modern Portfolio Theory (MPT) , in particular Asset Pricing Theory (APT) (Ross, 1976b), we can hedge any portfolio value by exploiting appropriate correlations between assets . Thus, we can hedge with anything that shows a variation in value opposite of that of the asset to be hedged, *e.g.*, stocks are often hedged with bonds and cash, while cash is often hedged with gold (= inflation hedge), etc.

Hedge Slippage

Thus, the asset being hedged is often not the asset underlying the traded futures contract and therefore there can be considerable (and costly) slippage between the required hedge and the actual hedge . This is easy to understand, when we recall what inexact systematic risk identification implies (*Cf.* Chapter 4). Suppose that the spot price A_0 of the asset being hedged is linearly related to the spot price S_0 of the asset underlying the futures contract, then

$$\Delta A_0 - \beta \Delta S_0 = 0 \tag{12.20}$$

Here

$$\beta = \frac{\Delta A_0}{\Delta S_0} \tag{12.21}$$

is the price beta, an inexact parameter of which the epistemic uncertainty range is to be determined by projective CLS identification , as in Chapter 4. Combining this uncertain parameter β with the certain hedge ratio, we have the inexact hedge ratio :

$$h = \frac{\Delta P}{\Delta S_0} \times \frac{\Delta S_0}{\Delta F_0}$$
$$= \frac{\beta}{e^{(r+c-q)T}} \tag{12.22}$$

which is the general form of the (imperfect) hedge ratio used in futures hedging . As we learned in Chapter 4, the epistemic uncertainty of the β, and thus of this hedge relationship can be measured in five equivalent ways, for example by the bounds on the CLS projection slopes $\widehat{\beta}_2^{LS} \leq \beta \leq \widehat{\beta}_1^{LS}$ (where $\widehat{\beta}_1^{LS} = \widehat{\beta}_2^{LS}/\rho_{12}^2$).

Very often cash-equivalent indices are used for passive hedging purposes of substantial institutional portfolios , like pension funds , endowment funds or large mutual funds . What is crucial in such a partial hedge is the existence of a close correlation between the portfolio value and the value of the index . Thus, one could use the S&P500 Index to hedge a particular stock portfolio fairly accurately when that portfolio's value is closely correlated to the S&P500, *i.e.*, their relationship shows a high bivariate coefficient of determination ρ_{12}^2.

The earlier formula above provides the hedge ratio for when the hedge is created by shorting an S&P500 ($\beta \approx 1.0$) Index *futures* , while the hedge ratio in the preceding Chapter 10 provided the hedge ratio for shorting an S&P500 Index *option* . Both contain an uncertain parameter, β, respectively $N(d_1)$. Transaction costs and ease of execution usually determines the choice between these different hedge instruments.

Basis Risk

But there are other risks in hedging with futures, like the basis risk . All of the variables involved in the hedge ratio must be measured as of the time that the hedge is lifted and *not* when the hedge is initiated. This means that the hedge ratio depends partly on what the basis is at some future date and the correct hedge ratio cannot be known with certainty, when the hedge is initiated (even when β would, hypothetically, be known with certainty).

Suppose an asset is "perfectly" hedged by shorting a futures contract at the current price F_0. The current value of the hedged portfolio (= portfolio asset + short position in the futures) is

$$V_0 = F_0 + (S_0 - F_0) \tag{12.23}$$
$$= S_0$$

When the hedge is lifted, at some future date t, with $0 < t < T$, the value V_t of this hedged portfolio will be the contracted value of the futures F_0 plus the basis $(S_t - F_t)$.

This is equivalent to the value of the asset S_t at that date, plus the profit on the short position of the futures $(F_0 - F_t)$. Thus

$$V_t = F_0 + (S_t - F_t)$$
$$= S_t + (F_0 - F_t) \tag{12.24}$$

If the futures hedge is lifted before the settlement day, when $0 < t < T$, the value of the combined portfolio V_t (= asset plus hedge) is uncertain, since it will be a function of what the basis $(S_t - F_t)$ is at that time. Therefore, lifting a hedge before settlement day is dangerous , since it forces one to speculate how much the basis will change between now and then. Only on settlement day, when $t = T$, it is not dangerous to lift the futures hedge, since on settlement day the basis is zero $(S_T - F_T) = 0$ and the value of the hedged portfolio V_T equals the current price of the futures contract F_0:

$$V_T = F_0 + (S_T - S_T) = F_0 \tag{12.25}$$

12.4.2   Portfolio Insurance?

How good is dynamic *portfolio insurance* by futures hedging? Following is the story of portfolio insurance gone awry on Monday, October 19, 1987, when the Dow Jones Industrial Average (DJIA) , a popular stock index (containing 30 blue chip stocks) in the United States, fell more than 500 points, or ca. 21%, because of market adjustment to a change in the fundamental intrinsic stock values . It started with a scare over the weekend that interest rates would rise, which depressed the intrinsic stock values, as calculated, say, by the Dividend Discount Model (*Cf.* Chapter 3), because the expected cost of capital had risen dramatically. When that Black Monday the financial markets opened, the market participants tried *en masse* to appropriately adjust their portfolio hedge ratios h to protect the value V_t of their portfolios. But their hedge ratio adjustment was too slow and they remained continuously underhedged (= too small δ), since their stock puts were not valued up in time (*Cf.* Fig. 2.), so that their portfolios continued to lose value. They were "chasing deltas" that kept getting away from them. The futures market on that Monday experienced a "gap "opening, where the opening price was nearly 10% below the preceding trading day's close. The futures price dropped before insurers could update their hedge ratios.

Why was their hedge ratio adjustment too slow, when both the spot and futures markets properly operated? Later investigations showed that both the stock market and the futures market had properly and efficiently executed the avalanche of sell orders , despite all the turmoil, thus the arbitragers performed correctly, although imprecisely. The information flows between the two markets were not fast enough. Current market prices were unavailable, with trade execution and the price quotation systems hours behind, which made the computation of correct hedge ratios impossible. Second, since the portfolio managers lifted their futures hedges before settlement day

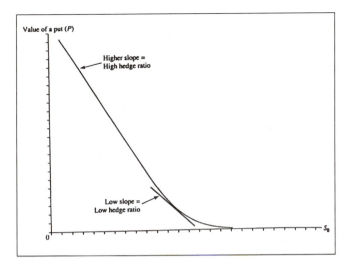

Figure 2   Hedge ratio δ of a put option increases as the stock price S_0 declines

to replace them by new future contracts, they continuously suffered severely from the then still imperfectly understood *basis risk*. Futures prices traded at steep discounts to their proper levels compared to reported stock prices, thereby making the sale of futures (as a proxy to equity sales) to increase hedging seem expensive. The $basis_t = S_t - F_t$, or cash-to-futures spread, was negative most of the day. When some insurers gambled that the futures price F_t would recover to its usual positive premium over the stock index S_t, and chose to defer futures sales, they remained underhedged. As the markets continued to decline, their leveraged portfolios experienced substantial losses.

At several times during that Monday and the next Tuesday morning, the participants of the futures market in the Chicago Board of Trade (CBOT) in Chicago, did not know the value of the Dow Jones Industrial Average Index as determined on the New York Stock Exchange (NYSE) in New York. Therefore, they couldn't know how much they should change their futures hedge position , and a vicious downward feedback spiral between the spot and futures markets was formed. On Tuesday, October 20, 1987, at noon, the Federal Reserve (= the central banking system of the U.S.) stepped in by announcing that there would be sufficient liquidity , *i.e.*, that the cash interest rate would remain unchanged and thus the actual cost of capital for the institutional stock investors would not rise. Thus a floor of unchanged intrinsic stock values appeared in the spot stock market in New York followed by a floor of corresponding unchanged futures values in the futures market in Chicago. The extra cash the Federal Reserve pumped into the markets for this *reassurance* was drained only two weeks later to avoid inflationary consequences . Thus, unlike in the 1930s, a major economic depression caused by lack of liquidity and high (real) interest rates and an enduring collapse of intrinsic stock values was avoided.

The Breeden Commission , which in 1987 - 88 investigated these market distortions , recommended that the stock and future markets should have "circuit breakers ," to interrupt trading for half an hour to slow down the trading when the stock market declined by 2.5%, so that both the spot and futures markets would stay in sync and trading and settlement would remain efficient. On October 27, 1997, these circuit breakers were triggered twice in the spot market, when the DJIA declined by 554 points, or 7.2%. Trading was first halted at midday when the index had declined by 350 points or 2.5%. The futures exchange continued to trade smoothly and the markets remained in sync. On the next day, October 28, 1997, the DJIA regained 337 points, or 4.73% of its value. It was the highest one-day jump since October 20, 1987, on that Tuesday afternoon when the Fed had stepped in after the paralyzing big crash on Black Monday.

12.5   Exercises

Exercise 119 *Refer to the data of the bond of the first Exercise in Chapter 3. Compare how you compute forward rates from spot rates by carefully rereading Chapter 3. Then compute the one-year forward rates . Plot the term structure and the one-year forward rates in separate graphs. Computing forward rates and a corresponding discount function from available spot rates is an essential activity for financial engineers , since all cash flows of swaps (= the most active sector of international banking) and similar financial instruments are valued using these forward rates.*

Exercise 120 *Suppose the spot Deutschemark /US dollar exchange rate is 1.820 D-Marks/US$, the US interest rate is 6.00% and the German interest rate is 5.45%, then what are the prices of the D-Mark/dollar forwards to be expired in three months? Explain your computations and how you would execute the transactions. With which transaction do you incur foreign exchange risk exposure and with which one can you avoid it?*

Exercise 121 *The following question is an application of the forward or futures pricing formula (= interest-rate parity condition) to currencies:*

$$F_0 = S_0 e^{(r_d - r_f)t} \tag{12.26}$$

$$\simeq S_0 \left(\frac{1 + r_d t}{1 + r_f t} \right) \tag{12.27}$$

Suppose that the spot Singapore dollar/US dollar rate is 1.4150, the US interest rate is 5.75% and the Singapore interest rate is 6.50%. What are then the prices of the S$/US$ forwards to be expired in one to three months? Use either the continuous or the discrete time formula and show all your calculations.

Exercise 122 *When we are dealing with a stock market Index and the Index pays dividend at an annual rate g, then the forward pricing formula is*

$$F_0 = S_0 e^{(r-g)t} \tag{12.28}$$

Suppose that the spot Nikkei-225 Index is 20,500 *Yen, the Japanese interest rate is* $r_f = 3.5\%$ *and the dividend pay-out rate is* 1.5%, *then what are the prices of the futures on the Nikkei-225 Index to be expired in one to three months?*

Exercise 123 *If the current March* 1996 *S&P500 futures price is* $570, *the volatility of the March* 1996 *S&P500 futures an estimated* 23%/*year, and the US interest rate* 6.5%, *what is the S&P500 futures call option price with strike price* $580 *to expire in six months?*

12.6   Bibliography

Heath, D., Jarrow, R. and Morton, A. (1992) "Bond Pricing and the Term Structure of the Interest Rates: A New Methodology," *Econometrica*, **60** (1), 77 - 105.

Hull, J. C. (1996) *Options, Futures and Other Derivatives*, 3rd ed., Prentice Hall International, Inc., New York, NY.

Marshall, J. F. and Bansal, V. K. (1992) *Financial Engineering: A Complete Guide to Financial Innovation*, New York Institute of Finance, New York, NY.

Ross, S. A. (1976a) "Options and Efficiency," *Quarterly Journal of Economics*, **90** (1), February, 75 - 89.

Ross, S. A. (1976b) "Arbitrage Theory of Capital Asset Pricing," *Journal of Economic Theory*, **13**, 341 - 360.

chapter:13,page:1

Chapter 13
SWAPS

13.1 Introduction

Three types of financial transactions take place in the cash and foreign currency (FX) markets: spot, forward and swap transactions, which are each defined as follows:

1. A *spot* transaction involves an agreement on price today, with settlement and actual delivery of the underlying asset usually only a few (one or two) business days later.

2. A(n *outright*) *forward* transaction involves an agreement on price today for settlement at some later date in the future (beyond the normal time lag for spot settlement, *e.g.*, for FX one or two weeks, or one through twelve months and sometimes, in OTC transactions, up to five, ten, or even 30 years). No money changes hands until delivery and settlement.

3. A *swap* transaction is a combination of spot and forward transactions, *e.g.*, a swap can consist of the sale of a bond with the simultaneous agreement to repurchase it at some date in the future, or the purchase of an amount of foreign currency with an agreement to resell it at some later date in the future.

Since a *swap* is any private agreement between two parties to exchange cash flows in the present and the future according to a prearranged formula and spot prices are equivalent to combinations of discounted forwards, it is easy to analyze swaps as portfolios of exact spot and forward spot contracts, even though swaps can be very complex transactions.

13.1.1 *Reasons for using Swaps*

The first swap was an interest rate swap negotiated in 1981 by the World Bank. Since 1981 the swap market has exploded and has become much more efficient. While in the early days of the swaps, bid-ask spreads were as high as 100 basis points, by the late 1980s, bid-ask spreads on interest rate swaps had narrowed to less than 10 basis points and swaps have become (almost) true and fair zero-sum games and thus (almost) exact arbitrage equilibrium models.

There are three general reasons for the popularity of swaps:

1. Swaps are a cost-effective way to transform a firm's existing risk profile by *synthetically* altering the balance sheet accounts.

2. Swaps are used for *structured financing, i.e.*, the process of issuing new securities to obtain cheaper borrowing cost, or to enhance investor return.

3. Swaps are expedient ways to exploit *asymmetric information, i.e.*, information about the firm that the capital market does not possess, to establish the firm's relative creditworthiness.

13.2 Valuation of Interest Rate Swaps

13.2.1 Interest Rate Swaps

In a "plain vanilla" *interest rate swap* one party A agrees to pay another party B cash flows equal to the interest at a *floating* interest rate (*e.g.*, the London Interbank Borrowing Rate or LIBOR) on a *notional principal* B_0 for a period of time T, and to receive cash flows equal to the interest at a fixed interest rate (= party A is long a fixed rate bond and short a floating rate bond). On the other hand counterparty B receives from party A cash flows equal to the interest at the agreed floating rate and pays interest at a fixed rate (= party B is long a floating rate bond and short a fixed rate bond). Such swaps are usually arranged by swap dealing intermediaries such as banks.

The *potential swap gain* from an interest rate swap is always

$$\text{Potential Swap Gain} = (r_A^{Fix} - r_B^{Fix}) - (r_A^{Float} - r_B^{Float}) \qquad (13.1)$$

where $(r_A^{Fix} - r_B^{Fix})$ is the difference between the interest rates facing parties A and B in the fixed rate markets, and $(r_A^{Float} - r_B^{Float})$ is the difference between the interest rates facing A and B in the floating rate markets.

Example 124 *Table 1. provides some illustrative market borrowing costs for firm A and firm B. Firm A is a better credit than firm B. The potential swap gain is* $120 - 70 = 50$ *basis points, when a bank brings these two swap parties together.*

TABLE 1.:	BORROWING	COSTS	
	Firm A	*Firm B*	*Credit Spreads*
Borrow fixed	$r_A^{Fix} = 10.0\%$	$r_B^{Fix} = 11.20\%$	$(r_B^{Fix} - r_A^{Fix}) = 1.20\%$
Borrow floating	$LIBOR + 0.30\%$	$LIBOR + 1.00\%$	$(r_A^{Float} - r_B^{Float}) = 0.70\%$

Table 2. shows the actual savings from a credit swap between firm A and firm B.

TABLE 2.:	SAVINGS	FROM SWAP
	Firm A	Firm B
A borrows fixed B borrows floating	−10.0%	−(LIBOR + 1.00%)
A receives fixed A pays floating B receives floating B pays fixed	9.9% −LIBOR	LIBOR −10.0%
All-in cost of funding	LIBOR + 0.10%	11.0%
Savings	0.20%	0.20%

With the swap firm A pays floating $LIBOR + 0.10\%$, while firm B pays 11.0% fixed.

Thus the potential gain of 50 basis points is divided up among the swap parties as follows. Firm A and firm B each gain 20 basis points from the swap. The bank which arranges this swap earns a fee of 10 basis points on the notional swap amount.

13.2.2 Valuation of Interest Rate Swaps

If there is no possibility of default (= no credit risk), an interest rate swap can be valued in three equivalent ways:

(1) a long position in one bond with a short position in another bond;

(2) a series of long and short positions in zero coupon bonds; and

(3) a series of long and short forward contracts.

We will now discuss these three equivalent valuations in turn.

Swap valuation by bonds

Thus, the value of a swap as a *combination of a long and a short bond* is

$$V_t = B_t^{Fix} - B_t^{Float} \tag{13.2}$$

The value of a swap is zero at the time when a swap is first negotiated and again at the end of its life: $V_0 = V_T = 0$. During its life a swap may have positive or negative values: $V_t <, =$, or > 0 for $0 < t < T$. Immediately after a *payment* or *reset date*, the floating bond's value is always equal to the notional principal. The value of the swap to the party which receives the fixed rate and pays the floating rate is

$$V_t = B_t^{Fix} - B_t^{Float} \tag{13.3}$$

The value of the swap to the party which receives the floating rate and pays the fixed rate is

$$-V_t = B_t^{Float} - B_t^{Fix} \tag{13.4}$$

This makes clear that a two party swap is a zero-sum or fair game, since the sum of the values of the swaps to the two parties is $V_t + (-V_t) = 0$ ($Cf.$ Frye, 1993).

The discount rates, used in valuing the bonds, should reflect the riskiness of the respective cash flows. This is usually a discount rate is used with a risk level corresponding to the floating rate underlying the swap. Often the floating rate underlying the swap is the LIBOR and the swap risk is the risk associated with loans in the London interbank market.

Remark 125 *Just as the prime rate is often the reference floating rate of interest in domestic financial markets, in particular between domestic banks and corporations, LIBOR is the reference floating rate of interest in international financial markets. LIBOR is the rate of interest offered by banks on deposits from other banks in the original Euro currency markets. One-month LIBOR is the rate offered on 1-month deposits, 3-month LIBOR is offered on 3-month deposits, etc. Soon, after January 1, 1999, when the European Monetary Union (EMU) became a fact and Europe had one monetary unit, the EURO, another reference floating rate may emerge, the EURO-IBOR = EURO Inter-Bank Offer Rate.*

Swap valuation by zeros

We'll now discuss the second way of valuing swaps. In Chapter 3 we showed that any bond can be decomposed into a *series of zero coupon bonds*. For the valuation, both the fixed and the floating rate bonds are usually converted into series of zero-coupon bonds using the term structure of interest rates. We illustrate this first conversion with an example adapted from Hull (1996). Suppose that under the terms of the swap, a party agrees to pay 6-month LIBOR and receive 8% fixed interest per annum (with semi-annual compounding) on a notional principal of $100 million. The swap has a remaining life of 15 months. The relevant discount rates with continuous compounding for 3-month ($T_1 = \frac{3}{12} = 0.25yrs$), 9-month ($T_2 = \frac{9}{12} = 0.75yrs$), and 15 month ($T_3 = \frac{15}{12} = 1.25yrs$) maturities are 10%, 10.5% and 11.0%, respectively. The 6-month LIBOR rate at the last payment date was 10.2% (with semi-annual compounding). Then the semi-annual cash flow on the fixed rate bond is

$$CF_t = \frac{1}{2} \times 0.08 \times \$100 million$$
$$= \$4 million \tag{13.5}$$

. Furthermore, the already determined and known

$$\text{first floating rate payment } =$$
$$= \$5.1 million \tag{13.6}$$

so that the value of the fixed rate bond is

$$B_t^{Fix} = 4e^{-0.10 \times \frac{3}{12}} + 4e^{-0.105 \times \frac{9}{12}} + 4e^{-0.11 \times \frac{15}{12}} + 100e^{-0.11 \times \frac{15}{12}} \tag{13.7}$$
$$= \$98.24 million$$

and the value of the floating rate bond is

$$B_t^{Float} = 5.1e^{-0.10 \times \frac{3}{12}} + 100e^{-0.10 \times \frac{3}{12}}$$
$$= \$102.51 million \tag{13.8}$$

Thus, the (present) value of the swap is

$$V_t = B_t^{Fix} - B_t^{Float}$$
$$= 98.24 - 102.51$$
$$= -\$4.27 million \tag{13.9}$$

If the bank had been in the opposite position of paying fixed and receiving floating, the value of the swap would be $+\$4.27 million$.

Swap valuation by forwards

There is a third equivalent way of valuing swaps. In the absence of credit risk (an important condition!), this value of the swap is equivalent to, and can be converted into, a *series of long and short forward contracts*, as we now demonstrate by using the preceding example. To do so, we must review a few technical financial conversions to derive the semi-annual compounding rates. If r_1 is the spot rate of interest for the period of T_1 years and r_2 the spot rate of interest applying to T_2 years, where $T_2 > T_1$, we know from Chapters 3 and 12 that the continuously compounding forward interest rate for the period of time between T_1 and T_2 is given by

$$_1f_2 = \frac{r_2 T_2 - r_1 T_1}{T_2 - T_1} \tag{13.10}$$

Thus, for our previous example, with continuous compounding, we have the forward rate $_1f_2$ between T_1 and T_2 is:

$$_1f_2 = \frac{0.105 \times \frac{9}{12} - 0.10 \times \frac{3}{12}}{\frac{9}{12} - \frac{3}{12}}$$
$$= 0.1075 \tag{13.11}$$

and the forward rate $_2f_3$ between T_2 and T_3 is

$$_2f_3 = \frac{0.11 \times \frac{15}{12} - 0.105 \times \frac{9}{12}}{\frac{9}{12} - \frac{3}{12}}$$
$$= 0.1175 \tag{13.12}$$

Next, these annual continuous compounding rates must now be converted into semi-annual compounding rates, because the swap payments will be made at the semi-annual reset dates.

Remark 126 *Recall from Chapter 2 that when ρ is the rate of interest with continuous compounding and r the equivalent rate with compounding n times a year, we must have, as a limiting approximation:*

$$e^{\rho T} = (1 + \frac{r}{n})^{nT} \tag{13.13}$$

Taking natural logarithms at both sides of the equation we find

$$\rho = n \ln(1 + \frac{r}{n}) \tag{13.14}$$

from which we find that, by approximation:

$$r = n(e^{\frac{\rho}{n}} - 1) \tag{13.15}$$

Thus, the two continuously forward compounding rates are converted to semi-annual compounding rates (in annual %!), as follows:

$$_1f_2 = 2(e^{\frac{0.1075}{2}} - 1)$$
$$= 0.1104 \tag{13.16}$$

and

$$_2f_3 = 2(e^{\frac{0.1175}{2}} - 1)$$
$$= 0.1210 \tag{13.17}$$

For the party receiving the fixed and paying floating interest, we subtract the floater from the fixed bond, so that a series of discounted payment differences results. The current value of the preceding swap is then, in millions of dollars

$$V_0 = (4.0 - 5.1)e^{-0.10 \times \frac{3}{12}} + (4.0 - \frac{1}{2} \times 0.1104 \times 100)e^{-0.105 \times \frac{9}{12}}$$
$$+ (4.0 - \frac{1}{2} \times 0.1210 \times 100)e^{-0.11 \times \frac{15}{12}}$$
$$= -\$4.27million \tag{13.18}$$

Thus, the swap is clearly a combination of series of discounted long and short forward contracts:

$$V_t = \sum_i (F_{t,i}^A - F_{t,i}^B)e^{-r_i T_i} \tag{13.19}$$

Remark 127 *At the time a swap is entered, its value is zero. Thus, the sum of the values of the forwards underlying the swap contract is also zero at that time. But this does not mean that the individual elements of that sum are zero. In general, some forwards will be positive and some will be negative. Therefore, a bank usually holds a large portfolio of many long and short forwards.*

To easily compute the values of these forward contracts, one needs a semi-annual continuous discount function based on the existing yield curve. However, in reality, one yield curve doesn't exist for all maturities and the same credit grade. Thus, in practice, a continuous yield curve has to be interpolated from various sub-yield curves, often from different maturity ranges and from different credit qualities.

13.2.3 Constructing a Swap Yield Curve

As we mentioned in Chapter 11, spot rates are usually provided as yields-to-maturity (YTMs), while forwards (futures) use term structure rates (zero-coupon rates). Since for the same credit quality, day count convention and maturity, there must be only one price, the *par yield curve* and the *zero coupon curve* must express the same price in different ways.* Thus, the only purpose of first constructing a complete yield (-to-maturity) curve, by bootstrapping and splining related market data, is to find a complete discount function for every given maturity to determine the time value of money. This sounds easier to do than it actually is, considering that there are many different kinds and varieties of financial market rates:

1. *Rates of different form*

- Add-on rates $(1 +_0 r_1 \times \frac{T}{360})$, or genuine discount rates $(1 +_0 z_1)^{\frac{T}{365}}$ (Eurodollar versus T-bill rates), with different day count conventions (*e.g.*, 360 versus 365 days)

- Exchange, or OTC forward rates (Eurodollar futures versus FRAs)

- Cash rates with different compounding frequencies (LIBOR 6-month, or LIBOR 1-month)

2. *Rates with different levels of credit risk*

- Risk-free rates (T-bill notes and T-bonds)

- Rates of exchange contracts with a clearing house for daily marking-to-market

- SWAP rates based on "A" to "AA" credit rating

- Rates of OTC instruments based on credit tiering (FRAs)

3. *Rates of different liquidity*

- Minimal bid-ask spreads on high volume transactions (so-called on-the-run Treasuries, first four contract months of Eurodollar and T-bond futures)

- Wider bid/ask spreads for low volume transactions (seasoned OTC financial instruments, nonstandard FRAs)

---

*Analogously, a speedometer of an automobile calibrated in miles in the United States will show a speed of $50 miles/hr$, while a speedometer calibrated in kilometers in Europe will show the same velocity as ca. $80 km/hr$. Both speedometers indicate the same driving speed.

4. *Rates of different maturities*

- Spot rates (Eurodollar and Federal Funds)

- Short term rates (Money market, FRAs, Futures)

- Medium term rates (Treasury, SWAP rates)

- Long term rates (Treasury, SWAP rates)

All these rates should be considered when a defined par yield curve is constructed via *conversion*, *e.g.*, using the following three conversion formulas,

$$(1 +_0 r_1 \frac{T}{360}) = (1 +_0 z_1)^{\frac{T}{365}} = e^{\rho \frac{T}{m}}, \tag{13.20}$$

via *bootstrapping* (when no rates exist for a particular maturity and these rates have to be found by interpolation), and via *splining* (linking rates at the same maturity by smoothing). Indeed, specialized financial engineers now operate in the financial markets, called *yield curve specialists*, who deal with this intricate and delicate matter. The construction of a complete yield curve is as much a science as an art, given the many available data sets and institutional quoting conventions. The resulting yield curve for the swap markets is thus an identified inexact model of the spot interest rates based on the mid-points of the empirical bid and offer rates.[†] Next, from the yield curve the *spot term structure* is found by computing the semi-annual zero-coupon rates. Fig. 1. provides a theoretical representation of this financial engineering process to identify a swap yield curve.[‡]

Notice the various segments for the short term spot rates, forward rates, long term Treasury rates, etc., which are used to identify first a par yield curve from and next a zero coupon curve, *i.e.*, a term structure of interest rates.

But sometimes a discount rate for a particularly sized initial period is needed. For example, when only zero rates exist for 1-month and 2-month maturities, but the first futures contract is a 1.5-month contract, the following interpolation formula is often used

$$z_{1.5m} = z_{1m} + \frac{T_{1.5m} - T_{1m}}{T_{2m} - T_{1m}}(z_{2m} - z_{1m}) \tag{13.21}$$

Remark 128 *Recall that when the yield curve is upward-sloping, because the financial markets expect short term rates to rise in the future, the term structure of zero-coupon rates lies above the yield curve (Fig. 4). When the yield curve is downward sloping, because the financial markets expect the short term rates to decline in the future, the term structure lies below the yield curve.*

[†]Different financial engineers do produce their own identified par yield curves for swap transactions. When these par yield curves would be truly exact, all financial engineers would realize one and the same yield curve for swap transactions. Because of the differences, there is a clear role for arbitragers within the swap markets.

[‡]In 1989, in New York, Fig. 1. was kindly provided by Position Management, Inc., a financial engineering consulting firm, specializing in the construction of swap yield curves.

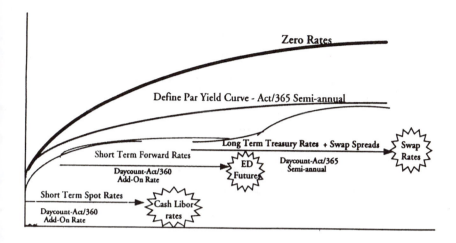

Figure 1 Financial engineering of a swap yield curve

13.2.4 *Computing the Discount Function*

A semi-annual *discount function* is generated from the term structure of interest rates of Fig. 1., for analyzing future and present value cash flows.

Example 129 *Take $_0r_1 = 10\%$ and the maturity $T_{0,1} = 90days$, then from the conversion formula:*

$$(1 +_0 r_1 \frac{T}{360}) = (1 +_0 z_1)^{\frac{T}{365}} \tag{13.22}$$

we first find

$$
\begin{aligned}
_0z_1 &= (1 + 0.10 \times \frac{90}{360})^{\frac{365}{90}} - 1 \\
&= 10.5328\%
\end{aligned}
\tag{13.23}
$$

and the discount function value $DF_{T_{0,1}}$ for $T_{0,1} = 90days$ is

$$
\begin{aligned}
DF_{T_{0,1}} &= \frac{1}{(1.105328)^{\frac{90}{365}}} \\
&= \frac{1}{(1 + 0.10 \times \frac{90}{360})} \\
&= 0.975609
\end{aligned}
\tag{13.24}
$$

The discount function calculates for each maturity the rate at which the future or face value of a bond is discounted to its present value (= market price by arbitrage)

$$PV_0 = FV_T \times DF_{T_{0,1}} \tag{13.25}$$

Therefore, this constructed discount function DF_T forms the basis for all swap valuations. The discount function DF_T is (usually) a monotonic, decreasing function of maturity T (Fig. 2).

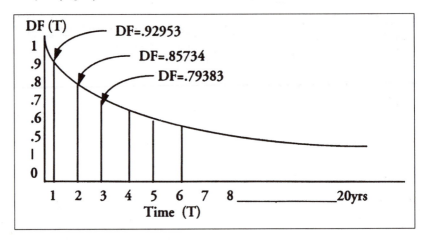

Figure 2   Discount function

13.3   Valuation of Currency Swaps

13.3.1   Quoting Conventions

According to the Bank for International Settlements (B.I.S.) in Basel, 61 percent of trading of convertible currencies takes place with respect to the U.S. dollar, *i.e.* the *anchor currency*. For example, the Singapore dollar and the Malaysian Ringgit are both quoted *vis-a-vis* the U.S. dollar. By quoting $n = 19$ currencies against one anchor currency there are only 19 exchange rates. Otherwise there would be

$$n \times (n-1)/2 = 19 \times (19-1)/2$$
$$= 171 \tag{13.26}$$

bilateral exchange rates. Fig. 1. provides the currency cross rates as recorded at the end of the trading day of July 3rd, 2000, and reported in *The Asian Wall Street Journal* of July 4th, 2000. The top row and the left column provides the bilateral exchange rates against the U.S. dollar.

CURRENCY CROSS RATES																		July 3	
	U.S.	A$	Pound	C$	RMB	Euro	FFr	DM	NK$	Rupee	Rph	Yen	NZ$	Won	Ring	Peso	S$	SwFr	NT$	Baht
U.S.		1.670	0.661	1.480	8.279	1.051	6.892	2.065	1.795	44.870	8950.00	106.150	2.137	1113.70	3.800	43.520	1.735	1.634	30.765	39.360
Australia	0.599		0.396	0.886	4.957	0.630	4.127	1.230	1.868	26.765	5359.26	63.583	1.279	668.88	2.275	26.060	1.037	0.978	18.422	23.569
Britain	1.514	2.528		2.241	12.534	1.592	10.434	3.111	11.802	67.530	23550.30	180.711	3.235	1686.14	5.752	65.889	2.621	2.473	48.578	59.591
Canada	0.676	1.128	0.446		5.593	0.710	4.656	1.388	5.266	30.178	6048.48	71.713	1.444	752.40	2.567	29.401	1.170	1.104	20.784	26.591
China	0.121	0.202	0.000	0.178		0.127	0.832	0.248	0.942	5.396	1081.10	12.822	0.258	134.53	0.458	5.257	0.209	0.197	3.716	4.754
Euro	0.981	1.599	0.628	1.408	7.875		6.555	1.955	7.415	42.490	8513.24	100.970	2.032	1059.351	3.614	41.396	1.647	1.554	29.284	37.439
France	0.148	0.242	0.096	0.215	1.201	0.153		0.296	1.931	6.482	1298.64	15.402	0.310	181.80	0.551	6.315	0.251	0.237	4.464	5.711
Germany	0.487	0.813	0.321	0.720	4.029	0.512	3.354		3.793	21.738	4355.41	51.657	1.040	541.97	1.849	21.179	0.843	0.795	14.972	19.154
Hong Kong	0.128	0.214	0.065	0.190	1.062	0.135	0.884	0.264		5.730	1148.14	13.817	0.274	142.87	0.487	5.583	0.222	0.210	3.947	5.049
India	0.0224	0.0374	0.0148	0.0331	0.1853	0.0235	0.1543	0.0460	0.1745		200.38	2.3783	0.0478	24.93	0.0851	0.9743	0.3388	0.0366	0.6887	0.8811
Indonesia	0.0001	0.0002	0.0001	0.0002	0.0009	0.0001	0.0008	0.0002	0.0009	0.0050		0.0119	0.0002	0.12	0.0004	0.0049	0.0002	0.0002	0.0034	0.0044
Japan	0.009	0.015	0.006	0.014	0.078	0.010	0.065	0.019	0.073	0.421	84.31		0.020	10.49	0.035	0.410	0.018	0.015	0.290	0.371
New Zealand	0.468	0.782	0.309	0.693	3.874	0.492	3.225	0.962	3.648	20.906	4169.60	49.878		521.21	1.778	20.367	0.810	0.765	14.396	18.420
S. Korea	0.0009	0.0015	0.0006	0.0013	0.0074	0.0009	0.0062	0.0018	0.0070	0.0401	8.04	0.0953	0.0019		0.0034	0.0391	0.0018	0.0015	0.0276	0.0353
Malaysia	0.263	0.440	0.174	0.390	2.179	0.277	1.814	0.541	2.052	11.757	2355.57	27.938	0.562	293.12		11.454	0.456	0.430	8.097	10.358
Philippines	0.023	0.038	0.015	0.034	0.190	0.024	0.158	0.047	0.178	1.024	205.65	2.436	0.049	25.59	0.087		0.040	0.038	0.797	0.904
Singapore	0.576	0.964	0.381	0.855	4.781	0.607	3.980	1.187	4.502	25.798	5166.93	61.305	1.234	643.20	2.194	25.134		0.944	17.763	22.732
Switzerland	0.612	1.022	0.404	0.906	5.067	0.644	4.219	1.256	4.772	27.343	5476.36	64.975	1.306	681.70	2.326	26.636	1.060		18.831	24.093
Taiwan	0.033	0.054	0.021	0.048	0.269	0.034	0.224	0.067	0.253	1.482	290.92	3.450	0.069	36.20	0.124	1.415	0.056	0.053		1.279
Thailand	0.026	0.042	0.017	0.038	0.210	0.027	0.175	0.052	0.196	1.135	227.30	2.697	0.054	28.30	0.097	1.106	0.044	0.042	0.782	

Figure 3   Currency cross rates of July 3, 2000, reported in *The Asian Wall Street Journal* of July 4, 2000

Not only simplifies the use of an anchor currency the FX quotations, it also reduces the possibility of *triangular arbitrage* and it increases the efficiency of the currency markets. If all currencies are traded against each other directly, the exchange rate of the Singapore dollar versus the U.S. dollar compared with the Malaysian Ringgit versus the U.S. dollar implies an exact exchange rate of the Singapore dollar versus the Malaysian Ringgit. If this implied rate differs from the direct quote of the Singapore dollar versus the Malaysian Ringgit, a potential opportunity for triangular arbitrage may occur. But when all cross rates are derived from the rates of the currencies versus the dollar anchor, there is only one available cross rate and thus no possibility of triangular arbitrage.

However, some international banks do specialize in the currently still existent (inefficient) cross rate quotes (*e.g.*, ABN-AMRO Bank). The bid-ask spread of a direct cross-rate quotation incorporates both bid-ask spreads from the two currencies quoted with respect to the dollar. Thus, a commercial bank has some room to undercut the size of the total spread, provided it has enough cross-rate swap business to make such a business profitable.

There are American (or direct) and European (or indirect or reciprocal) terms of quotation:

American terms: the dollar price of one unit of foreign exchange, for example, $US\$0.58 = S\$1.00$, and $US\$0.58 = A\$1.00$.

European terms: the foreign currency price of one U.S. dollar, for example, $S\$1.73 = US\$1.00$ and $A\$1.73 = US\$1.00$.

Currency quotations are generally in American terms, in particular in the markets for FX futures and options on FX futures (*Cf.* Fig. 5 for an example of the foreign currencies quoted in the table published daily in *The Asian Wall Street Journal*).

All FX trading involves two prices, a bid, or buying price and an offer, or selling price. Whether an exchange rate represents a bid price or an offer price depends on the currency used for reference.

Example 130 *If you bid for Singapore dollars with U.S. dollars, that is the same as offering U.S. dollars for Singapore dollars. When a trader quotes Singapore dollar against the U.S. dollar (European terms) at a bid/offer price of $(S\$1.575 - 1.580)/US\$1$ it is natural to think of the small number, $S\$1.575$, as the bid price and the large number, $S\$1.580$, as the offer price. But bid and offer for what? The Singapore dollar? Answer: no! The $S\$1.575/US\$1$ quote is the bid price for the U.S. dollar, while $S\$1.580/US\$1$ quote is the offer (or asked) price for the U.S. dollar. The FX traders' objective is to make money. So, the trader wants to give away as few Singapore dollars as possible, when he purchases U.S. dollars. Hence his bid for the U.S. dollar of $S\$1.575$. On the other hand, he wants to acquire as many Singapore dollars possible, when he sells U.S. dollars. Hence he offers to sell $US\$1$ for $S\$1.580$.*

13.3.2 Valuation of Currency Swaps

In the absence of default risk, a *currency swap* can be decomposed into a portfolio position with two bonds, similar to an interest rate swap. The only difference is that one bond is in one currency, while the other is in a different currency. Thus, in general, the value of a currency swap is:

$$V_t = S_t B_t^F - B_t^D \qquad (13.27)$$

where B_t^F is the value of the foreign denominated bond, measured in the foreign currency, for example, in Japanese Yen. S_t is the spot exchange rate, expressed as number of units of domestic currency per unit of foreign currency. For example, in American terms, $S\$/Yen$. B_t^D is the value of the domestic bond underlying the swap. For example, in Singapore dollars, $S\$$.

Thus, the value of a currency swap can be computed from:

(a) the term structure of interest rates in the domestic currency,

(b) the term structure of interest rates in the foreign currency, and

(c) the spot exchange rate.

For simplicity, suppose the term structure is flat both in Japan and in Singapore. The Japanese (continuously compounding) interest rate is $r_f = 4\%/year$ and the similar Singapore rate is $r_d = 6\%/year$. A bank has negotiated a currency swap, where it receives $5\%/year$ in Yen and pays $7\%/year$ in Singapore dollars once a year (*i.e.*, it is long a Yen bond and short a Singapore bond). The notional principals in the two currencies are S$10 million and $1,400$ million Yen, respectively. The swap will last for another three years and the current cross exchange rate is $75 Yen = S\$1$. Now the present value of the domestic Singapore bond is:

$$B_t^D = 0.7e^{-0.06} + 0.7e^{-0.06 \times 2} + 10.7e^{-0.06 \times 3}$$
$$= S\$10.217 million \tag{13.28}$$

and the present value of the foreign Yen bond is:

$$B_t^F = 70e^{-0.04} + 70e^{-0.04 \times 2} + 1,470e^{-0.04 \times 3}$$
$$= 1,435.60 million\ Yen \tag{13.29}$$

Thus, the value of the swap in Singapore dollars is:

$$V_t = S_t B_t^F - B_t^D$$
$$= \frac{1,435.60}{75} - 10.217$$
$$= S\$8.92 million \tag{13.30}$$

If the bank had been paying Yen and receiving Singapore dollars, the value of the swap would have been $-V_t = -S\$8.92 million$.

The decomposition into a *series of long and short forwards* is now relatively easy. The payment periods are the same and the term structures in this example are both flat, so that the value of the swap is:

$$V_t = (\frac{70}{75}e^{-0.04} - 0.7e^{-0.06}) + (\frac{70}{75}e^{-0.04 \times 2} - 0.7e^{-0.06 \times 2})$$
$$+ (\frac{1470}{75}e^{-0.04 \times 3} - 10.7e^{-0.06 \times 3})$$
$$= (\frac{70}{75}e^{(0.06-0.04)} - 0.7)e^{-0.06} + (\frac{70}{75}e^{(0.06-0.04) \times 2} - 0.7)e^{-0.06 \times 2}$$
$$+ (\frac{1470}{75}e^{(0.06-0.04) \times 3} - 10.7)e^{-0.06 \times 3} \tag{13.31}$$

But this equals:

$$V_t = (70F_1 - 0.7)e^{-0.06} + (70F_2 - 0.7)e^{-0.06 \times 2} + (1470F_3 - 10.7)e^{-0.06 \times 3} \tag{13.32}$$

where each forward contract

$$F_i = \frac{1}{75}e^{(0.06-0.04)T_i} \tag{13.33}$$

is just the compounded spot exchange rate, in Singapore dollars. It is compounded at the interest rate differential $r_d - r_f = (0.06 - 0.04)$. Therefore, this currency swap can also be valued as a series of long forward contracts and short spot contracts. This demonstrates how the value of a currency swap can be computed from the term structure of forward rates and from the term structure of domestic interest rates. The term structure of the forwards incorporates the interest rate differentials between the two countries.

13.4   Risks of Swap Contracts

13.4.1   Market and Credit Risk

Thus far, we've discussed swaps without credit risk, but most swaps involve both market risks and credit risks, like any other securities (*Cf.* Jarrow and Turnbull, 1995):

1. The *market risk* is the possibility that the interest or exchange rates may move into a direction such that the value of the swap becomes negative to the bank. In that case, the bank has to pay a positive amount to get out of the swap.

2. The *credit risk* is the possibility that the bank's counterparty may default when the value of the swap to the bank is positive.

Example 131 *From the bank's perspective, in a fixed for floating interest rate swap, when interest rates fall, the parties paying fixed to the bank become a source of credit risk, while, when interest rates rise, the parties paying floating to the bank become sources of credit risk. So, credit risk of an interest rate swap hinges foremost on the volatility of the interest rates.*

Conceptually, if the probability of the fixed interest rate going to state i is p_i, the swap value to the bank in state i is V_i, and the probability of the counterparty to swap A defaults in state i is p_i^A. Then, the counterparty A's credit risk to the bank can be measured by a series of weighted options:

$$\text{Credit Risk of } A \ = \sum_i p_i p_i^A \max[V_i, 0] \tag{13.34}$$

Here the *value of the credit risk* is computed by a summation of (risk-neutral) probabilities multiplying the empirical option values. This is another example of how credit risk can be decomposed into option risk, and then priced by regularly traded options (*Cf.* Chapter 10)!

13.4.2 Duration of a Swap

The value of a swap will change as interest rates change and duration is the first-order sensitivity of fixed-income contracts (*Cf.* Chapter 11). Therefore, the *duration of an interest rate swap* is:

$$D^V_{Mod} = D^{Fix}_{Mod} - D^{Float}_{Mod} \qquad (13.35)$$

Since the duration of the fixed-rate bond is large and the duration of the floating rate bond is small (the duration must be less than the time until the next reset date), the duration of the swap is always dominated by the duration of the fixed-rate bond.

13.5 Exercises

Exercise 132 *Create a vanilla interest rate swap on a $150mln notional principal between this fixed bond and a floating bond with an initial rate of 5.0%, to be reset annually. What is the value to the party receiving fixed and paying floating? What is the value of the swap for the counter-party?*

Exercise 133 *A $100 million interest rate swap has a remaining life of 10 months. Under the terms of the swap, 6— month LIBOR is exchanged for 12% per annum (compounded semi-annually). The average of the bid and ask rate being exchanged for 6—month LIBOR in swaps of all maturities is currently 10% per annum with continuous compounding. The 6-month LIBOR rate was 9.6% per annum two months ago. What is the current value of the swap to the party paying floating? What is its value to the party paying fixed?*

Exercise 134 *The following is an example of an international currency swap. Suppose that the term structure of interest rates is flat in both the United States and Singapore. The current U.S. dollar interest rate is 8% per annum while the Singapore interest rate is 6% per annum. The current exchange rate is S$1.40 = US$1. Under the terms of a swap agreement, an international bank pays 3% per annum in Singapore dollars and receives 7% per annum in U.S. dollars. The notionals in the two currencies are US$15 million and S$20 million. Payments are exchanged every half year with one exchange having just taken place. The swap will last two more years. Create a table showing the value of the swap to the international bank for various exchange rates (from 1.30S$/US$1 to 1.50S$/US$1 in increments of S$0.02) and various U.S. interest rates (6% to 10% with increments of 50 basis points. Assume that all interest rates are continuously compounded.*

Exercise 135 *The following is a risk management application of swaps, in particular an example of balance sheet gap management (Cf. Brown & Smith, 1995, Chapter 3). Consider the risk management problem faced by the ABC company, a financial services corporation, whose balance sheet is as follows.*

COMPANY ABC's BALANCE SHEET AND A/L DURATIONS		
Item	Market Value	Duration (years)
Assets		
Cash	200	0.00
5-yr term loans, valued at par to yield 10%	800	4.17
10-yr amortizing mortgages valued at par to yield 10%	1000	4.73
Total Assets	2000	
Liabilities		
5-yr, floating-rate note with semi-annual reset to LIBOR	1200	0.50
(current LIBOR =7%)		
10-yr, zero-coupon bond issued to yield 7%	600	10.00
Total Liabilities	1800	
Net worth	200	

1. This company is interest rate sensitive (Why?). Compute the duration gap of this company.

2. How can you immunize ABC's duration gap by cash hedging? Would that be advisable? Why or why not?

3. How can you immunize ABC's duration gap by using swaps? Assume that the fixed swap rate is currently 7%. You may want to use the spreadsheets of the Exercises in Chapter 11 for the appropriate duration calculation!

13.6   Bibliography

Brown, K. and Smith, D. J. (1995) "Swap Applications" and "Pricing Interest Rate and Currency Swaps," Chapters 3 and 4 in *Interest Rate and Currency Swaps: A Exercise*, The Research Foundation of The Institute of Chartered Financial Analysts, Charlottesville, VA, pp. 41 - 55 and 61 - 81.

Cox, J. C., Ingersoll, Jr., J. E. and Ross, S. A. (1985) "A Theory of the Term Structure of Interest Rates," *Econometrica*, **53**, March, 363 - 384.

Frye, J. (1993) "Underexposed and Overanxious," *Risk*, **5** (2), March, 42 - 46.

Hull, J. C. (1996) *Options, Futures and Other Derivatives*, 3rd ed., Prentice Hall International, Inc., New York, NY.

Jarrow, R. A. and Turnbull, S. M. (1995) "Pricing Derivatives on Financial Securities Subject to Credit Risk," *Journal of Finance*, **50** (1), March, 53 - 85.

chapter:14,page:1

Chapter 14

MULTI - CURRENCY INVESTMENTS AND EXACT PERFORMANCE ATTRIBUTION

14.1 Introduction

This Chapter pulls together several themes of the preceding Chapters and consists of four sections. The first two sections are devoted to exact cash growth analysis of multi-currency portfolios. The first section is without market risk, while the second section introduces the market risk. The third section is devoted to portfolio optimization within this exact growth accounting framework. It is a special application and clear illustration of Markowitz' section on semi-definite covariance matrices in Chapter 3 "Capabilities and Assumptions of the General Model " of his book (Markowitz, 1992, pp. 42 - 43).* The fourth section of this Chapter discusses exact portfolio performance attribution for the global investor. All four sections are based on the *exact cash growth cum risk accounting* model of Los (1998a & b; 1999).

Since the floating of the Thai baht on July 2, 1997, currency and credit crises in Thailand, the Philippines, Indonesia, Malaysia and Hong Kong have dramatically increased interest in multi-currency investment management in Southeast Asia. Such complex investment management requires an exact, unified accounting framework for performance analysis of multi-currency portfolios, which involve various market assets, currencies and cross-currency hedging swaps.[†]

---

*This was kindly pointed out to me by Professor Harry Markowitz in a personal letter of January 13, 1999, in reaction to my statement in Los (1998b, p. 189) that "Markowitz 'conventional mean-variance optimization of portfolios....requires that the central risk matrix is positive definite, *i.e.*, nonsingular (Markowitz, 1952, 1987)." Professor Markowitz corrected me by writing: "In fact, however, Markowitz (1987) explicitly permits singular covariance matrices, **C**. The section titled "Semidefinite Covariance Matrices, "pages 42 and 43, gives reasons why it is important to allow |**C**| = 0. (Your application is an additional reason). Chapter 7 demonstrates that once a non-singular $\overline{\mathbf{M}}$ (sub) matrix is found, subsequent $\overline{\mathbf{M}}$ matrices will also be non-singular even though the total **M** matrix is singular. Chapter 8 shows how the simplex algorithm provides the initial non-singular **M**." "Since Markowitz (1987) is out of print you may not have actually seen a copy. Please find one enclosed " Hereby I thank Professor Markowitz for his generosity. My only response to his comment is that one doesn't need the iterative simplex algorithm to solve the optimization problem, as Chapter 6 and again Section 4 of this Chapter, when I extend the Markowitz procedure with some tensor algebra, clearly demonstrates. The Kuhn-Tucker Theorem is used to solve the problem explicitly and the plotting of the Efficiency Frontier is direct.

[†]The flip side is that such cross-currency hedges facilitate the risk of *currency contagion, i.e.*, the

The four key components of the performance of a multi-currency investment portfolio are:

1. *Market selection*;
2. *Currency selection*
3. *Security selection*; and
4. *Hedge selection*.

The global investor should be able to account for the separate impact of each of these key components on the portfolio's performance, both in terms of return and of risk. In this Chapter, for simplicity, the first section discusses market selection, currency selection and hedge selection, while the third section discusses some security selection. All four components can be inserted into the same mathematical framework.

The continuously compounding *cash accounting* framework of Karnosky and Singer (1994) and Singer and Karnovsky (1995) accommodates only *return maximizing* investment strategies. But modern portfolio management requires *return/risk optimizing* investment strategies, *i.e.*, investment strategies which seek the most desirable combination of high investment returns and low risks.

By using simple tensor (Kronecker) algebra, Los (1998b) extended Singer and Karnovsky's exact accounting framework to include market risk and thus the opportunity to use Markowitz' mean-variance portfolio optimization of Chapter 6 within their exact accounting framework.[‡] For the empirical example, we use historical data from a simple portfolio of investments in three Asian countries of Singapore, Malaysia and Indonesia, using monthly data from June 1993 to June 1997.

Karnosky and Singer (1994) and Singer and Karnosky (1995) use an extension of the Capital Asset Pricing Model (CAPM) to complement the original *exact performance attribution* accounting framework of Ankrim (1992), Brinson, Hood and Beebower (1986) and Brinson, Singer and Beebower (1991). As we saw earlier, the foundation of the CAPM's *performance attribution* is the idea that an asset's rate of return consists of a nominal risk-free cash rate (= real risk-free cash rate plus a premium to compensate for inflation) and a premium to compensate for the (non-cash) asset risk.

The usefulness of this unified, exact, multi-currency, performance attribution framework is its ability to accommodate the complete set of financial instruments - bonds stocks, options, futures, swaps - that is now widely used in the management of international corporate balance sheets and of global investment portfolios. As has been discussed in the Chapters 3 and 9, 11, 12 and 13, fundamental instruments (cash,

---

spreading of currency risk via the cross-currency swap linkages.

[‡]Empirical credit risk can be incorporated into the same portfolio optimization framework, with a *caveat*. Credit risk distributions are asymmetric: they tend to be skewed to the left with long left tails. Consequently, the use of only means and symmetric variances to determine an efficient portfolio frontier may be misleading. The higher moments measures of skewness and kurtosis play an important role in credit risk distributions.

bonds, stocks) and derivative financial instruments (options, futures and swaps), as well as ongoing firms, projects, etc. can (and should) be valued in terms of *discounted expected cash flows*. The usual prediction assumption is one of inertia: the first and second moments of the asset return distributions remain the same, at least for the next period (*Cf.* Chapter 5).

14.2 Multi - Currency Investment Return Accounting

14.2.1 Investment Strategy Return Attribution

According to the exact cash accounting framework of Singer and Karnosky (1994, 1995), at time t an investor can earn three possible investment returns: (1) investment in a fundamental asset in country i, *e.g.*, a stock or a bond, earning a *local rate of return* $r_i(t)$, (2) a *cash swap* with swap rate of return $c_j(t) - c_i(t)$, with $c_j(t)$ the cash rate in country j into which the notional principal is swapped, and $c_i(t)$ the cash rate in country i out of which the notional principal is swapped and (3) the *foreign currency* (FX) *appreciation* rate $\varepsilon_j(t)$ of country j.[§] Thus one particular *bilateral investment strategy* at time t is represented by the *strategic rate of return*

$$s_{ij}(t) = r_i(t) + [c_j(t) - c_i(t)] + \varepsilon_j(t) \tag{14.1}$$

Notice that such a strategy is again equivalent to the CAPM sum of a risk premium and a cash return (*Cf.* Chapter 7), *i.e.*, the local market i *risk premium* $[r_i(t) - c_i(t)]$ and the *cash return* on currency j, $[c_j(t) + \varepsilon_j(t)]$:

$$s_{ij}(t) = [r_i(t) - c_i(t)] + [c_j(t) + \varepsilon_j(t)] \tag{14.2}$$

This is also equivalent to the sum of a local market i return, the return on a currency forward cross hedge and the FX j appreciation rate, since

$$\begin{aligned} s_{ij}(t) &= r_i(t) + [\{c_1(t) - c_i(t)\} - \{c_1(t) - c_j(t)\}] + \varepsilon_j(t) \\ &= r_i(t) + [f_i(t) - f_j(t)] + \varepsilon_j(t) \\ &= r_i(t) + f_{ij}(t) + \varepsilon_j(t) \end{aligned} \tag{14.3}$$

The *return on a currency forward* is $f_i(t) = c_1(t) - c_i(t)$ (*Cf.* Chapter 12), with $c_1(t)$ the cash return of the base currency, *e.g.*, the US dollar. The return on a *currency forward cross hedge* $f_{ij}(t) = [f_i(t) - f_j(t)]$ consists of the difference between the return on the long domestic forward $f_i(t)$ and the return on the short foreign forward $f_j(t)$.

[§]The U.S. dollar is the *base currency* or numéraire throughout this discussion.

14.2.2 Exact Cash Growth Accounting

In cash investment terms, an initial investment $P(0)$, e.g., of $100mln$, invested in a strategy earning $s_{ij}(t) = 18\%$, grows in period t as follows

$$\begin{aligned} P_{ij}(t) &= P(0).e^{s_{ij}(t)} \\ &= P(0).e^{r_i(t)+[c_j(t)-c_i(t)]+\varepsilon_j(t)} \\ &= 100.e^{0.10+0.16-0.05-0.03} \\ &= 100.e^{0.18} \\ &= \$119.72mln \end{aligned} \qquad (14.4)$$

Thus a domestic investor in country i, who invests in an risky asset to earn a total rate of return $r_i(t) = 10\%$

$$\begin{aligned} P_{ij}(t) &= P(0).e^{r_i(t)} \\ &= 100.e^{0.10} \\ &= \$110.52mln \end{aligned} \qquad (14.5)$$

But, in addition, the investor can swap out of the domestic cash into foreign cash of country j. The *total cash rate* earned in the foreign country j is

$$c_j(t) - c_i(t) + \varepsilon_j(t) = 0.16 - 0.05 - 0.03 = 8\% \qquad (14.6)$$

Thus the total of the investment growth is

$$\begin{aligned} P_{ij}(t) &= 110.52e^{c_j(t)-c_i(t)+\varepsilon_j(t)} \\ &= 110.52e^{0.08} \\ &= \$119.72mln \end{aligned} \qquad (14.7)$$

Thus the *market selection* decision involves *risk premium management*, while the *currency selection* involves *global cash management*. Market risk premium management (or *country fund management*) compares the risky country rates with the available cash rates - $[r_i(t) - c_i(t)]$ - to determine the optimal asset investment strategy. Global cash (or treasury) management compares the available cash rates in the various countries and their respective exchange rates - $[c_j(t) + \varepsilon_j(t)]$ - to determine the best *cash overlay* strategy.

This particular cash accounting representation includes options, since any option can be represented by a combination of a risky asset and cash borrowing, as we learned in Chapter 9. This accounting representation also includes both domestic and foreign currency futures, e.g.,

$$\begin{aligned} P_{ij}(t) &= P(0).e^{c_j(t)+\varepsilon_j(t)} \\ &= 100.e^{0.16-0.03} \\ &= 100.e^{0.13} \\ &= \$113.88mln \end{aligned} \qquad (14.8)$$

and cross-currency swaps, *e.g.*,

$$P_{ij}(t) = P(0).e^{c_j(t)-c_i(t)}$$
$$= 100.e^{0.16-0.05}$$
$$= 100.e^{0.11}$$
$$= \$111.63mln \qquad (14.9)$$

Thus, in this cash accounting framework, both the spot, on-balance sheet items, as well as the derivative, off-balance sheet instruments, are included.

The terminal value of capital $P(T)$, at the end of the investment horizon T, implementing one particular investment strategy $s_{ij}(t)$, can now be represented by the following expression, which concatenates the growth factors of the successive periods:

$$P_{ij}(T) = P(0) \prod_t^T e^{s_{ij}(t)}$$
$$= P(0) \prod_t^T e^{r_i(t)+[c_j(t)-c_i(t)]+\varepsilon_j(t)} \qquad (14.10)$$

Example 136 *A* $100mln *investment invested over five years with successive growth rates of* 10%, -40%, 5%, 12% *and* 1%, *respectively, grows as follows:*

$$P_{ij}(5) = 100.e^{0.10}.e^{-0.40}.e^{0.05}.e^{0.12}.e^{0.01}$$
$$= 100.e^{-0.12}$$
$$= \$88.69mln \qquad (14.11)$$

which demonstrates the devastating effects of a stock market crash of 40% *in the second year.*

14.2.3 Strategy Return Matrices

An $n \times n$ asymmetric *strategy return matrix* at time t is a matrix containing all n^2 bilateral investment strategies

$$\mathbf{S}(t) = \{s_{ij}(t); i,j = 1, ..., n\} \qquad (14.12)$$

For example, for $i, j = 1, 2, 3$ we have the 3×3 asymmetric strategy return matrix at time t

$$
\mathbf{S}(t) = \begin{bmatrix} s_{11}(t) & s_{12}(t) & s_{13}(t) \\ s_{21}(t) & s_{22}(t) & s_{23}(t) \\ s_{31}(t) & s_{32}(t) & s_{33}(t) \end{bmatrix}
$$

$$
= \left[\begin{pmatrix} r_1(t) \\ r_2(t) \\ r_3(t) \end{pmatrix} - \begin{pmatrix} c_1(t) \\ c_2(t) \\ c_3(t) \end{pmatrix} \right] \begin{bmatrix} 1 & 1 & 1 \end{bmatrix}
$$

$$
+ \left\{ \left[\begin{pmatrix} c_1(t) \\ c_2(t) \\ c_3(t) \end{pmatrix} + \begin{pmatrix} \varepsilon_1(t) \\ \varepsilon_2(t) \\ \varepsilon_3(t) \end{pmatrix} \right] \begin{bmatrix} 1 & 1 & 1 \end{bmatrix} \right\}' =
$$

$$
\begin{bmatrix} r_1(t) + \varepsilon_1(t) & r_1(t) - c_1(t) + c_2(t) + \varepsilon_2(t) & r_1(t) - c_1(t) + c_3(t) + \varepsilon_3(t) \\ r_2(t) - c_2(t) + c_1(t) + \varepsilon_1(t) & r_2(t) + \varepsilon_2(t) & r_2(t) - c_2(t) + c_3(t) + \varepsilon_3(t) \\ r_3(t) - c_3(t) + c_1(t) + \varepsilon_1(t) & r_3(t) - c_3(t) + c_2(t) + \varepsilon_2(t) & r_3(t) + \varepsilon_3(t) \end{bmatrix}
$$

$$(14.13)$$

Table 1. provides an actual empirical example of such a matrix of pure return strategies for June 1997 with Singapore, Malaysia and Indonesia as the three investment countries of interest. It shows the annualized monthly rates of return on the indices of their respective stock markets in Singapore, Kuala Lumpur and Jakarta; the respective 30-day bank lending rates; and the appreciation rates of the Singapore dollar, the Malaysian ringgit and the Indonesian rupiah.

TABLE 1:	RETURN (%)	STRATEGIES,	IN JUNE 1997
$\mathbf{S}(t) =$	1. Singapore	2. Malaysia	3. Indonesia
1. Singapore	44.2	34.8	45.3
2. Malaysia	48.0	38.7	49.1
3. Indonesia	87.8	78.4	**88.9**

Strategy matrix $\mathbf{S}(t)$ in Table 1. shows the decompositions in terms of the breakdown in stock market returns, swap returns and FX appreciation rates:

$$
\mathbf{S}(t) = \begin{bmatrix} 33.4 + 10.8 & 33.4 - 3.9 + 7.9 - 2.6 & 33.4 - 3.9 + 14.5 + 1.3 \\ 41.3 - 7.9 + 3.9 + 10.8 & 41.3 - 2.6 & 41.3 - 7.9 + 14.5 + 1.3 \\ 87.6 - 14.5 + 3.9 + 10.8 & 87.6 - 14.5 + 7.9 - 2.6 & 87.6 + 1.3 \end{bmatrix}
$$

$$(14.14)$$

Notice that on the diagonal of this investment strategy return matrix $\mathbf{S}(t)$, we find all strategies for the simple buy-and-hold strategy of investing in country

i, where the total rate of return is the combination of what is earned in the stock market and what is earned on the currency. Thus, in June 1997 Singapore earned 44.2% at an annualized monthly rate on domestic investments, namely 33.4% in the stock market and10.8% on the Singapore dollar appreciation.[¶] In contrast, the off-diagonal elements contain the strategies of buying stock in country i and swapping out of it into the cash of country j. What is earned in such a strategy is a combination of stock market earnings, swap earnings and exchange rate earnings. Thus, in June 1997, an investor would earn a 33.4% in the Singapore stock market, but by swapping from the Singapore dollar into the Indonesian rupiah, the investor could earn an extra $14.5 - 3.9 = 10.6\%$ on the cash swap and 1.3% on the rupiah appreciation. Consequently, the total rate of return on his strategy would have been 45.3% at an annualized rate (*i.e.*, 113 basis points more, on an annualized basis, than what was earned by staying fully invested in Singapore).

Table 1. shows that, in June 1997, the dominant maximizing return strategy , which disregards market risk, was to fully invest in the Jakarta stock market, since it gained 87.6% at an annual rate and the rupiah appreciated 1.3% at an annual rate. In June 1997, when you were invested in the stock markets of Singapore or in Kuala Lumpur, an investor could have picked up some extra basis points by swapping into Indonesian rupiahs. This would have been very advantageous to an investor in the Singapore stock market, who could have picked up 10.6% in the cash swap, but less so for an investor in the Kuala Lumpur stock market, who could have picked up only $14.5 - 7.9 = 6.6\%$ on an annualized basis. Two days into July 1997, this particular dominant and very profitable cash management strategy of swapping into Indonesian rupiahs started to fall apart, when Southeast and East Asia entered the enormous volatility of the regional Asian financial crisis.

14.3 Portfolio of Multi - Currency Investment Strategies

14.3.1 Growth Accounting of Portfolio Investments

Let's now extend the accounting framework to include portfolios of strategic investments. Since, by first order approximation,[∥] the portfolio value grows as follows in period t:

$$P_{ij}(t) = P(0)(1 + s_{ij}(t))$$
$$= P(0)e^{s_{ij}(t)} \tag{14.15}$$

[¶]Rounding errors prevent exactness of some summations in the digit behind the decimal point. The base currency in this example is again the US dollar.

[∥]The approximation is more accurate when the periods $t = 1, 2, ..., T$, and thus the periodic rates $s_{ij}(t)$, are smaller. For example, daily valuations are more accurate than weekly valuations, which are more accurate than monthly valuations, which are more accurate than quarterly valuations, etc. An increasing number of global financial firm is able to compute daily valuations of their portfolios, thanks to electronic accounting systems, and as is strongly recommended by the Association for Investment Management and Research [AIMR, 1997, p. 66].

the *value accumulation of a portfolio* of investment strategies in period t can be represented by

$$P(t) - P(0) = \sum_{i,j} w_{ij}[P_{ij}(t) - P(0)]$$

$$= P(0) \sum_{i,j}^{n} w_{ij} s_{ij}(t) \tag{14.16}$$

where w_{ij} is the share of the investment capital allocated to strategy $s_{ij}(t)$ with 100% investment allocation $\sum_{i,j}^{n} w_{ij} = 1$. Thus, the portfolio rate of return in period t is (*Cf.* Chapter 6):

$$s_p(t) = \sum_{i,j}^{n} w_{ij} s_{ij}(t) \tag{14.17}$$

But, then the value of a portfolio at time t is:

$$\begin{aligned}
P(t) &= \sum_{i,j} w_{ij} P_{ij}(t) \\
&= P(0)[1 + \sum_{i,j}^{n} w_{ij} s_{ij}(t)] \\
&= P(0) e^{\sum_{i,j}^{n} w_{ij} s_{ij}(t)} \\
&= P(0) e^{s_p(t)} \tag{14.18}
\end{aligned}$$

Combining the preceding equations, we find that, by first order approximation, the terminal value of the capital invested in a portfolio of investment strategies is:

$$\begin{aligned}
P(T) &= \sum_{i,j} w_{ij} P_{ij}(T) \\
&= P(0) \prod_{t}^{T} e^{\sum_{i,j}^{n} w_{ij} s_{ij}(t)} \\
&= P(0) \prod_{t}^{T} e^{s_p(t)} \tag{14.19}
\end{aligned}$$

14.3.2   *Vectorization of a Sequence of Strategy Matrices*

By using the simple linear algebra of Chapter 4, the cash accounting system of the preceding Section 2.3 can be generalized in matrix form. Using the definition of a bilateral investment strategy, the strategy matrix $\mathbf{S}(t)$ at time t for $i, j = 1, 2, ..., n$, is

$$\begin{aligned}
\mathbf{S}(t) &= [\mathbf{r}(t) - \mathbf{c}(t)]\iota_n' + \{[\mathbf{c}(t) + \varepsilon(t)]\iota_n'\}' \\
&= [\mathbf{r}(t) - \mathbf{c}(t)]\iota_n' + \iota_n[\mathbf{c}(t) + \varepsilon(t)]', \tag{14.20}
\end{aligned}$$

where $r(t)$, $c(t)$ and $\varepsilon(t)$ are $n \times 1$ data vectors of asset rates, cash rates and FX appreciation rates at time t, and ι'_n is a $1 \times n$ unit vector, *i.e.*, a vector consisting of n units, $\iota'_n = [1, 1, ..., 1]$.

The 3−dimensional $n \times n \times T$ historical investment *strategy array* S represents a *sequence* of strategy return matrices

$$\mathbf{S} = \{\mathbf{S}(t); t = 1, ..., T\} \tag{14.21}$$

For example, S is a $n \times n \times T = 3 \times 3 \times 60$ array. *Vectorization* of this 3−dimensional investment strategy array S facilitates the analysis of the time series of (presumed) stationary strategy return matrices. Let's first *vectorize* one strategy return matrix $\mathbf{S}(t)$. The notation $vec(\mathbf{S}(t))$ means the $n^2 \times 1$ strategy vector, whose first n elements constitute the first column of $\mathbf{S}(t)$: $s_1(t)$; the second n elements constitute the second column of $\mathbf{S}(t)$: $s_2(t)$; *et cetera*. Thus,

$$vec(\mathbf{S}(t)) = [s_1(t)', s_2(t)', ..., s_n(t)]' \tag{14.22}$$

i.e., a vector of stacked columns of $\mathbf{S}(t)$.

Next, the 3−dimensional $n \times n \times T$ historical investment *strategy array* S is the *sequence* of such strategy matrices $\mathbf{S} = \{\mathbf{S}(t); t = 1, ..., T\}$. Thus, vectorization of the strategy array S produces an $n^2 \times T$ matrix:[**]

$$
\begin{aligned}
\mathbf{VEC(S)} &= [vec(\mathbf{S}(1)), vec(\mathbf{S}(2)), ..., vec(\mathbf{S}(T))] \\
&= [\iota_n \otimes \mathbf{I}_n][\mathbf{r} - \mathbf{c}] + [\mathbf{I}_n \otimes \iota_n][\mathbf{c} + \varepsilon] \\
&= \mathbf{H} \begin{bmatrix} [\mathbf{r} - \mathbf{c}] \\ [\mathbf{c} + \varepsilon] \end{bmatrix}
\end{aligned} \tag{14.23}
$$

where $\mathbf{r}$ is the $n \times T$ matrix of T observations on the rates of return of n country assets, $\mathbf{c}$ is the $n \times T$ matrix of observations on the n cash rates, and ε is the $n \times T$ matrix of T observations on the n currency appreciation rates, all with $T > 2n$. Consequently, $[\mathbf{r} - \mathbf{c}]$ is the $n \times T$ matrix of T observations on the n country risk premia and $[\mathbf{c} + \varepsilon]$ is the $n \times T$ matrix of observations on the n country cash earning rates.

The $\mathbf{VEC(S)}$ matrix of the three Asian countries, *i.e.*, the annualized monthly time series of strategy vectors for Singapore, Malaysia and Indonesia for the five years from July 1993 through June 1997, contains $n^2 = 9$ strategies over $T = 60$ periods. Thus, in our empirical example, $\mathbf{VEC(S)}$ is an $n^2 \times T = 9 \times 60$ matrix.

$\mathbf{H}$ is the crucial $n^2 \times 2n$ *selector matrix*, which embodies the exact cash accounting identities:

$$\mathbf{H} = [\; [\iota_n \otimes \mathbf{I}_n] \quad [\mathbf{I}_n \otimes \iota_n] \;] \tag{14.24}$$

[**]When A is an $m \times n$ matrix and B a $p \times q$ matrix, then the *Kronecker product* of these two matrices is defined by $A \otimes B = [a_{ij}B]$ and $vec(AB) = (B' \otimes I)vec(A) = (I \otimes A)vec(B)$. For proof cf. Dhrymes (1978), pp. 519. For a compilation of useful Kronecker product results, cf. Los (1984), pp. 543-548.

where both $[\iota_n \otimes \mathbf{I}_n]$ and $[\mathbf{I}_n \otimes \iota_n]$ are $n^2 \times n$ matrices consisting of ones and zeros. Here ι_n is the $n \times 1$ unit vector and $\mathbf{I}_n$ is the $n \times n$ identity matrix. The matrix $[\iota_n \otimes \mathbf{I}_n]$ contains the accounting identities for the n risky asset returns ($= n$ country returns), while the matrix $[\mathbf{I}_n \otimes \iota_n]$ contains the accounting identities for the cash overlays, $i.e.$, the n FX appreciation rates and n cash rates.

Remark 137 *In September 1999, in joint collaborative discussion, Leow (1999) and Los (1999) generalized the accounting identity matrix* $\mathbf{H}$ *further to include the extra securities selection level. When* $m = $ *number of risky assets or securities and* $n = $ *number of countries* = *number of FX series (relative to the base currency, i.e., the U.S. dollar)* = *number of (default) risk-free cash assets, then the* $mn^2 \times (m+1)n$ *selector matrix is:*

$$\mathbf{H} = \left[\begin{array}{cc} [\iota_n \otimes \mathbf{I}_{mn}] & [\mathbf{I}_{mn^2} \otimes \iota_n] \end{array} \right] \qquad (14.25)$$

where $[\iota_n \otimes \mathbf{I}_{mn}]$ *is the* $mn^2 \times mn$ *matrix containing the accounting identities for the* m *risky assets (stocks, bonds, real estate, etc.) in each of the* n *countries. The matrix* $[\mathbf{I}_{mn^2} \otimes \iota_n]$ *contains the accounting identities for the* mn *cash overlays with* n *FX appreciation rates and* n *cash rates. Still, further generalization of this cash growth accounting identity matrix is possible. It is enlightening to contemplate the important role this complex matrix* $\mathbf{H}$ *of cash growth accounting identities plays within the context of modern, multi-national investment finance, in particular for total portfolio risk management. Other, related accounting identities, play similar, although somewhat lesser roles. For example, Chapter 1 provided the history of the original simple, exact, book value (now market value) accounting identity* $E = A - L$, *which in Chapter 11 metamorphosed into the portfolio immunization (or hedging) identity, still an important tool for first order asset/liability risk management:*

$$D^E_{Mod} = D^L_{Mod} + \frac{A}{E} \cdot (D^A_{Mod} - D^L_{Mod}) \qquad (14.26)$$

To find the market risks involved in the various investment strategies, we compute the data covariance matrix of all the strategies from the deviations from the investment horizon means. The means of each of the n strategies are given by the $n^2 \times 1$ vector

$$\overline{\mathbf{VEC(S)}} = \frac{\mathbf{VEC(S)}.\iota_T}{T}$$
$$= \mathbf{H} \left[\begin{array}{c} [\bar{\mathbf{r}} - \bar{\mathbf{c}}] \\ [\bar{\mathbf{c}} + \bar{\varepsilon}] \end{array} \right] \qquad (14.27)$$

where ι_T is the $T \times 1$ unit vector. Let's have a look at our empirical data. Table 2. displays the (transposed) vector for the average returns, earned by the nine strategies.

TABLE 2:	AVERAGE	RETURN	STRATEGIES	(%)	7/92	-	6/97		
$\overline{s}_{ij} =$	$\overline{s}_{11}$	$\overline{s}_{21}$	$\overline{s}_{31}$	$\overline{s}_{12}$	$\overline{s}_{22}$	$\overline{s}_{32}$	$\overline{s}_{13}$	$\overline{s}_{23}$	$\overline{s}_{33}$
$\overline{\text{VEC(S)}}' =$	8.7	11.6	9.0	10.3	13.2	10.6	13.2	16.0	13.4

In Table 3. this average return strategy vector is reconstituted into the matrix of (5 year) average strategy returns.

TABLE 3:	AVERAGE RETURN STRATEGIES (%), 7/92 - 6/97		
	1. Singapore	2. Malaysia	3. Indonesia
1. Singapore	8.7	10.3	13.2
2. Malaysia	11.6	13.2	**16.0**
3. Indonesia	9.0	10.6	13.4

Thus, in the five year period July 1992 through June 1997, the *maximizing average return strategy* would have been to invest in the Kuala Lumpur stock market and to swap into the Indonesian rupiah. On average, this strategy would have earned a 16% return per year. Indeed, we just noticed that, on average, Malaysia had the largest stock market risk premium, while Indonesia earned most on its cash (versus the US dollar).

14.3.3 Strategy Risk Matrices

Thus far, we haven't discussed the risks of multi-currency portfolio management. However, this can be done in the context of the mean-variance portfolio optimization framework of Chapter 6. We first need to compute the *strategy risk matrix*, *i.e.*, the covariance matrix of the strategy rates of return. The $n^2 \times T$ matrix of deviations from the means are given by:

$$\mathbf{DEV(S)} = \mathbf{VEC(S)} - \overline{\mathbf{VEC(S)}}.\iota_T'$$
$$= \mathbf{H}\left[\begin{array}{c}[\mathbf{r}-\mathbf{c}]\\ [\mathbf{c}+\varepsilon]\end{array}\right][\mathbf{I}_T - \frac{\iota_T\iota_T'}{T}] \tag{14.28}$$

where ι_T is the $T \times 1$ unit vector and $\mathbf{H}$ is the $n^2 \times 2n$ selector matrix, which represents the Singer and Karnosky (1994, 1995) system of exact accounting identities (*Cf.* Chapter 1). We can now compute the $n^2 \times n^2$ data covariance, or *strategy risk matrix* of the n^2 investment strategies:

$$\Sigma = \frac{\mathbf{DEV(S)}.\mathbf{DEV(S)}'}{T}$$
$$= \frac{\left\{\mathbf{H}\left[\begin{array}{c}[\mathbf{r}-\mathbf{c}]\\ [\mathbf{c}+\varepsilon]\end{array}\right][\mathbf{I}_T - \frac{\iota_T\iota_T'}{T}]\right\}\left\{\mathbf{H}\left[\begin{array}{c}[\mathbf{r}-\mathbf{c}]\\ [\mathbf{c}+\varepsilon]\end{array}\right][\mathbf{I}_T - \frac{\iota_T\iota_T'}{T}]\right\}'}{T}$$
$$= \mathbf{H}\Phi\mathbf{H}' > 0 \tag{14.29}$$

where Φ is the $2n \times 2n$ risk premium - cash return covariance matrix.

Remark 138 *The fact that the $2n \times 2n$ matrix Φ is a positive definite matrix (i) testifies to the fact that the financial markets are incomplete; and (ii) makes mean-variance portfolio optimization possible. Only when Φ would be a singular matrix, financial markets would be complete (Cf. Chapter 8 for complete financial markets). But then no further portfolio optimization would be possible, and the financial markets would be in an ideal efficient equilibrium.*

The strategy risk matrix Σ can also be decomposed into its various *financial market correlation risks*, using Kronecker products:[††]

$$\Sigma = \iota_n \iota_n' \otimes [\Sigma_{rr} + \Sigma_{cc} - \Sigma_{rc} - \Sigma_{rc}'] + [\Sigma_{cc} + \Sigma_{\varepsilon\varepsilon} + \Sigma_{c\varepsilon} + \Sigma_{c\varepsilon}'] \otimes \iota_n \iota_n'$$
$$+ \iota_n \otimes [\Sigma_{rc} + \Sigma_{r\varepsilon} - \Sigma_{cc} - \Sigma_{c\varepsilon}] \otimes \iota_n' + \iota_n' \otimes [\Sigma_{rc} + \Sigma_{r\varepsilon} - \Sigma_{cc} - \Sigma_{c\varepsilon}]' \otimes \iota_n \quad (14.30)$$

where Σ_{rr} measures all normal stock markets covariance risk, Σ_{cc} measures all cash markets covariance risk and $\Sigma_{\varepsilon\varepsilon}$ all the foreign exchange markets risks, under the assumption of stationarity.[‡‡] The asymmetric matrices Σ_{rc}, $\Sigma_{r\varepsilon}$ and $\Sigma_{c\varepsilon}$ measure the covariance risks between the stock and cash markets, between the stock and foreign exchange markets, and between the cash and foreign exchange markets, respectively. Therefore, this expression accounts exactly for all the market risks involved in multi-currency portfolio management, as can be seen when we arrange these submatrices according to the fundamental data covariance matrix in Table 4, which should not be confused with the strategy risk matrix Σ.

TABLE 4:	DATA	COVARIANCE	MATRIX
Data series	**r**	**c**	ε
r $(n \times T)$	Σ_{rr}	Σ_{rc}	$\Sigma_{r\varepsilon}$
c $(n \times T)$	Σ_{rc}'	Σ_{cc}	$\Sigma_{c\varepsilon}$
ε $(n \times T)$	$\Sigma_{r\varepsilon}'$	$\Sigma_{c\varepsilon}'$	$\Sigma_{\varepsilon\varepsilon}$

Table 5. provides the 9×9 five year holding period strategy risk matrix Σ for Singapore, Malaysia and Indonesia. This strategy risk matrix is computed from the annualized rates of return over the 5−year period July 1992 - June 1997.

[††]When A is an $m \times n$ matrix and B a $p \times q$ matrix, then the *Kronecker product* of these two matrices is defined by $A \otimes B = [a_{ij}B]$ and $vec(AB) = (B' \otimes I)vec(A) = (I \otimes A)vec(B)$. For proof cf. Dhrymes, 1978, pp. 519. For a compilation of useful Kronecker product results, cf. Los, 1984, pp. 543-548.

[‡‡]This assumption of stationarity, $\bar{s}$ =constant and Σ_{ij} =constant, was broken, for example, on July 2nd, 1997, when the fall in the Thai baht triggered a series of negative breaks in the various ASEAN financial markets, which spread by contagion.

TABLE 5.:	STRATEGY	RISK	MATRIX	Σ	(9×9)			
Strategies	s_{11}	s_{21}	s_{31}	s_{12}	s_{22}	s_{32}	s_{13}	s_{23}	s_{33}
s_{11}	3187.1	3326.8	2618.7	2997.0	3136.6	2428.6	3154.7	3294.4	2586.4
s_{21}	3326.8	6159.7	3207.9	3250.2	6083.1	3131.3	3356.9	6189.8	3238.0
s_{31}	2618.7	3207.9	5611.9	2667.3	3256.4	5660.5	2709.3	3298.4	5702.4
s_{12}	2997.0	3250.2	2667.3	3033.9	3287.1	2704.3	3021.5	3274.7	2691.8
s_{22}	3136.6	6083.1	3256.4	3287.1	6233.7	3407.0	3223.6	6170.1	3343.4
s_{32}	2428.6	3131.3	5660.5	2704.3	3407.0	5936.2	2576.0	3278.7	5807.9
s_{13}	3154.7	3356.9	2709.3	3021.5	3223.6	2576.0	3260.6	3462.7	2815.1
s_{23}	3294.4	6189.8	3298.4	3274.7	6170.1	3278.7	3462.7	6358.2	3466.7
s_{33}	2586.4	3238.0	5702.4	2691.8	3343.4	5807.9	2815.1	3466.7	5931.2

Since the square roots of the diagonal elements of the strategy risk matrix in Table 5 provide measures (= standard deviations) of the strategy risks, we observe that over the period July 1992 through June 1997, the *minimum average risk strategy* has been strategy s_{12}: to invest in the Singapore stock market and to swap into Malaysian ringgit. Its standard deviation was $\sigma_{s_{12}} = \sqrt{3033.9}\% = 55.08\%$.

Table 6. provides the average return/risk $(\bar{s}_{ij}/\sigma_{s_{ij}})$ profile of these nine strategies. Notice that, in June 1997, the $(i,j) = (1,3)$ strategy was the best, according to this (Sharpe's) ratio (Cf. Chapter 7): invest in the Singapore stock market and swap into a cash overlay of Indonesian rupiahs.

TABLE 6:	AVERAGE	RETURN	RISK	PROFILES	7/92	-	6/97		
$i,j =$	1,1	2,1	3,1	1,2	2,2	3,2	1,3	2,3	3,3
$\bar{s}_{ij}/\sigma_{s_{ij}} =$	0.154	0.147	0.120	0.187	0.167	0.137	0.231	0.200	0.174

Over the period July 1992 through June 1997, the *maximum average return/risk strategy* was strategy s_{13}, to invest in the Singapore stock market and to swap into Indonesian rupiah, with only $\bar{s}_{13}/\sigma_{s_{13}} = 0.2312$. Notice that none of the nine strategies produced enough average return to compensate for even one quart of the average market risk in these three Southeast Asian countries in the past five years!

14.3.4   Singularity of Strategy Risk Matrix

The computed determinant of this empirical strategy risk matrix Σ, $i.e.$, the product of its nine eigenvalues, is positive definite:

$$|\Sigma| = \prod_i^9 \lambda_i$$

$$= (-1.5809 \times 10^{-6})(3.945 \times 10^{-7})(-8.2587 \times 10^{-6})(1.206 \times 10^{-4})$$

$$(193.15)(385.22)(2766.4)(8154.3)(34213.0)$$

$$= 1.5307 \times 10^{-5} > 0 \tag{14.31}$$

Although this empirical strategy risk matrix Σ is empirically positive definite and appears to be of full rank, its computed determinant $|\Sigma|$ is extremely small. A little sensitivity testing with the precision levels demonstrates that its empirical (uncertain) $rank(\Sigma) \approx 5$ and there are five stable eigenvalues and four extremely small unstable ones. This suggests that there are four exact relationships, or planes, among the nine data series ($Cf.$ Chapter 5).

Indeed, a little algebra proves that the strategy risk matrix Σ must singular, $i.e.$, it is not of full rank (Los, 1998b, 1999). This fact has stymied a lot of portfolio managers, who try to use this matrix Σ in mean-variance portfolio optimization. The strategy risk matrix Σ is exactly singular, since it has the same rank as the deviations-from-the-means matrix $\mathbf{DEV(S)}$:

$$rank\left\{\mathbf{DEV(S)}\right\} = rank\left\{\mathbf{H}\begin{bmatrix}[\mathbf{r} - \mathbf{c}] \\ [\mathbf{c} + \varepsilon]\end{bmatrix}[\mathbf{I}_T - \frac{\iota_T \iota_T'}{T}]\right\}$$

$$\leq Min\left\{rank\,(\mathbf{H})\,,rank\begin{bmatrix}[\mathbf{r} - \mathbf{c}] \\ [\mathbf{c} + \varepsilon]\end{bmatrix},rank\begin{bmatrix}\mathbf{I}_T - \frac{\iota_T \iota_T'}{T}\end{bmatrix}\right\}$$

$$= Min\{2n - 1, 2n, T - 1\} = 2n - 1 < n^2 \tag{14.32}$$

since $\mathbf{H}$ is the $n^2 \times 2n$ selector matrix of rank $2n - 1$, $\begin{bmatrix}[\mathbf{r} - \mathbf{c}] \\ [\mathbf{c} + \varepsilon]\end{bmatrix}$ is a risk-premium and cash return $2n \times T$ matrix of rank $2n$, and $\begin{bmatrix}\mathbf{I}_T - \frac{\iota_T \iota_T'}{T}\end{bmatrix}$ is the deviations producing $T \times T$ matrix of rank $T - 1$, where it is required that $T > 2n$.

This algebraic result can be illustrated for our empirical example by computing the rank of the selector matrix $\mathbf{H}$ for the three Asian countries. Since $\mathbf{H}$ consists of zeros and ones only, this is easily done:

$$rank(\Sigma) = 2n - 1 = 5 < n^2 = 9 \tag{14.33}$$

This is the case also for the 300×300 covariance matrix in RiskMetrics^{TM}, as Professor Mark Garman confirmed, when he revealed the instability and unreliability of RiskMetrics^{TM}'s information matrix Σ^{-1} in a Research Seminar on March 7, 1996 at the Nanyang Technological University in Singapore. My conclusion was also corroborated by e-mail on April 23, 1998 by Peter Zangari of J. P. Morgan, Inc.

Cf. Proposition 7 of Dhrymes (1978), p. 437.

Thus, despite the empirical appearance of a full rank, due to the imprecision of finite computers registers, the strategy risk matrix Σ can't be reliably inverted for use in the classical Markowitz' mean-variance analysis (Markowitz, 1952, 1991, 1999), since it is algebraically singular!

However, this does not prevent Markowitz' mean-variance analysis, since the CAPM approach of separating the risk premium from the cash overlay return provides an exact portfolio optimization solution, as we'll discuss in the next Section.

14.4 Multi - Currency Portfolio Optimization

The following section is inspired by Markowitz 'discussion of the problems for portfolio optimization caused by semi-definite data covariance matrices in Chapter 3 "Capabilities and Assumptions of the General Model " of his book (Markowitz, 1992, pp. 42 - 43).

14.4.1 Extended Markowitz Procedure

Let's now see how we can exploit the accounting identities to get around the problem of the singular strategy risk matrix. The *mean portfolio rate of return* for the investment horizon T, $\bar{s}_p$, is the weighted linear combination of all the n^2 mean rates of return of the strategies, $\bar{s}_{ij}$, which we find in the mean vector $\overline{\mathbf{VEC(S)}}$

$$
\begin{aligned}
\bar{s}_p &= \mathbf{w}'\overline{\mathbf{VEC(S)}} \\
&= \mathbf{w}'\mathbf{H}\left[\begin{array}{c} [\bar{\mathbf{r}} - \bar{\mathbf{c}}] \\ [\bar{\mathbf{c}} + \bar{\varepsilon}] \end{array} \right] \\
&= \mathbf{v}'\left[\begin{array}{c} [\bar{\mathbf{r}} - \bar{\mathbf{c}}] \\ [\bar{\mathbf{c}} + \bar{\varepsilon}] \end{array} \right]
\end{aligned}
\tag{14.34}
$$

$\mathbf{w}$ is a $n \times 1$ vector of *portfolio allocation weights*, such that the sum of the weights equals unity: $\mathbf{w}'\iota_{n^2} = 1$, where ι_{n^2} is the $n^2 \times 1 = 9 \times 1$ unit vector; $\mathbf{v}$ is the $2n \times 1 = 6 \times 1$ vector of the combined portfolio allocations $\mathbf{v} = \mathbf{H}'\mathbf{w}$, such that $\mathbf{v}'\iota_{2n} = 2$. The overall *strategy portfolio risk*, σ_{pp}, is the variance of the portfolio rates of return,

$$
\begin{aligned}
\sigma_{pp} &= \mathbf{w}'\Sigma\mathbf{w} \\
&= \mathbf{w}'\mathbf{H}\Phi\mathbf{H}'\mathbf{w} \\
&= \mathbf{v}'\Phi\mathbf{v}
\end{aligned}
\tag{14.35}
$$

Notice that the first $n = 9$ combined allocations v_i, $i = 1, 2, ...9$, refer to the strategy choice of how much of the capital to invest in which stock market to earn a risk premium, while the second $n = 9$ allocations $v_{.j}$, $j = 1, 2, ..., 9$, refer to the strategy choice of how much of the capital to invest in which currency to earn a cash return. The $2n \times 1$ vector $\mathbf{v}$ exhausts the capital allocation based on these two fundamental

---

The portfolio allocation weights form a stochastic vector, as we encountered in Chapter 8

choices of investments in stock markets and in currencies, because of the following accounting identities:

$$\mathbf{v}' = \mathbf{v}'\left[\begin{bmatrix} \iota_n \\ \mathbf{0} \end{bmatrix} + \begin{bmatrix} \mathbf{0} \\ \iota_n \end{bmatrix}\right] \text{ with} \tag{14.36}$$

$$\mathbf{v}'\begin{bmatrix} \iota_n \\ \mathbf{0} \end{bmatrix} = \mathbf{w}'\mathbf{H}\begin{bmatrix} \iota_n \\ \mathbf{0} \end{bmatrix} = \mathbf{w}'\iota_{n^2} = 1 \text{ and} \tag{14.37}$$

$$\mathbf{v}'\begin{bmatrix} \mathbf{0} \\ \iota_n \end{bmatrix} = \mathbf{w}'\mathbf{H}\begin{bmatrix} \mathbf{0} \\ \iota_n \end{bmatrix} = \mathbf{w}'\iota_{n^2} = 1, \tag{14.38}$$

Now the procedure has once again become similar to Markowitz' nonsingular mean-variance analysis, which we again solve using the familiar Kuhn-Tucker Theorem for constraint optimization (*Cf.* Chapter 6). First, form the Lagrangian with the *three* accounting identities:

$$\begin{aligned} L(\mathbf{v}, \lambda_1, \lambda_2, \lambda_3) &= \mathbf{v}'\Phi\mathbf{v} + \lambda_1\left[1 - \mathbf{v}'\begin{bmatrix} \iota_n \\ \mathbf{0} \end{bmatrix}\right] \\ &+ \lambda_2\left[1 - \mathbf{v}'\begin{bmatrix} \mathbf{0} \\ \iota_n \end{bmatrix}\right] + \lambda_3\left[\bar{s}_p - \mathbf{v}'\begin{bmatrix} [\bar{\mathbf{r}} - \bar{\mathbf{c}}] \\ [\bar{\mathbf{c}} + \bar{\varepsilon}] \end{bmatrix}\right] \end{aligned} \tag{14.39}$$

Next, to find the optimum of this Lagrangian, set the $2n + 3$ partial first derivatives equal to zero, *i.e.*, the derivatives with respect to the $2n$ elements of the allocation vector $\mathbf{v}$ and to the three Lagrangian multipliers λ_1, λ_2 and λ_3.

In Los (1998b) it is found that the optimal Lagrangian multipliers λ_1^{opt}, λ_2^{opt} and λ_3^{opt} are given by

$$\begin{bmatrix} \lambda_1^{opt} \\ \lambda_2^{opt} \\ \lambda_3^{opt} \end{bmatrix} = 2.\Delta^{-1}.\begin{bmatrix} 1 \\ 1 \\ \bar{s}_p \end{bmatrix}$$

where the 3×3 symmetric and positive definite matrix Δ is such that

$$\Delta = \begin{bmatrix} [\iota_n'\ \mathbf{0}]\Phi^{-1}\begin{bmatrix} \iota_n \\ \mathbf{0} \end{bmatrix} & [\mathbf{0}\ \iota_n']\Phi^{-1}\begin{bmatrix} \iota_n \\ \mathbf{0} \end{bmatrix} & [[\bar{\mathbf{r}}-\bar{\mathbf{c}}]'\ [\mathbf{c}+\bar{\varepsilon}]']\Phi^{-1}\begin{bmatrix} \iota_n \\ \mathbf{0} \end{bmatrix} \\ [\iota_n'\ \mathbf{0}]\Phi^{-1}\begin{bmatrix} \mathbf{0} \\ \iota_n \end{bmatrix} & [\mathbf{0}\ \iota_n']\Phi^{-1}\begin{bmatrix} \mathbf{0} \\ \iota_n \end{bmatrix} & [[\bar{\mathbf{r}}-\bar{\mathbf{c}}]'\ [\bar{\mathbf{c}}+\bar{\varepsilon}]']\Phi^{-1}\begin{bmatrix} \mathbf{0} \\ \iota_n \end{bmatrix} \\ [\iota_n'\ \mathbf{0}]\Phi^{-1}\begin{bmatrix} \bar{\mathbf{r}}-\bar{\mathbf{c}} \\ [\bar{\mathbf{c}}+\bar{\varepsilon}] \end{bmatrix} & [\mathbf{0}\ \iota_n']\Phi^{-1}\begin{bmatrix} \bar{\mathbf{r}}-\bar{\mathbf{c}} \\ [\bar{\mathbf{c}}+\bar{\varepsilon}] \end{bmatrix} & [[\bar{\mathbf{r}}-\bar{\mathbf{c}}]'\ [\bar{\mathbf{c}}+\bar{\varepsilon}]']\Phi^{-1}\begin{bmatrix} \bar{\mathbf{r}}-\bar{\mathbf{c}} \\ [\bar{\mathbf{c}}+\bar{\varepsilon}] \end{bmatrix} \end{bmatrix} \tag{14.40}$$

So that by substitution, the optimal fundamental choice allocations are determined to be

$$\mathbf{v}^{opt} = \frac{\Phi^{-1}\left[\lambda_1^{opt}\begin{bmatrix} \iota_n \\ \mathbf{0} \end{bmatrix} + \lambda_2^{opt}\begin{bmatrix} \mathbf{0} \\ \iota_n \end{bmatrix} + \lambda_3^{opt}\begin{bmatrix} [\bar{\mathbf{r}} - \bar{\mathbf{c}}] \\ [\bar{\mathbf{c}} + \bar{\varepsilon}] \end{bmatrix}\right]}{2} \tag{14.41}$$

Remark 139 *The $(2n + 3) \times (2n + 3)$ matrix of partial second derivatives is positive definite, since the full rank $2n \times 2n$ covariance matrix $\Phi > 0$, so that the optimum is, indeed, a constrained minimum.*

We have now the two equations of Markowitz' Efficient Portfolio Frontier for $2n$ investment strategy choices, which can again be plotted in a two-dimensional graph. For every portfolio strategy return $\bar{s}_p^{opt}$ there is a corresponding portfolio strategy risk σ_p^{opt}:

$$\bar{s}_p^{opt} = \mathbf{v}^{opt\prime} \left[\begin{array}{c} [\bar{\mathbf{r}} - \bar{\mathbf{c}}] \\ [\bar{\mathbf{c}} + \bar{\mathbf{e}}] \end{array} \right]$$

$$\sigma_p^{opt} = \sqrt{(\mathbf{v}^{opt})\Phi'\mathbf{v}^{opt}}$$

With each optimal average strategy return $\bar{s}_p^{opt}$ corresponds an optimal level of risk σ_p^{opt}, or, vice versa, with each level of risk σ_p^{opt} corresponds an optimal average investment strategy return $\bar{s}_p^{opt}$. The corresponding Efficient Strategy Portfolio Frontier for our empirical $n = 3$ Asian countries - Singapore, Malaysia and Indonesia - example is displayed in Fig. 1.. Notice that we've also indicated by arrows where the average maximum return, respectively, the average maximum risk-adjusted returns are in this $2-$ dimensional space, relative to the Frontier and relative to the Global Minimum Variance (GMV).

Table 7. displays the corresponding optimal GMV allocations computed for the same our $n = 3$ example. Notice the fundamental choice allocations $\mathbf{v}^{opt}$ for the three countries' equity markets in the left column $(v_i, i = 1, 2, 3)$ and for the three countries' cash overlays in the top row $(v_i, i = 4, 5, 6)$. The 3×3 quadrangle in the middle of Table 7. contains the strategic investment allocations $\mathbf{w}$, for $w_{ij}, i, j = 1, 2, 3$.

TABLE 7:	OPTIMAL	GMV	STRATEGY	ALLOCATIONS
		1. Singapore	2. Malaysia	3. Indonesia
	Fundamental choices	$v_4 = 0.37$	$v_5 = 0.80$	$v_6 = -0.16$
1. Singapore	$v_1 = 0.98$	0.36	0.78	-0.16
2. Malaysia	$v_2 = -0.10$	-0.04	-0.08	0.02
3. Indonesia	$v_3 = 0.12$	0.05	0.10	-0.02

Table 8. provides several examples of optimal portfolio allocations chosen as average return points (e.g., $\bar{s}_p^{opt} = 2.0, 6.0, 8.0, 9.0, 10.0, 12.0$ and 16.0% at an annual rate) on the same Efficient Strategy Portfolio Frontier in the $2-$ dimensional average

---

= Fig. 1 in Los, 1998b.
= Table 13. in Los, 1998b.

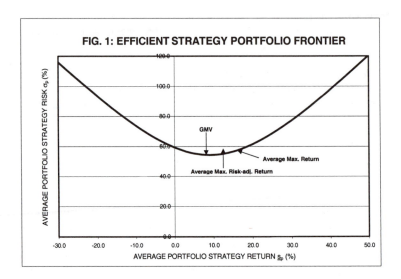

Figure 1

strategy risk/return $(\sigma_p^{opt}/\overline{s}_p^{opt})$ space of Fig. 1. The GMV investment strategy is indicated by bold numbers. The GMV strategy for this $n = 3$ Asian portfolio results in a Markowitz pair of $(\overline{s}_p^{opt}, \sigma_p^{opt}) = 9.0, 54.4)$ (in percent, at an annual rate), which has a lower return and a lower risk than the maximum average return/risk strategy $(\overline{s}_{13}, \sigma_{s_{13}}) = (13.2, 57.1)$ combination of Table 6.

TABLE 8:	EXAMPLES	OF	OPTIMAL	PORTFOLIO	ALLOCATIONS			
Average return	$\overline{s}_p$	2.00	6.00	8.00	9.00	10.00	12.00	16.00
Avg. risk premium	$\overline{r}_p - \overline{c}_p$	3.18	3.21	3.23	3.24	3.25	3.26	3.30
Avg. cash return	$\overline{c}_p + \overline{e}_p$	-1.18	2.79	4.77	5.76	6.75	9.74	12.70
Average risk	σ_p	57.4	54.9	54.4	54.4	54.4	54.9	57.4
Choice	v_1	0.95	0.97	0.97	0.98	0.98	0.99	1.01
allocations	v_2	-0.13	-0.11	-0.11	-0.10	-0.10	-0.09	-0.08
	v_3	0.18	0.15	0.13	0.12	0.12	0.10	0.07
	v_4	1.92	1.03	0.59	0.37	0.14	-0.30	-1.19
	v_5	0.82	0.81	0.80	0.80	0.79	0.79	0.77
	v_6	-1.75	-0.84	-0.39	-0.16	0.06	0.52	1.42
Strategy	w_{11}	1.83	1.00	0.57	0.36	0.14	-0.30	-1.20
allocations	w_{21}	-0.24	-0.12	-0.06	-0.04	-0.01	0.03	0.09
	w_{31}	0.34	0.15	0.08	0.05	0.02	-0.03	-0.09
	w_{12}	0.78	0.78	0.78	0.78	0.78	0.78	0.78
	w_{22}	-0.10	-0.09	-0.09	-0.08	-0.08	-0.07	-0.06
	w_{32}	0.15	0.12	0.11	0.10	0.09	0.08	0.06
	w_{13}	-1.66	-0.81	-0.38	-0.16	0.06	0.51	1.43
	w_{23}	0.22	0.10	0.04	0.02	-0.01	-0.05	-0.11
	w_{33}	-0.31	-0.12	-0.05	-0.02	0.01	0.05	0.10

For a more extensive and realistic global portfolio allocation example, the two Markowitz frontier equations have been used to plot the Efficient Strategy Portfolio Frontier in Fig. 1. in Chapter 6, for the investment horizon June 1992 through October 1997 and for a portfolio of $n^2 = 81$ investment strategies, with budget allocations between $n = 9$ countries: Hong Kong, Indonesia, Japan, Malaysia, Philippines, Singapore, Thailand, Germany and the U.S.A..

The corresponding optimal Global Minimum Variance (GMV) portfolio allocations are displayed in the Table 9. Notice the two series of **v** capital allocation weights: the stock market allocations $\mathbf{v}_{i\cdot}, i = 1, 2, ..., 9$ are displayed in the left column (summing up to 100%) and the currency overlay allocations $\mathbf{v}_{\cdot i}, i = 1, 2, ..., 9$ are displayed in the top row (also summing up to 100%). The investment strategy allocations $w_{ij}, i, j = 1, 2, ..., 9$ are again in the middle quadrangle of Table 9.

TABLE 9: OPTIMAL GMV STRATEGIC ALLOCATIONS FOR ASIAN COUNTRIES WITH USA AND GERMANY
Average portfolio return = 12.5% June 1992 - October 1997
Average portfolio risk (stdev) = 25.0%

		Hong Kong	Indonesia	Japan	Malaysia	Philippines	Singapore	Thailand	Germany	USA	
	cash return weights	v_1	v_2	v_3	v_4	v_5	v_6	v_7	v_8	v_9	
	risk premium weights	-2.4%	-58.4%	9.5%	47.4%	40.7%	-112.4%	13.8%	27.3%	134.4%	100.0%
Hong Kong	v_1 -13.1%	0.3%	7.6%	-1.2%	-6.2%	-5.3%	14.7%	-1.8%	-3.6%	-17.6%	-13.1%
Indonesia	v_2 -16.8%	0.4%	9.8%	-1.6%	-8.0%	-6.9%	18.9%	-2.3%	-4.6%	-22.6%	-16.8%
Japan	v_3 5.9%	-0.1%	-3.4%	0.6%	2.8%	2.4%	-6.6%	0.8%	1.6%	7.9%	5.9%
Malaysia	v_4 7.3%	-0.2%	-4.3%	0.7%	3.5%	3.0%	-8.2%	1.0%	2.0%	9.8%	7.3%
Philippines	v_5 6.2%	-0.1%	-3.6%	0.6%	2.9%	2.5%	-6.9%	0.9%	1.7%	8.3%	6.2%
Singapore	v_6 15.7%	-0.4%	-9.2%	1.5%	7.5%	6.4%	-17.7%	2.2%	4.3%	21.2%	15.7%
Thailand	v_7 3.6%	-0.1%	-2.1%	0.3%	1.7%	1.5%	-4.1%	0.5%	1.0%	4.9%	3.6%
Germany	v_8 11.7%	-0.3%	-6.9%	1.1%	5.6%	4.8%	-13.2%	1.6%	3.2%	15.8%	11.7%
USA	v_9 79.4%	-1.9%	-46.4%	7.6%	37.7%	32.3%	-89.3%	11.0%	21.7%	106.8%	79.4%
	100.0%	-2.4%	-58.4%	9.5%	47.4%	40.7%	-112.4%	13.8%	27.3%	134.4%	200.0%

14.5 Exact Investment Performance Attribution

Nowadays, the monitoring and measurement of the value-added performance of an active value-adding portfolio manager is based on the exact accounting of the value added by active portfolio management in comparison to passive portfolio management:

- *Passive portfolio management* occurs when the portfolio's capital is invested in a portfolio benchmark, or market index. A *portfolio benchmark* is a weighted average (often weighted by capital) of the assets in that particular market. There are now several hundreds of benchmarks and the selection of the appropriate benchmark has become quite an art.

- *Active portfolio management* occurs when the active portfolio allocations deviate from the passive portfolio allocations.

As we noted in the Introduction, there are four essential portfolio management decisions to which value can be attributed: market selection, currency selection, security selection and hedge selection:

1. *Market selection* determines the market risk premium relative to the aggregate passive benchmark local currency return of the portfolio.

2. *Currency selection* determines the currency risk premium relative to the aggregate passive benchmark cash return, in base currency terms, *e.g.*, in U.S. dollar terms.

3. *Security selection* determines the security risk premium relative to the market risk premium (= the original CAPM idea).

4. *Hedge selection* determines the hedge return of the portion of the portfolio hedged into, or out of, the local currency relative to the unhedged cash position.

Each of these portfolio management decisions can be active or passive. Consequently, there are in total $2^4/2 = 16/2 = 8$ potential combinations of market and currency exposures available to a global portfolio manager and to which his performance can be exactly attributed. (Because of the symmetry of the hedges there are $16/2 = 8$ and not 16 potential combinations).

We will now present the complete accounting framework for such *exact performance attribution analysis*, which is a vectorization of Exhibit 8 in Singer and Karnosky (1995, p. 91). The corresponding portions of the value added that can be attributed to each active portfolio selection decision are given by the following expressions, in both summation and matrix notation:

1. Market selection return =

[active market weightsw_i - passive market weights $\overline{w}_i$] $\times$

$$\left[\begin{array}{l} \text{passive local currency market risk premiums } (\overline{r}_i - \overline{c}_i) \\ \text{- index local currency market risk premiums} \end{array} \right]$$

$$= \sum_i^n \{(w_i - \overline{w}_i) [(\overline{r}_i - \overline{c}_i) - P_{rc}]\}$$

$$= (\mathbf{w} - \overline{\mathbf{w}})' [(\overline{\mathbf{r}} - \overline{\mathbf{c}}) - P_{rc}] \tag{14.42}$$

for all countries $i = 1, ..., n$; P_{rc} is the scalar, aggregate, passive, benchmark index for local currency return premiums.

Example 140 *For the three Asian countries portfolio, we have the 5−year average for the stock market risk premia, in percentage:*

$$\overline{\mathbf{r}} - \overline{\mathbf{c}} = [\mathbf{r} - \mathbf{c}] \frac{\iota_T}{T}$$

$$= \left(\begin{array}{c} 6.2 \\ 12.9 \\ 17.0 \end{array} \right) - \left(\begin{array}{c} 2.7 \\ 6.6 \\ 13.3 \end{array} \right)$$

$$= \left(\begin{array}{c} 3.5 \\ 6.3 \\ 3.7 \end{array} \right) \tag{14.43}$$

where ι_T is the $T \times 1$ unity vector. Thus, in the period July 1992 through June 1997, on average, the stock market gained most in Indonesia, 17.0%, and least in Singapore at 6.2%. But their stock market risk premia did not differ much, 3.7% versus 3.5%, respectively. On average, Malaysia had the largest stock market risk premium: 6.3%.

2. Currency selection return =

Passive benchmark weights and returns are indicated by bars over the variables, signifying that they represent weighted averages.

$$\begin{bmatrix} \text{active currency weights } (w_i + h_i) \\ \text{- passive currency weights } (\overline{w}_i + \overline{h}_i) \end{bmatrix} \times$$
[passive cash return $(\overline{c}_i + \overline{\varepsilon}_i)$ - benchmark index cash return P_c]

$$= \sum_i^n \left\{ \left[(w_i + h_i) - (\overline{w}_i + \overline{h}_i) \right] \left[(\overline{c}_i + \overline{\varepsilon}_i) - P_c \right] \right\}$$

$$= \left[(\mathbf{w} + \mathbf{h}) - (\overline{\mathbf{w}} + \overline{\mathbf{h}}) \right]' \left[(\overline{\mathbf{c}} + \overline{\varepsilon}) - P_c \right] \qquad (14.44)$$

where h_i are the currency hedge weights into (positive) or out of (negative) currency i and P_c is the scalar, aggregate, passive, benchmark index for cash returns, in base-currency terms.

Example 141 *For our empirical Asian example, we have the 5-year average for the cash earnings*

$$\overline{\mathbf{c}} + \overline{\varepsilon} = [\mathbf{c} + \varepsilon] \frac{\iota_T}{T}$$

$$= \begin{pmatrix} 2.7 \\ 6.6 \\ 13.3 \end{pmatrix} + \begin{pmatrix} 2.5 \\ 0.2 \\ -3.6 \end{pmatrix}$$

$$= \begin{pmatrix} 5.2 \\ 6.8 \\ 9.7 \end{pmatrix} \qquad (14.45)$$

On average, the Singapore dollar appreciated, while the Malaysian Ringgit remained about even and the rupiah depreciated versus the US dollar. On cash international investors could gain, on average, most in Indonesia at 9.7%, followed by Malaysia at 6.8% and Singapore at 5.2%.

3. *Security selection return =*
[passive market weights $\overline{w}_i$] $\times$
$$\begin{bmatrix} \text{active local currency market returns } r_i \\ \text{- passive local currency market returns } \overline{r}_i \end{bmatrix}$$

$$= \sum_i^n \left[\overline{w}_i (r_i - \overline{c}_i) - \overline{w}_i (\overline{r}_i - \overline{c}_i) \right]$$

$$= \sum_i^n \left[\overline{w}_i (r_i - \overline{r}_i) \right] \qquad (14.46)$$

$$= \overline{\mathbf{w}}' (\mathbf{r} - \overline{\mathbf{r}}) \qquad (14.47)$$

And finally,

4. *Currency hedge selection return =*
[passive currency weights $\left(\overline{w}_i + \overline{h}_i\right)$] $\times$
$\left[\begin{array}{l} \text{active local currency cash returns } c_i \\ \text{- passive local currency cash returns } \overline{c}_i \end{array}\right]$

$$= \sum_i^n \left\{ \left[\left(\overline{w}_i + \overline{h}_i\right)\left(c_i + \overline{\varepsilon}_i\right)\right] - \left[\left(\overline{w}_i + \overline{h}_i\right)\left(\overline{c}_i + \overline{\varepsilon}_i\right)\right]\right\}$$

$$= \sum_i^n \left[\left(\overline{w}_i + \overline{h}_i\right)\left(c_i - \overline{c}_i\right)\right] \tag{14.48}$$

$$= \left(\overline{\mathbf{w}} + \overline{\mathbf{h}}\right)'\left(\mathbf{c} - \overline{\mathbf{c}}\right) \tag{14.49}$$

In addition to these analytical accounting terms, there are a two non-analytical "filler" cross-product terms, which close the cash growth accounting system, but cannot be attributed to the value added of each active portfolio selection decision:

5. *Market cross-product return =*
[active market weights w_i - passive market weights $\overline{w}_i$] $\times$
$\left[\begin{array}{l} \text{active local currency market returns } r_i \\ \text{- passive local currency market returns } \overline{r}_i \end{array}\right]$

$$= \sum_i^n \left\{\left(w_i - \overline{w}_i\right)\left[\left(r_i - \overline{c}_i\right) - \left(\overline{r}_i - \overline{c}_i\right)\right]\right\}$$

$$= \sum_i^n \left\{\left(w_i - \overline{w}_i\right)\left(r_i - \overline{r}_i\right)\right\} \tag{14.50}$$

$$= \left(\mathbf{w} - \overline{\mathbf{w}}\right)'\left(\mathbf{r} - \overline{\mathbf{r}}\right) \tag{14.51}$$

6. *Currency cross-product return =*
$\left[\begin{array}{l} \text{active currency weights } \left(w_i + h_i\right) \\ \text{- passive currency weights } \left(\overline{w}_i + \overline{h}_i\right) \end{array}\right] \times$
$\left[\begin{array}{l} \text{active local currency cash returns } c_i \\ \text{- passive local currency cash returns } \overline{c}_i \end{array}\right]$

$$= \sum_i^n \left\{\left[\left(w_i + h_i\right) - \left(\overline{w}_i + \overline{h}_i\right)\right]\left[\left(c_i + \overline{\varepsilon}_i\right) - \left(\overline{c}_i + \overline{\varepsilon}_i\right)\right]\right\}$$

$$= \sum_i^n \left\{\left[\left(w_i + h_i\right) - \left(\overline{w}_i + \overline{h}_i\right)\right]\left(c_i - \overline{c}_i\right)\right\} \tag{14.52}$$

$$= \left[\left(\mathbf{w} + \mathbf{h}\right) - \left(\overline{\mathbf{w}} + \overline{\mathbf{h}}\right)\right]'\left(\mathbf{c} - \overline{\mathbf{c}}\right) \tag{14.53}$$

The market selection return (1), the security selection return (3) and the market cross-product return (5) together produce the *total market return:*

$$\sum_{i}^{n} [w_i(r_i - \overline{c}_i) - \overline{w}_i(\overline{r}_i - \overline{c}_i)] \tag{14.54}$$

$$= \mathbf{w}'(\mathbf{r} - \overline{\mathbf{c}}) - \overline{\mathbf{w}}'(\overline{\mathbf{r}} - \overline{\mathbf{c}}) \tag{14.55}$$

The currency selection return (2), the currency hedge selection return (4) and the currency cross-product return (6) together produce the *total currency return:*

$$\sum_{i}^{n} \left\{ [(w_i + h_i)(c_i + \overline{\varepsilon}_i)] - [(\overline{w}_i + \overline{h}_i)(\overline{c}_i + \overline{\varepsilon}_i)] \right\} \tag{14.56}$$

$$= [(\mathbf{w} + \mathbf{h})'(\mathbf{c} + \overline{\varepsilon})] - [(\overline{\mathbf{w}} + \overline{\mathbf{h}})'(\overline{\mathbf{c}} + \overline{\varepsilon})] \tag{14.57}$$

These complete exact global performance attribution computations are easily implemented in an EXCEL spreadsheet. Sponsors and global investors can use this performance attribution accounting system to closely *ex post* monitor the investment performance of their portfolio managers and to identify the strengths and weaknesses of their active value-adding portfolio management. Some portfolio managers are fine country selectors, others good security selectors. Still others know how to select currency or cash hedge overlays to add value.

An example of the portfolio performance analysis of value-added attributions of market selection, currency selection and security selection for a global equity portfolio in 1989 is given in Table 10..

= Table 12. in Karnosky and Singer, 1994, p. 41.

A. Portfolio performance summary		
MSCI Global Equity Index		16.97%
Market selection	−0.75%	
Currency selection	5.63	
Security selection	1.65	
Exchange rate differences	−0.03	
Intramonth effect	1.16	
Total value added		7.66%
Global equity portfolio		24.63%

B. Attribution of added value (basis points)

Country	Market Selection	Currency Selection	Security Selection	Total
Australia	−8	11	19	22
Austria	−6	−2	0	−8
Belgium	−16	19	2	5
Canada	−8	19	5	16
Denmark	−3	−4	0	−7
Finland	1	−1	0	0
France	−5	−9	20	6
Germany	29	22	6	57
Hong Kong	3	−1	−7	−6
Italy	17	−21	0	−4
Japan	89	297	25	411
Netherlands	14	14	11	39
New Zealand	−34	4	13	−17
Norway	−3	−2	0	−5
Singapore	2	1	−5	−2
Spain	−25	22	19	16
Sweden	−3	−3	0	−7
Switzerland	16	18	−8	26
United Kingdom	21	4	22	47
United States	30	173	43	246
Cash	−185	NA	0	−185
Subtotal	−75	563	165	653
Exchange rate differences				−3
Intramonth effect				116
Total active contribution				766

Note: Totals may not sum because of rounding.

NA = not applicable.

TABLE 10.: Global Equity Portfolio, 1989 (Base currency = U.S. dollar)

Another example for a global bond portfolio in 1992 is given in Table 11..

= Table 15. in Karnosky and Singer, 1994, p. 48.

A. *Portfolio performance summary*
Salomon Brothers World
    Goverament Bond Index   5.53%
Market selection   0.24%
Currency selection   3.09
Security selection   0.48
Exchange rate differences   −0.16
Intramonth effect   −0.09
    Total value added   3.56%
Global bond portfolio   9.09%

B. *Attribution of added value (basis points)*

Country	Market Selection	Currency Selection	Security Selection	Total
Australia	1	5	0	6
Belgium	−7	14	1	9
Canada	39	1	−10	31
Denmark	−14	18	9	14
France	−1	16	−24	−9
Germany	17	33	18	68
Italy	−5	47	0	41
Japan	−23	−16	−14	−53
Netherlands	13	6	7	26
Spain	−5	−28	2	−31
Sweden	−4	23	0	19
Switzerland	1	−3	0	−2
United Kingdom	−10	68	4	62
United States	19	124	53	196
Cash	3	NA	0	3
Subtotal	24	309	48	381
Exchange rate differences				−16
Intramonth effect				−9
Total active contribution				356

Note. Totals may not sum because of rounding.

NA = not applicable.

TABLE 11.: Global Bond Portfolio, 1992 (base currency = U.S. dollar)

The following Exercises provide a few more empirical examples of exact portfolio performance attribution based on European and Asian country data.

14.6　Exercises

Exercise 142 *(a) Compute the U.S. dollar returns for all combinations of market and currency strategies based on the following return data and select the best combi-*

nation strategy. (b) Perform an exact value added performance attribution analysis (in basis points) on the same accounting data, given the indicated portfolio strategy.

MULTICURRENCY PORTFOLIO RETURN SUMMARY (%)

Country	Passive Returns					Actual Returns		
	Local Currency Market Returns	Local Currency Cash Returns	Local Exchange Rate Returns	Local Market Risk Premium	Cash Return in U.S. Dollars	Local Market Returns	Market Risk Premium	Cash Return in U.S. Dollars
	(1)	(2)	(3)	(1-2)	(2+3)	(4)	(4-2)	(2+3)
Germany	7.00	5.00	1.00	2.00	6.00	6.80	1.80	6.00
U.K.	10.50	11.25	-3.00	-0.75	8.25	12.25	1.00	8.25
Japan	9.50	9.00	-1.00	0.50	8.00	10.50	1.50	8.00
U.S.	8.40	7.50	0.00	0.90	7.50	9.00	1.50	7.50
U.S. cash	7.50	7.50	0.00	0.00	7.50	8.00	0.50	7.50
Benchmark	8.85	8.19	-0.75	0.66	7.44	8.11	1.58	7.89

MULTICURRENCY PORTFOLIO STRATEGY SUMMARY (%)

Country	Market Strategy			Currency Strategy			
	Passive Index Weight	Active Weight w_I	Over/ Under	Active Weight w_I	Currency Hedging +h_I	Currency Weight =w_i+h_i	Over/ Under
Germany	25	60	35	60	-50	10	-15
U.K.	25	10	-15	10	45	55	30
Japan	25	10	-15	10	15	25	0
U.S.	25	15	-10	15	-10	5	-20
U.S. cash	0	5	5	5	NA	5	5
Total	100	100	0	100	0	100	0

Exercise 143 (a) When the local asset, forward, and foreign exchange markets and their corresponding rates of return are independent of each other, the dynamic development of an initial investment $A_0 = \$200mln$ can be exactly accounted for by a local asset growth factor, a cash swap factor and a currency translation factor. Write out algebraically such a strategic factorization of capital growth and explain the resulting formula. (b) Is the assumption of market independence a realistic one? Why or why not? (You may want to illustrate your answer concisely with an example of the developments in the Southeast Asian financial markets since the hand-over of Hong Kong by imperial Britain to communist China, on 1 July 1997)

Exercise 144 The Head Trader of the Westpac Banking Corporation, Inc., "Australia's First Bank," established in 1817, with A\$140 billion in global assets and ranked as one of the top ten companies listed by market capitalization on the Australian Stock Exchange, provides you, an international financial analyst, with the following Southeast Asian multi-currency portfolio summary for the period 1993 - 1998. The base currency for the international operations of this international bank is assumed to be U.S. dollars. (a) With disregard for the risks involved, can you, ex post, select the best historical investment strategy in this five year period? How? (b) What are two major shortcomings of your historical multi-currency portfolio analysis? How would you proceed to resolve them?

MULTICURRENCY PORTFOLIO RETURN SUMMARY (%)

Country	Local Currency Market Returns	Local Currency Cash Returns	Exchange Rate Returns	Local Market Risk Premium	Cash Return in U.S. Dollars
	Passive Returns				
	(1)	(2)	(3)	(1-2)	(2+3)
Australia	-13.020	8.354	-4.481	-21.374	3.872
Hong Kong	-14.821	6.411	0.032	-21.233	6.444
Indonesia	-5.889	17.449	-4.601	-23.338	12.848
Japan	1.392	1.820	-1.387	-0.427	0.432
Malaysia	-1.156	6.245	0.845	-7.401	7.090
Philippines	10.657	9.789	-7.971	0.868	1.818
Singapore	-0.177	2.778	3.553	-2.956	6.331
South Korea	14.953	14.436	2.800	0.517	17.236
U.S.	32.298	5.664	0.000	26.634	5.664
U.S. Cash	5.664	5.664		0.000	5.664

14.7   Bibliography

Dhrymes, P. J. (1978) *Introductory Econometrics*, Springer Verlag, Inc., New York, NY.

Gastineau, G. L. (1995) "The Currency Hedging Decision: A Search for Synthesis in Asset Allocation," *Financial Analysts Journal*, May - June, 8 - 17.

Karnosky, D. S. and Singer, B. D. (1994) *Global Asset Management and Performance Attribution*, The Research Foundation of The Institute of Chartered Financial Analysts, Charlottesville, VA.

Leow C. B. (1999) *Optimal Global Investment Strategy*, MSc thesis in Corporate and International Finance, Department of Economics and Finance, Durham University, UK, September

Los, C. A. (1984) *Econometrics of Models with Evolutionary Parameter Structures*, Ph.D. dissertation, Columbia University, University Microfilms International, Ann Arbor, MI, January.

Los, C. A. (1998a) "Optimal Asian Multi-Currency Strategy Portfolios With Exact Risk Attribution," Asia-Pacific Risk and Insurance Association, *The Second Annual Conference Proceedings*, 19 - 22 July 1998, Singapore, pp. 153 - 187. (Received an Outstanding Paper Award).

Los, C. A. (1998b) "Optimal Multi-Currency Investment Strategies With Exact Attribution in Three Asian Countries," *Journal of Multinational Financial Management*, **8** (2/3), September, 169 - 198.

Los, C. A. (1999) "Comment on "Combining Attribution Effects Over Time"," *The Journal of Performance Measurement*, **4** (1), Fall 1999, 5 - 6.

Markowitz, H. M. (1952) "Portfolio Selection," *Journal of Finance*, **7** (1), 77 - 91.

Markowitz, H. M. (1992) *Mean-Variance Analysis in Portfolio Choice and Capital Markets*, Blackwell, Oxford, UK (original 1987).

Singer, B. D. and Karnosky, D. S. (1995) "The General Framework for Global Investment Management and Performance Attribution," *The Journal of Portfolio Management*, **21** (2), 84 - 92.

Singer, B. D., Terhaar, K. and Zerolis, J. (1998) "Maintaining Consistent Global Asset Views (with a Little Help from Euclid)," *Financial Analysts Journal*, January/February, 63 - 71.

Appendix A
ALGEBRAIC GEOMETRIC MEASUREMENTS OF THE BIVARIATE MODEL

First, we establish the bivariate uncertainty relationship, or Noise/Signal ratio, between the coefficient of determination ρ_{12}^2 and the projection slope angles θ_1, θ_2 and θ_3, as observed in Figure 1.

Proposition 145

$$\frac{N}{S} = \frac{1 - \rho_{12}^2}{\rho_{12}^2}$$

$$= \frac{\sin \theta_2}{\sin \theta_1 \sin \theta_3} \tag{A.1}$$

Proof. For the bivariate case, we have the relationship between the coefficient of determination ρ_{12}^2 and the projection slope coefficients β_2 and β_1.

$$\rho_{12}^2 = \frac{\sigma_{12}^2}{\sigma_{11}\sigma_{22}}$$

$$= \left(\frac{\sigma_{12}}{\sigma_{11}}\right)\left(\frac{\sigma_{12}}{\sigma_{22}}\right)$$

$$= \tan \theta_3 \tan \theta_1$$

$$= \frac{\tan \theta_1}{\tan(\theta_1 + \theta_2)}$$

$$= \frac{\beta_2}{\beta_1} \tag{A.2}$$

, which is the relationship we found in chapter 3. By expanding the tangential expressions into sinusoidal expressions by the well-known relationship

$$\tan \theta_i = \frac{\sin \theta_i}{\cos \theta_i} \tag{A.3}$$

, we find

$$\rho_{12}^2 = \frac{\sin \theta_1 \cos(\theta_1 + \theta_2)}{\cos \theta_1 \sin(\theta_1 + \theta_2)} \tag{A.4}$$

By substituting this expression into the bivariate Noise/Signal ratio, expanding the result using some other well known trigonometric expressions, and by canceling terms, we find

$$\frac{N}{S} = \frac{1 - \rho_{12}^2}{\rho_{12}^2}$$

$$= \frac{1}{\rho_{12}^2} - 1$$

$$= \frac{\cos\theta_1 \sin(\theta_1 + \theta_2) - \sin\theta_1 \cos(\theta_1 + \theta_2)}{\sin\theta_1 \cos(\theta_1 + \theta_2)}$$

$$= \frac{\cos\theta_1 \left[\sin\theta_1 \cos\theta_2 + \cos\theta_1 \sin\theta_2\right] - \sin\theta_1 \left[\cos\theta_1 \cos\theta_2 - \sin\theta_1 \sin\theta_2\right]}{\sin\theta_1 \cos(\theta_1 + \theta_2)}$$

$$= \frac{\left(\cos^2\theta_1 + \sin^2\theta_1\right)\sin\theta_2}{\sin\theta_1 \cos(\theta_1 + \theta_2)}$$

$$= \frac{\sin\theta_2}{\sin\theta_1 \cos(\frac{\pi}{2} - \theta_3)}$$

$$= \frac{\sin\theta_2}{\sin\theta_1 \sin\theta_3} \tag{A.5}$$

■

Next, we establish the relationship between the conventional t-statistic, the epistemic uncertainty in the data, as measured by the determinant of the data covariance matrix $|\Sigma|$, and the Noise/Signal ratio for the bivariate case $\frac{N}{S}$.

Proposition 146

$$t = \frac{\beta_2}{\sqrt{\frac{\tilde{\sigma}_{11}}{\sigma_{22}}}}$$

$$= \frac{1/\beta_1}{\sqrt{\frac{\tilde{\sigma}_{22}}{\sigma_{11}}}}$$

$$= \frac{\sigma_{12}}{\sqrt{|\Sigma|}}$$

$$= \sqrt{\frac{S}{N}} \tag{A.6}$$

Proof. Let's first look at the bivariate t-statistic for β_2:

$$t = \frac{\beta_2}{\sqrt{\frac{\tilde{\sigma}_{11}}{\sigma_{22}}}} \tag{A.7}$$

Substituting the appropriate expressions in for β_2 and $\tilde{\sigma}_{11}$ we find

$$t = \frac{\frac{\sigma_{12}}{\sigma_{22}}}{\sqrt{\frac{\left(\sigma_{11} - \frac{\sigma_{12}^2}{\sigma_{22}}\right)}{\sigma_{22}}}}$$

$$= \frac{\frac{\sigma_{12}}{\sigma_{22}}}{\sqrt{\frac{\left(\sigma_{11}\sigma_{22} - \sigma_{12}^2\right)}{\sigma_{22}^2}}}$$

$$= \frac{\sigma_{12}}{\sqrt{\left(\sigma_{11}\sigma_{22} - \sigma_{12}^2\right)}}$$

$$= \frac{\sigma_{12}}{\sqrt{|\Sigma|}} \tag{A.8}$$

But then also:

$$t = \frac{\sigma_{12}}{\sqrt{|\Sigma|}}$$

$$= \frac{\sqrt{\frac{\sigma_{12}^2}{\sigma_{11}\sigma_{22}}}}{\sqrt{\left(1 - \frac{\sigma_{12}^2}{\sigma_{11}\sigma_{22}}\right)}}$$

$$= \sqrt{\frac{\rho_{12}^2}{\left(1 - \rho_{12}^2\right)}}$$

$$= \sqrt{\frac{S}{N}} \tag{A.9}$$

Similarly

$$t = \frac{1/\beta_1}{\sqrt{\frac{\tilde{\sigma}_{22}}{\sigma_{11}}}} \tag{A.10}$$

Again, substituting the appropriate expressions in for β_1 and $\tilde{\sigma}_{22}$ we find

$$t = \frac{\frac{\sigma_{12}}{\sigma_{11}}}{\sqrt{\frac{\left(\sigma_{22} - \frac{\sigma_{12}^2}{\sigma_{11}}\right)}{\sigma_{11}}}}$$

$$= \frac{\frac{\sigma_{12}}{\sigma_{11}}}{\sqrt{\frac{\left(\sigma_{11}\sigma_{22} - \sigma_{12}^2\right)}{\sigma_{11}^2}}}$$

$$= \frac{\sigma_{12}}{\sqrt{\left(\sigma_{11}\sigma_{22} - \sigma_{12}^2\right)}}$$

$$= \frac{\sigma_{12}}{\sqrt{|\Sigma|}} \tag{A.11}$$

■

    This clearly demonstrates that the bivariate t-statistic is independent of the direction of projection, since it depends only on the value of the observed data covariance σ_{12} and the magnitude of the determinant $|\Sigma|$,which is a measure of the magnitude of the model uncertainty, *i.e.* the lack of linear dependency. The bivariate t-statistic assesses the quality of the information in the covariance σ_{12} against the bivariate system uncertainty in the data measured by $|\Sigma|$. Similar expression can be developed for trivariate and other multivariate cases.

Appendix B
FLOW CHART OF LINEAR MODEL IDENTIFICATION

The following flow chart summarizes the recipe for linear model identification in ten easy Steps. At the bottom there are two pathways via Step 9A or via Step 9B.

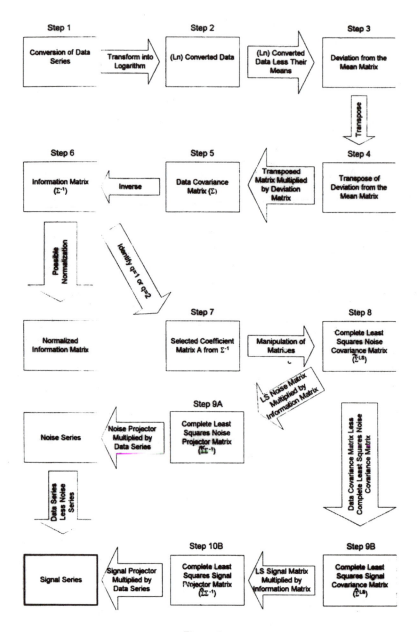

Figure 1

Appendix C
3D NOISE/SIGNAL RATIO

The 3D Noise/Signal ratio for the $q = 2$ signal projectors is derived from the $3D$ Noise/Data ratio (*Cf.* Chapter 5).

Proposition 147

$$3D \; Noise/Data \; Ratio = \frac{|\Sigma|}{\sigma_{11}\sigma_{22}\sigma_{33}} \geq 0$$

and

$$3D \; Noise/Signal \; Ratio = \frac{|\Sigma|}{\sigma_{11}\sigma_{22}\sigma_{33} - |\Sigma|} \geq 0$$

Proof. Using a simple Theorem of linear algebra, we measure the volume of the system noise "box" relative to the volume of the data "box." (*Cf.* Fraleigh and Beauregard, 1987, p. 304) The system noise "box" measures how much the projected exact signals differ from each other. The volume of the data "box" is given by the volume spanned by the 3×3 identity matrix $\mathbf{I}$, representing the orthogonal frame of reference for the three data measurements, which is unity.

$$3D \; Noise/Data \; Ratio = \sqrt{|(\widehat{\mathbf{P}}_1^{CLS} + \widehat{\mathbf{P}}_2^{CLS} + \widehat{\mathbf{P}}_3^{CLS})'(\widehat{\mathbf{P}}_1^{CLS} + \widehat{\mathbf{P}}_2^{CLS} + \widehat{\mathbf{P}}_3^{CLS})|}$$

$$= \begin{vmatrix} 1 & \frac{\sigma_{12}}{\sigma_{22}} & \frac{\sigma_{13}}{\sigma_{33}} \\ \frac{\sigma_{12}}{\sigma_{11}} & 1 & \frac{\sigma_{23}}{\sigma_{33}} \\ \frac{\sigma_{13}}{\sigma_{11}} & \frac{\sigma_{23}}{\sigma_{22}} & 1 \end{vmatrix}$$

$$= \frac{\sigma_{11}\sigma_{22}\sigma_{33} - \sigma_{33}\sigma_{12}^2 - \sigma_{22}\sigma_{13}^2 - \sigma_{11}\sigma_{23}^2 + 2\sigma_{12}\sigma_{13}\sigma_{23}}{\sigma_{11}\sigma_{22}\sigma_{33}}$$

$$= \frac{|\Sigma|}{\sigma_{11}\sigma_{22}\sigma_{33}} \geq 0$$

Thus the 3D Noise/Data ratio is equal to the system uncertainty as measured by the determinant $|\Sigma|$, divided by the product of the three data variances. The 3D noise/signal ratio follows immediately. ∎

Remark 148 *Normalization of the three $q = 2$ signal projectors does not change the value of the Noise/Data ratio. For example, when we normalize on the first elements, we also have*

$$
\begin{vmatrix}
1 & 1 & 1 \\
\frac{\sigma_{12}}{\sigma_{11}} & \frac{\sigma_{22}}{\sigma_{12}} & \frac{\sigma_{23}}{\sigma_{13}} \\
\frac{\sigma_{13}}{\sigma_{11}} & \frac{\sigma_{23}}{\sigma_{12}} & \frac{\sigma_{33}}{\sigma_{13}}
\end{vmatrix}
= \frac{|\Sigma|}{\sigma_{11}\sigma_{22}\sigma_{33}}
$$

Corollary 149

$$
3D\ Noise/Data\ Ratio = 1 - \rho_{12}^2 - \rho_{13}^2 - \rho_{23}^2 + 2\rho_{12}\rho_{13}\rho_{23} \geq 0
$$

Proof. Write out the expression

$$
3D\ Noise/Data\ Ratio = \frac{|\Sigma|}{\sigma_{11}\sigma_{22}\sigma_{33}}
$$

$$
= 1 - \frac{\sigma_{12}^2}{\sigma_{11}\sigma_{22}} - \frac{\sigma_{13}^2}{\sigma_{11}\sigma_{33}} - \frac{\sigma_{23}^2}{\sigma_{22}\sigma_{33}} + 2\frac{\sigma_{12}\sigma_{13}\sigma_{23}}{\sigma_{11}\sigma_{22}\sigma_{33}}
$$

$$
= 1 - \rho_{12}^2 - \rho_{13}^2 - \rho_{23}^2 + 2\rho_{12}\rho_{13}\rho_{23} \geq 0
$$

where $\rho_{ij}^2 = \frac{\sigma_{ij}^2}{\sigma_{ii}\sigma_{jj}}$, for $i, j = 1, 2, 3, i \neq j$ are the familiar coefficients of bivariate determination. ∎

Thus the 3D Noise/Data ratio and the 3D noise/signal ratio, *completely* account for all bivariate information, including the systematic interaction, measured by the $\rho_{12}\rho_{13}\rho_{23}$ term.[*]

Remark 150 *The theoretical minimal and maximal values of the 3D Noise/Data ratio are zero and unity respectively. The theoretical maximal value of the 3D Noise/Data ratio would occur when there is absolutely no systematic relationship between any of the three variables and all $\rho_{ij}^2 \to 0$ for $i, j = 1, 2, 3, i \neq j$. Then no measured (observed) system exists and all data are noise, $|\Sigma| \to \sigma_{11}\sigma_{22}\sigma_{33}$, and the 3D Noise/Data ratio $\frac{N}{S} \to 1$.*

C.1   Bibliography

Fraleigh, J. B. and Beauregard, R. A. (1987) *Linear Algebra*, Addison - Wesley Publishing Co., Reading, MA, 1987.

---

[*]The factor 2 results from the symmetry of the covariance matrix.

Appendix D
1986 MANIFESTO FOR IDENTIFICATION OF MODELS FROM INEXACT DATA

D.1 Background

If there is a point in collecting data at all, building models from data is a necessity. Models serve to condense and clarify data, for insight into the mechanisms generating data, and for prediction, synthesis, etc. At the moment, modeling is a quasi - monopoly of statisticians, but it should be really a matter of mathematical engineering.

The decision is essential.

The present paradigm used by working statisticians is to look at the data as a sample output of a (hypothetical, not verified) probabilistic "machine." They ask "is the sample big enough?", "should I get more data?", etc. The tool for this type of work is elementary probability theory.

The mathematician and engineer, separately or together, are interested in what the data can tell us about the underlying system, not in the noise overlaid on the data. Their questions are, "do we have enough information in the data about the system?" and "how is the data related to the system?" The tools for this work are pure and applied mathematics and computers.

Taking a scientific view of the modeling problem, it is not hard to show that the standard statistical paradigm - all data is a sample - is a prejudice. Prejudices may be true but usually they are not. Scientific research organized around prejudice is a dead end. It is, unfortunately, hard to explain this fact of life to practitioners; for example, to modeling and data analysis groups at banks.

Thus an awkward situation has arisen:

(i) The research opportunity is extremely clear.

(ii) Research must be undertaken against considerable entrenched inertia of those who would most benefit by new knowledge.

Something like this has happened before; think, for example, of Mendelian genetics.

D.2   Proposed Research Path

If we agree to the scenario just outlined, the research approach to be followed is quite obvious.

(i) Study the consequences of prejudice. Find out what parts of a model depend on prejudice (subjective assumptions) and what parts are determined by data. Are all the conventional assumptions needed and used in the modeling process? Can the data speak for itself? Can we use modeling theory to answer the question of data quality? Is some aspect of data analysis necessarily always prejudiced?

(ii) Development of prejudice-free schemes. Computing power is beginning to approach awesome magnitudes. Can we use massive computing so as to squeeze out all possible information from the data about the latent model?

The information we are looking for is not the same thing that statisticians look for (sample variability). The standard statistical approach is known to be wrong (in most cases, not always). It is also known that in the absence of noise in the data the modeling problem is purely mathematical and therefore solvable; in fact, it has been solved in many interesting cases. Thus prejudice - free modeling should be possible. Exactly how to achieve this is the research core of the proposal.

Let us note that this is a great argument for mathematical engineering. Current statistical practices reflect the fact that for the past 100 years computation was a real bottleneck. And much of theoretical statistics (R. A. Fisher's work in the early 1920's) was developed as a kind of home-made mathematics.

This is now all changed. It is reasonable to begin to "reengineer" mathematically the whole spectrum of statistical procedures, with elimination of prejudices as the main organizing principle, and using the powers of modern mathematics and of modern computing.

D.3   Biographical Background

R. E. Kalman (D.Sci., Columbia, 1957) is a (the?) world leader in mathematical and scientific engineering. In 1985 he became the first laureate of the Kyoto Prize in High Technology (known as the "Japan Nobel Prize"). C. A. Los (Ph.D., Columbia University, 1984) is Senior Economist and econometrician at the Federal Reserve Bank of New York.

Appendix E
LIST OF (COMPUTATIONAL) FINANCE JOURNALS ON THE INTERNET

Electronic links are available via http://www.helsinki.fi/WebEc/journals.html. Last updated on 29 February 2000

E.1 Electronic Journals

- *Applied Financial Economics*
  - *Applied Mathematical Finance*
  - *Computational Economics*
  - *Computers in Higher Education Economics Review*
  - *Derivatives*
  - *European Finance Review*
  - *European Journal of Finance*
  - *Finance and Development*
  - *Finance & Stochastics*
  - *Financial Counseling and Planning*
  - *Geneva Papers on Risk and Insurance Theory*
  - *International Review of Economics and Finance*
  - *International Finance*
  - *International Journal of Finance and Economics*
  - *International Journal of Theoretical and Applied Finance*
  - *International Review of Economics and Finance*
  - *International Review of Finance*
  - *International Review of Financial Analysis*
  - *Journal of Banking and Finance*
  - *Journal of Corporate Finance*
  - *Journal of Economic Dynamics and Control*
  - *Journal of Economic Literature (classification system)*
  - *Journal of Economics and Finance*
  - *Journal of Empirical Finance*
  - *Journal of Finance*
  - *Journal of Financial Abstracts (many leads for research)*

- *Journal of Financial and Quantitative Analysis*
- *Journal of Financial Economics*
- *Journal of Financial Intermediation*
- *Journal of Financial Markets*
- *Journal of International Financial Markets, Institutions and Money*
- *Journal of International Money and Finance*
- *Journal of Money, Credit and Banking*
- *Journal of Monetary Economics*
- *Journal of Multinational Financial Management*
- *Journal of Real Estate Finance and Economics*
- *Journal of Risk and Insurance*
- *Journal of Risk and Uncertainty*
- *Journal of the Royal Statistical Society Series B (Statistical Methodology)*
- *Journal of the Royal Statistical Society Series C (Applied Statistics)*
- *Journal of Time Series Analysis*
- *Kyklos*
- *Pacific-Basin Finance Journal*
- *Review of Financial Studies*
- *Risk Management and Insurance Review*
- *Studies in Nonlinear Dynamics and Econometrics*

Index